THE CANADIAN ECONOMY

PROBLEMS AND OPTIONS

Co-edited by

R. C. BELLAN

Department of Economics
University of Manitoba

W. H. Pope

Department of Economics
Ryerson Polytechnical Institute

McGraw-Hill Ryerson Limited

Toronto   Montréal   New York   St. Louis   San Francisco
Auckland   Bogotá   Guatemala   Hamburg   Johannesburg
Lisbon   London   Madrid   Mexico   New Delhi   Panama
Paris   San Juan   São Paulo   Singapore   Sydney   Tokyo

PREFACE

This book is the outgrowth of deep concern felt by its co-editors about the poor performance of the Canadian economy during the past decade. The unemployment rate has been unacceptably high; the jobs worked at by many Canadians have been far inferior to those for which they were qualified by their training, education, skill and personal capacity. An inflation rate of the order of ten percent per annum has become a settled feature of the national economy, eroding the real value of people's savings, bringing about inequitable redistributions of real income, and generating a widespread malaise. Concern about inflation has prompted behaviour on the part of individuals, business firms and public authorities which aggravates the problem of constantly rising prices and creates new problems. As a nation, we have regularly spent much more in the rest of the world than we have earned there and have borrowed huge amounts of money from foreigners to sustain the external value of our dollar. Thus, we have created monstrous current account deficits in our balance of payments. We now must make very large payments of interest to foreigners and we are passing on a legacy of indebtedness to future generations of Canadians which will oblige them to make similar payments.

International comparison confirms the adverse judgment that is dictated by our own accounts and statistics. While Canada has been compiling its sorry record, other countries have had lower unemployment and inflation rates, have piled up balance of payments surpluses, and have achieved year-to-year growth rates far in excess of ours. Although in 1960 Canada's per capita income was second only to that of the U.S., by 1977 it was eleventh among western world countries.

Harry Pope and Ruben Bellan both believed very strongly that this negative development of the Canadian economy was attributable primarily to misguided public policy. Each tried in his own way to bring about a redirection of policy. Harry Pope engaged in a lengthy correspondence with officials of the Bank of Canada and the federal Department of Finance, urging abandonment of the policy of raising interest rates to attract foreign funds. Ruben Bellan wrote a series of articles in the *Toronto Star* in which he argued that contemporary inflation was essentially of a cost-push variety which could not be liquidated by fiscal-monetary restraint, that such restraints caused unemployment without curbing the inflation, and that there was a strong possibility that they actually aggravated the inflation in addition to causing the unemployment.

At Harry Pope's suggestion, he and Ruben Bellan joined forces to produce a publication that would contribute to a better understanding of the Canadian economy. What they proposed was a book that would describe the main elements of the Canadian economy, the problems it confronts, and the options available for dealing with them. Written in simple, non-technical language, it would be thoroughly intelligible to university undergraduates and to members of the general public.

The writing would be done by established Canadian experts, each writing a chapter on a topic on which he or she was a recognized authority. By providing factual information about the Canadian economy, and dispelling myths, the book would, it was hoped, contribute to the formulation of policies which would foster the fullest realization of Canada's potentialities.

Edie Franks, Sponsoring Editor of the College Division of McGraw-Hill Ryerson, gave the project her enthusiastic support. The result, then, is this book.

R.C. Bellan
W.H. Pope

PART A

THE ECONOMY

Chapter 1

The Resource-Based Industries

J. McConnell,
Department of Geography, University of Saskatchewan

Canadians as a rule begin thinking about primary resource industries with two preconceptions in mind. The first is that these industries are at present, and have been historically, the backbone of the Canadian economy. The second is that Canada is resource-rich, endowed by nature with large reserves of resources which, if rationally (sensibly) developed, will ensure the economic security of Canadians far into the future. The term "preconception" is used deliberately here because these ideas about Canada are introduced to Canadian students long before any analysis of the national economy begins. Every Canadian child learns that Canada has more than half the world's fresh water, that the North is a vast storehouse of resources, that three of every five sheets of North American newsprint come from Canadian forests, that prairie farmers feed the hungry of the world, that the Grand Banks are the world's greatest fishing ground, etc., etc. The effect of these two preconceptions is to give the resource industries prominence when thinking about the Canadian economy begins, and to lend special importance to any economic measures that can be supposed to have a beneficial effect on these industries. Any adequate geographic analysis of Canada's resource industries must begin by examining these preconceptions. Is Canada a storehouse of natural resources? Are the resource industries the backbone of the Canadian economy?

In chronological order of their development, the primary resource sectors of the Canadian economy are: fish and fur-gathering, farming, forestry, mining and energy production. The growth of each of these activities in Canada was paralleled by increase in settlement, by urban development and by the growth of manufacturing and service industries. It is difficult, however, to show how growth in every resource industry directly produced corresponding growth in the other sectors of Canada's economy. The development of New France may be used as illustration. As the value of the fur trade to France grew, so did the size and complexity of the settlements along the St. Lawrence. However, the trade itself brought very little capital or employment to the colony. Indeed, French law restricted the participation of colonials in the trade. Wealth, employment and even political and social power within New France were derived primarily from the provision of services to, or for, the administration of the colony and from the development of a local agricultural and industrial economy. Neither the colonial administration nor the local economy were directly and closely linked to the fur trade. It is not the purpose here to review the history of the introduction of each of the primary resource sectors, but to put forward the argument that, in most instances, developments in the resource sector did not induce a corresponding growth in other sectors of the domestic Canadian economy. If this is true, the resource sectors cannot be viewed as having provided the basis of a unified Canadian economy in the past. What is suggested is that the Canadian economy had, historically, two parallel parts, a resource economy and a domestic economy, and that these interrelated on the level of a world or metropolitan economy, but relatively little on an in-Canada level. This suggestion is supported if the resource sectors of the Canadian economy are examined geographically.

Some major resources of Canada are important only to specific regions, and the basic geography of Canada imposes problems for the interregional integration of resources or the benefits to be derived from them. Fish from the maritime provinces is produced in excess of national demand, and is far away from the small and dispersed market that is Canada. To reach its most lucrative foreign markets, it is not necessary that fish touch any place but the maritime port closest to the producer. It need not even be funnelled through any maritime entrepôt. The same is true for prairie wheat. Wheat goes through eastern ports or Vancouver, but it is not necessary that it do so. Many prairie producers argue that the system of grain export would be strengthened, and no actual loss in employment caused, if the bulk of Canadian export grain moved through Churchill and Prince Rupert. Western oil and gas illustrate the same point. No facilities were built to move Alberta oil to eastern markets while it was cheaper to supply this market from offshore sources and sell surpluses to nearby American markets. Even today, with international oil prices escalating steadily, there is little economic sense in supplying the whole of the dispersed domestic market from domestic sources. Proposed projects such as a trans-Canada oil pipeline, or even the extension of the gas pipeline to the Maritimes, are generally justified with the argument that such a facility will mean that no foreign government, or corporation, can create shortages by denying supplies to Canada. They are not justified by economic arguments. Quebec hydroelectric power, B.C. lumber and Saskatchewan potash production have similarly few relationships with the domestic Canadian market.

It would be fair to say that most of the products of these resource industries, i.e., fish, wheat, oil, gas, hydroelectricity and potash, are exported in their raw state; there are few significant forward linkages to the Canadian economy. The linkage industries that do exist beyond the region of resource production—flour mills, oil refineries, fertilizer producers in central Canada, fish wholesalers in central Canada or the west—exist only to meet domestic demand. They are unaffected by the size or growth rate of the specific resource industry from which their supplies come, and they in turn cannot, through technological or other efficiency gains, influence the growth of the resource industry.

It is obvious that the relationship of the resource industries to the domestic economy cannot be judged solely on the basis of forward linkages to the secondary sector. The return to resource industry employees, who in turn provide demand for the products of the secondary sector, might be supposed to generate domestic growth. Also, the demand by resource industries for goods and services, ranging from transportation systems to financial institutions, might enlarge the base of a domestic economy.

The raw or only primarily processed resources of Canada, lacking a national industrial or domestic market, have been directed to foreign markets. This has meant that a substantial portion of the final market price is absorbed by the cost of transportation. Canada's geographic size, its northern climate and the wide dispersal of its resources serve to enhance this cost. Also, with the possible exception of nickel during a period of the industry's history, the resources of Canada have had to compete in foreign markets with other actual or potential producers. These factors in combination have put a premium on low, or low-cost, labour input to resource production. The low return to labour in the fish and fur industries discouraged extensive immigration to Canada. The immigrants who provided the labour in the developing forest and farm industries generally arrived in Canada pulled by the carrot of land and pushed by intolerable conditions at home. The final incentive for some, as Professor Innis has described it, was the very low fares on timber boats.[1] Many of the jobs in the resource industries were part-time and as such were poorly paid since often they were not a sole source of income. In mining, the contrast in demand for labour between the development and the operating phases of mines, coupled with the usually short life of specific mines, called for an impermanent and mobile labour force. In general, the labour force in many resource industries could, and still can be, described as small, low-paid, fluctuating in numbers and geographically mobile. These characteristics have limited the effective demand generated by this group for products of the secondary sector.

The exception to this generalization is agriculture. At the time when agriculture ceased to be a subsistence activity and became a staple or surplus producing activity in Canada, it had a large, growing and relatively stable labour force. Moreover, agriculture generated a large demand for goods. The growth of a secondary manufacturing sector in Canada, as well as the growth of Canada's population, can in part be related to expansion of the output of agricultural staples. However, as an export dollar earner, agriculture has been a notably unstable performer. Farm incomes fluctuate widely and with them farmers' demand for goods. Also, the range of agricultural products produced in Canada is small, and of those which can be produced here, Canada's output is only a small fraction of world production. In the case of wheat, our largest agricultural export, we produce between 4 per cent and 5 per cent of the world's total, and only 30 to 40 per cent of the United States' production.[2] Canada's agricultural industry thus represents only a small fraction of the world's total and a minor part of North America's market for inputs to agriculture. To add to the problem of smallness, Canada's market is widely scattered, with parts more accessible to foreign rather than domestic suppliers in terms of simple transport cost. Hence, the demand created by agriculture has been difficult for Canadian manufacturers to meet. This situation has been steadily worsening since the 1930s as a result of the steady decline in the size of the agricultural labour force.

The demand for services by the resource sector has been large. The Canadian transportation and communications system was created initially in response to this demand. The large capital expenditures on the system were, however, not expected to be justified by the level of revenue generated by the resource sector alone. Rather, the planners and investors hoped that a resource industry and the demands that it generated would foster secondary industry in Canada. The design of the railway system— to tie the regions of Canada together rather than to move raw products most efficiently—reveals their intent. The transportation system itself created a large demand for labour and goods. It was the basis of the growth of a domestic steel industry and was for many decades one of the largest employers in the country. The lack of growth in the secondary sector that depended on resources and the fluctuations in income from raw resource sales forced much of the rail transportation system into eventual bankruptcy. Since the 1930s, the system has been rationalized and been maintained as a subsidized national service. The transportation system, then, is maintained primarily because of its value to the total economy, including the resource sector, and not purely by the income generated in the resource sector. This is especially true of the extensive road network built since the Second World War. It was built by the public either to enable the development of specific resource industries, or in the hope that access would on its own foster such development.

For capital and financial services, the resource sector of the economy has, for the most part, sought sources outside the country. Canada has developed a large, centralized and sophisticated banking system, but that system has provided little to the resource sector. The major part of the activity of Canadian banks has been in low-risk, short-term investments. The money needed to finance long-term and relatively high-risk ventures, such as expansion of manufacturing or major mineral or energy development projects, has usually come from outside Canada. Even long-term investments in services, such as those undertaken by provincial or municipal governments, have often been financed in foreign money markets. The fact that foreign sources have provided much of the development capital in the resource sector has had consequences for the research service area, as well. A small fraction of Canadian GNP has been invested in research, and the proportion of research money spent in Canada in the resource area that comes from the private sector is exceptionally low. Indeed, it would be fair to say that when Canadians want capital and technology for resource development, they first look abroad.

In view of the above, it is difficult to view the resources of Canada as absolutely basic to the Canadian economy in the sense that they directly and totally sustain other sectors of the economy. Neither the manufacturing sector nor the service sector is wholly dependent upon or, in a good many cases, even closely related to, the products or the needs of the resource industries. Rather, a large part of the resource sector, with its foreign markets and foreign sources of capital and services, is one economy in Canada; the domestic economy, with its large social capital investment, its large transportation and communications system and its large service and smaller manufacturing labour forces, is another. The basic connection between the two is that both exist within the political, economic unit that is Canada. The resource industries use the economic infrastructure of Canada as they need it, pay royalties and taxes to the governments of Canada and are ultimately dependent upon decisions made by these governments. The domestic economy treats the resources as a capital asset. They are, on the one hand, sold off for cash, which is used to help sustain the domestic economy. On the other hand, the future of the resources is mortgaged to provide present capital flows to the domestic economy. This situation makes it essential that there be a large reservoir of resources for Canadians to sell or mortgage. The preconception that Canada is a treasurehouse of resources is, therefore, essential to any optimistic view of Canada's future. It thus becomes essential to examine this preconception.

All students of resources are early acquainted with the division between renewable and non-renewable. In Canada, fish, fur, forests, farms and some varieties of energy production are renewable resources. The future growth of renewable resource production and income depends upon several factors. These are: firstly, the existence of unused capacity —e.g., unfarmed arable land, uncut forests, etc.; secondly, technological changes which would lead to increased productivity per unit of area; and, finally, a rise in selling prices greater than accompanying changes in production costs. These same factors influence the future of the non-renewable resources: minerals and fuels. In the case of these, since the resource is by definition being depleted, unused capacity in the form of undeveloped or undiscovered quantities of the resource have to be much more extensive than is the case for renewable resources. Because of this need to estimate undiscovered quantities, the non-renewable resources must be dealt with in a different manner than the renewable. Further, since each of the renewable resources has a distinct geographic and economic character, the potential of each should be analyzed separately.

An aspect of resource evaluation which cannot be analyzed with any degree of accuracy but which should be borne in mind by any analyst is the problem of resource definition. At any time, a new resource may be defined and found to be present in Canada in marketable quantities. A case in point is the post-war development of uranium for use as a fuel. By the same token, the possibility exists that an at-present valuable resource might be rendered relatively worthless by the discovery of replacement materials or new, larger and cheaper sources of supply outside Canada. The possibility of easily recoverable nickel on the continental shelves poses such a threat to one of Canada's major metallic mineral exports.

Canada's oldest resources, fish and fur, show little if any unused capacity, and both, as industries, have severe problems inherited from the past. The resources are widely scattered and have traditionally been harvested by a scattered and poorly paid labour force. Within this century, the prices of fish and fur have not kept pace with other price rises, particularly those associated with what is now considered to be required for an adequate standard of living, e.g., housing, health, transportation and education. As a result, the labour force in these activities has become steadily more impoverished. With little money available in fishing, there has been little incentive to develop the small, unused Canadian capacity largely found in the under-exploited inland fishery, or to attempt to expand the fishery to offshore waters. There have been no gains in production per unit of area in the fishery. For many decades, there has been talk of either sea or inland fish farming but low prices for fish have discouraged serious research or capital investment. The case of fur production is similar. There is little unused capacity available to trappers, and what there is may well be essential to the maintenance of animal populations at present being harvested. The price of furs has fluctuated widely within this century; since, until recently, trapping fur-bearing animals has been treated largely as a free activity with no barriers to entry, there has been a swelling and shrinking of the labour force with price fluctuations. The unstable prices have discouraged fur farming, an activity in which Canada, in any case, has no apparent comparative advantage. Furthermore, with the expansion of industrial, recreational and forestry activities in Canada, the land available for wild fur production is diminishing.

Recent gains in the overall income of the fishing industry have been a product of rises in price. Insofar as these reflect a decline in world supply relative to a stable or growing demand, they are probably permanent. In Canada, overall income has been improved and future gains in income assured, to an extent, by the extension of the territorial waters. The new Canadian authority within the two-hundred-mile limit will, it is hoped, encourage the expansion of Canadian participation in the offshore fishery. The gains in income cannot, however, be taken as betokening a period of growth in the fishing industry. The higher incomes still do not make wage rates or rates of return on capital competitive with other sectors of the economy. The best that can be said is that fishing as an industry may in future pay its way, and that an assured position in world markets could open the way for investment in secondary industries linked to fishing.

Fur trapping is rarely a sole source of income, but it requires a fairly large capital outlay. In this century, the size of this capital outlay has been growing steadily. Social and employment pressures are such that it is almost invariably necessary for a trapper to carry on most of his life in a place other than the trapline. Thus, the costs of dual housing and heavy transportation expense inevitably make trapping an expensive business. Attempts to stabilize fur prices have had indifferent success and marginal incomes are generally declining. Trapping will persist as a traditional occupation for some and will supplement the incomes of many others, but it will not be a growing source of personal or national income.

The forest industry in Canada has been the largest net earner among the renewable resource industries in this century. In 1978, the value of all forest products was about $9 billion, and this yielded a net positive balance of payments of some $1.8 billion.[3] The unused capacity of the forest lands of Canada is not large. Areas of forest at present unused are generally in relatively inaccessible areas, and are for the most part of poorer quality than those being harvested. Generally, the price of access is too great to be justified by potential profit from the forest alone, and where access is developed it will be on the basis of some other activity. For example, in Northern Saskatchewan, roads are now being built to new uranium mines. These provide access to forests north of the Churchill River, but no immediate development for anything but the local market is planned. The trees in this area, as is the case in the northern portions of the other provinces and in the Mackenzie District of the Northwest Territories, are too small to be of much value for lumber and too sparse to be an economic source of pulp. Even if these at present unused forests were developed they would add, at the most, twenty per cent to the present total volume of wood production.

It is the hope of the Canadian Council of Resources and Energy Ministers that the output of the forest industries in Canada will be increased by fifty per cent by the year 2000. This estimate is largely based on the hope of increases in yields per unit of area by the use of improved silviculture techniques. These have not yet been proven technically and have not been shown to be cost-effective. Also, the question as to whether such undertakings would be the best use of capital must be considered. Basic to a positive evaluation of this question is the probable future price of forest products. Competitive sources of some forest products, especially paper, make it doubtful that prices will rise substantially; in the case of other products, such as lumber, posts and poles, alternative materials may limit possible price gains.

It is probable that the next two decades will see a rise in the income from forest production, but it is unlikely that this rise will be large. There are no great untapped resources. Efficiency growths will be expensive and unspectacular, and rises in price above rises in operating costs seem unlikely. Canada does not look rich in forest resources.

The same kind of general statements might be made about agriculture. According to the 1976 census, there were a total of 300,118 farms in Canada, with a total acreage of 166 million.[4] Of these farms, almost two-thirds (196,380) had sales of farm products totalling less than $25,000.[5] If the long-term average relationship of costs to sales in agriculture of 5:8 is assumed, it is apparent that two-thirds of Canada's farms yielded incomes of less than $10,000. Since most farms absorb the labour of more than one person, the personal income from agriculture is, in the main, well below the national average.

The amount of agricultural land in Canada is small, and is scattered from coast to coast across the southern edge of the country. Only 7.2 per cent of Canada is in farms, and only 4 per cent is improved land. The only two extensive areas of farmland are in the southern prairies and in the Great Lakes-St.Lawrence Lowland in Ontario and Quebec. Of the areas in farms only two, a small area in southern British Columbia and another in southern Ontario, do not have climatic limitations which severely restrict the range of mid-latitude crops which can be grown. It would be fair to say that Canada has a small, scattered, poorly endowed agricultural resource, operated by a scattered, poorly paid labour force.

These problems—the size and distribution of the land base, the limitations placed on agriculture by climate, and the low rate of return to its labour—severely limit the potential growth of Canadian agriculture. The largest proportion of Canada's farmers are involved in fulfilling some of the demands of local markets, dairy production being by far the largest activity in this category. The best-endowed land in Canada, that in southern Ontario and Quebec and in southern British Columbia, surrounds the country's largest urban markets and is largely oriented toward their needs. These areas provide a few products—the major ones being fruit and tobacco—to the national market, but they achieve no net balance of exports over imports in any commodities produced. A net positive balance of payments in agriculture for the country as a whole is approached or maintained only by the large grain exports of the prairies. The potential of growth is dependent upon the ability of agriculture to supply more of the commodities now being imported, to increase exports in commodities other than grains, and to increase grain exports. The potential for import replacement is small since most imports are items not grown in Canada for climatic reasons. Most commodities produced in Canada are also produced in the United States, which is in most commodities a surplus producer. The potential to increase income from the production of grains as well as other commodities, given a market, is dependent again upon the trio of new land, new technology or higher prices.

Significant increases in the amount of agricultural land in Canada are unlikely. Inadequate climate, poor soil, or both, characterize all areas not at present in farms, and make farming marginal in about twenty per cent of the area at present in farms. The areas where climatic amelioration through irrigation, or soil improvement through drainage or other mechanical techniques can be practised are small, and the cost of such projects is high.

The decades since the Second World War have witnessed a steady increase in the per acre yields of most grain crops, and there is a widely held belief that this will continue. Projections of grain export figures reported on Canadian radio and television have reached as high as forty million tonnes for the 1990s. Such a figure would represent a doubling of output and would require startling gains in productivity. Such productivity gains would involve higher inputs of energy and fertilizers, and the continuous use of land now fallowed at least one year in three. The cost of the first of these may be higher than the probable benefits, and the second is a procedure which is as yet not accepted by farmers. In any case, the possibility of implementing these procedures would require higher prices for grains.

The general rise in the price of food in North America in the last decade has in large part reflected rises in production costs but not increases in agricultural incomes. The increase in the prices of export commodities, particularly grains, is to some extent more apparent than real since it reflects, in part, declines in the value of North American currencies. Recent attempts to regulate international grain prices at levels that would reflect production costs in the major exporting countries have been unsuccessful. The market for our wheat is unstable because two major importers, China and Russia, could leave the market at any time; many third world buyers could not stand substantial price rises. It appears unlikely, therefore, that any substantial net growth in agricultural income could be based on growth in export earnings. As suggested above, without substantial price increases, the investment in added productivity might not be justified.

Throughout this century, agriculture has responded to low prices and incomes by increasing labour efficiency. The number of farmers has declined drastically and the size of farms has grown greatly. There is no sign at present of this trend reversing itself. Should it continue, the farm population, now numbering less than one million in Canada, will continue to decline in size and will concomitantly lose much of its impact on the economy and the political structure of the country. Whether the rate of research and technological investment in agriculture will continue at its present high level in view of such a decline cannot be easily estimated. It appears unlikely, however, that agriculture as a resource industry can be regarded as a likely basis for future growth in the Canadian economy.

Hydroelectric power is the renewable resource contribution to Canada's energy needs. Between 1960 and 1975, the output of hydro power doubled in Canada and, since 1975, with the opening of such producers as the La Grande project in Quebec, it has continued to grow. It now constitutes a major export commodity for the provinces of New Brunswick, Newfoundland, Quebec, Ontario, Manitoba and British Columbia. New technologies in long distance power transmission have underlain this gain, and seem to assure that much of Canada's water power resources can be profitably tapped. Power development is in itself a major success story in Canada, but when viewed as a contribution to growth in the Canadian economy or as a basis of future wealth, the picture is less rosy.

While hydro power production more than doubled in 15 years, the production of thermal power more than quadrupled. Behind the growth in power production has been a spectacular rise in the demand for power. With satiation of some aspects of the market, and with a new drive toward conservation triggered by possible fossil fuel shortages, the growth rate in demand is slowing. At the same time, the cost of bringing new sources of hydro power on stream is increasing. At present, untapped sources are for the most part far from consumption centres, which increases transmission costs, and are in regions where climate or other technical problems make construction extremely expensive. Also, these untapped resources are not as large as imagination would make them. Most of Canada's highly touted resource, water, is in lakes and swamps. Running water is the basis of all water uses save recreation, and in this, Canada is not well served relative to other areas. Canada's annual runoff is about one-third that of the United States, and much of it is in northern areas where annual variations in runoff are great. This entails huge engineering costs to pond water and provide for regular flows, especially in the winter season when demand is high and runoff is lowest. In general, it can be concluded that hydro power production will not keep up with rises in demand and that increases in the total production of hydro power will be gained at ever-escalating costs.

There is a great deal of talk today about other renewable resources being used as energy sources. Vegetation used directly as fuel or as a source of gas or liquid fuels such as methane or alcohol is one such source. Solar energy used directly is the other major one. Large-scale development of either in Canada is problematic, however. The growth rate of vegetation in much of Canada is relatively low, and in the most favoured areas, production is largely directed to valuable timber or food crops. In the case of direct solar energy production, it is unfortunate that Canada's period of high demand coincides with the period of lowest solar input. The problem of storage is the major technical problem involved in solar energy use, and Canada would encounter a huge storage problem. At best, in Canada these renewable resources could contribute to the conservation of other energy resources in some regions. This may become an increasingly worthwhile goal; however, even if Canada achieves that goal, it could not therefore be viewed as energy-rich.

The resources which at present command the greatest amount of interest and which are seen as being of the greatest future value to Canada are the non-renewable resources: fuels and minerals. Since, as has been pointed out, the future of these is largely dependent upon either undiscovered supplies or undeveloped technologies, the scope for speculation about a rosy or bleak future is unlimited. Some reasonable estimates of the potential of some resources can be made, however, and these give some idea of the broad limits of future growth.

It is unlikely that future exploration will add substantially to Canadian coal reserves. This fuel source can become much more important than it is now only as a result of new mining technology or further spectacular rise in the price of other fossil fuels. The reserves of oil and gas in promising shallow strata on the land mass of Canada are generally known. Further growth may come from deeper drilling, from exploration on the continental shelves, or from transfer zones. These sources are, however, far more expensive both to explore and to exploit than historic sources.[6] New technologies may produce better returns from already known sources, but for the foreseeable future, the costs of oil from such areas as the tar sands and the heavy oil fields in the Lloydminster-Cold Lake region will remain very high relative to the actual production costs of Middle-East or Caribbean oil. The capital costs of implementing the development of heavy oil or tar sands, of bringing south the limited amounts of oil and gas at present proven in the Arctic or of delivering western Canadian fuels to Quebec and Maritime markets are huge relative to the capital cost of other developments. Such investments will not only distort investment patterns in Canada, but will leave the economy vulnerable in the event of stabilization or actual decline of offshore oil prices. Canada's predicted oil reserves, even including these high cost sources, are usually presented in terms of how many years they would supply a growing domestic market. There is little talk of Canada's being an exporter in the long term. The benefit we gain from possession of our oil and gas must come from some advantage that Canadians would gain in their other economic endeavours by having cheaper fuels. Oil and gas, like coal, are not resources which, if sold, would buy our future.

Uranium has been touted as a major fuel resource in the last decade. Certainly, the proven reserves in Ontario and Saskatchewan are large, and the amount of exploration going on, especially in Keewatin, would indicate that large further reserves are probable. If Atomic Energy of Canada and the regulatory bodies in the United States, France and West Germany are to be believed, the technologies for mining, refining and energy production are known and are efficient. Plans to meet the energy needs of these three countries include large-scale atomic developments, and all are at present willing to invest in Canadian uranium development. In Canada, only Ontario perceives an immediate need for atomic energy development, so the export market looks excellent. The only cloud on the horizon for the nuclear business arises from the apparent inadequacy of its supposedly proven technology and the growth of an antinuclear movement. Those opposed to nuclear development question the safety of the nuclear fuel cycle at all points; the apparent inability of people in the business to answer their questions satisfactorily combined with the technological problems bedevilling the industry have led to the cancellation or postponement of several nuclear projects in Europe and North America. The potential of uranium is certainly there but the development remains questionable.

Canada produces a wide range of minerals and in the case of some is a major world producer. Among the metallic minerals, copper, gold, nickel, iron, lead, silver and zinc are produced in large quantities and bring large returns. Among the non-metallics, asbestos and potash are Canada's major products. In 1975, the metallics contributed over $4 billion and the non-metallics, close to $2 billion to the GDP in the primary sector. The bulk of Canada's production in all of these major minerals is exported in a raw or semi-processed state. Canada's production of minerals in general and of the major export minerals in particular has grown steadily in this century, and the minerals industry is generally viewed as a major growth sector in the Canadian economy. Indeed, it is in reference to minerals and the future of minerals development that phrases like "treasurehouse of resources," and "golden resource future" are most frequently heard. An analysis of the broad limits of future growth in minerals does not deny the prospect of some expansion in mineral production but suggests that a rapid or sustained boom is unlikely.

In the years from 1969 to 1973, the production of most of the major metallic minerals grew in dollar value as well as quantity. Between 1973 and 1975, the quantities produced declined for all, while dollar value continued to rise.[7] In the last decade, there has been little net growth, measured in constant dollars, of Canada's output of its major metallic and non-metallic minerals. There are no new major mineral development projects at present underway. In the short term, then, there is little chance for substantial growth in income from mineral production. For the long term, one must examine possible future developments.

The bulk of the minerals in easily accessible and easily mined regions of Canada is probably already known. Large deposits in more remote or difficult areas are also known for the most part. This is reflected in the fact that most of the major mineral deposits developed since the Second World War were known earlier in the century. The iron ore of Labrador and the base metals of Pine Point were known before the First World War. The development of at present known reserves is conditional on generally higher prices, or new technologies, or an expanded transportation system. The first of these is dependent upon factors outside Canada: the rate of world consumption and the development of alternative sources in other countries.

Since the mining industry is dominated by large multi-national companies, new technology is not developed with any specific regional reference and confers no national advantage on any one country; a company is likely to pursue technology which will produce the highest possible return on investment, be it in Canada or Guatemala. The third factor, transportation, has been developed in Canada deliberately to encourage resource development, and the growing northern road network has been an important factor in maintaining growth in the minerals industry. The roads have generally followed actual mineral discoveries or the promise of discoveries and have, in a sense, subsidized development. They have also stimulated exploration. This process of stimulating growth through roads to resources cannot, however, go on indefinitely. Transportation connections in the more remote regions of the country—Ungava and the Northwest Territories, for example—are much more expensive to build and maintain than those in areas further south and, barring the unlikely event of very large and profitable mineral finds, are much less likely to produce growth in any of the resource industries. Thus, the role that small-scale mineral developments have played in maintaining or increasing rates of mineral production in the immediate past may decline in the future.

The long-term future of minerals, then, depends primarily upon developments in both demand and technology that will occur outside of Canada. The only immediate potential for growth based on mineral exploitation would appear to be in the performance of additional processing functions in Canada or in the development here of mineral-based manufacturing industries. The fact that these have not developed in the past leads one to question if there is now any comparative advantage which would make these types of industry the best in which to invest available capital. The answer to this question would require an analysis of the manufacturing sector of the Canadian economy and is beyond the scope of this study. A good many knowledgeable individuals, and at least one national political party, urge that we adopt an industrial strategy aimed at expanding manufacturing activity which is based on our natural resources. The fact that this strategy is so widely advocated lends credence to the view that Canada's endowment of natural resources, mineral and other, is not in itself a sufficient guarantee of future economic growth.

Conclusion

Perhaps the best summary statement about the natural resources of Canada is in Dr. Kenneth Hare's introduction to the centennial volume on Canada produced by the Canadian Association of Geographers: "Instead of praising in fulsome language the prodigality of nature, Canadians should perhaps wonder how nature managed to put so little of use into an area so large."[8] This warning about our view of the natural abundance of Canada was timely and accurate, but it has been little heeded or used as a starting point for analysis. Rather, rhetoric that extols our natural wealth appears to be a necessary part of political speeches and seems, more tragically perhaps, to underlie much that passes for economic policy.

This brief study has attempted to demonstrate two key characteristics of the Canadian economy. The first is that the resource sector of the economy is not closely integrated with, or absolutely basic to, the secondary and tertiary sectors. Indeed, it is isolated from these sectors insofar as it is dependent almost wholly on foreign capital and technology and external markets. The second is that the resource base of Canada is not large now and appears unlikely to be much larger in the future. In the past, royalties collected on the basis of natural resources contributed to the development of a large secondary and tertiary economy and the maintenance of a relatively high standard of living; future royalties may be distinctly smaller. The future will require, on the one hand, that Canadians develop the attitudes, technologies and institutions necessary to integrate more closely the two sectors of the national economy and, on the other hand, that they reject ideas and plans based either on the dream that the status quo can go on indefinitely or on theories which suggest that magic solutions like manipulating the money supply will conjure up both resources and production based on those resources.

---

[1] H. A. Innis and W. T. Easterbrook. "Fundamental and Historical Elements" in *The Canadian Economy, Selected Readings*, J. J. Deutsch, B. S. Keirstead, K. Levitt, R. M. Will, eds., Macmillan, Toronto, 1961, pp. 440-448.

[2] J. Paxton, ed. *The Statesman's Yearbook 1977-78*. Macmillan, London, 1978, Table, p.xiii.

[3] John Fraser. Minister; *Environment Canada News Release*, 02/15/01/80, 4662, Ottawa.

[4] Statistics Canada, *1976 Census of Canada*, Agriculture Graphic Presentation, 1978. Ottawa. Unnumbered pages.

[5] Ibid., Unnumbered pages.

[6] D. H. Root, L. J. Drew. "The Patterns of Petroleum Discovery Rates," *The American Scientist*, Vol. 67, No. 6, 1979, pp. 448-452.

[7] *Canada Year Book 1976-77*. Minister of Supply and Services, Ottawa, 1977, Table 12.4, pp. 614-15.

[8] F. K. Hare. Introduction in *Canada, a Geographical Interpretation*. J. Warkentin, ed., Methuen, Toronto, 1968, p. 7.

Chapter 2

Energy[1]

John F. Helliwell,
Department of Economics, University of British Columbia

Energy Production, Energy Trade and Energy Use

Energy Production and Trade in Canada and the United States

Table 1, which is based on data and forecasts published by the International Energy Agency, shows production, net imports and, by inference, consumption in both Canada and the United States of the five main sources of primary energy: crude oil, natural gas, coal, nuclear electricity and hydro. Actual data are reported for 1960, 1973 and 1976, and IEA forecasts (which are based on 1977 submissions to IEA by the federal governments of both countries) for 1980, 1985 and 1990. The Table 1 figures for oil and gas production suggest, and data for exploration and reseves confirm, that Canadian oil and gas reserves have been developed later than their United States counterparts. In 1960, before the "Ottawa Valley Line" was established (in 1961, following the recommendation of the Borden Commission) to provide a protected market (west of the Ottawa Valley) for Canadian crude oil, Canada had net oil imports more than half as large as domestic production. By comparison, U.S. net oil imports in 1960 were less than 20 per cent of domestic production. With the protection of the Ottawa Valley line, and with increasingly easy access to U.S. markets in the late 1960s and early 1970s, Canadian oil production increased almost fourfold between 1960 and the mid-1970s.

Natural gas and coal production, in the historical period, show themselves as much more important in the United States than in Canada, chiefly because there were large markets close by large deposits. Indeed, the Canadian steel industry, centred in southern Ontario, and thermal production of electricity by Ontario Hydro are heavily dependent on coal imported from nearby U.S. deposits. When Canadian natural gas production eventually started to grow dramatically—it increased more than fivefold between 1960 and 1973—the impetus came partly from the increasing

	1960	1973	1976	1980	1985	1990
Canada						
Oil	26.4	99.5	81.1	81.3	76.1	89.7
Gas	11.6	62.1	57.4	67.7	73.2	66.3
Coal	5.8	12.0	14.1	21.3	29.9	37.1
Nuclear	—	3.9	4.4	8.9	16.9	29.3
Hydropower	33.5	49.7	57.2	61.3	73.4	87.4
Total	77.3	227.2	214.2	240.5	269.5	309.8
United States						
Oil	382.8	511.2	454.8	517.8	516.1	457.0
Gas	293.8	514.5	453.6	385.1	379.4	386.1
Coal	251.9	346.8	388.8	506.0	613.0	719.0
Nuclear	0.1	20.6	46.3	86.0	187.3	292.2
Hydropower/ other	36.3	67.8	73.9	80.0	82.4	97.6
Total	964.9	1,460.9	1,417.4	1,574.9	1,778.2	1,951.9

[a]Source: IEA estimates of primary energy production and trade for Canada and the United States, 1960-1990. All data are annual flows measured in millions of net metric tonnes of oil equivalent (Mtoe).
[b]Conversion factors: crude oil, 1 million barrels per day = 50.35 Mtoe for Canada, 49.1 for the United States; gas, 1 trillion cubic feet = 23.11 Mtoe for Canada, 23.89 for the United States; coal, 1 million metric tonnes = 0.69 Mtoe for hard coal, 0.34 for lignite; electricity, 1 TWh = .086 Mtoe.

stocks of proven gas reserves discovered in the search for oil but primarily from the development of pipeline transmission systems designed to serve U.S. as well as Canadian markets. In a similar way, the forecast expansion of Canadian coal production by 175 per cent between 1976 and 1990 (the actual increase is likely to be much smaller) is in large measure based on shipping western Canadian metallurgical coal to Japanese and Korean markets, along with greater use of western Canadian coal in Ontario.

Hydroelectricity has been, and will continue to be, of about equal absolute size in Canada and in the United States, and hence of far greater relative importance in the much smaller Canadian economy (about 10 per cent of the U.S. in both population and GNP). Relative to total energy requirements, nuclear energy has played similar roles in both countries, with 1976 and forecast 1990 nuclear capacities in the U.S. about ten times as large as in Canada.

In the forecast period, Canada's natural gas exports were assumed to taper off as existing contracts expire in the late 1980s and early 1990s. They thus ignore the 3.75 tcf of new gas exports approved in December

Table 1b Net imports of energy into Canada and the United States[a,b]

	1960	1973	1976	1980	1985	1990
Canada						
Oil	14.5	−11.5	10.1	19.1	34.1	31.5
Gas	−2.4	−23.7	−21.9	−23.6	−20.5	−5.1
Coal	7.2	3.4	2.0	0.7	−3.1	−5.0
Total	19.3	−31.8	−9.8	−3.8	10.5	21.4
United States						
Oil	70.0	284.5	353.3	506.3	571.6	696.3
Gas	0.3	12.2	18.3	33.9	54.2	52.3
Coal	−21.4	−20.6	−38.7	−50.0	−59.0	−62.0
Total	48.9	276.1	332.9	490.2	566.8	686.6

[a]Source: IEA estimates of primary energy production and trade for Canada and the United States, 1960-1990. All data are annual flows measured in millions of net metric tonnes of oil equivalent (Mtoe).
[b]Conversion factors: crude oil, 1 million barrels per day = 50.35 Mtoe for Canada, 49.1 for the United States; gas, 1 trillion cubic feet = 23.11 Mtoe for Canada, 23.89 for the United States; coal, 1 million metric tonnes = 0.69 Mtoe for hard coal, 0.34 for lignite; electricity, 1 TWh = .086 Mtoe.

1979 for delivery to the United States between 1980 and 1987. Additional exports beyond 1987 are also likely, but have not yet been approved. Total primary energy demand is forecast to grow by 38 per cent between 1976 and 1985, and oil production is forecast to fall, thus causing forecast oil imports to reach about .7 million barrels per day in 1985. The oil supply forecast appears to involve about 1.5 million barrels per day (Mb/d), of which more than .4 is presumed to come from oil sands and heavy oil

Table 2a Total primary energy use per capita in Canada
and selected other OECD countries

	1960	1973	1976	1980	1985	1990
Canada	5.36	8.78	8.87	9.78	10.94	12.27
United States	5.60	8.30	8.10	9.20	10.00	10.70
United Kingdom	3.26	4.00	3.70	4.02	4.29	4.62
Sweden	3.64	5.79	6.05	6.40	7.21	7.24
Norway	2.50	4.80	5.05	5.76	6.55	7.20
New Zealand	2.29	3.27	3.48	3.87	4.67	5.20
Germany	2.63	4.37	4.21	5.03	5.70	6.40
Japan	1.02	3.15	3.24	3.91	4.88	5.70

Table 2b Total primary energy use in relation to GNP
(Canada and the United States) or GDP (other countries)

	1960	1973	1976	1980	1985	1990
Canada	1.93	1.96	1.87	1.80	1.71	1.64
United States	1.51	1.51	1.51	1.41	1.41	1.37
United Kingdom	1.85	1.67	1.52	1.41	1.32	1.24
Sweden	1.30	1.34	1.32	1.19	1.16	1.09
Norway	1.31	1.54	1.41	1.24	1.20	1.12
New Zealand	1.26	1.36	1.40	1.51	1.67	1.69
Germany	1.25	1.27	1.20	1.23	1.11	1.04
Japan	1.33	1.33	1.34	1.32	1.28	1.26

plants. The 1985 and 1990 estimates of natural gas production appear to involve some production from frontier deposits (i.e. Mackenzie Delta, Arctic Islands or East Coast Offshore), amounting to 2 per cent of total production in 1985, and 15 per cent in 1990. The 1985 and 1990 forecasts of conventional oil production [estimated to be down to .7 million barrels per day (Mb/d) 1990] and of non-frontier natural gas production are intended to represent maximum sustainable production from non-frontier sources. As I shall indicate later, they are serious underestimates of what non-frontier suppliers will be willing and able to produce. Thus the Table 1 figures are likely to overestimate oil imports, to underestimate gas exports, and to overestimate production of oil sands and very heavy oils.

The forecasts in the table were all prepared before the doubling of world oil prices in 1979. To the extent that these price increases eventually show up in prices for Canadian energy production and consumption, future energy demands are likely to be smaller, and some types of domestic energy production larger, than shown in Table 1.

International Comparisons of Primary Energy Use

Table 2 shows total primary energy use, per capita and in relation to real gross national product, for Canada and the United States, along with comparable measures for other OECD countries. Sweden and Norway were selected because they have, like Canada, northern climates, high standards of living, and heavy energy use associated with their forest industries. New Zealand has a slightly milder climate, but shares with Canada and the Nordic countries a heavy use of hydroelectricity (and also the presence of electricity-intensive aluminium smelting), and a substantial forest industry. Canada is more sparsely populated than the comparison countries, with 2 inhabitants per square kilometre, compared to 12 for Norway and New Zealand, 20 for Sweden, 23 for the United States, 247 for Germany and 299 for Japan. The latter two countries are included for comparison to show the effects that their rapid industrial growth have had on energy use patterns.

All of the countries show past and future increases in the per capita use of primary energy. Canada's average annual increases (in absolute terms) are larger than those for all of the other countries, for past as well as future periods. In terms of the ratio of energy to output of goods and services, most countries show constant or increasing energy use between 1960 and 1973, a period during which the relative price of energy fell in all countries. From 1973 to 1976, most of the countries show falling energy-intensity of output, and from 1976 to 1990 all countries except New Zealand forecast substantial declines in energy intensity.

The forecast drop in the ratio of energy use to output is of the same order for Canada as for most of the other countries. What is somewhat surprising is that the gap between Canada and other countries actually widens, in proportionate terms, from 1976 to 1990. To the extent that Canada's past energy intensity was due to low-cost and low-priced energy, the gap should be squeezed as prices move toward the world levels, as they are assumed to do in the forecast assumptions underlying Table 2.

International Comparisons of Electricity Use

The high and rising per capita energy consumption figures for Canada require further investigation and explanation. It is useful to split electricity and other forms of final energy, if only because of the difficulty of preparing and interpreting primary energy statistics for electricity. The problem is one of finding a suitable "oil-equivalent" measure of the electricity obtained from nuclear, hydro and geothermal power. The IEA procedure is to use average efficiences of thermal generation facilities in each country or in some of its neighbouring countries. For countries such as Canada, Sweden and Norway that have had large and low-cost hydro sites (often far from major centres of population) and have attracted large electricity-intensive industries (such as aluminium smelters) as a consequence, the use of "oil equivalent" measures based on thermal generation may exaggerate the figures for total energy use. To isolate the impact that earlier availability of low-cost hydro sites may have on current patterns of electricity use and total energy use, Table 3 shows per capita electricity use, the relative importance of electricity as a fraction of total primary energy, and total primary energy use excluding electricity. The table shows that Canada, Norway and Sweden, all predominantly hydro countries, use much more than average amounts of electricity, especially for industrial use. New Zealand, the other predominantly hydro country, shows something of the same pattern for households, but the corresponding pattern for industrial use is not evident in the 1976 data even though about 15 percent of New Zealand's electricity was being consumed by the country's new aluminium smelter. The rising energy/GDP ratios forecast for New Zealand in Table 2b imply further shifts to energy-intensive industry to an extent that seems implausible.

Even after all electricity is eliminated from primary energy use, in the last column of Table 3, the figures still show Canada as high as the United States, on a per capita basis, and much higher than all of the 16 other countries. If similar calculations are done for 1990, they show per capita non-electricity energy use of 7.1 for Canada compared to 5.8 for the United States, and much less for all other countries. The calculations excluding electricity naturally understate the energy-intensiveness of electricity-intensive countries like Canada, yet even in this case the official forecasts show that Canada is expected to be increasingly more energy-intensive than other countries. The calculations that underlie this forecast almost surely understate the long-term effects of energy conservation if Canadian energy prices and costs rise until Canadian users face roughly the same energy costs as in other countries.

So much for the broad patterns of national energy supply and demand. To understand better the workings and effects of Canadian energy policies, it is essential to know something of the regional distribution of energy resources and energy demands. In the simplest terms, it is enough to know that Alberta accounts for 86.5% of Canada's oil production (Saskatchewan, with 9.6%, produces most of the rest) and 84% of natural gas production (British Columbia, with 10.6%, produces most of the rest).

Table 3 1976 electricity use in Canada and other OECD countries
(in thousand kWh per capita)

	Population mid-1976 (millions)	House-hold use	Indus-trial use	All uses	Electricity as percent of TPE[a]	TPE per capita excluding electricity
Canada	23.143	2.98	5.14	12.28	38%	5.43
United States	215.118	2.80	3.35	9.91	32%	5.51
United Kingdom	56.001	1.52	1.79	4.60	34%	2.44
Sweden	8.219	2.42	4.97	10.52	40%	3.62
Norway	4.027	4.84	10.03	18.62	59%	2.13
New Zealand	3.116	2.69	2.25	6.71	44%	1.94
Germany	61.513	1.17	2.61	5.11	31%	2.94
Japan	112.768	0.87	2.71	4.34	20%	2.17

[a]TPE = total primary energy

Canada's coal production is 42% in Alberta, 31% in B.C., and 19% in Saskatchewan. Thus, Canada's hydrocarbon production is almost entirely from the three most westerly provinces. The major centres of population, industry and energy use are in Ontario and Quebec, although energy use is much more evenly spread than is production. Ontario accounts for 31.4% of Canada's oil consumption, 46.6% of natural gas consumption, and 51% of coal consumption. Quebec, which had until 1976 received all of its crude oil from offshore sources and is only partially served by natural gas transmission systems, accounts for 29.7% of oil consumption, 5.5% of natural gas, and 2% of coal. The east coast Maritime provinces account for 13.2% of Canada's oil consumption (all imported), no natural gas, and 3% of coal. They account for 7% of Canada's coal production. East Coast offshore oil and gas drilling has so far led to some discoveries but no production.

Although the distribution of hydroelectric installations is somewhat uneven across the country, with Quebec and British Columbia having the major resources, all of the provinces generate the balance of their own requirements from nuclear (in Ontario, and planned for Quebec) and from conventional thermal installations. Thus, there is little net interprovincial or international trade in electricity, beyond the large block of power (almost 10% of Canadian production) going from Labrador to Quebec on long-term contract.

Energy Pricing and Revenues

Federal Energy Pricing Policies

The federal government came by its oil and gas pricing strategy in bits and pieces, starting with a fortuitous timing of events in 1973. Exports of crude oil came under direct control (under the existing powers of the National Energy Board) in March of 1973, in response to concern that the rapid growth of export demands (85% increase from 1970 to 1973) might deprive Canadian refineries of their crude oil supplies. In September of 1973, in response to consumer complaints about higher oil prices unmatched by rising costs, domestic oil prices were frozen at $3.80 per barrel, and a special charge levied on exports, one month before the Middle East war and the ensuing oil embargo.

Then world oil prices started to climb dramatically, and the other main elements of the Canadian pricing policy fell into place in response to distortions coming about when the oil price controls really started to bite. Thus, in January 1974, it was agreed between federal and provincial governments that oil should have the same price (except for transport costs) throughout the country, and an import compensation scheme was developed to subsidize refineries using higher cost imported oil. The pressure to raise natural gas prices came primarily from the provincial governments in Alberta and British Columbia.

Pre-emptive action by British Columbia and pressure from Alberta forced the federal government to act, through the NEB, to set gas export prices closer to those for crude oil. Table 4 shows the main policy-determined increases in domestic wellhead prices for oil, Toronto city-gate prices for natural gas and natural gas export prices.

Table 4 Policy-determined prices for Canadian crude oil and natural gas 1973-1980

Date when new prices were established	Crude oil wellhead price ($/bbl)	Natural gas prices (Can. $/mcf)	
		Toronto city-gate wholesale price	Export price
Sept. 1973	3.80		
April 1, 1974	6.50	0.62	
Nov. 1, 1974		0.82	
Jan. 1, 1975			1.00
July 1, 1975	8.00		
Aug. 1, 1975			1.40
Nov. 1, 1975		1.25	1.60
July 1, 1976	9.05	1.405	
Sept. 10, 1976			1.80
Jan. 1, 1977	9.75	1.505	1.94
July 1, 1977	10.75		
Aug. 1, 1977		1.68	
Sept. 20, 1977			2.16[a]
Jan. 1, 1978	11.75		
Feb. 1, 1978		1.85	
July 1, 1978	12.75		
Aug. 1, 1978		2.00	
May 1, 1979			2.30[a]
July 1, 1979[b]	13.75		
Aug. 1, 1979		2.15	2.80[a]
Nov. 4, 1979			3.45[a]
Jan. 1, 1980	14.75		
Feb. 1, 1980		2.30	
Feb. 17, 1980			4.47[a]
Aug. 1, 1980	16.75		
Sept. 1, 1980		2.60	
Jan. 1, 1981	17.75	2.60[c]	4.94 (as of April 1, 1981)

[a]Beginning with the September 1977 export price increase, export prices of natural gas are listed in US, rather than Canadian dollars.
[b]In December, 1978, previously agreed price increases of $1/bbl for oil and of 15¢/mcf for gas, originally scheduled to be implemented Jan. 1 and Feb. 1, 1979, respectively, were deferred until the mid-1979 dates shown in the table.
[c]Does not include federal tax.

The Regional Distribution of Oil and Gas Use and Revenues

Turning to the broader aspects of the revenue effects of energy prices, it is difficult to make a complete accounting but easy to show the striking size of the changes in Canadian regional income flows that have resulted from energy price increases since 1973. It is necessary to consider only oil and gas, because, as I have already indicated, there is little interprovincial trade in electricity.

In 1977, the world value of Canada's 585 million barrels of oil production was about 8.8 billion Canadian dollars, and the 2.5 trillion cubic feet of gas production had an export value of about $6 billion. This amounts to about 7% of Canada's 1977 GNP. Alberta received an average price of about $10.25 per barrel (about two-thirds of the landed price of offshore crude) for the 450 million barrels of oil exported from the province and an average border price of about $1.60/mcf (about two-thirds of the export value) for the 1.8 tcf of gas exported from the province. These gross revenues of about 7.5 billion dollars in 1977 are big by any standard, whether in relation to population (Alberta had 8% of Canada's mid-1977 population of 23.7 million, so 1977 oil and gas revenues amounted to about $4000 per capita) or in relation to past experience. In 1977, the Alberta government received more than $2.1 billion in production royalties on oil and natural gas, more than 35% of the total amount received in the previous thirty year history of the oil industry in Alberta. More dramatically, Alberta royalty revenues of $6.2 billion over the 1974-1977 period were more than three times as large as all previous royalty revenues.

The large size and rapid growth of actual and potential oil and gas revenues explain why their distribution among producing firms, governments and consumers has been such an active source of debate, legislation and jurisprudence in Canada since 1973. The intricacies of the conflicts and compromises in taxation, regulation and development are much too in-

Table 5 Distribution of incremental revenues from crude oil

	With no additional exploration	With additional exploration equal to 50% of additional revenues
Federal government	27.0%	3.0%
Provincial governments	48.4%	44.0%
Industry share:		
Reinvested		50.0%
Not reinvested	24.6%	3.0%
	100.0%	100.0%

volved to unravel in a brief survey. There are many analyses available, although none has yet appeared with the full objectivity and clarity that only hindsight can bring. To fill in this part of my survey, I shall only indicate the key features of the fiscal debate as part of my general description of the interests and investments of the main participants.

Players and Instruments

The first and most obvious point to make is that oil and gas have much in common with each other, but little in common with electricity and coal. Nuclear energy is in a different world again. Thus, I shall have to treat them separately, starting with oil and gas.

Oil and Gas

Oil and gas resources in Canada are almost entirely owned by the Crown, and developed under lease by predominantly foreign-owned firms. Natural resources fall within provincial jurisdiction under the British North America Act, so that the "Crown" for these purposes means the provinces south of 60 degrees latitude and the federal government for resource deposits in the Yukon and Northwest Territories.

Federal Fiscal Tools

For the oil and gas resources that lie within the provinces, the federal fiscal instrument is the federal corporation income tax. The key changes that have been made in the federal corporation income tax since 1973 started with the disallowance of royalty payments to provinces as a deductible expense in 1974, and continued with a number of measures designed to refund or defer income tax for income reinvested. Table 5 shows how, according to federal government calculations, the resulting system divides incremental revenues from an increase in the wellhead price of crude oil.

Provincial Fiscal Tools

The main provincial fiscal instrument for oil and gas is the production royalty, although land sales and bonus bids for production rights can be a very important source of revenue, especially in the current fiscal regime, where taxes and royalties are both structured to favour reinvestment of current revenues.

The Constitutional Issue

The key constitutional issue that has arisen (especially in Saskatchewan) relates to provincial attempts to design production royalties that are flexible enough to permit firms to recover the costs of producing from high-cost deposits while allowing the Crown to collect a high proportion of the resource value from low-cost deposits. In a recent controversial decision, the Supreme Court of Canada decided in favour of firms that were appealing the Saskatchewan legislation on the grounds that it amounted to an indirect tax. Under the British North America Act, both federal and provincial governments may levy direct taxes, but only the federal government may levy indirect taxes. The provinces also levy a corporation income tax which, for most provinces, including the three main oil and gas provinces, is collected by the federal government. The provinces continued to let royalties be deductible for their own corporation income taxes, and also offered some compensation for extra federal income tax incurred because of the non-deductibility of provincial royalties. The provinces continue to argue that the federal action was an unjustified and discriminatory infringement of the provincial ownership of natural resources.

The federal government has, as described earlier, developed a number of new taxes and subsidies relating to crude oil, and these now are large relative to corporation income tax receipts for oil and gas. For example, in the 1976-77 fiscal year, the revenues were $660 million from the oil export charge, $558 million from a federal gasoline tax of $0.10 per gallon, and $862 million in corporation income tax from oil and gas companies. The offsetting expenditures were $945 million in oil import compensation payments and $484 million in additional equalization payments.

The additional equalization payments arise because the federal government makes transfer payments to provinces with less than average revenues, and the average is increased when provincial oil and gas revenues increase. The items listed above are not the whole story of federal involvement. In the same accounting, the federal government notes 1976-77 energy research and development expenditures of $120 million (still 75% on nuclear energy and uranium), energy conservation expenditures of $67.5 million and "other energy projects" expenditures of $475.6 million. The latter item probably includes some but not all of the federal government's entrepreneurial investments in energy development.

The Federal Government as Oil and Gas Developer

The main federal investments in energy production include: almost 50% shareholding in Panarctic Oils Ltd., the main explorer in the Arctic Islands and the driving force behind the Polar Gas pipeline proposal; 100% ownership of Atomic Energy of Canada Limited; 15% equity in the Syncrude oil sands project; and other energy investments undertaken by Petro-Canada Ltd., formed in 1976 as the federal government's 100%-owned vehicle for direct investment in oil and gas development. In November 1978, Petro-Canada made by far its largest expenditure, $671 million (U.S.) to acquire Phillips Petroleum's 48% controlling interest in Pacific Petroleums Ltd. of Calgary, which in 1976 was Canada's fourth largest producer of natural gas and ninth largest producer of oil. Subsequent purchases raised Petro-Canada's holding to 100%. It is estimated, based on 1977 data, that with the amalgamation of Pacific Petroleums' operations, Petro-Canada's production would be Canada's sixth largest in crude oil (including natural gas liquids) and second largest in natural gas. The continuing controversy surrounding Petro-Canada's purchase involves issues of public versus private ownership, foreign versus domestic control, and new capital investment versus takeovers as means of establishing a presence. The problems raised by the further blurring of federal government roles have not received much public attention, but are of potential importance. For example, Petro-Canada, through its new control of Pacific Petroleums, is now the dominant shareholder in Westcoast Transmission, a federally regulated company that is a 50% partner in the Alaska Highway natural gas pipeline. It is difficult to see how, in these circumstances, the federal government can avoid, and be seen to avoid, compromising conflicts of interest.

A final and most important class of federal instruments is based on the federal power to tax and regulate international trade. These powers are of especial importance in the case of oil and gas, where international trade has been such an important and controversial part of the industry's development. The National Energy Board is the chief federal agency overseeing energy trade and development; its approval of energy exports and pipeline projects is a necessary but not sufficient condition for federal government approval, because proposals must also receive cabinet approval. The NEB also recommends to the government the levels of the natural gas export price and the oil export price described in the previous section.

Provincial Governments as Oil and Gas Owners and Developers

The provincial governments start with resource ownership as their primary policy instrument in oil and gas development, but there have been three other main types of instrument. First, Alberta has long controlled the export of oil and gas from the province through the hearings and decisions of the Alberta Energy Resources Conservation Board (AERCB). Second, prices for gas production have been forced up by means of changes in the Arbitration Act, and prices for Alberta users have been lowered by means of rebates paid to natural gas users by the Alberta government. In British Columbia, the wholesale prices for B.C. users of natural gas have been kept low (less than half of the export price at the end of 1979) by having the Crown-owned British Columbia Petroleum Corporation buy all gas from B.C. producers and sell at one price in the domestic market and another price in the export market. Outside B.C. and Alberta, natural gas prices to Canadian users are based on the Toronto city-gate price, which is usually set by negotiation between the federal and provincial governments. Third, the provincial governments have been directly involved in numerous corporate ventures intended to support provincial revenue or development goals.

The Oil and Gas Industry

The chief participants in the oil and gas industry are the firms that discover, develop, process, produce, transport and distribute the oil and gas. The oil industry is vertically integrated from exploration right through to the gasoline pump, with most of the crude oil production and almost all of the refining and marketing activity in the hands of the major international oil companies. Natural gas is much more dispersed, with a large group of firms (including the major international firms that dominate oil) in exploration and development, three large transmission companies (Nova, formerly AGTL, Westcoast Transmission and TransCanada Pipelines) and a large number of provincially regulated natural gas distribution companies. With different firms at the top and bottom ends of the pipeline, regulatory hearings for natural gas transmission tariffs reflect a broader range of interests than do the corresponding hearings for Interprovincial Pipelines. The latter firm is controlled by the largest of the firms that use it as a common carrier for the oil that they either produce or buy in Alberta and refine in Ontario.

The main policy instrument available to the producing firms is political and administrative influence, acquired through financial and personal contacts, supported by privileged access to expertise and data and enforced by actual or threatened mobility. By their mobility, the firms force competition between the resource-owning jurisdictions. Thus, when the federal and provincial governments both moved strongly to increase oil and gas taxes and royalties in 1974, there was a sharp reduction in drilling activity and there were much-publicized, but not very large, movements of drilling rigs from Canada to the United States. Shortly afterward, there were important tax and royalty concessions by both levels of government, and the pace of drilling activity soon increased to record levels. To the extent that the producing firms can suppress competition among themselves when they deal with governments, the producing firms could jointly have enough leverage to obtain supernormal returns. Assessing the evidence on this point is not easy, as the concept of supernormal returns (i.e., returns greater than those necessary to attract the necessary pool of capital, labour and enterprise) is itself not easy to define, and must be measured over the whole producing life of the resource, a time long enough to permit the relative bargaining strengths of the producing firms to ebb and flow several times.

How Are the Economic Rents Being Divided?

Table 6 shows the distribution of economic rents (i.e., the amount by which the market value of the oil and gas exceeds the opportunity costs of all the capital, labour, materials and enterprise needed to develop them) over the past and future production from the (conservatively estimated stocks of) conventional oil and gas deposits in western Canada. The results are based on an assumed world oil price of about $35 (or $30 US) in 1980, then rising to the end of the century at 2% annually in real terms.[2] The three cases in the table show the economic rents under three different assumptions about domestic oil prices. In all cases, domestic natural gas prices have their current relationship with domestic crude oil prices— about 85% of btu equivalence at the Toronto city gate. The "Federal Conservative" results assume domestic oil price increases of $4 per barrel in 1980, with subsequent increases of $4.50 per year until 1983, and then $5.50 per year until the domestic oil price reaches 85% of the world level. The "Alberta" case goes to world prices in $7 annual increments starting in 1980. The "Federal Liberal" case increases oil prices by $2 per year until a "Made in Canada" price of $25 (in 1980 Canadian dollars) is reached and thereafter maintained. (*But see note to Table 6 on page 33.*)

Canadian economic rents from crude oil and natural gas (as shown in column 7) are higher in case 1 than in case 2. This is so in spite of the fact that economic waste through inefficient use is substantially higher (as shown in column 4) when oil and gas are priced much below their world values. Thus, under current tax and royalty provisions, and with the high degree of foreign ownership of the non-frontier oil and gas resources, the efficiency losses from the lower prices are outweighed by the redistribution gains in favour of Canadian consumers.[3] If the policy of low prices is carried too far, especially when the production from the low-cost non-frontier sources falls far in relation to the supplies of imported and synthetic crude (for which world prices are paid to the producers), then the efficiency losses become large enough to swamp the redistribution gains. This is shown by the case 3 results.

The general effect of a lower price policy for crude oil is to transfer money from the federal government, the provincial governments in the producing provinces, and the producing firms, to Canadian energy consumers. The large negative economic "rents" accruing to the federal government are due primarily to the compensation payments on imported oil, which reach $5 billion per year by 1985 in case 3, on average import volumes of 450 thousand barrels per day. In the "Alberta" case, by contrast, the import subsidy goes to zero in 1985, and imports average 250 thousand barrels per day.

Table 6 Net economic rents from conventional and synthetic crude oil and natural gas under alternative pricing policies
(Present values in billions of end-1980 Canadian dollars)

		Total Rent (1)	All Producers (2)	Canadian Consumers (3)	After (Waste of) (4)	Federal Government (5)	Provincial Governments (6)	Total Canadian Rents (7)
1. Federal Conservative Case Domestic oil price increases $4.50/ barrel annually to 1983, then $5.50/ year to 85% of world price	Oil	270	62	75	7	12	121	222
	Gas	233	31	60	28	35	92	194
	Total	503	93	135	35	47	213	416
2. Alberta Case Domestic oil price increases $7.00/ barrel annually to 100% of world price	Oil	270	69	42	5	30	129	216
	Gas	231	33	49	22	37	98	191
	Total	501	102	91	27	67	227	407
3. Federal Liberal Case* Domestic oil price increases $2.00/ barrel annually to 1990, then larger increases to approach $25 in 1980 prices	Oil	219	38	202	31	−118	98	190
	Gas	237	20	105	78	26	73	208
	Total	456	58	307	109	−92	171	398

Meaning of Columns: Column 1 is the sum of 2, 3, 5, 6, and net economic rents accruing to U.S. purchasers of Canadian natural gas exports.
Column 7 is the sum of 3, 5, 6, and 21.5% of column 2, where 21.5% was the value estimated in 1976 as the Canadian equity ownership proportion in non-frontier natural gas and crude oil production.

* Under the National Energy Program, unveiled at the end of October 1980, the $2 per barrel increases continue in 1981, 1982, and 1983. ''. . . Thereafter, until the end of 1985, price increases will take place at the rate of $2.25 every six months. Commencing in 1986, the price will be raised at the rate of $3.50 every six months, until it reaches its appropriate quality-determined level relative to the oil sands 'reference price' [the lesser of $38 a barrel, effective January 1, 1981, and escalated annually thereafter by the Consumer Price Index or the international price]. If by 1990 the conventional oil price is still below that for reference price oil, consideration should be given to a more rapid rate of escalation.'' (National Energy Program, p. 27]

Electricity, Nuclear and Coal

The electricity situation is far removed from that of oil and gas. In each province, except Alberta, there is a dominant electric utility that generates, transports and distributes the bulk of the electricity sold in that province. Most of the Crown corporations and the few remaining privately owned utilities are subject to some form of provincial regulatory control. There are some interprovincial and international grid connections, and hence some potential for NEB control of exports, but the trade flows tend to be incidental to the planning and operation of the utilities.

Nuclear energy, by contrast, is dominated by the federal government, which has played key roles in the international marketing of uranium, the design, construction and sale of the CANDU reactor and the associated heavy water plants, and the regulation of trade and safety of nuclear materials. The provincial utilities, on the other hand, are the only potential Canadian users of nuclear generators.

Coal is used by provincial utilities and steel plants (chiefly in Ontario) for thermal power generation and steel making, respectively; it is produced in the same provinces that produce the oil and gas, with the important addition of the Maritimes. The eastern coal production, like that in many other countries, is a subsidized declining industry. The western coal production growth has been chiefly of metallurgical coal for export. The coal for Ontario is mainly imported. While there is clearly a substantial prospect for increasing coal exports, and for some increasing use of coal for conventional thermal generation of electricity, the longer term energy use of coal may well lie as a source of petrochemical feedstock, of liquid fuels and of synthetic gas. In the meantime, there appears little prospect that coal will play a significant role in the design and implementation of federal energy policies. A national coal policy has been promised, but it is uncertain what the federal government can contribute beyond some support for improved transportation facilities.

Federal Oil Supply Policies

The main elements of the 1976 federal energy policy strategy, as it related specifically to oil supplies, were:

1) To move domestic oil prices toward international levels.

2) To double, at a minimum, exploration and development activity in the frontier regions of Canada over the following three years (1976-79), under acceptable social and environmental standards.

3) To reduce net dependence on imported oil in 1985 to one-third of total Canadian oil demands. The 1985 import target since has been changed to be the lesser of 800,000 barrels per day or one-third of total demand.

4) To reduce the rate of energy demand growth to 3.5% over the ten years 1976-1985.

Specific measures that have been taken by the federal government include:

1) Direct investment in the Syncrude oil sands plant (15% of equity), coupled with tax concessions and a guaranteed market at world prices for Syncrude output. This policy was developed in great haste when rapidly rising costs apparently threatened the continuation of the project in early 1975. An economic analysis of the costs and benefits suggests that the complex package of tax, royalty and investment terms was such as to involve a substantial net transfer from the federal government to the Alberta government and, to a lesser extent, to the producing firms.

2) Extension of the Interprovincial Pipeline oil pipeline system eastward across the 'Ottawa Valley Line' to Montreal. The federal government has since adopted a policy that crude oil prices should be the same in Montreal and Toronto, with a corresponding federal subsidy to cover the costs of operating the line between Toronto and Montreal. Under these circumstances, the throughput of the line becomes a federal policy variable.

3) Providing additional tax credits for frontier drilling, to the extent that a company in a taxable position need find no more than 7 cents of every dollar it spends on well costs of over $5 million. The federal government has also announced new policies for allocating exploration and production rights for oil and gas on federal lands. The new policy involves some bidding for rights, a 10% production royalty, and a Progressive Incremental Royalty (PIR) intended to get a higher Crown return on more valuable deposits. The policy is intended to encourage early frontier development rather than to obtain high eventual returns.

4) The federal government, through its national oil company Petro-Canada, attempted in mid-1978 to acquire control of Husky Oil, a U.S.-controlled firm with important reserves of heavy oil deposits. In the upshot, control of Husky was acquired by Alberta Gas Trunk Line, now Nova. Both Petro-Canada and Nova expressed interest in accelerating Husky's plans for a plant to upgrade Lloydminster-type heavy oils to make them more suitable for conventional refineries. Petro-Canada's subsequent takeover of Pacific Petroleums in November 1978 supplied a new direct federal participation in heavy oil development, as Pacific had already been actively considering the construction of an $800 million heavy oil upgrading plant in Alberta.

Electricity

While capital expenditures for electricity generation are forecast by the federal government to account for over 60% of their 1977 forecast of 1976-1990 energy capital expenditures, totalling over 180 billion 1975 dollars, the federal government has little scope for affecting the main electric power decisions in Canada. The key issues relate to the amount and type of new generating capacity to be provided, and the rate structures employed to distribute the costs of electricity to the users. In contrast to oil and gas, where primary concern focuses on the distribution of economic rents between regions of the country, and between Canadians and the mainly foreign-owned oil companies, the distribution issues in electricity arise mainly between classes of user within each province. The economic costs of inefficient provincial electricity supply and pricing policies are thus borne almost entirely by residents of the same province.

The federal government has two indirect roles in electric power planning, the first being the integrated forecasting of all energy supplies and demands, and the second the production and regulation of nuclear reactors.

Inflated Estimates of Electricity Demand Growth

In the function of integrated supply and demand forecasting, the federal government has no doubt found itself in an embarrassing position. On the one hand, the estimates of capital expenditures and system expansion are based on the plans of the major provincially based electricity supply utilities. On the other hand, the demand forecasts used by the utilities in their 1975 expansion plans surveyed by EMR are so high as to be inconsistent with any of EMR's equation-based forecasts. Part of the problem is that the provincial utilities tend to have considerable freedom to expand their systems according to their own estimates of demand and then to set pricing schedules that recover their total costs and encourage the expansion of demand to meet the level of pre-built capacity. The existence of excess capacity thus tends both to perpetuate itself, by delaying the rate structure reforms required to match future marginal costs and revenues. It can be argued that the combination of high general inflation rates and high interest rates is putting enough financial pressure on the provincial utilities that, on their own initiative, they are likely eventually to wish to use rate structure reform to cut the rate of growth of their expenditures in order that a higher degree of financial self-sufficiency be recovered. In the meantime, however, there is the prospect of an extended period of excess electricity supply, with capital and operating costs at unnecessarily high levels and with rate structure reforms delayed as a way of absorbing the excess capacity.

Nuclear Energy

The federal government's second main role in electricity planning is as developer, regulator and seller of nuclear generation facilities. This involves several conflicts of interest, as reduced electricity demands mean fewer sales of CANDU reactors. Similarly, tighter safeguards on the domestic and foreign use and control of uranium and radioactive wastes mean fewer sales of CANDU reactors. The Canadian federal government, its Crown corporations and its regulatory agencies probably have a deeper involvement in, and commitment to, nuclear power than does the national government in any other country. As has been shown in hearings before the Ontario Royal Commission on Electric Power Planning, there is considerable mistrust of the nuclear industry, and little public faith in the federal government's ability to deal objectively with the issues. On the touchy question of nuclear wastes, the federal government has recently commissioned a report from outside experts, and the government of Saskatchewan has recently had a Royal Commission on the safety of potential uranium mining projects in the province. Both reports concluded that the risks were manageable, although anti-nuclear groups have presented counterevidence on the nuclear waste issue to the Resources Committee of the House of Commons.

The economic analysis of nuclear power is bedevilled by the fact that so much of the past and current development is directly or indirectly financed by government in ways that make comparable costing difficult or impossible to achieve. For example, 70.6% of federal direct research expenditure on energy (excluding Atomic Energy Control Board grants) in 1972-73 was on nuclear energy. This issue, as well as the related issues of government involvement in exports of uranium and reactors, must lie beyond the scope of my survey. What is apparent, however, is that even the direct costs of nuclear power generation are very high, and that reductions in the expected growth of electricity demand will be matched by very substantial reductions in the planned program of nuclear power development.

Energy and the Structure of the National Economy

The potential difficulties in digesting and financing large energy investments were first studied in relation to the Mackenzie Valley pipeline proposals of the early 1970s, and have since been raised with respect to the EMR estimates of $180 billion of energy-related capital expenditures between 1976 and 1990. The EMR estimate is that this will amount to about 6% of Gross National Product in the mid-1980s, much higher than the average of 3-4% before 1970. Based on my earlier analysis of the expenditure forecasts, it is possible to reduce the $180 billion to a figure that is more in line with what is likely to happen, as well as more in line with past experience.

If we take the electricity expenditure estimates of $80 billion (all these figures are in 1975 prices), this reduces the total to $150 billion, even if all of the other figures are left untouched. These include oil sands and heavy oil expenditures of almost $15 billion, equal to approximately seven Syncrude-sized plants; pipeline expenditures of $26 billion, equal to the estimated 1975 dollar costs of four Alaska Highway pipelines; and conventional oil and gas development expenditures of $23 billion. The latter figure is large, but possible if one assumes that the potential non-frontier supplies are much larger than EMR has forecast. The oil sands and heavy oil estimate must be correspondingly reduced. Eight billion dollars would cover Syncrude, plus Syncrude expansion or a separate plant of Syncrude size, the Imperial Oil project at Cold Lake, and 200,000 barrels per day of other heavy oil production and upgrading. The actual total, in terms of 1975 prices, is almost bound to be less than $8 billion unless there is a large expansion of exports of oil. The pipeline estimate should be cut to about $10 to $12 billion, unless an Alaska Highway oil line is added or the Arctic islands are developed for export markets.

With these rough adjustments, which are consistent with my earlier comments about the likely shape of energy investments, the total drops to less than 130 billion 1975 dollars, which is 4.0% of EMR's estimate of total GNP (also in 1975 dollars) between 1976 and 1990. Their estimates of the size of GNP are also likely to be high, but probably not, in aggregate, by more than 15% or so. Thus the "energy-dominated" economy does not appear likely, unless governments permit themselves to get committed to unnecessarily large capital expenditures for uneconomic energy projects.

Technology, Scale and Energy Policies

Throughout this survey, examples have been given of federal or provincial government involvement in large-scale high-technology energy supply or petrochemical projects that seem likely to involve higher costs and excess supply. On the other hand, it has been argued that there are relatively unstudied "soft" energy supply sources that could, even in the Canadian context, meet the energy demands of a "conserver society." These alternative "soft energy paths," with their associated scaling-down of energy demands, have received some federal government policy support through the Office of Energy Conservation in the Department of EMR, and through the federally financed Science Council of Canada.

Aside from the apparent glamour of large scale developments, their scale and complexity, combined with the scale and complexity of regulatory processes, encourage a symbiotic relation between government and industry. Although the necessity and desirability of this symbiosis are certainly open to question, it clearly has some attractions to both government and industry.

Conversely, the establishment of a framework that fosters smaller-scale alternatives is a difficult and risky business for governments, who have little chance of receiving much political credit. Especially when there is an air of "energy crisis," governments feel pressure to "do something," and not just to let things happen. It is a feature of smaller-scale and decentralized alternatives that the government can itself do little more than establish a framework (e.g., establish tax, royalty and pricing policies, and constrain the power of both public and private energy monopolies) and let the consequences follow.

---

[1] This chapter is a much abridged and slightly updated version of "Canadian Energy Policy," *Annual Review of Energy*, 1979, 4:175-229 (Reproduced by permission of Annual Reviews Inc., Palo Alto, CA.). All footnotes, references, acknowledgements, and additional tables are to be found in the full version.

[2] This table is based on Table 1 of J.F. Helliwell "The Distribution of Energy Revenues Within Canada: Functional or Factional Federalism?", Resource Paper No. 48, February 1980 (Vancouver: UBC Programme in Natural Resource Econonomics). The notes to that table explain the assumptions in more detail.

[3] The possibilities for using taxation changes rather than low prices as means of obtaining a better distribution of energy revenues are assessed in J. F. Helliwell "Taxation and Energy Policy" in Canadian Tax Foundation *Proceedings of the Thirty-First Annual Conference*, Toronto, November 1979 (also available as Resources Paper No. 47, UBC Programme in Natural Resource Economics, January 1980).

Chapter 3

The Industrial System[1]

John N.H. Britton,
Department of Geography, University of Toronto

The current pattern and level of Canadian economic development closely reflects its settlement history. Natural resource endowment has initiated the development process throughout the globe's sparsely populated regions, and Canada fits this pattern, demand for Canada's resources having been derived from three distinct sources. At the earliest stage, the importance of colonial powers in exploration and trade was pre-eminent and was the origin of Harold Innis' "Staple Theory." Shifting staples and growth in domestic demand characterized the second stage from the nineteenth century through to the Great War, significant immigration in the first half of the nineteenth century having laid the basis for manufacturing development later in the century. The low level of technological sophistication of industries in the early decades of the twentieth century enhanced the possibilities for their establishment in a young country needing equipment for transport, farming and other activities. With the exception of petrochemicals, Canada's basic manufacturing industries have their roots in this phase of development. During the most recent stage, major demands for Canadian resources have again been external.

In contrast to other economically small countries of the new world, Canada has indeed been fortunate that a wide range of primary products has been available as a succession of staples and as a stimulus to the emergence of primary manufacturing industries during the twentieth century. Canada's energy resources, market size and the accessibility of U.S. markets combined to encourage a basic industrialization. Unfortunately, however, many of Canada's resources are non-renewable, or, as is the case with forest products, are exploited in a non-renewable fashion.

Each stage of Canada's development has left its imprint on the industrial structure. The first stages created minimal domestic linkages apart from the commercial and administrative systems required to expedite the export of commodities. During the second stage, local resources were used in Canada to manufacture the tools required to "open up" the hinterland. Manufacturers of railways equipment and machinery for farm and mine, smelting and metallurgy were established to a small extent in the Maritimes, especially Sydney, but mainly in central Canada, Hamilton and Sault Ste. Marie, emerging as major steel centres that have endured to the present. Transportation and communications equipment came to be a major component of the Canadian industrial scene, complementing those industries that refined and handled primary raw materials. A modest development of hydro power had occurred by 1900, for example, in the St. Maurice Valley, but it is in the latter stage of Canadian development that basic and large-scale manufacturing industry has evolved to take advantage of hydro power (e.g., the Saguenay and Kitimat) and to accommodate the needs of the petroleum age—petrochemicals and automobiles are located in Central Canadian market centres but with increasing petrochemical development in the West.

Over the past three decades, substantial economic growth has again been made possible by immigration and the consequent growth of the domestic market. There have also been important changes in the structure of the economy. Tertiary industries are now a major source of jobs. Between 1951 and 1971, for example, the proportion of the work force in the tertiary sector in Canada increased from 38 to 50 per cent. Secondary industries (construction and manufacturing), registering the impact of productivity improvements and other competitive influences, now employ 35 per cent of the work force, down from 40 per cent in 1951. Primary sector employment has declined even more dramatically as technical changes have contributed to much greater productivity, sharply reducing the need for labour input. Productivity improvements in the goods-producing sectors, together with part-time work and greater female participation in the services, have been important factors in the pattern of employment change. Growth of output in manufacturing, distribution and the resource industries has also been a major factor, as firms in these activities have stimulated the emergence of specialized business and technical firms to serve them. Thus, Canada's industrial activities have generated a white-collar-office concentration especially in the Toronto region, but secondarily in Montreal, Calgary and Vancouver.

In addition to these jobs in the tertiary sector, there has been expansion of employment in public administration and social, community and personal services, but these jobs, many of which are in the public sector, serve to distribute white-collar employment more extensively throughout urban Canada. It is the business services (advertising, for example), and corporate head offices that are truly localized in metropolitan Toronto, and these activities are a direct expression of the concentration of Canadian industrial power in Southern Ontario.

While there has been a history of industrial growth in recent decades, there are now problems to be faced in Canada. Labour-intensive industries in manufacturing which are concentrated in Quebec now face increasing competition from low-wage countries. Furthermore, the fact that the resource industries and capital-intensive industries in primary manufacturing have been weak stimuli to domestic high technology suppliers of capital equipment in secondary manufacturing is now a major deficiency in Canada's industrial structure. In short, Canada's manufacturing industries are not fulfilling their potential, which means that the Ontario regional economy, perhaps for the first time, is under pressure to develop new industrial competence or suffer de-industrialization. Unfortunately, the worry one should have about Canadian manufacturing also spills over into the tertiary sector which is highly dependent upon demand from manufacturing industry.

Locational Organization of Manufacturing Industry

The geographic pattern of Canadian economic activity is one of spatial concentration in the heartland of Ontario and Quebec, with 42 per cent of the country's jobs being located in Ontario and another 29 per cent in Quebec. There is substantial variation in the location of the components of the industrial economy even when it is considered on a provincial basis; output of mining is highly concentrated in Alberta, for example, (48 per cent) while retail sales, though concentrated in Ontario and Quebec, reflect the population pattern. More than half of Canada's manufacturing output comes from Ontario, with more than a quarter of the remainder from Quebec (Figure 1). It is no surprise, therefore, that white-collar jobs involved in producer services follow a similar spatial concentration. Such occupations as computer programmers, EDP operators, advertising salesmen and mathematicians, statisticians and systems analysts are equally or more spatially concentrated than manufacturing output or total employment.

The *industrial growth* of recent decades has not generated major changes in the manufacturing map: for example, Ontario's share of value added increased from 51 to 54 per cent (1952-72). Quebec's share declined from 31 per cent to 27 per cent; Alberta (2.4 per cent to 3.4 per cent) and British Columbia (7.5 per cent to 8.7 per cent), made small gains. The concentration tendency in Ontario is broadly based, ranging through transportation (effects of auto pact and aerospace) to petrochemicals, while relative expansions in the western provinces were specifically in chemicals and equipment manufacture (oil industry-related) in Alberta and in petroleum and coal, non-metallic minerals and pulp and paper in British Columbia.

Despite Canada's industrial diversity, the concentration of manufacturing in Southern Ontario and in the other industrial regions of Cen-

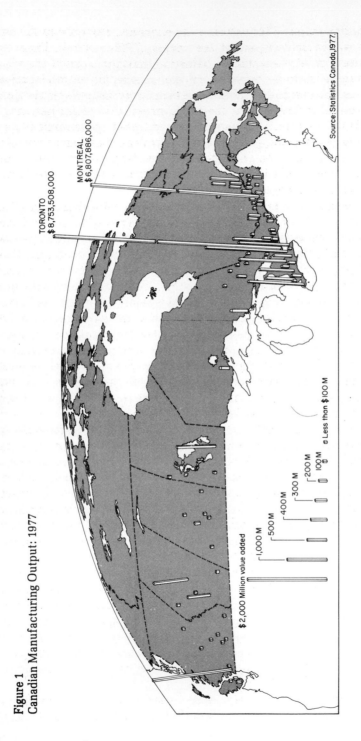

Figure 1
Canadian Manufacturing Output: 1977

TORONTO
$8,753,508,000

MONTREAL
$6,807,886,000

$2,000 Million value added

1,000 M
500 M
400 M
300 M
200 M
100 M
Less than $100 M

Source: Statistics Canada, 1977.

tral Canada dominates. This pattern is an economic response to the east-west form of the settled part of the country. This narrow, linear settlement pattern creates substantial industrial transport costs if the whole Canadian market is to be served from one geographic set of locations. Nevertheless, the present distribution of manufacturing reflects the domination of central locations over the development of a wider network of regional plants. In effect, industries have adapted, geographically and economically, by accepting a location pattern that has higher transport costs but lower production costs derived from larger plants, longer production runs, newer technology and industrial concentration itself, given the historical and current influence of the tariff.

Manufacturing is comprised of a broad and ever-widening range of activities. It includes both the bakeries and creameries to be found in any substantial urban centre, providing the perishables that require immediate delivery to consumers, and the breweries, soft drink-bottling plants, brickworks and cement works that supply regional markets with products whose heavy costs of transportation strongly favour production in or very near major points of sale. These are all processing industries that are widely distributed across Canada. Processing industries also include those dependent upon raw materials—for steel, pulp and paper, petroleum products, various other metals, meat products, (in market locations), canned food and wines—at the sources of major material inputs, depending upon supply, production and transport factors. In fact, non-central industrial locations in Canada largely owe their existence to the resource base which has allowed primary processing to develop.

While the locational pattern of *primary manufacturing* generally reflects its need for proximity to resource locations (transport cost reasons), or cheap land or power, the pattern is more complex as evidenced by the fact that there are processing industries located in central regions. The steel industry, for example, shows that market proximity dominates the mix of transport costs associated with assembling raw materials and supplying a diversified, but basic, product. Similarly, although wood industries are identified with British Columbia and paper with British Columbia, Ontario and Quebec, the location of resource-based industries at sub-provincial scales illustrates both the link between industry and the resource regions (Canadian Shield or Western Mountains) and the presence of segments of resource-based industries in market locations. Most resource locations and primary manufacturing centres generate only small amounts of local consumer industry and local industrial services; in the aggregate, these locations do not detract from the strength of the industrial heartland, which is built on both secondary manufacturing and processing industry.

The main focus of this chapter is *secondary manufacturing* which includes the production of consumer goods such as clothing, furniture, automobiles and household appliances. These industries are concentrated in the two central provinces with Quebec containing relatively more of the labour-intensive industries, such as clothing and furniture, and Ontario having relatively more of the capital-intensive industries, such as the production of automobiles and household appliances. But it should be emphasized that, in some instances, "manufacture" is little more than the assembly of components imported from another country—the U.S., in most cases. The fabrication of capital goods—ships, aircraft, agricultural equipment, machinery for factory and office—is also included as part of secondary manufacturing. Shipyards are located mostly in the Maritime provinces and Quebec.

The locational concentration of secondary manufacturing reflects a complex interrelationship of factors, including the historical evolution of economic development, especially the progressive agglomeration of plants in the major manufacturing regions of metropolitan Toronto, the Golden Horseshoe of Lake Ontario, southwest Ontario and Metropolitan Montreal. These agglomerations also reflect the regional and local development of urban and industrial infra-structure in general; specifically, they offer skilled labour, managerial, engineering, and other technological services for industry, component and auxiliary suppliers.

Canada reflects the world-wide trend to regional industrial concentrations—especially in Central Canada—and a simple interpretation, as implied above, suggests that within these regions, high levels of geographic accessibility are the basis of the input-output dependence of industries, as reflected in the flows of intermediate products, components and services. Following this logic, Canada would appear to reflect, through localization and urbanization factors, the same locational and regional development forces as have been inferred or observed in some of the major industrial regions elsewhere in the world. Industrial regions like those in Canada's heartland, however, may have weaker internal connections of the direct, input-output type, though they have labour market, service, infra-structural and visibility advantages—the external economies of agglomeration. Nevertheless, a variety of direct product linkages has developed within Canada's industrial regions—such as basic steel supplies—which foster industrial clustering because of saving in delivery cost, speed and access to wholesalers. But when higher-valued industrial inputs are considered, the range of distances that separates supplying and buying plants is much greater because of the technological content of the products involved and also because of a less elastic demand with respect to transport cost. Reinforcing this geographic attenuation of input-output links is the impact that multi-locational firms have on the flow of industrial products. Despite their geographic separation, interdependent plants in a firm generate interregional flows of material, components and service inputs.

In this connection, research on material linkages in the Montreal region shows that only one-third of industrial purchases and sales are made within the region. Size of establishment modifies the pattern: small establishments (1-25 workers) have the strongest local connections (54 per cent of purchases) while large establishments (over 101 workers) make less than one-third of their purchases locally and are less dependent on wholesalers than is true of smaller establishments. The largest establishments, however, dominate the aggregate of industrial activity and intra-firm economies are confirmed to explain non-local linkages.

Research on the material input linkages of secondary manufacturing firms in southern Ontario has identified three linkage classes of firms:

1. "Independent" plants, such as small- to medium-sized machinery plants in Toronto or the Lakeshore and simple fabricators which depend upon regional inputs.
2. "Dependent" plants, for which most flows are of high value and are from distant sources, often from elsewhere within the same corporation. Auto parts plants of U.S. ownership are a prime example.
3. "Intermediate" plants, which take advantage of local and regional sources of industrial inputs and depend as well upon long distance linkages.

Toronto itself contains plants in the "dependent" category; thus, corporate factors often are shown to over-ride access to the region's wholesalers and component manufacturers. In the periphery of Toronto's urban field, however, the proportion of "dependent" plants is at its greatest. This same pattern is echoed when the sources of routine office services are examined: as metropolitan access declines so does the independence of branch plants, especially when under U.S. ownership. The branches in more distant industrial towns in southern Ontario demonstrate to the greatest degree the substitution of long-distance corporate flows for regional connections, thereby perpetuating the low level of development and regional industrial integration of these centres.

Foreign Ownership and Tariffs

Multi-locational firms in Canadian secondary manufacturing thus attain particular significance, not only because dominant control is located outside the country, but because it is often in the firms' best interests to maintain a strong intracorporate (international) dependence for a wide variety of inputs—components, capital equipment, managerial and professional services. The impact on the industrial heartland is to reduce the internal strength of Canada's industrial complexes in ways not immediately obvious: thresholds for the emergence of firms supplying specialized components and services in Central Canada are not met and/or high costs are passed on to those firms buying from these minimum-scale specialists.

A major agent contributing to the locational concentration of secondary manufacturing has been the attraction of American branch plants to the central industrial regions. Being located close to the American Manufacturing Belt has assisted the maintenance of intracorporate links and the behaviour of foreign plants has to be considered as a key element in the evolution of Canada's industrial regions and in the level of development and performance of the Canadian industrial system in general. This significance is derived in large part from the *amount* of foreign capital employed in manufacturing, because from capital invested directly has come economic dependence and foreign control of Canadian economic activities. Canada is a hinterland economy, an economic periphery to the United States, and this status is entrenched in the strength of U.S. direct investment in Canada. An understanding of the performance of the Canadian economy, especially of its manufacturing, must start first with understanding this unique degree of U.S. control.

Over half of Canada's manufacturing capacity consists of foreign-owned branch plants, ownership, in most instances, being lodged in the U.S. (Table 1). Foreign ownership is the case, particularly in industries such as smelters and pulp and paper plants that sell much of their product in the U.S., and industries that employ advanced technology developed in other countries, such as the automobile and household appliance industries. A large fraction of the aerospace industry is Canadian-owned, as are Canada's shipyards.

The greatest concentrations of foreign control are found in mining and manufacturing, notably in the higher-technology (non-traditional) industries; lower levels of foreign control of assets occur in retail and wholesale trade and in the large service sector. Foreign-controlled investments are associated on average with larger-sized firms in Canada and this in turn appears related to higher labour productivity in U.S.-controlled manufacturing plants. As we will see, this "positive" effect is more apparent than real and signals the weakness of domestic firms.

The level of American investment is a direct result of the application of tariffs against a wide variety of imports, especially finished goods. Tariffs were introduced 100 years ago and most writers have followed the argument that tariffs were motivated by a Canadian infant industry policy. Naylor, however, has argued that Canadian policy in 1879 was a deliberate abandonment of Canadian industrial *firms* and industrial *entrepreneurial ability* to the inroads of foreign capital. Canada introduced tariffs although Canadian firms were beginning to produce in competition with imports, the Canadian problem being competition for capital be-

Table 1 Ownership of Canadian Manufacturing, 1970

Group	Establishments: Foreign-Controlled, by percentage	Average Size of Establishments (number of production workers) Foreign	Domestic	Value of Shipments Foreign-Controlled, by percentage	Average Size of Canadian Establishments as a Percentage of Average Size of Foreign Establishments
Food and Beverage	8.8%	92	18	33.2%	19.6%
Tobacco	—	—	—	—	—
Rubber and Plastics	23.0	140	26	72.7	18.6
Leather	8.4	123	43	20.2	35.0
Textiles	12.6	179	42	46.8	23.5
Knitting Mills	9.4	120	59	18.4	49.2
Clothing Industry	2.8	131	37	9.8	28.2
Wood	5.0	98	19	25.1	19.4
Furniture and Fixtures	2.6	94	14	16.8	14.9
Paper & Allied Industries	32.3	211	110	49.3	52.1
Printing and Publishing	2.1	55	13	11.9	23.6
Primary Metals	27.5	339	173	45.9	51.0
Metal Fabrication	11.3	74	20	39.9	27.0
Machinery Industry	31.0	120	27	71.6	22.5
Transportation Equipment	21.4	398	40	86.8	10.1
Electrical Products	42.8	146	70	64.6	47.9
Non-metallic Minerals	15.9	72	20	51.6	27.8
Petroleum and Coal Products	67.0	100	11	97.9	11.0
Chemicals	46.7	55	18	81.3	32.7
TOTAL	11.9%	124	25	52.0%	20.2%

Source: Statistics Canada, *Domestic and Foreign Control of Manufacturing Establishments in Canada, 1969 and 1970*, Cat. No. 31-401, Information Canada, Ottawa, March 1976, pp. 42-45.

tween industrial firms and commerce. The commercial staples had proved to be profit-makers in the past and commercial interests were relieved of industrial competition for capital when direct foreign investment in manufacturing was accelerated by the tariff.

Northeastern U.S. was already an industrial power by the last quarter of the 19th century and once the branches of U.S. firms had arrived, changes in the U.S. organization of production were imported. Over the years several peaks in merger activity in the U.S. were transmitted into Canada. This access of U.S. business trends to Canada and the expansion of the Canadian market after the Second World War ensured that larger amounts of U.S. capital would be invested in Canada. Now Canadian industry is well stocked with the subsidiaries of multinational corporations and American domestic companies.

U.S. direct investment in Canadian secondary manufacturing was assisted by the proximity of the Canadian market and the Canadian assembly of imported components is now common. Other manufacturing investments, however, were motivated by the prospect of non-Canadian sales; this is especially true for forest products, mineral production and other resource products.

Tariffs have been reduced in recent decades, owing to the Kennedy and Tokyo agreements under GATT (General Agreement on Tariffs and Trade). Nevertheless, negotiations have made little impact on non-tariff barriers to trade. While high tariffs on finished goods generally have encouraged U.S. firms to establish branches in Canada, often as miniature replicas of the product range of the parent firm, schemes like the Auto Pact and the agricultural machinery agreement have integrated Canadian and U.S. production. These have not been an unqualified success for Canada. Exports have increased, but imports have increased more: furthermore, Canada's auto production embodies a proportionally large amount of unskilled labour while U.S. production is characterized by a proportionally large skilled complement in the work force (Table 2).

The auto pact has rationalized Canadian production lines and improved

Table 2 Labour Skill Levels in Automotive Industry

Skill Level	Vehicle Assembly		Parts Production	
	Canada	U.S.	Canada	U.S.
Skilled	2%	8%	10%	10%
Semi-skilled	23%	43%	38%	56%
Unskilled	75%	49%	52%	34%

Source: J. Shepherd, *The Canada-U.S. Auto Pact: A Technological Perspective* (Science Council of Canada 1978) p. 11, using data from 1976 Review by Department of Industry, Trade and Commerce.

productivity but also, it has institutionalized auto trade deficits and has negotiated away any possibility of a relative improvement in Canadians' jobs and incomes. The Auto Pact simply did *not* protect Canada's share of the industry as it was supposed to do and, technologically, it is incapable of responding to current problems. Auto firms in Canada, are singularly poorly equipped to undertake relevant research and product development. Independent Canadian auto parts manufacturers are poorly served by the Pact; parts are imported into Canada from the U.S. in such quantities that auto trade imbalances are created. In part, at least, this demonstrates the lack of access that Canadian independents have to the market of the "Big Four" auto assemblers, reflecting the strength of inter- or intracorporate arrangements developed between U.S.-controlled firms: 60 per cent of parts consumed is either bought from "captive" suppliers or produced by the "Big Four."

Other tariff reductions have occurred under remission schemes, such as the defence production sharing agreement with the United States. The overall effect is that, of the total of end-products imported into Canada in 1976, over 63 per cent entered duty-free (44 per cent if auto-pact imports are excluded). This represents a remarkably high level of non-protection; other countries allow very much lower proportions of end-product imports to enter duty-free (e.g., in 1970: U.S.: 6.8 per cent; U.K.: 16 per cent; EEC: 3.2 per cent; Japan: 3.6 per cent). Canada is thus a very confusing environment: Canadian tariffs are waived under several agreements; Canada tends to be in increasing end-product trade deficit; tariffs that are in place protect the Canadian market for both domestically owned firms and the branches of foreign-owned firms.

Manufacturing Performance

Given the geographic pattern of Canadian manufacturing and its ownership structure, the core question remains, "How well does industry perform?" While the easy answer to this question is "poorly," supplying a full answer is a complex task. Manufacturing is comprised of a complex set of interdependent firms bound together by flows of materials, income and information. Furthermore, it generates income and employment growth and creates knowledge and thus increased human capacity (development). This is a brief definition of an *industrial system,* the economic entity whose performance we must assess. Adopting this focus for our thinking means that we are forced to ask questions about interdependent relationships among firms, regions, ownership groups and industries. Economists writing on trade performance (one indicator of an industrial system's success) are concerned with a macroscopic view of the external performance of the economy, usually in terms of sectors. But they rarely consider such matters as the responses of different groups of firms to new market opportunities, although judgment of such reactions may be central to the evaluation of the possible effects of tariff changes. Likewise, many industrial economists refer to aspects of the performance of firms without clearly specifying the importance that should be attached to the degree of interdependence between firms. Questions like these are basic to an understanding of the form and performance of Canada's industrial system.

Canada's trade balance in secondary manufactures is found to be negative persistently. An obvious line of enquiry is through factors affecting the degree of international dependence of firms in Canada. Imports of intermediate goods can be related to the locus of control (foreign ownership), export levels can be evaluated in terms of products (stage in product life cycle), and these to control locations, scale factors, level of R & D intensity, industrial levels of professional and technical employment, and so on. Because imports of some intermediate goods substitute for feasible domestic production (and even potential exports) with a system that, like Canada's, is relatively open, it becomes important to evaluate very carefully the determinants of international corporate purchases. Of equal importance is that Canada has been experiencing increasing difficulty over several decades in the production and export of goods that embody high levels of skill and technology.

Total merchandise trade as a percentage of GNP generally improved over the 1955-70 period but the achievements of the late 1960s reflect strongly the temporary surplus earned in the early years of the Auto Pact. A rather poorer performance picture is created by the movement of the relative trade balance for *manufactures* (proportion of GNP), if the effect of the subsequent losses in auto trade are considered; the negative balance of manufactures never recovered to its level of the early 1950s. Resource-based manufactures (Figure 2) (a positive series) have trended upwards and non-auto secondary manufactures (a negative series) have trended downwards since 1950, while the products of non-auto high-technology manufactures have a slight downtrend in a strongly negative series. In recent decades, therefore, resources continued to be the positive force in Canada's merchandise trade while, contrary to the trends in world trade patterns, Canada has slipped to a less advanced comparative industrial position. Worldwide increases in trade and economic development were just not reflected in Canada's economic position: Canada became more dependent on its current staples but there has been no demonstration yet that Canada has begun to take the additional steps required to make resources the foundation for future development.

Canada has a wide variety of structural economic problems to face. If we accept that economic development depends on industrialization in Canada just as it does elsewhere in the world then the first among these

Figure 2
Selected Elements of Canadian Trade Balance: Per Cent Value of Shipments

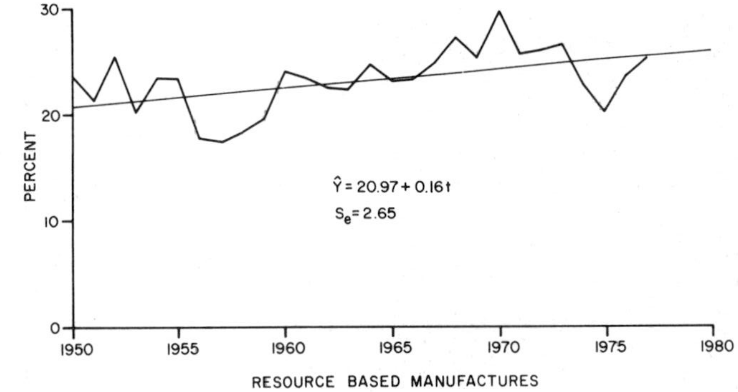

30
20
10
0
PERCENT
1950
1955
1960
1965
1970
1975
1980
Ŷ = 20.97 + 0.16t
Se = 2.65
RESOURCE BASED MANUFACTURES

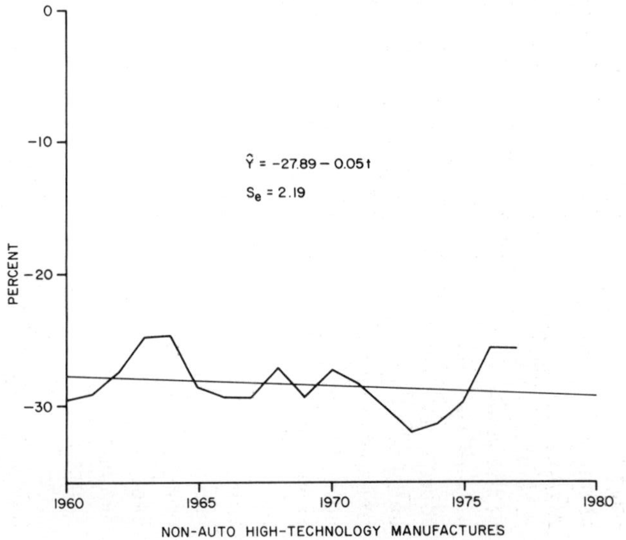

0
-10
-20
-30
PERCENT
1960
1965
1970
1975
1980
Ŷ = -27.89 – 0.05t
Se = 2.19
NON-AUTO HIGH-TECHNOLOGY MANUFACTURES

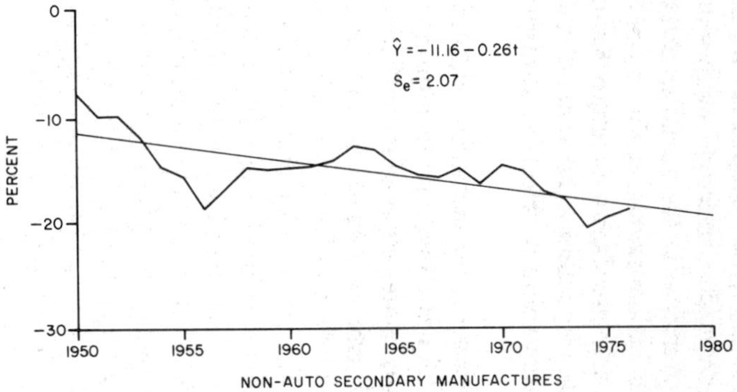

0
-10
-20
-30
PERCENT
1950
1955
1960
1965
1970
1975
1980
Ŷ = –11.16 – 0.26t
Se = 2.07
NON-AUTO SECONDARY MANUFACTURES

Source: Statistics Canada

problems is Canada's evident industrial stagnation (at a semi-industrial stage) while other economies have been developing. In 1955, Alfred Maizels in his book *Industrial Growth and World Trade* (London: 1953) placed Canada among a group of semi-industrial economies that were at about the same level in regard to the *value of manufacturing production per capita* and *finished manufactures as a share of exports.* These measures locate economies in terms of the domestic importance of manufacturing production and in terms of the international penetration achieved by this sector; true industrialization requires high values in both dimensions. Semi-industrial economies are characterized by high-medium per capita indices and inferior export positions for finished goods, while non-industrial economies have low values on both scales. Over the years to 1973 the Canadian population approximately doubled in size but in industrial terms Canada more or less stagnated when compared with the rest of the 1955 group of industrial and semi-industrial economies (allowing for the export-creating but development-inhibiting effects of the Auto Pact). Smaller European economies gained relative to Canada (Figure 3); Sweden achieved particularly dramatic advances in development. Given Canada's economic size, her industrialization has to be recognized as a very weak response to the possibilities. Highly industrialized countries consolidated their positions and semi-industrial economies converged on the first group. Despite her larger size and greater industrial development, Canada clustered with Australia and New Zealand, which are also high-income economies highly reliant on primary exports, to pay for manufactured imports of end products—despite substantial domestic levels of manufacturing employment.

Canada's pattern of economic growth within the OECD group is distinctive: first rank in employment growth and ninth rank in output increase in the period 1955-1968. In other words, Canada's *performance* differs considerably from that of most industrial economies and this is part of the explanation of her trading position. Canada's dominant role as a primary resource hinterland is illustrated by the relatively greater development of resource-based industries and the comparatively small production of professional goods, electrical machinery, plastics, and the like.

One expression of Canada's manufacturing problems is her pattern of imports. Canada imports *finished* goods from (a) cheap labour areas, (b) cheap labour and technologically superior areas, and from (c) technologically superior traders that have more or less similar wage rates, e.g., the U.S.A. If Canada is in trade deficit in secondary manufactures with *all* of these types of trading partners, we can be assured that minor relative improvements in labour productivity and adjustment of the dollar's foreign exchange rate and of Canadian wage scales will by themselves do little for Canada's negative trade balance. Given our wage levels and our aspirations, we are just too heavily committed to conventional

Figure 3
International Industrialization: Production and Exports of Manufactures: 1955-1973

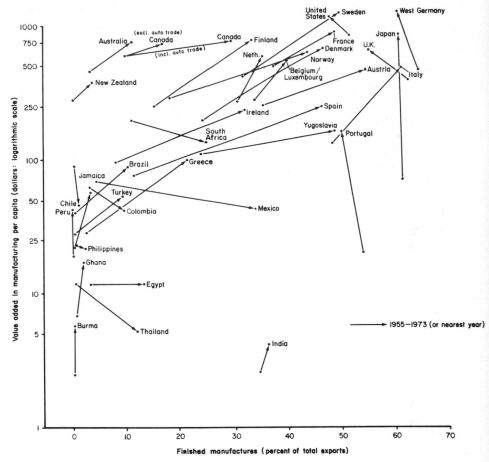

Source: Science Council of Canada, *Uncertain Prospects*, Ottawa, 1977

products of traditional industries and to technologically mature products. The Canadian economy has failed to achieve the technological level it could have achieved or should aspire to, given prevailing education levels, wage rates, and so on. Canada could have specialized (within the area of secondary manufacturing) in innovation-intensive products for which the small size of the domestic market would not have presented major direct or indirect cost burdens. This applies particularly to capital goods required for resource exploitation. There is, of course, a middle ground in which Canada could expand between high performance products which are innovation-intensive and those which are relatively simple mass-market items. This ground is occupied by goods whose markets are protected by transport costs and innovation, and by design-based products that are in the early and growth stages of the product cycle. These can be finished goods (consumer and capital goods), components and subassemblies which could lay claim to continental and possibly international markets.

While Canada's poor industrial situation is partly indicated by the types of products that firms turn out—goods with low export potential—the other part of the explanation lies in the combination of high labour cost and inferior productivity. Canada is not cost-competitive against a wide variety of imported goods; removal of the productivity gap has to occur in at least some of the firms that are passive in exploring opportunities for import substitution or for the export of secondary manufactures. The economy is characterized by a serious structural fault. There is an apparent maladaptation of Canada's secondary industrial make-up to the country's size, education levels and wage rates, as well as to world prices and the performance rating of goods.

Employment Issues

While there has been much change in the nature of employment throughout the entire industrial world, Canada has relinquished jobs in the goods-manufacturing sectors faster than its competitors have (see Table 3).

As noted, the consequent pattern is one of a service emphasis and it is possible that this may be a symptom of the emergence of "post-industrial" economy and society. This designation is a dangerous one, however, as it is the qualitative distribution of jobs in society that is the critical factor in identifying a truly progressive pattern of economic change. Industrial and sectoral data alone do not reveal enough about the type (quality) of activities that employees are performing, and comparisons with the United States, which has progressed further along the growth path in service employment, require that occupational data be examined.

The evidence points to a low level of *both* blue-collar and white-collar jobs in Canada today; comparisons with the U.S.A. reveal an origin of worry about the comparative performance of Canada's industrial economy. The relatively poorer quality of jobs in Canadian manufacturing and the inferior *future* potential of this sector show that Canada is failing to generate the technical jobs that are required for industrial success under contemporary economic conditions. In essence, Canada has fallen victim to Pavitt's warning that

> a healthy growth in services depends on the efficiency of manufacturing industry; otherwise growth in the relative importance of service employment may reflect a "de-industrial

Table 3 Professional and technical jobs in selected
high technology industries—Canada and U.S.A.
(As percentage of total jobs)

	Canada Professional and Technical 1961 1971	U.S.A. Professional and Technical 1960 1970	Canada Engineers 1961 1971	U.S.A. Engineers 1960 1970
Chemicals	12.9% 10.5%	15.5% 18.5%	2.6% 2.4%	3.8% 4.3%
Primary metals	6.3 6.4	5.6 6.7	1.9 2.3	1.9 2.1
Machinery	8.3 9.1	9.5 13.3	2.7 3.3	4.2 6.2
Electrical Products	13.2 11.4	15.3 18.1	4.5 4.6	6.9 8.1
Transport Equipment	6.6 5.3	12.2 14.1	2.3 2.7	6.0 6.8
All manufacturing	5.0 5.3	6.9 9.1	1.2 1.6	2.7 3.3

society'', rather than a "post-industrial society'', and the
quality of the services will inevitably be low. [2]

A likely effect of Canada's industrial problems is increasing economic
and social disillusionment among those who are young and educated on
the grounds that the country's industrial system is not producing the demands for their skill, in manufacturing or services, in the manner occurring in the better developed economies. Instead of enjoying an expansion
of the relative importance of superior types of position, *Canada has experienced a marked relative contraction* in managerial posts and an increase in professional and technical jobs of only 6 per cent—as opposed
to a 32 per cent increase in the U.S.—within manufacturing. Since technological development (economic development) and increased export potential rely heavily on these skilled occupations, these patterns are critical
for Canada's industrial future. Decline in employment shares or increases
below U.S. levels occurred for the professional and technical job category in every high-technology industry. Given the leading position of the
U.S. and its slower technological growth in the 1960s, Canada should
have done better. It has forgone many important opportunities.

Human Resources versus Natural Resources
and Problems of Corporate Development

Some opinions imply Canada will do rather well with resource-based industries on the one hand and a growing services sector on the other. Various misconceptions lie behind these views and it is important that they be rejected. There are several reasons:

1. Unless manufacturing and/or resource industries create a sufficient surplus, improvements in publicly provided services (health, education, etc.) will be impossible. Ultimately, the size of the whole non-market sector is dependent upon the level of *surplus* earnings in the domestic and export market, hence Canada cannot do without an effective manufacturing sector.
2. Increasingly, computerization and word-processors are reducing the need for employees in routine office jobs.
3. A large proportion of the jobs in the service industries is directly dependent upon demands created in manufacturing industry (for producer sevices), and the role of manufacturing workers in demanding consumer services is also very significant.

That Canada is generating proportionally fewer opportunities for the highly skilled than most developed economies means that there is an *underutilization of human resources.* Why is this so? The conventional view would have us believe that Canada's comparative advantage is such that *natural* resources are the basis of the country's strength and that it would be costly or at least unneccessary to develop a differently based economic structure. There are two problems with this view. First, it is historical, a reflection of the past and the present, and not necessarily an indication of the future situation toward which we should be heading. Second, that it is true of the past and present means that there has been a comparative failure of the Canadian economy to develop an industrial structure in which human, especially corporate, resources are able to assert themselves more strongly in Canada's international profile. We come back, therefore, to the question, "Why has Canada persistently underdeveloped its corporate resources, and underutilized and underdeveloped the other human resources that it has generated?"

Before answering this question, two other lines of argument must be considered. First, what is Canada's likely *future* international strength in natural resources? In other words, "How pressing is the problem of underdeveloped use of human resources in the industrial system?" Second, "Is there evidence from the industrial system to support the contention that there is corporate failure in Canada?"

Canada is very well-endowed with natural resources and the advantages are well-known of having natural gas, oil, many minerals, copper and nickel in very large quantities and so on; they are revealed in international trade figures. The capital-intensive phases of extraction and processing generally occur in Canada but even here there are problems.

Japanese purchasing agreements, for example, usually stipulate the shipment of copper concentrate from an earlier stage of processing. Generally, Canada does not have well-developed forward resource-linkages; that is, there is little manufacture past early-stage processing (concentrates, ingots, pulp, timber, newsprint). This fact, and the import dependence of Canadian resource industries on capital equipment, for exploration, extraction and processing, mean that there are substantial opportunities being lost in Canada for *the interdependent use of human and natural resources* at the manufacturing stage. Underdevelopment of the industrial system compared with its potential would be another way of describing the situation.

Canada's level of resource exports, currently, is not large enough to offset our trade deficit in respect to services and other goods; we now compete with an increasing array of producers of non-petroleum staples —hard-dealing countries whose exports most often are based on *one* product and who also are regarded as having a "comparative advantage" in natural resources. And here more competitors are coming! As well, there are major problems of exploitation at the resource frontier which require not only large amounts of capital for their solution but also new technology and corporate competence. Given the poor realization of the possibilities of both downstream resource profits and of domestic linkages between capital-equipment producers and resource sectors, Canada has placed herself in a domestically weak position; it will be difficult to keep renewing resource staples. Canada has been taking a "free ride" on resources for the past three decades; payment should have been made in technological development.

The future of Canada's resource base lies in the development of new exploration, extraction, processing, delivery and utilization technologies. From where will this capability come? From the record, it appears that imports will be the primary source. In the future, however, Canada will be unable to afford the luxury of importation without incurring further opportunity costs of the sort revealed at present by our employment structure, trade balance and weak dollar. There is every reason for Canada to continue to have a strong resource component in its "comparative advantage"; an unchanging "comparative advantage," however, carries with it continued heavy economic and social costs because it reflects a failure to develop a technologically more competent economic structure, particularly in the manufacturing sector and the non-consumer services.

There is evidence to support the hypothesis that *problems of corporate underdevelopment* in Canada are at the core of the failure to use fully the country's human resource potential. The high level of net outflows of dividends and royalties reflects the single-minded way in which Canada has obtained international access to industrial capital and industrial technology through direct foreign investment. A further effect of industrial decisions on purchasing, influenced by the foreign-domestic mix of capital and technology, is that there are very heavy net imports of managerial and professional services (MPS). In 1970, Canada spent (directly) $1016.5 million on MPS, estimated to be 23 per cent of the salaries paid to managers, engineers, salesmen and clerks in manfacturing and mining. As 90 per cent of MPS imports are made by *foreign-controlled companies,* and 75 per cent by intracorporate, we have here a very clear indication of the significance of foreign companies in respect to the leakages from the industrial system. These leakages are the direct or indirect results of the openness of the system, particularly the economic permeability of the Canada/U.S. border. All these net trade deficits are of both short-run significance and long-run importance since they signal a reduced opportunity to produce, innovate and grow. The nature and scale of industrial inputs signal the level of *potential* for achieving import substitution and also indicate the degree of technological dependence that pervades the system. Imported components embody the technology that Canada does not have, at least in a form that would provide a basis for Canadian replication, improvement or replacement with second-generation products. There is no chance of a development cycle occurring in Canada if current products continue to be replaced by imports of new components embodying more recent technology. When replacement by new imports occurs, domestic production of currently standard components (former imports) has no export potential; significant Canadian development has, once again, been pre-empted.

We can take the case of MPS imports to illustrate some of Canada's corporate problems in developing its human resources: the evidence indicates the high level of foreign, corporate substitution of MPS imports in place of domestically supplied services. The substitution is a reasonable choice from the corporation's perspective but does *not* coincide with Canada's interests. Every import for which there is a potential domestic supply point has the negative aspects described above: reduced multiplier effects and retarded developmental potential. The consequence of these negative impulses working through the system is that the "possible domestic supply" is weakened and reduced in size to the point where an increasing number of functions *have* to be imported by *domestic* firms; otherwise they have to do without. The short-and long-term effects are a reduced number of jobs and reduced innovative and export potential in Canadian technical and financial service activities. MPS imports, in effect, have developmental implications that parallel the impact that imports of goods have on the production phase of the industrial system. A high level of intracorporate and other imports anywhere in the industrial system reduces opportunities for domestic supply firms to emerge or expand. Imports of MPS and intermediate goods are therefore important

in their own right because of their significance for employment opportunities, trade balance and so on, but especially because they are the
means by which the development of domestic technological strength is
stifled by foreign-owned firms. Where they are competing, domestic
firms tend to walk a narrow line between being (1) out-paced in product
innovation and technology replacement, or (2) successful in bearing costs
of some product development, licencing, or the purchase of new product
or production technology. But the number taking an aggressive stance
with respect to innovation and international marketing is insufficient. Not
all areas of secondary manufacturing are marked by the presence of large
foreign firms, of course. However, in few of Canada's non-traditional industries are we particularly successful.

Dependency and Technological Underdevelopment

So far we have concentrated on assessing the patterns of inputs to the industrial system and have recognized that there is an ownership dualism in
Canada that has constrained development impulses: foreign-owned firms
tend to be Canadian parts of the U.S. industrial system, while a small domestic system carries on with only part of the range of industrial tasks expected in a high-income country of 24 million. What makes the impact of
the foreign firms so substantial is that they are large, and collectively they
dominate. This impact operates in two ways. First, they are mass producers in the main and have large market power. Smaller Canadian producers, usually not endowed with the corporate resources of their
competitors, survive through finding product, performance and locational
niches, chiefly in Canadian markets. This effect is alarming—the domestic industrial system is much smaller than it is generally perceived to be!
Growth and development potentials are constrained. Second, given their
size and corporate resources, foreign-owned plants in secondary manufacturing are poor exporters; world production mandates of multi-
nationals have only infrequently been vested in Canadian subsidiaries.
Canadian producers are poor exporters, too, estimates *of export performance* (excluding transport equipment) for secondary manufacturers
giving foreign firms a 9.5 per cent export rate and domestic firms an 11.3
per cent rate. However, more important than this difference is the fact
that more than half of these "export sales" by foreign companies were intracorporate transfers. *In 1969, only 4 per cent of the sales of foreign subsidiaries located in Canada were free-market exports!*

In point of fact, foreign firms in secondary manufacturing do not produce much that could be exported to arms'-length buyers. How do we
know? Given Canada's wage-cost position, only products in the early and
early-growth phases of the product cycle are export candidates of sec-

ondary manufacturers. But the volume of imports of these items (e.g., electrical goods and electronics from the Far East), the lack of exports by foreign firms in Canada and the *intracorporate* domination of what exports there are by these firms together reveal that foreign firms are not capable of exporting because they do not have the appropriate products. Furthermore, there was never any intention by the majority of these firms to export from Canada. This should not really come as a surprise because U.S. firms freely admit the pre-emptive market strategies that lie behind their investment in subsidiaries. Foreign firms in secondary manufacturing are predisposed to be *importers* of corporate-built components and the majority are *not* destined to be competitors in foreign markets.

The problem stands; because of its tariff and other policies, Canada has obtained a large foreign-controlled industrial sector that under-contributes to the Canadian industrial system. Worldwide changes in technology and jobs have overtaken the situation that Canada allowed to evolve and the past strength of Canada's dependence upon resource exports has a less certain future. There is no doubt about the reality of the "third wave of industrialization", about the more advanced economic, technological and occupational structures that are being found elsewhere in the developed world; nor is there doubt about shifts in Canada's resource base that place greater emphasis on the need to develop technological and managerial expertise.

The search for explanations of Canada's massive and growing imports of secondary manufactures in part lies in past and present levels of R & D activity and in the supporting industrial activities that generate new products, processes, and export and domestic sales. Basically, R & D is underdeveloped in Canada—less than 1 per cent of GDP compared with the U.S. level of 2.5 per cent.[3] Only one-third of R & D funds come from the business sector, compared with 40-50 per cent in other OECD countries, and the business sector is a weaker performer of R & D, too; it does 40 per cent of the country's research, compared with 50-65 per cent done by the business sector in OECD countries. The Canadian R & D pattern, however, is worse than these data appear to indicate: 57 per cent of R & D expenditures are made by subsidiaries because they are the firms large enough to fund this type of work. Furthermore, the impact of the R & D undertaken by foreign-controlled firms on exports is very limited. Subsidiaries that function in a relatively autonomous way do tend to export either the products or processes in which they differ from their parent. But the R & D of most subsidiaries is primarily concerned with adapting the technology of the parents. The impact on exports is negligible: about *half of the subsidiaries doing R & D* in Canada had exports amounting to less than 15 per cent of sales in 1976. The reason for this pattern lies in the market constraints that apply to product lines derived from imported technology.

Understandably, given their small average size, domestic firms as a group are also poor R & D performers; otherwise Canada's trade situation would be much better. Nevertheless, research reveals that the R & D expenditures of domestic companies *relative to their level of sales* is higher than those of their foreign counterparts. This *relatively* more effective R & D performance of domestic firms has an unfortunate corollary in that the size of R & D units in Canada is also very small.

Although R & D establishes the technological base for much innovative capability, the design and engineering of products and the costs of initial marketing activities are of much greater importance than often is acknowledged by the emphasis on R & D activity in Canadian literature. Canada probably lags behind the U.S. in design and engineering expenditures, reflecting a highly underdeveloped level of innovative capability in Canada. This particular problem is the more troublesome as recent research on the export performance of firms in Canada shows that these factors are vital to export success.

The evidence points to Canada's need for increased expenditure on R & D, but probably more important is the need for Canada to undertake *new* product development where design and engineering are needed in order to sell domestically and internationally. The present situation seems to reflect the dominance of product modification among subsidiaries (hence little call for design work) and the difficulty most firms have in developing domestic innovative capability. The problem of stimulating domestic firms to act in a progressive way is deep-seated; nevertheless, some economists emphasize that the signs of Canadian industrial underdevelopment, including poor productivity and low efficiency, are themselves the products of tariffs and that free trade would provide the solution. Will opting for free trade help? Free trade might be the desirable long term state, but how good is it as a policy instrument? Unfortunately, removing tariffs will not necessarily increase output and improve efficiency for the majority of firms. Other consequences of a change in tariffs would be a variety of social and economic costs which may also be unacceptable. Probably the most important observation to make about the free-trade option is that no changing of tariffs will improve productivity or efficiency unless industries have products saleable in the U.S. and other foreign markets; the capability to design, produce and market these products must exist *before* tariff change!

Unfortunately proponents of free trade rarely embrace a social and economic view of the evolution of Canadian society that jibes with the corporate, occupational, economic and technological situations here and developments occurring elsewhere in the world. In particular, their case ignores the present and resultant internal and external operations of Canada's industrial system—the inter-firm dependencies that operate now, or those which could have been operating, and how present interdependencies will change under free trade.

Policies and Options

Given the complexity of changes in the *international* industrial system, knowing the present significance of foreign ownership in Canada's industrial system, and bearing in mind the need for structural and functional change in Canadian industry, it is vital that Canada embark on a deliberate long-term policy of technological and industrial development. To develop a technological strategy for Canada the goal must be to converge on a set of policy guidelines that are justified in terms of the analysis of Canada's problems of industrial performance and behaviour. In the light of this, a consistent techno-industrial strategy is an imperative.

Firms survive or fail according to performance criteria, "the market" identifying the survivors and winners. But provincial and federal governments, together with their Crown corporations and utilities, also establish conditions of success for individual firms or industries through their power to award significant contracts, to make loans or to buy companies. Therefore, a consistent policy context is required. Furthermore, there are still doubts that Canadian firms always receive the contract considerations other governments give their national firms. There is concern, too, that the capital demands by a few firms/projects, employing many workers, have been given preferred treatment compared with the needs and prospects of a large number of smaller firms. The objective must be to see that both large and small projects are supported because they are important to the attainment of Canadian economic and technological goals. But these goals, the policy and the instruments must be specified and given a fair trial and consistent support. A variety of government agencies and private commentators agree; there is, however, only partial political endorsement of this position. Short-term considerations dominate.

We must be clear about the policy options. It is realistic to expect that there will be more direct action on industrial problems by federal and provincial governments. Government purchases amount to about $30 billion per year and both levels have announced support for Canadian purchasing. This approach achieves more than just job creation; it provides a basis for establishing technological competence. At a minimum, this competence will enable us to produce substitutes for imports and it may lead to export capability. Some *resource developments* will also require governmental involvement and the Science Council has argued the importance of Canada's developing its own technology for dealing with oceans, oil-sands, satellites, pipelines and Arctic resources. Support for programs of increased *R & D and innovation* is a commitment that all governments must make but so far this support has not been available on a sufficiently long-run and predictable basis to encourage "new and sustained activity." Provincial science and technology advisory bodies now exist; for example, the Alberta Oil Sands Technology and Research Administration is to speed up and finance oil sands research and to ensure domestic ownership of the technology. There are also new co-operative ventures between industry and universities, and this emergence of *innovation centres* may mean greater technological stimulation and availability of information firms, especially small firms with their inherent disadvantages in undertaking market assessment, product innovation, absorbing new technology and adopting effective product designs. Ultimately, changes must be encouraged in the *organizational structure of Canadian firms.* The underdevelopment of complexes of firms focussing on core companies is a sign of industrial immaturity. Too many Canadian firms in electronics or the computing field, for example, are trying to "go it alone" rather than be involved in sub-contracting arrangements with larger companies. In the aerospace industry, however, a superior model of organization and development has emerged and economic strength has resulted. Joint ventures between foreign and domestic companies may furnish foreign market connections and make capital resources available. There is always the danger, however, that such arrangements may merely become another form of foreign take-over.

In a real sense, all the policy measures mentioned here are designed to generate an environment in which Canadian managerial ability and innovative capability can develop. Clearly, Canada needs a new National Policy, one that will seek to establish a techno-industrial strategy that is relevant to the times; fortunately there is strengthening public opinion in favour of this policy development.

---

[1] The research assistance of Andrew Reed is gratefully acknowledged.
[2] Keith Pavitt, "Technical Change," *Futures,* August, 1978.
[3] Canada recently adopted a 2.5 per cent goal but there is little chance of this being realized without innovative policy instruments.

Chapter 4

Transportation

Ingrid Bryan,
Department of Economics, Ryerson Polytechnical Institute

Canada's immense geographical spread, together with the bulk and weight of its leading products, ensure that transportation will always be a paramount national issue. Its first settlers located themselves near ocean, lake or river and thus could use watercraft, then the most efficient means of transportation available. The Great Lakes-St. Lawrence River system was a major transportation artery that furnished effective access deep into the continental interior, particularly after canals on the St. Lawrence enabled vessels to circumvent the river's rapids.

While waterways were gifts of nature and vessels were privately owned, a considerable outlay of public funds was nevertheless required in connection with water transportation. Canals were mostly public works; the government arranged for dredging of river channels where required, provided navigation aids, built and maintained port facilities. The advent of the railway made effective transportation available during the winter months and to areas remote from water, thereby fostering a huge extension of the range of economic activities that could be carried on and vast enlargement of their geographic extent. The railway required, however, financial support from government, particularly in the raising of the immense capital sums needed to finance the construction of lines and the acquisition of rolling stock. This, governments were prepared to provide, because of the fallout of benefit for the public as a whole that was anticipated from the availability of rail transportation.

The inevitably monopolistic character of railway operations generated the possibility of consumer exploitation in the form of charges which furnished exorbitant profits. As well, the composition of railway costs created the possibility of severe discrimination among different users. Fixed costs constitute a very large fraction of total costs. Every charge for service must at least cover the variable cost involved and include some contribution toward the fixed cost. The railway could decide just how big a contribution to exact from each user toward its fixed cost; its allocation of fixed cost among different users could therefore be arbitrary, unfair and harmful to the overall national interest. A regulatory authority was therefore established to protect users generally against the possibility that the general level of charges was excessive and against the further possibility that the rates charged to different users were unfairly and undesirably discriminatory. The authority, as well, frequently insisted on cross-subsidization; i.e. it required railways to provide services that were in themselves uneconomic in order to promote a public interest, such services being subsidized by the railways' other, profitable operations.

Direct regulation of railway rates probably started with the Crow's Nest Pass Agreement of 1897, under which the Canadian Pacific Railway agreed to hold constant the rates on grain and grain products from the prairie provinces to the Lakehead (and on certain settlers' supplies inbound from eastern Canada) in return for federal subsidies for the construction of a branch line into British Columbia. Since that time there has been almost continuous warfare between users of transport and the railways over freight rates, with the railways occasionally giving in to certain groups of transport users, sometimes in return for federal government subsidies. Examples of this are the Crow's Nest Pass Agreements, which became law in 1925, the Maritimes Freight Rates Act of 1927, which provides for a 30 per cent reduction to transport users on some preferred freight movements in the Maritimes, and the movement of feed grains from west to east which has been subsidized since 1941.

In the post-World War II period, trucking provided an alternative to railways for many transport users that attracted much of the most profitable traffic. Regulatory barriers, particularly the ingrained structure of cross-subsidization, increased the difficulty of meeting this competition head-on. The railways attempted to recoup some of their losses by nominally ''general'' rate increases which in fact would have been largely applied in Western Canada and the Maritimes where truck competition was limited and the railways had near-monopoly power. Central Canada, well-served by the trucking industry, was relatively little concerned by railway freight rate increases; it was Western Canada and the Maritimes that vigorously opposed them. The McPherson Royal Commission was appointed to deal with some of these problems. Following its recommendations, the *National Transportation Act* of 1967 was passed. This Act constituted a major change in philosophy of transport regulation in Canada, by emphasizing efficiency and by recognizing the virtues of competition. The regulatory control over railways was decreased and the railways gained considerable freedom in setting rates.

Since the passage of the *National Transportation Act,* two developments have been pulling transport policies in opposing directions: one towards more regulation and one towards less regulation. The call for more regulation has come from the western provinces which feel that the *National Transportation Act* with its provisions of relatively free (unregulated) transport markets unfairly favours the central provinces where plenty of competition guarantees low freight rates. At the Western Economic Opportunities Conference in 1973, the western provinces called for amendments to the Act that would establish regional development as a goal for transport policy. In response, the Federal government introduced Bill C-33 in the form of an amendment to the *National Transportation Act* which affirms that transport policy should be an instrument of support for the achievement of national, regional, social and economic goals. The Bill has not yet been adopted.

The opposing pressure on transport policies calling for less regulation originated in the so-called Chicago School. Economists belonging to the Chicago School argue that regulation seldom achieves its objectives with costs that substantially exceed the modest benefits that it yields. Experience has shown that regulation tends to raise prices to transport users instead of lowering them. Regulation is frequently of more benefit to the producer than the consumer, as regulators become identified with the welfare of the regulated firms. It is also contended that regulation protects inefficiencies and distorts the allocation of resources. The solution, according to the Chicago School, is not to try to improve regulatory control but to deregulate the economy. Any excess profits reaped by an unregulated natural monopoly can be confiscated by an excess profits tax.

There are cases where indeed deregulation appears to have offered substantial benefits, perhaps particularly in transportation. An oft-quoted example is the airline industry in California, which is not regulated. Although only a few companies operate on the main routes, price competition has resulted in fares which are about two-thirds of fares on comparable routes subject to regulation by the Civil Aeronautics Board. There is also some evidence that the quality of service in terms of frequency and regularity is better than in regulated markets.

Urban Transportation

The most important means of transportation in urban areas are buses, subway trains, private automobiles and taxis. Each has its advantages and drawbacks and is particularly suited for some specific transportation purposes. While private automobiles can be used in urban centres of any size, each of the others, depending as it does upon passenger revenue, can be operated only in an urban centre of at least some minimum size. These minima will be different for each type of conveyance. Taxis will likely be found in even very small towns; a bus system will be viable only in a fairsized city; a subway is economic only in a big city where traffic of the order of 20 thousand persons per hour must be conveyed along some routes.

In those cities which are large enough to support public transit systems there is a strong likelihood that, from a purely economic point of view, the private automobile plays a larger role than it should while public transit and taxis both play smaller roles. Because they place great store in the privacy and comfort of a private automobile—and dislike waiting for a bus—a great many people use automobiles for journeys which they could have made far more economically by public transit. The cost of public transit is not an important factor: surveys have indicated that relatively few motorists would switch to public transit even in response to a substantial reduction in transit fares. During peak periods of travel, severe traffic congestion tends to occur because too many motorists are using the same thoroughfares at the same time, with the result that each imposes cost upon the others in the form of extra time spent and extra fuel consumed. The motorist will not, in all likelihood, take these costs into account when he decides whether or not to use his car.

The waste of congestion could be eliminated if enough motorists could be induced not to drive their cars along main thoroughfares during the periods of maximum travel demand. One suggestion, technologically feasible but probably unacceptable politically, would be to charge motorists for the use of city streets, with higher rates imposed for driving along central streets and during the periods of maximum demand. Every car could be equipped with an electronic identifier; a counting machine at every corner would record the movement of every vehicle, noting the time of day. The owners would be billed periodically, at the rates fixed for the streets on which they had driven and the times of day that they had driven on them. Given that such charges were going to be made, motorists who had no strong need to drive on central streets at key times would refrain from doing so, and those people who did need—or badly wanted—to drive on those streets at those times would be able to do so conveniently, without being held up by any excess of traffic.

Less far-fetched, but also less effective, procedures for deterring traffic congestion would be to charge very high fees for downtown parking and to impose steep excise taxes on gasoline. Presumably, fewer people would go downtown by car to work or shop if downtown parking was very expensive; on the other hand, this would not deter motorists who drove through the downtown area, and thereby contributed to its traffic problems, but did not park there. Steep taxes on gasoline would deter some people from driving their cars downtown and thereby help reduce traffic problems, but would obviously be unfair instruments for relieving downtown traffic congestion since they would equally burden motorists who did all their driving elsewhere.

Taxicab fares are generally regulated by local public authorities who specify the number of cabs that may operate. The substantial profits earned in the industry indicate that the volume of service provided is less than optimum. In Toronto in 1980, a licence to operate a cab, which could be sold by the original recipient, had a market value of the order of $50,000. If there were no restriction on entry into the industry, a larger number of cabs would enter with the result that excess profits would decline to zero and a licence would have no value. The fact that a licence sells for a very large sum is a clear indication that the industry is providing less service than is socially desirable. More cabs should be allowed, the optimum number being the one such that the marginal cab earned no excess profit whatever so that the right to operate it had zero value.

Intercity Passenger Transportation

The problems encountered in intercity passenger transportation differ from the urban problems of congestion and pollution. They are more typical regulatory problems, such as the need for subsidies and the control of competition. Three problems will be discussed here: subsidization of rail services, regulation of domestic air carriers and airport investments.

Subsidization of Railway Passenger Service

Passenger trains virtually monopolized intercity transportation until the 1920s. The Depression and the Second World War delayed the real impact of cars and buses until the late 1940s. By 1951, the rail share had dropped to 15 per cent of total traffic while cars had 72 per cent. Today, automobiles probably have a share of close to 85 per cent, with railroads having less than 5 per cent and the remaining 10 per cent shared by aircraft and buses. The railroads have made some half-hearted attempts to fight off further erosion of their passenger base. CN aggressively tried to improve its services and lowered fares in the mid-60s (the "red, white and blue" plan), which temporarily held up the tide but did not make passenger trains profitable. In 1977, the Liberal government attempted another rescue operation by integrating CN and CP passenger services in *Via Rail,* designed to make services more efficient and to end costly duplications. However, costs remain greater than revenues for all Canadian passenger services; the federal subsidy paid to the railways in 1977 was $198 million.

The reasons for the decline in the popularity of passenger trains are easy to document. For trips involving a distance of over 500 miles, the aircraft has become the dominant mode because of the saving in time costs. For trips of less than 500 miles, modal choice is more difficult to predict, as it depends on local conditions. If the time taken to commute to and from the airport at both ends is high, and if rail offers frequent and fast downtown to downtown services, trains may indeed hold their own. In general, to be profitable, passenger trains would have to operate at high speed, on medium-distance runs, and between densely populated areas.

CN attempted to enter this type of market with the introduction of the Turbo on the main Montreal-Toronto run. The Turbo was aerodynamically designed and powered by jet-turbine engines which made the train capable of a speed of 160 mph. It was, however, beset with endless problems involving the heating and electrical systems. Furthermore, because of track conditions (too many curves and level crossings), it averaged only 89 mph in service. In 1979, a Turbo caught fire and the service was discontinued.

Given that all non-commuter passenger trains lose money, it is not surprising that the Canadian Transport Commission has been inundated with applications from the railways for discontinuance. From 1967 to the end of 1976, there were 72 such applications before the Commission; only eleven, however, were approved, all being cases where passengers were few and substitute means of transport were available. One example was the London-Windsor service which had a daily average of two passengers; another, the service between Dauphin and Winnipegosis in Manitoba which, in 1974, had an average of 10 passengers. This last service cost the taxpayer $754 per passenger mile.

Continuation and subsidization of passenger train services has little economic justification on most routes but is a political issue. Even though most people never use a passenger train, it is thought to be bad for a community if the service ceases. As long as the subsidies needed to keep trains running come from general tax revenues, the communities affected voice strong opposition to rail closure, as the availability of rail services is for them, in effect, a free good. However, if the user-pay principle were introduced, i.e., that a community should bear some of the cost of keeping its railway service operating, some of the vehement opposition to rail closings would likely be silenced. And this further issue arises: if subsidies to passenger trains are used as a form of regional policy, is the provision of rail passenger services the most efficient means of assisting a needy community?

The future of passenger trains may appear somewhat brighter at present. Before the substantial increases in energy prices that began in 1973, airlines spent 10 cents of every revenue dollar on fuel, intercity buses spent 7 cents and trains, 3.8 cents. The huge increases in energy prices have therefore had the largest effect on airline costs and the least effect on rail costs. If this is translated into prices, some modal switch in favour of trains may be expected.

Domestic Air Fares and the Question of Regulation

The airline industry in Canada, as in most other countries, has been subject to stringent regulation of entry and price competition. Regulation has usually been promoted for two reasons. In the first place, it was believed that the industry was a natural monopoly and therefore could not be expected to function competitively. Secondly, governments have usually had a direct stake in the welfare of the industry in the form of full or partial ownership of an air carrier (e.g., Air Canada). Where this is the case, it is unlikely that a government will allow competition which may lower the profits of its own airline.

The 1960s brought changes in the industry which led to critical questioning of the type of regulatory environment that the industry had come to assume and rely on. First, the development of charter services on international routes led to substantial reduction in the cost of flying abroad and demand for the introduction of similar services on domestic routes. Second, two states in the United States, Texas and California, allowed price competition and relatively easy entry of airline operations within their borders. It was only a matter of time until it became known that competition forced fares in these markets to roughly two-thirds the level in comparable markets subject to regulation, without any loss in the quality of service. In 1977, the Air Transport Committee of the Canadian Transport Commission could no longer resist public pressure for change; since then, Canada's airlines have introduced a variety of plans under which passengers may travel at rates far below the regular fare.

Airport Investments and Congestion

Airport investments have become a controversial issue since the building of the Mirabel airport and the proposal for a new airport at Pickering, outside of Toronto. The alleged justification of both of these projects was the congestion problems at Dorval and Malton. Construction of the new Pickering airport was prevented by a well-organized citizens' movement, the protestors rallying around an anti-growth, anti-pollution platform. Their opposition had additional grounds. Even if existing airports are congested, the question which needs to be examined is whether or not the building of new airports is the most efficient means of getting rid of the problem.

The traditional remedy for the problem of facilities being crowded at some times and empty at others is the introduction of peak-load pricing. peak times, these could include the construction of off-site terminals and which helps to spread demand over the day (and night) and therefore reduces the need for additional capacity. Peak-load pricing is not practised in Canada, but has been used at London's Heathrow and Gatwick airports since 1972. The regulatory agency which administers the construction and running of Canada's airports, the Canadian Air Transport Administration (CATA), levies two types of fee, one on passengers (the airport tax) and one on aircraft. The tax on aircraft is in the form of a a landing fee which is assessed on the basis of the weight of the aircraft and the type of flight; it ranges from $1.30 for a small Cessna to $600 for a Boeing 747. This fee schedule, however, does not deter the same small Cessna from using the airport at the busiest time of the day. Peak-load pricing would impose a prohibitive charge for the landing and take-off of small aircraft at peak times and would therefore contribute to more efficient utilization of facilities by passenger aircraft.

There are, as well, ways to reduce passenger congestion of the terminal facilities. Apart from the rescheduling of departures and arrivals to off-peak times, these could include the construction of off-site terminals and measures such as very high parking fees to discourage senders and greeters. There is no evidence that, in evaluating the need for new airports, CATA examined such alternatives.

Intercity Cargo Transportation

The major share of freight transportation, measured in terms of operating revenues, is held by trucking (44 per cent), followed closely by rail (41 per cent) (1976). Only ten years earlier, rail had the major share (55 per cent) with trucking second (30 per cent). The share of water in the same time period decreased marginally (from 3 to 2 per cent).

Water Transport

The use of freight revenues as a measure understates the importance of water carriers, as they transport bulk commodities at relatively low freight rates. Indeed, taking ton-miles as the measure, one study showed that water carriers surpassed CP rail and carried very nearly as much freight as CN—and this in a nine-month shipping season, as opposed to year-round haulage by rail. More than half of the tonnage moved domestically by water consists of three categories of commodity: wheat and other grains (22 per cent), fuel oil (19 per cent), iron ore (17 per cent). Other commodities moved by water in substantial volume are logs, gasoline, sand and gravel, limestone and salt.

The water transport industry can be divided into three sectors: Great Lakes shipping, coastal shipping and Arctic shipping. Arctic shipping includes seasonal cargo movements on the Mackenzie River, as well as transportation of Arctic resources and coastal shipping among Arctic communities.

The Great Lakes shipping industry consists of a Canada-owned fleet of bulk carriers comprised of 19 companies, many of which are still family-owned. A small amount of general cargo is carried between Valleyfield, Hamilton, Windsor, Sarnia and Thunder Bay by package freighters owned by the Canada Steamship Lines. The coastal industry consists of tugboat operators on the West Coast and a "mixed bag" of small operators of various types of vessel on the East Coast.

The Water Transport Committee of the Canadian Transport Commission must license all water carriers and has jurisdiction over rates for general cargo and passenger traffic. Since 1977, licences to operate in coastal waters are restricted to Canadian ships. However, it appears that the regulatory control exercised is negligible. There is no evidence that it is particularly difficult to get a licence, and the Committee's control over rates is not important since most of the cargo is in bulk and is therefore not subject to CTC jurisdiction. The inland and coastal shipping industry appears to be competitive and relatively healthy.

Trucking

Interprovincial trucking was technically placed under the jurisdiction of the CTC by the *National Transportation Act* of 1967. However, the powers to restrict entry and regulate rates have never been assumed. Before they could be used, the federal government would have to take back the power to regulate extraprovincial undertakings, a power given to the provinces in 1953.

All provinces except Alberta control entry into the industry (through the granting of operating authority and licences) and control rates charged in intraprovincial trucking. Alberta truckers dislike the absence of regulation and have apparently attempted to persuade the provincial government to assume its regulatory powers, so far to no avail.

Provincial entry regulations appear to impose a high cost on users of trucking services. Various estimates indicate that rates in regulated provinces are 10 to 20 per cent higher than those in Alberta. One indication that these higher rates are translated into high profits for the truckers is a report in the *Financial Post* of a recent investigation of the Ontario Highway Transport Board by the Standing Resources Development Transport Committee of the Ontario Legislature. In this hearing, it was shown that trucking licences "are traded on a sort of a black market" and "several examples were given of permits which cost $700 to obtain from the government being sold for many thousands of dollars." [1] The fact that people are willing to pay many "thousands of dollars" to gain entry into the industry is an indication that a trucking licence is a licence to make supernormal profits. It is likely therefore that deregulation of provincial trucking would provide considerable benefit to consumers of transport services.

The New Transport Policy and Discriminatory Rates

Railway freight rates are an old Western grievance which has been resurrected, most prominently at the Western Economic Opportunities Conference held in Calgary in 1973. According to the *National Transportation Act* of 1967, railroads are essentially free to set their rates at whatever figures they wish, the presumption being that competition from other modes of transportation will prevent the rates from being exorbitant. Where a shipper does not have access to an alternative mode of transportation, he may appeal to the Commission and they will fix the rates that the railway may charge him.

Price discrimination is a common feature in most modes of transportation, being known in transport circles as "charging what the traffic will bear." This can be done if the transport firm possesses some form of monopoly power. For maximum profit, the rate for each commodity should be set in accordance with the elasticity of demand for transportation, with high elasticity of demand favouring a low rate, and low elasticity favouring a high rate. People in western Canada feel that they have relatively inelastic demand for rail service since there is little competition from either water or truck over the relatively long distances involved. As a result, the West feels that it has to bear a disproportionate share of the fixed costs of the railways. Westerners have complaints, as well, relating to specific freight charges. They argue, for example, that rates for the export of raw materials are lower than the rates for processed products, which encourages production close to the market (in eastern Canada) with a consequent loss of manufacturing jobs for westerners. The Crow's Nest Pass rates are both damned and lauded. They are lauded because they enable the grain farmer to get a higher net return for his grain. They are damned because these higher grain prices raise the cost of feedgrains for western livestock producers and are therefore hurting their industry.

However, demand for transportation is not necessarily inelastic merely because there is little competition in transport modes. If the demand and supply for a product are very elastic, a transport firm cannot charge a high freight rate because then the commodity will be priced out of the market and the transport firm will earn no revenue whatever. Indeed, careful analysis shows that many of the western complaints are difficult to substantiate. Further, even if commodities exported from the West are charged very high freight rates, the welfare implications are not straightforward. It is possible that the burden will fall mostly on the eastern consumer and/or producer, depending on the relative elasticities of demand and supply. It is almost impossible to prove who bears the major part of the burden. It is very likely that freight rates have been overemphasized as factors affecting the development of manufacturing in the West. One exception, though, should be noted: Crow Rates, discussed below.

Grain Transport and the "Holy Crow"

The grain transport system is antiquated, being basically unchanged since the early part of the century. The farmer uses his own vehicle to deliver grain to the nearest elevator, located on a rail branch line, usually close to his farm. At each elevator, the grain is loaded onto individual rail cars, which are then assembled into trains for the long haul to Vancouver or

Thunder Bay. Given the economies of scale in elevator operations and the cost advantages of trucks over railways on hauls less than 100 miles, an efficient system would concentrate grain collection in a few large terminals; the railways could then assemble a complete train at each terminal. Such a system would involve large-scale abandonment of branch lines and increase in cost for farmers because they would have to truck their grain longer distances. Any attempt at such rationalization would therefore meet with substantial resistance from farmers.

The difficulties experienced with grain transportation are partly attributable to the Crow Rates, as well. As indicated earlier, the Crow Rates stem from the Crow's Nest Pass Agreement of 1897 between the CPR and the federal government, under which the CPR agreed to lower the rate on moving grain to the Lakehead in return for a federal subsidy toward the cost of a rail line from Lethbridge to the Kootenay Valley in British Columbia; in 1925, the 1899 rates became statutory. According to the findings of the Snavely Commission, appointed in 1975, the Crow Rates, which vary from 14 to 26 cents per hundredweight, do not even cover the railways' variable costs. A realistic rate today would probably range from 70 to 80 cents per hundredweight. Grain moving at the low statutory rates account for 30 per cent of the railways' ton-mile output but only 12 per cent of rail revenue. The losses reported by the railways on grain haulage —even after receiving a federal subsidy for operating uneconomic branch lines—totalled $90 million in 1974.

The effects of the Crow Rates are many. In the first place, the railways have had no incentive to maintain track on uneconomic branch lines, or to invest in box-cars for grain. Furthermore, since the westbound route through the Rockies is more expensive to run than the eastbound route to Thunder Bay, it is in the interest of the railways to encourage eastward movements, given that, under the Crow Rates, the revenues are the same. This apparently has led to underinvestment by the railways in switching yards at the port of Vancouver compared to the port of Thunder Bay, which in turn has led to underinvestment by west coast port operators in grain cleaning capacity. All of these factors produced a crisis in grain transportation in the mid-1970s, with the result that several sales commitments could not be honoured.

Between 1961 and 1967, there were few rail line abandonment proceedings, and in the following year, the Canadian Transport Commission (CTC) began paying subsidies to the railways for losses incurred on branch lines which were run as a public service. In 1974, the federal government guaranteed a basic network until the year 2000 (category A lines); the railways were allowed to abandon 525 miles (category C lines); and a commission under Chief Justice Hall was appointed to decide what to do with the remaining 6283 miles (category B lines).

The Hall Commission presented its report in 1977. It recommended that another 2165 miles of B lines be abandoned over the next five years, that 1813 miles be retained within the basic network, and that the remaining 2344 miles be placed under the jurisdiction of a new regulatory agency, to be called the Prairie Rail Authority. The Commission also recommended a program of compensation to railways for losses attributable to grain transportation and some contributions to the provinces toward the cost of road maintenance. The Commission considered that this would be necessary since highway trucking would play a more important role following branch line abandonment. The Commission also investigated the familiar complaints about the structure of freight rates, and recommended that rates be set at levels which did not discriminate against the natural advantages of private producers. The precise meaning of this recommendation was not explained.

Apart from a healthy scepticism that the new Prairie Rail Authority would do a better job than the CTC, the most controversial recommendation was that the Crow Rates should be retained. The implication is that grain transport will have to be subsidized to perpetuity, and that distortions will worsen as the spread between the fixed Crow Rates and other rates widens because of inflation, which keeps raising the latter. Obviously Crow Rates prevent rationalization of western grain hauling; however, their abolition is a highly sensitive political issue.

The Carriage of International Trade

This section of the chapter will examine the problems involved in deepsea transport. It will not provide a complete picture of the carriage of goods in international trade, since some cargo is now carried by air and, in the case of Canada's trade with the United States, little is carried in deep-sea bottoms; most moves by rail, truck or lake carrier. However, many of the problems encountered in road and rail transport have already been discussed. Suffice it to say that the problems encountered in the American part of the journey are similar to those in the Canadian part, though in many cases the interaction of two regulatory agencies makes problems more difficult.

There are three broad categories of deep-sea shipping: liquid bulk, carried by tankers; dry bulk (for example, ores and grains) carried by bulk carriers; and general cargo, carried by liners. The services of tankers and bulk carriers are purchased on the open market at competitive prices, the cost of a time or a voyage charter being set on exchanges that are quite similar to commodity exchanges. Liner services, on the other hand, are usually cartelized and controlled by shipping conferences, a shipping conference being an association of shipping lines which operates on a regularly scheduled basis on a given route; each route usually has two conferences, one inbound and one outbound. A conference attempts to limit entry, to fix prices and to tie its customers to its services through loyalty contracts. These have a similar effect to the "agreed charges" in railway operations whereby a transport user receives a lower rate from a carrier in return for a promise to give all his business to that carrier.

Of the tonnages loaded from Canadian ports, most is bulk cargo (grains, 20 per cent; ores, 30 per cent; other bulk cargo, 40 per cent) with liner cargo accounting for only 10 per cent of tonnage. On the import side, petroleum products make up 40 per cent of the tonnage, coal and other bulk cargoes, 50 per cent, and liner cargos, 10 per cent. However, the share of liner cargoes in the *value* of exports and imports is substantially higher than 10 per cent, since liner cargoes consist of relatively high-valued manufactured and semi-manufactured products.

Recent developments in shipping technology have led to larger and more specialized ships such as supertankers, LNG (liquefied natural gas) carriers, reefers (refrigerated cargo carriers), containerships, OBO (ore/bulk/oil) carriers, and other types of combination carriers. These changes in ship design have led to corresponding changes in port use and port design. The importance of small inland ports and also of inner city ports has declined. Many of today's ships cannot clear the Seaway, while others find it more economical to unload at Halifax or Montreal, the cargo being carried by rail to its final destination. Inner city ports are no longer suitable since they can no longer provide storage facilities for containers; nor do they have the room needed to accommodate large bulk carriers or tankers. These factors have led to the decline of the Port of Toronto and other Great Lakes ports and have boosted the development of the Maritime ports (Halifax and Saint John).

Canadian Shipping Policy: Investment

In 1878, Canada was fourth among the ship-owning nations of the world in terms of tonnage owned and operated. With the development of steel hulls, Canada started to lose her competitive advantage, largely because she had no steel industry; by the early 20th century, her tonnage had declined by 50 per cent. In 1917, during the First World War, the Dominion government launched a large ship-building program, with the ships to be operated by a Crown corporation—the Canadian Government Merchant Marine. The Marine incurred heavy losses in the 1920s as a consequence of rising construction costs, falling freight rates and lack of inbound cargo. By 1936, the total losses from the venture reached $95 million—a very large amount at that time.

World War II again altered the situation. A total of 400 ships was built during the War, many being owned and operated by Park Steamships, a fully owned government subsidiary. At the end of the War, Canada again had the fourth largest merchant marine in the world. The government announced in 1945 that it planned to sell as many ships as it could to Canadians and lay up the remainder. Purchasers of the ships were under obligation not to transfer any to foreign registry. The Canadian Maritime Commission was established, with responsibility for finding procedures whereby the fleet could be maintained on a permanent basis. The death blow fell, however, when the United States offered for sale at very low prices hundreds of merchant ships that had been built during the War. This made it possible for other countries to venture into the shipping industry and freight rates fell sharply. The Canadian government made it clear that it was not prepared to subsidize the Canadian fleet, and, as well, made it possible for shipowners to transfer their vessels to British registry, presumably to take advantage of lower wage rates. Since then Canada has been without a merchant-marine, the government pursuing a *laissez-faire* policy in the belief that it will provide Canadians with shipping services at the lowest possible cost. Scarce public funds have been diverted from shipping to other purposes, and Canada has been able, supposedly, to benefit from the low freight rates that foreign shipowners were able to offer, thanks to the large subsidies provided them by their respective governments.

It should be added, however, that even though Canada has no deep-sea fleet, many Canadian corporations have an active interest in shipping, usually pursued through subsidiaries. For example, Canadian Pacific has two subsidiaries: CP Bermuda Ltd., involved in chartering operations, and CP Steamships Ltd., which owns and operates container ships under the British flag. CN has acquired an interest in the Canadian-owned Cast shipping group, involved in a regular nonconference service on the North Atlantic.

Since the demise of the Canadian merchant marine, there has been pressure on the federal government to revive it, by enabling ships to operate under the Canadian flag, through tax concessions and/or subsidies, or by direct investment. The renewed interest in a Canadian fleet can probably be attributed to nationalist sentiment, reinforced by strong pressure from the Seafarers' International Union; the Union has even guaranteed a ten-year strike-free period in the event of a fleet being established. A fairly powerful shipping lobby also urges that we have a Canadian merchant marine. Recent developments in world shipping markets leading to reduction in competition and increase in shipping rates have also cast doubt on the wisdom of a continued policy of *laissez-faire*.

Canadian Shipping Policy: Regulation

The freight rates charged by liners on scheduled runs are usually set by conferences which are in essence cartels and therefore involve the possibility of collusive gouging of users. Governments generally have accepted their existence on the grounds that open competition would produce undesirable instability. The Canadian government adheres to the general practice: the *Shipping Conference Exemption Act* in effect exempts conferences from our anti-combines legislation, allowing them to restrict entry and control prices. Under the Act a shipper who objects to a rate being charged him may appeal to the Canadian Transport Commission, which can thereupon conduct an investigation. Such investigations have been few and proceed in leisurely fashion; eight have been launched since 1967, with only one finally concluded. None of these involved shipping rates.

---

[1] The *Financial Post,* April 7, 1979, Special Report on Land Transport, "What Deregulation Means to Business."

Chapter 5

The Financial System

Norman Cameron,
Department of Economics, University of Manitoba

The financial system performs three functions in any economy. It provides a payments mechanism for everyday transactions in the rest of the economy; it channels funds from savers to borrowers and allows savers to change the type of assets they hold; it provides a vehicle through which the government can exercise some control over real output and employment in the economy as a whole.

The financial system consists of all financial markets and those persons who participate in them, whether as principals, or as agents such as stockbrokers and life insurance salesmen. It includes the markets in which savers lend directly to borrowers from non-financial sectors, e.g., a household buying a Canada Savings Bond, and also includes the markets in which savers lend indirectly—by depositing in institutions such as banks, which in turn lend the funds to borrowers. This category includes the markets for deposits of banks, trust companies and credit unions, as well as those for mutual fund shares, life insurance policies and pension entitlements.

The share of savers' funds which flows directly to non-financial, ultimate borrowers, as opposed to indirectly through one or more intermediaries, varies over time with the state of financial development and with relative interest rates. In Canada in the 1970s, roughly two-thirds of the total net savings flow (i.e., of savings not directly reinvested in housing or physical assets by the saver) has made its way to the ultimate borrowers through intermediaries. For the 1980s, one can expect more or less the same.

This definition of the Canadian financial system includes a large measure of foreign activity, both by foreign individuals and institutions in Canada, and by Canadian individuals and institutions abroad. Despite the protectionist noises made by many nations in the last few years, the world economy is interconnected as never before, and world financial markets are even more so. This shows up clearly in the flow of funds figures: non-residents accounted for 14 per cent of all Canadian financial assets bought by non-financial groups over the period 1962-1978, and, on the other side of the balance sheet, they did almost 9 per cent of the total borrowing by non-financial groups. The international activity of Canadian financial institutions is equally important.

This chapter is organized as follows. In the next and major section, I survey the institutions and the markets of the financial system. The second section contains a description of how the Bank of Canada is able to use control of supply in the currency and deposit market to help stabilize the nation's output and price levels. In the third section, I discuss five problems of current concern in financial markets. The final section contains a brief look ahead.

Survey of Institutions and Markets

Origins and Development

In 1867, the list of financial intermediaries included the banks, some insurance companies, building societies and mortgage loan companies. They bought and sold a very limited range of assets and liabilities. There was a well-developed inter-merchant trade credit system, and also a large number of private bankers. The Toronto Stock Exchange listed 18 stocks and the Montreal Exchange from 30 to 50, mainly of banks, utilities and mining companies.

Now Canada has a well-developed financial system with a broad range of financial assets and institutions, handling large flows of funds quickly and efficiently. At the centre is the Bank of Canada, which controls the level of chartered bank cash reserves and provides lender of last resort facilities both to them and to the money market dealers. There are currently 11 chartered banks operating under the federal Bank Act, and one federally chartered savings bank in Montreal. There are almost 4,000 local credit unions and caisses populaires, grouped into 30 regional or provincial centrals and operating under special provincial legislation. There are 95 trust and mortgage loan companies, 49 of which operate under the federal Trust Companies Act and Loan Companies Act. There are 31 companies licensed under the federal Small Loans Act as moneylenders or small loans companies. There are 248 federally registered companies in the fire and casualty insurance business, and 167 in life insurance. Ontario alone lists 151 provincially licensed insurers. A large range of mutual funds are regularly listed in the financial papers, with investments from gold to Treasury bills to stock options and everything in between. Dozens of other financial corporations act as specialized lenders simply under provincial or federal companies acts.

There are several distinct types of secondary markets in which previously issued assets change hands. The money market is operated mainly by a group of 15 investment dealers who have and use special borrowing privileges with the Bank of Canada. This market handles transfers and placements of large negotiable short-term assets such as Treasury bills and corporate term notes. There are five stock exchanges (in Toronto, Montreal, Vancouver, Calgary, and Winnipeg) and a nation-wide over-the-counter market run out of the offices of the major investment dealers. These firms also constitute the bond market. A secondary mortgage market is the most recent development.

The government is involved in several ways. The Alberta Treasury Branches and the less active Ontario Savings Office act as savings banks. The Canada Mortgage and Housing Corporation acts as a major mortgage lender to selected types of borrower. The Federal Business Development Bank and the Canada Development Corporation supply loan and equity funds to the private sector. The federal government dominates the pension sector both with its own pension scheme for the civil service and with the Canada Pension Plan. The Quebec Pension Plan handles the equivalent flow of funds for residents of that province. In addition, there are over a hundred government loan schemes in existence.

Government supervision and regulation of the financial system is done through several types of organization. The Bank of Canada, the Super-intendent of Banks, the Canada Deposit Insurance Corporation and the federal and provincial Superintendents of Insurance supervise the banks, the trust and loan companies, and the insurance companies to ensure their solvency. Credit unions are supervised by special branches of provincial governments. Stock markets and investment companies are supervised by provincial securities commissions, generally taking their lead from the Ontario Securities Commission. Trusteed pension plans are supervised mainly by provincial pension commissions.

The goal of most of the regulation has been to protect the investor by licensing salesmen and agents, by prohibiting dangerous investment prac-tices by intermediaries, by forcing timely and full disclosure, and by regu-lar inspections and audits. Trust companies may not borrow more than 20 times their capital; under the new Bank Act, the same limitation will apply to foreign bank subsidiaries. For each type of institution there is a list of ineligible assets, though pension plans, trust companies and insur-ance companies may hold up to 7 per cent of their assets in such other-wise ineligible forms under "basket clauses" in their controlling legislation.

The new Bank Act and an expected revision to the federal Trust Com-panies Act will give more emphasis to competition among different types of institutions. Banks are now allowed directly into leasing and factoring, though not into trustee functions, securities underwriting or non-banking computer services; it is anticipated that the trust companies will be given broader powers in respect to commercial lending. Conversion of other in-stitutions into banks (e.g., IAC Ltd. into the Continental Bank) is now made easier through the substitution of letters patent for Parliamentary charter, as was done for federal trust companies in 1970.

A non-coincidental thrust of much of the legislation at both federal and provincial levels has been to prevent significant further entry by foreigners. The invasion of the commercial loan market by foreign bank affiliates operating simply under provincial companies acts caught both sets of regulators very much by surprise.

The growth process of the Canadian financial system has been accompanied by the gradual relaxation of legal constraints on the range of activity of financial intermediaries, a cumulative tightening of the rules on trading practices and disclosure, continual growth in market size and a continual drop in most transactions costs with advances in communications technology.

Reflecting this development, the intermediation ratio (of Canadian assets of financial intermediaries to Canadian GNP) has risen from 31 per cent in 1870 to 138 per cent in 1975 and 162 per cent in 1978 ($370 billion of assets: $230 billion of GNP). Branches of banks, credit unions and trust companies have spread to the point where there is now one branch for every 1800 residents.

The history of this development is shown in Figure 1, which traces the relative growth of financial intermediaries since 1870. The financial system is more than just this list of financial intermediaries, but they form the core of it and the modern end of the chart deserves close scrutiny. Several features stand out.

1. The government share has been growing rapidly. This reflects mostly the expansion of the Central Mortgage and Housing Corporation in the mortgage market of the mid-1970s, and of the public pension plans (both civil service pensions and the Canada and Quebec Pension Plans). The expansion of the CMHC seems to have halted, but the share of the pension sector will undoubtedly continue to grow over the next twenty years.

2. The growth of private sector trusteed pension plans has been as dramatic as that of government pension schemes. If group annuities of life insurers were added, the growth would be much larger.

3. The increasing variety of credit instruments available is reflected in part by the increasing variety of institutions in Figure 1, but only in part. Almost all types of institutions now offer a wider variety of instruments than they did in 1960, and generally participate in a wider variety of financial markets both as buyers and as sellers.

4. The banks' success since 1968 in reversing the long decline in their market share has been remarkable, though it is greatly understated in Figure 1 since none of the banks' rapidly growing foreign currency business is included in calculating their share.

Figure 1
Shares of Total Financial Intermediary Assets,
1870-1978

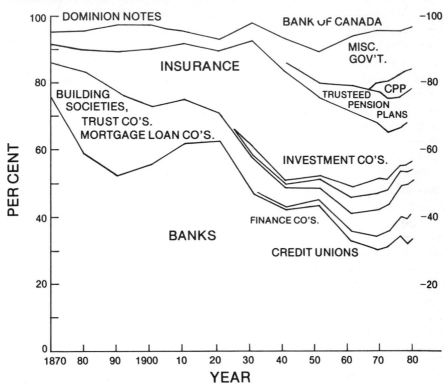

Sources: Neufeld (1972); Statistics Canada; Bank of Canada Review

The Mortgage Market

Individual financial markets are not very well described by Figure 1, since
there is a great deal of overlap between the different institutions. Indeed,
individual markets are difficult to discuss in the financial sector because
of the problem of defining the boundary of any one market. However, the
mortgage market is one of the most easily recognizable. Mortgage loans
are those which give the lender the right to seize real estate in the event of
default by the borrower. These loans are used typically to finance the
purchase of land and buildings.

Residential real estate accounts for over half of the average household's assets, and mortgage borrowing from other sectors alone has run at
almost two-thirds of total household borrowing for the years 1976-1978.
In the latest survey of consumer finances by Statistics Canada (for May
1977), 42 per cent of households had mortgage debt outstanding, in an av-

erage amount of over $18,000. While the ratio of this figure to average income, 115 per cent, is lower than the ratio of 125 per cent between average mortgage debt and average income that existed in the mid-1960s, the high interest rate levels that go with high inflation have made the servicing of even the lower debt ratios a much heavier burden for new homebuyers.

Table 1 shows the most recent breakdown of total mortgage holdings by financial intermediaries. This market is clearly no longer dominated by the life insurers and the trust and mortgage companies as was the case in the early years in Chart 1, though the trust companies still control almost two-fifths of the total when their holdings through pension plans and estate, trust and agency funds are included. The Central Mortgage and Housing Corporation is playing a smaller role now in financing, restricting itself mainly to limited-dividend, low-cost, multiple-unit housing (see the chapter on housing policy). The banks are still catching up from the years before 1968 when they were excluded from the mortgage market by a combination of the 1954 Bank Act (which prohibited banks from holding conventional mortgages) and the ceiling interest rate on mortgages insured under the National Housing Act. They now hold over half of all mortgages insured under the National Housing Act.

The mortgage market has been quite innovative in the 1970s in response to the increasing competition from credit unions and new trust companies. The credit unions had long had open mortgages, and this idea caught on with other institutions in 1978. In the early 1970s, lenders managed to combine the benefits of long-period amortization with the flexibility of a short-term instrument by making the mortgage rate renegotiable after five

Table 1 Institutional Holdings of Mortgage Loans:
Shares by Type of Institution, June 1979 (%)

Trust Companies	21.8%	Other estate, trust and agency funds of trust	
Banks[1]	16.4	co's.	9.3%
Life insurers[2]	14.1	REITS[3] and MIC's[4]	1.3
Credit unions and Caisses Populaires	12.5	Central Mortgage and Housing Corp.	7.5
Mortgage loan co's.	8.5	Miscellaneous	2.8
Trusteed pension plans	6.0		100%

Source: Statistics Canada, CS61-006.
Notes: 1. Including Montreal City and District Savings Bank (0.8%)
       2. Including segregated funds (1.1%)
       3. Real Estate Investment Trusts
       4. Mortgage Investment Companies

years. Since then, three-year and even one-year renegotiable mortgages have become popular as well, and it should not be very long before a floating rate mortgage appears. Graduated payment mortgages have already appeared, as have reverse income mortgages, which allow homeowners to borrow in the form of an annuity against the security of their equity in their own home.

From a long-term point of view, the most important development has probably been the growth of a secondary market for mortgages, i.e., a market in which a firm which has loaned money to a homebuyer on a mortgage basis sells the mortgage to another investor. This allows institutions like the smallish Fort Garry Trust Company to enter the mortgage market in a big way as a loan originator (i.e., a lender to actual homebuyers) without having to raise a huge volume of funds, and it allows other institutions to invest in mortgages at relatively low cost even when they do not have a large branch network to help them locate prime borrowers. In short, it allows the same specialization and division of labour that Adam Smith described in 1776 in the making of pins. It also decreases what limited market power any of the participants now have.

Government and Business Financing

The government sector has never been very limited in its sources of funds, except at the most junior levels. Now that the provinces have taken over and centralized most of the borrowing for their municipalities, even this group has open to it a range of borrowing alternatives from short-term tax-anticipation notes to bank loans to long-term bonds in any of a range of currencies and capital markets. Some of the provinces also tap the savings bond market. In each case, there are a large number of buyers in what is a broad, competitive and essentially international market. Government crown corporations have benefitted as much as the governments themselves from these extra sources, and hydro-related foreign borrowing in the 1970s has been very large.

The corporate business sector, and particularly large firms, have benefitted the most from the increasing competition in the financial system in the last ten years. As always, large firms have open to them the options of issuing stock or bonds for long-term assets, and of using banks, acceptance houses or trade credit for shorter-term needs. They can now consider, as well, such alternatives as foreign currency loans, term loans from their local banker for terms of up to 15 years, leasing contracts from a variety of institutions, term-preferred shares and income debentures, commercial paper or a banker's acceptance, and even a special fund for projects such as movie-making or oil-drilling programs. The government's tax treatment of term-preferred shares, income debentures and the special funds has been so generous that these have been much cheaper for many borrowers than regular loans.

The business sector's response to these new options is shown in Figure 2. Business firms have switched to much greater reliance on bank loans, many of which are for much longer terms than before. This has been at the expense of mortgage and bond issues. Much of the increase in public stock issues is in fact term-preferred shares, which are unlike normal equity financing in that they have a specific redemption date. To the extent that these instruments are regarded as debt instruments by the issuers, the shift from bonds to other types of financing in Figure 2 is overstated. The use of bankers' acceptances and commercial paper has remained small. Only some 200 companies use the former, and the latter is currently restricted by the Bank of Canada Act to firms in the manufacturing and resource sectors.

Smaller firms have less flexibility in borrowing than their larger cousins do. For their short-term financing needs, they are therefore tied to their

Figure 2
Financing of Private Non-Financial Corporations:
Shares by Type of Liability

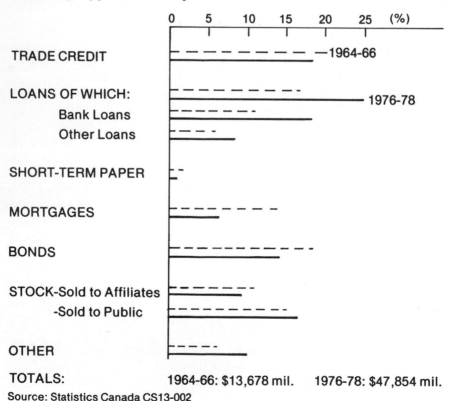

TOTALS: 1964-66: $13,678 mil. 1976-78: $47,854 mil.
Source: Statistics Canada CS13-002

local bank or near-bank or trade supplier, as has been the case for the last century. For longer-term financing needs, the banks' decision to offer term loans of up to 15 years has given these firms an alternative to mortgage financing which is cheaper to arrange and more flexible to use. The keen competition among the banks, credit unions, the new and powerful Caisses d'Entraide in Quebec, and especially the host of foreign bank affiliates which have invaded the commercial and term loan market, has recently made term borrowing as easy for smaller businesses as it has ever been.

Equity financing for small businesses is more of a problem area. After the long stock market boom of the 1960s, there were 45 major Canadian venture capital firms in business helping to finance new and expanding small firms with a combination of long-term loans and equity funds. Now the number has dwindled to 15, many of them (such as RoyMark, Triarch, Canadian Enterprise Development Corp. and TD Capital Group) being wholly or partly owned by the same banks that are now so active in term lending. Few of them are interested in financing the start-up of new firms, a type of financing which is being left to the Federal Business Development Bank. The FBDB has developed a strong program of management assistance for small businesses—a necessary ingredient of most start-up financing programs.

Markets for Savers

The markets in which financial intermediaries raise their funds have become much more competitive in the 1970s, and the rates of return to savers reflect this. In the short-term end and at the wholesale level, the money market is a single market in which Treasury bills, finance company and commercial paper, bankers' acceptances, provincial government paper, and the large denomination deposits of the banks and near-banks all compete for their place in the sun. Right beside it is another flourishing market in foreign currency deposits. In all of these markets, the size of the borrower's branch network or head office confers no advantage, as funds flow quickly to the highest rates. Intermediary margins are kept very small.

At the retail end where the general public deals, personal savings markets have changed beyond recognition since the days before 1967 when the banks offered only one type of personal savings deposit, set a single rate of interest through the Canadian Bankers Association, and adjusted it infrequently. The increasing threat posed by the trust companies and credit unions, which now have almost three-quarters as many branches as the chartered banks, and the liberating effects of the 1967 Bank Act revision have caused a revolution in the retail savings market. Households can now put their savings in fixed term deposits for various terms of up to five years, the pattern of yields for different terms basically reflecting yields in the government bond market; they can also put their savings in non-chequable notice deposits whose yields adjust frequently in response to changes in the money market. As foreign bank subsidiaries enter the Canadian retail savings market, we can expect further innovation of the sort already produced by the Bank of British Columbia, by the Continental Bank, and by the trust companies and credit unions.

Longer-term savings vehicles have also increased in number and variety. Individual life annuities are now available with benefits tied to the value of a segregated asset portfolio. New tax rules have made savings plans and registered pension plans very popular. These long-term funds are invested in a wide range of assets from money-market securities to mortgages and stock, and even other mutual funds. Stock options and futures contracts have also appeared for those eager to take greater risks.

Taken as a whole, our financial system is in the midst of rapid change at the wholesale level. Both new products and new types of institutions are being developed to suit more exactly the needs of different groups of borrowers and lenders. Existing financial institutions are branching out into a wider range of activities, despite often vigorous protests from those whose turf is being invaded. The banks in particular seem ready to take over trust, underwriting, and computer operations business from other firms as soon as they are allowed. They already have subsidiaries in mortgage lending, term lending, venture capital financing and leasing.

More of this sort of change is to be expected in the future as financial firms start to realize the potential of the new communications technology. On-line computerized accounting involves a heavy fixed cost, but lends itself easily to an approach being pioneered in Canada by the new Continental Bank and by some of the credit unions: the consolidation of all of any one customer's business, both deposits and loans, into one accounting record overseen by a customer service representative. This is the beginning of personal portfolio management for customers by banks. The importance of the banks may increase, but existing regulations may prevent the banks from establishing such full-line service and thus leave the field open to credit unions and trust companies to pioneer.

The Monetary Control Mechanism

The financial system is a set of markets so closely connected by overlapping forces of demand, supply and arbitrage that there is a quite stable set of relationships among their interest rates. A disturbance in any one market has ripple effects on almost all other markets, the net effect being that the whole structure of interest rates moves, instead of simply the one interest rate in the market being directly affected.

One of these financial markets is special in that the supply of the asset traded and held is determined not by borrowers' eagerness to raise funds, but by the Bank of Canada's desire for greater stability of incomes, employment and prices. This is the market for currency and chartered bank deposits (the media of exchange or "money" in Canada). The Bank of Canada controls the currency directly and, through two features of the Bank Act, exercises effective control over the total of bank deposits in the country. The two features are the requirement that banks hold cash reserves at least equal to 4 per cent of notice deposits and 12 per cent of demand deposits (to be decreased to 3 per cent and 10 per cent respectively by 1985), and the requirement that these cash reserves be in the form of coin, Bank of Canada notes and deposits in the Bank of Canada.

Since the banks are never interested in holding idle excess cash reserves at zero interest, and since the act of lending them out creates deposits which must be held by someone, the total of bank deposits is always up against the limit imposed by the volume of bank cash reserves available. The Bank of Canada can therefore expect an increased supply of deposits to follow reliably whenever it creates more cash reserves by adding to its assets.

The Bank of Canada has a few other tools with which to control the banking system, but they are much less important. A secondary reserve requirement was added in the 1967 Bank Act, but it has (properly) fallen into disuse since 1975. Its main effect is to create a captive market for Treasury bills. The Bank Rate (at which banks infrequently borrow from the Bank of Canada) now floats just above the Treasury bill rate; until March 1980, it was adjusted infrequently and served as a sort of announcement device to reveal whether the Bank of Canada was going to go along with or resist market interest rate changes. Moral suasion is used on occasion to ensure that particular classes of bank borrowers do not get squeezed out in periods of tight credit.

Control of the money supply is a powerful though uneven regulator of the rest of the economy. Whenever the money supply is increased faster than the demand, the extra money is like a hot potato. Whoever is holding it buys something else with it instead. If the something else is consumer durables, then that sector expands output. If the something else is financial assets, then the rise in their prices lowers the cost of funds in financial markets; more firms decide to add to capacity, and the capital goods sector expands.

The Bank of Canada does not have absolute control over the volume of currency and demand deposit balances in the chartered banks. The banks may always manage to get additional cash reserves, thereby making possible an increase in their loans and deposits. However, attempts by the banks to get extra cash reserves from sources other than the Bank quickly run into prohibitive marginal costs. One method of getting additional cash is to persuade the public to deposit more of its currency in banks. A way of getting more use out of the same quantity of cash reserves is to try to persuade customers to switch deposit types, from demand to notice or from Canadian currency to foreign currency deposits. Banks are generally already pursuing those avenues to the margin of profitability, however, so that there is little extra room left.

In summary, there is little doubt that the Bank of Canada can exert influence over the real sector through its control over the money supply. Monetary policy is a matter of hot dispute among economists on different grounds. First, it is not clear how fast monetary policy effects occur, how reliably, and how the total effect is spread over time. Second, there is dispute over exactly what the Bank of Canada should set as its monetary target: either an explicit rate of growth of money balances or, more vaguely, a growth rate sufficient to keep the interest rate on government bonds at a specified level, or some combination of the two (the current strategy used by the Bank).

Problems and Options

The individual markets of the financial system are among the more competitive markets in the Canadian economy, both because of the large number of participants in most of them and because of the availability of close substitutes in nearby markets. There are a few exceptions, as in the personal credit market and the securities underwriting business, but they are just that: exceptions.

The problems of the financial system have generally been not too serious in the 1970s. For the next decade, they are likely to become much more important, simply because the amount of financing which will be needed—for new energy projects and plant expansions—is expected to be double that of the 1970s in real terms (but see the chapter on energy). It will be much more important that borrowers be able to compete freely for savers' funds, so that less productive investments do not crowd out more productive ones. At the same time, the savings required to fund future pension benefits will continue to grow rapidly. Combining the savings needed for pensions with borrowing needed for the energy projects of the 1980s while satisfying the needs of savers and borrowers will require the undistracted ingenuity of the financing firms.

The most serious current problem is that posed by inflation in the mortgage market. Serious future problems will arise because of the degree of segmentation of financial markets which still exists, and because of the confusing role that the government has played with its tax policy in particular. Finally, there is a pension problem posed by a rapidly aging work force in a society which now regards pensions as a basic right but has not decided how to pay for them. Problems arising out of the conduct of monetary policy are dealt with in other chapters.

Inflation and Financial Markets

The response of financial markets to inflation can be easily summarized.

All available evidence confirms that as extra inflation of x per cent comes to be expected over some time horizon, current nominal interest rates for that time period will rise by approximately x per cent. This adjustment provides an extra amount of current interest income just sufficient to offset the decrease in purchasing power of the fixed nominal principal sum by x per cent per year.

The implications are not as easy to describe. Holders of short-term fixed interest assets will be protected from inflation only once it comes to be expected; they will be vulnerable to unanticipated inflation just like most others in the economy. Those who hold longer-term fixed interest assets can expect to earn higher interest rates after a lag equal to the remaining term to maturity of their assets. In the meantime, they will be receiving reduced real interest rates; as well, the market price of their assets will fall immediately to compensate for the attraction of the higher nominal rates currently being paid on new, substitute assets.

The response of lenders has been either to shift towards shorter-term assets, or to insist on renegotiation clauses in determining the interest rates on longer-term assets. For instance, it is now almost impossible to float a mortgage loan at an interest rate fixed over the whole amortization period.

Borrowers benefit from inflation because it reduces the purchasing power of fixed nominal value debts, and inflates the values of their assets relative to their debts. The cost is that they will also have a more difficult cash flow problem. Nowhere is this more serious than in the mortgage market, as an example will show. Mortgage payments are a form of level-payment annuity which combines interest and principal payments in different proportions over the life of the mortgage. The combined payment is designed to be a relatively stable share of total income to suit normal family budgets. For a family with an income of $20,000 per year growing at 2 per cent per year, a mortgage of $40,000 amortized over 25 years at 5 per cent interest (the rate in the mid-1960s) would require 14 per cent of income to service in the first year, dropping gradually with growing income to 8.6 per cent in the last year. If 8 per cent more inflation comes to be expected, so that the nominal income grows at 10 instead of 2 per cent and the same mortgage is amortized at 13 instead of 5 per cent, the mortgage payments require 26 per cent of income in the first year, but only 2 1/2 per cent in the last year. Such a pattern of payments does not suit most households, and for some the burden of payments in the early years would be such that they could not borrow at all.

The problem is made more serious by the drastic increase in house prices in the early 1970s, and efforts to solve it have run aground on the difficulty of reducing the early payments while ensuring that the ratio of loan principal to house value does not climb too high to protect lenders in the event of default. The real solution to this problem lies not in some form of indexing in financial markets, but in reducing the level of inflation.

Segmentation

Most financial markets are national, but there are some barriers to the flow of funds between markets and in some cases between regions which prevent efficient allocation of funds. The most obvious is the Canada Pension Plan, which forces Canadians to contribute to a government intermediary which in turn is a captive lender to the provincial governments. The Quebec Pension Plan at least allows funds to be invested in a wider range of assets. A glance at figure 1 will confirm that these plans already involve a large portion of the country's total financial assets; discussion below will suggest that the share is likely to rise in the future.

Reference has already been made to the artificial market for federal Treasury bills which is created by the secondary reserve requirement imposed on the chartered banks.

A less obvious source of segmentation which has been remarked on by many observers over the years is the large portion of the gross savings of the economy which is directly reinvested in physical assets by the firm doing the saving. Most such projects, especially those partly financed externally, are appropriate uses of scarce savings. Some, however, have not had the close scrutiny which exposure to financial markets normally provides; and some of these are inferior to other projects which have to be forgone because investment funds for them are not available.

Regional segmentation has not been too serious a problem, except in the view of those regional groups who would like to see all of their region's funds stay in the region. The Alberta Heritage Fund so far appears to be a device which has essentially that effect; so do the credit unions and the new Caisses d'Entraide in Quebec. The latter in particular emphasize very strongly the local reinvestment of funds.

The form which much of the saving of the household sector takes is a source of some segmentation, though of a mild sort. Much of personal saving is contractual, in that wealth is accumulated through a regular series of payments, according to a contract arranged some time previously. Debt repayments, life insurance premiums and many retirement savings plan and pension plan contributions are of this sort. Together they accounted for almost three-quarters of personal saving in Canada in 1978[1] and the pension contribution part is likely to grow further.

This type of contractual saving is itself insensitive to the size of yields elsewhere in the financial system; nevertheless, it is not a problem as long as the intermediaries that take in the public's money have a wide range of choice of investment assets, and as long as no one class of borrower is consistently shut out. In fact, the trust and insurance companies that take in the bulk of such funds are limited in the range of assets that they can hold, though less so now than for most of their history. Life insurers and pension funds may hold only very limited amounts of shares or bonds of companies which have not had a stable earnings record for the previous five years; these may be held only under a basket clause for otherwise ineligible assets, the sum of such assets being restricted to 7 per cent of the total of all assets. Use of this basket clause provision has been quite limited, however, so that life insurance companies and pension funds are not significant sources of finance for either new businesses or those in strongly cyclical industries.

A more serious limitation on the use of the funds put into retirement savings plans is that they be used on or before age 71 to buy a retirement annuity, on pain of being taxed in full at personal tax rates. The consumers' and trust company groups managed to get the legislation loosened to allow more forms of retirement annuity than just a guaranteed life annuity from one of the life insurance companies, but the choice is still narrow. When the universal pension system puts an adequate floor under retirement incomes, this degree of enforced caution in the handling of private savings may be recognized as excessive. It certainly does not help the financial system to allocate savings flows efficiently.

Governments, Regulations and Tax Policy

Governments have always had a significant presence in the financial system, either replacing private intermediaries, supplementing them, regulating them or, in the last fifteen years especially, redirecting flows of funds through tax incentives. All of this is in addition to the role of governments as important borrowers.

The objectives of the new tax policies have been a mixture of meeting revenue needs, reallocating flows of funds, and gaining short-term political advantage. Indeed, one of the complaints about federal tax policy in the late 1970s was that it was increasingly being formed in the Privy Council Office rather than in the Department of Finance[2].

Whatever the reason, the result has been a wide diversity of tax rates for different assets both for the same investor and across investors, ranging from full marginal personal tax rates (often on purely nominal returns) to large negative rates. In the extreme case of the frontier drilling funds in 1978-79, high-income investors could recoup all of their investment in the form of tax rebates, risk-free, even if the drilling program produced nothing.

The major tax initiatives currently in effect or in prospect are as follows. The capital gains tax is levied at half personal rates on increases in nominal value, though it is payable only at date of sale and principal residences are exempt. Unused capital losses from investments can be transferred against other income, but only in a limited range of cases. The transfer was disallowed in 1972, then allowed from 1974 for Multiple Unit Residential Buildings, films and drilling funds. For most of 1980, this privilege was disallowed again for MURB's. In 1976, a similar transfer of capital losses (from one taxpayer to another) through financial leases was disallowed. In 1974, the personal income tax system was indexed to allow for inflation, though the extra nominal interest income which compensates holders of fixed-nominal-value assets for extra expected inflation was still taxed at full marginal rates. Then the first $1,000 of interest, dividend and capital gains income was exempted from personal tax, as was the first $1,000 of pension income.

Periodically throughout the decade, the limits were raised on contributions to registered retirement savings plans. The newer Registered Home Ownership Savings Plans have effectively provided a rate of subsidy for investment in owner-occupied housing equal to the investor's marginal tax rate.

In the second half of the decade, intermediaries found a way of sheltering much of their income from corporate tax through term-preferred shares and income debentures, and they passed on much of the benefit to borrowers in the form of very low interest rates on such instruments. This privilege was to be limited, in the 1978 budget, to those with maturities over ten years. The defeated Tory budget of December 1979 proposed to extend the privilege to smaller businesses through a new class of small business development bond. This measure has been reintroduced temporarily by the Liberals in 1980. This exactly reverses the effect of the 1976 decision to disallow transfer of capital losses on financial leases.

In October 1979, the Conservative government introduced legislation to allow homeowners to deduct mortgage interest from taxable income, even though the implicit income from home ownership (and any capital gains) was already tax-exempt. This legislation was not passed before the government's defeat in December 1979.

In sum, federal tax policy has severely distorted the pattern of relative rates of return from different uses of funds at the cost of significant horizontal inequity among investors, a steady and large tax drain on the federal budget, and not much in the way of extra allocative efficiency to show for it. In particular, the emphasis seems out of tune with the financing needs of the 1980s. Given the current state of the real estate market in most of Canada, new single-family dwellings hardly seem a priority. The effect of limiting capital loss transfer penalizes especially the small or expanding business which does not have any immediate prospect of income of its own against which to offset capital losses, but which could derive financial benefit from the transfer of the tax benefit to someone else.

The Pension Problem

One of the more dramatic changes recorded in Figure 1 has been the rapid rise of pension funds. Relative to previous decades, we are clearly going to great lengths to make provision for our retirement. Yet the public discussion is of the pension problem, not the pension achievement. The difficulties are three. First, future retirement income needs will rise rapidly relative to GNP since the fraction of the population comprised of those over 65 is expected to double by 2030. The $16 billion accumulated to date by the Canada and Quebec pension plans would be dissipated in benefits by the turn of the century, and by 2030 as much as 14 per cent of GNP would be needed to continue the entitlements on a pay-as-you-go basis.

Second, serious inequities have arisen in current pension schemes, in that members of different pension plans have widely different amounts of protection against inflation. Before retirement, members whose pension entitlements are tied to final salary levels are protected in that their salary usually rises with inflation. Those in 'defined-contribution' plans are protected only insofar as their contributions earn more and pay out more, thanks to the higher interest rates that prevail during a period of inflation. Since a large proportion of pension funds are invested in long-term fixed value assets that were issued when interest rates were lower, this is of only limited benefit.

Retirement benefits are formally indexed to price levels for two-thirds of the members of public sector pension plans, but for only 5 per cent of private plan members[3]. There have been many *ad hoc* adjustments in the private plans to compensate for inflation after it happens, but they have been far less than equivalent to formal indexing.

The third difficulty has been the inflexibility of pension plans for members who change jobs. Currently, most pension plan contributions are vested in members only at age 45 and after 10 years of service, so that those leaving the plan before that point generally forfeit contributions made on their behalf by the employer. Members who leave their contributions in formula pension plans find their final pension tied to their salary as of the date that they left, i.e., not indexed at all after that point.

The cure to some of these difficulties, short of avoiding inflation in the first place, is to index pension benefits before and after retirement. This "solution" puts the pension funds in a bind, however, because the funds with which to do this are not necessarily there when needed. Employers are not happy about the idea either; many of them agreed to specific and fixed pension benefits in the belief that contributions would earn high rates of return, not recognizing that the high interest rates which make them so easily affordable result from that same inflation which erodes their value after retirement. The private pension industry is currently discussing a proposal which would have much the same effect as indexing: they would use all of a pension fund's earnings above 3 per cent to supplement the pensions of those already retired[4]. To increase portability between private plans, 15 life insurance companies are also trying out a set of rules for the transfer of pension entitlement between any of the plans they manage. Standing in the wings is the federal government, which may decide either to force such features as early vesting on the private plans, or to broaden the existing public pension schemes in order to replace much of the private system.

A look ahead

The system faces gradual but substantial change over the next decade, as three developments come together: on-line computerized financial market trading, such as the Computer Assisted Trading System currently on trial in the Toronto Stock Exchange; consolidated, computerized customer accounts which integrate customers' borrowing and investing activity; and the use of home television terminals that provide access to large banks of current financial information beyond that furnished in the financial pages of newspapers. Marginal transactions costs should fall as exchanges of paper are replaced by exchanges on magnetic tape. Many of the facilities available to the wholesale markets should become feasible for use in the retail sector, as well. Financial supermarkets seem likely to replace specialized institutions, though it is not clear whether the chartered banks will be allowed to take on this role. If not, the credit unions and trust companies, to say nothing of the foreign bank affiliates, have been and will be more than willing to take advantage of the opportunity.

---

[1] *Financial Post,* June 9, 1979, p. 8.
[2] *Financial Post,* August 26, 1978, p. 1.
[3] *Financial Post,* Dec. 22, 1979, p. 54.
[4] *Financial Post,* Sept. 22, 1979, p. 1.

Chapter 6

The Labour Force

Sally F. Zerker,
Social Sciences, York University

The labour force of a country, very broadly defined, is that part of the population which enters into the national labour market. Data collection agencies that employ refined data-gathering methods and apply sophisticated statistical calculations are able to provide more exact definitions. Thus, for example, Statistics Canada's monthly labour force survey does not cover the Yukon and Northwest Territories and excludes persons living on Indian reserves, inmates of institutions and full-time members of the armed forces. On the other hand, labour force information derived from the decennial Canadian census relates to all persons 15 years and over throughout the entire country.

If allowance be made for the above qualifications, the following is a useful definition: the labour force is composed of all persons fifteen years of age or over who are employed or unemployed. Those persons who are neither employed nor unemployed are considered not to be in the labour force. The employed include all those who work for pay or profit, either in an employer-employee relationship or are self-employed, together with those who are unpaid while contributing to family work on farms, business firms or professional practices. The unemployed are persons who are without work (at the time of the monthly survey), who had actively looked for work during the four preceding weeks and who are available for work. Persons who had been laid off but were expecting to return to their old job, or had a new job that would start in four weeks' time or less, are also considered unemployed—provided that they are available for work.

Information about the Canadian labour force should not be viewed merely as a collection of numerical summaries. It should instead be seen as perhaps the most informative possible indicator of economic activity and social trends. If there existed a continuous, historical, labour force series from the earliest arrival of Europeans in Canada, we could no doubt learn a great deal about our economic history using only this exceptionally instructive record. The labour force would at first be composed, preponderantly, of native people who were vital to the prosecution of the fur trade; the gradual economic diversification and geographical extension of settlement which occurred would be indicated by gradual changes in significant features of the labour force. Moreover, analysis of employment and unemployment records would inform us about the existence and severity of regional disparities, as well as the economy's cyclical performance. Knowledge of labour force characteristics, through both time and space, would contribute invaluably to our understanding of Canadian society.

Size and Recent Rate of Growth

Unfortunately we do not have, and can never have, a consecutive record of the Canadian labour force from its very beginning; we have only recently begun to collect the statistical data. Only since 1946 at the national level, and since 1966 at the provincial level, have labour force surveys been conducted. Substantial revisions to survey procedure were made in 1976 to enhance the quality and increase the range of data collected, particularly with respect to information relating to the dynamics of the labour market. The benefit of a broad range of material about the Canadian labour force is therefore a quite recent development.

Table 1 shows that the nation's labour force currently consists of approximately 11 million persons. It constitutes something less than half the population, which at the last census (taken in 1976) numbered almost 23 million persons. Population size is not the only variable that affects the size of the labour force. Wages and prices also have significant impact, since both factors enter into people's decision to seek work. The level of technology and consequent degree of automation will also affect the demand for labour and thus the size of the labour force. Such factors have been instrumental in enlarging the proportion of the Canadian public that has entered the labour force in recent years; the series on participation rates indicates how large that increase has been.

Distribution by Province, Sex and Age

Over the period 1966-78, no dramatic shift occurred in the distribution of the Canadian labour force among the ten provinces (see Table 2). Overall, the labour force grew by about 45 per cent between 1966 and 1978, with some increase occurring in every province. Significantly smaller than average increases occurred in Quebec, Manitoba and Saskatchewan, so that each of these provinces contained a smaller fraction of the nation's labour force than it had contained in 1966. The most rapid increases occurred in Alberta and British Columbia, while Ontario's labour force grew only slightly faster than the average rate. The labour force of each of these provinces was therefore a larger fraction of the national total in 1978 than

Table 1 Canadian Labour Force, Population, Growth and Participation

Year	Labour Force (1000's)	Index Labour Force 1966 = 100	Population	% increase inter-censal period	Partici-pation rate
1966	7493	100.0	20,014,880		57.3
1967	7747	103.3			57.6
1968	7953	105.9			57.6
1969	8194	108.9			57.9
1970	8395	111.3			57.8
1971	8639	114.2	21,568,311	7.8	58.1
1972	8897	117.1			58.6
1973	9276	121.3			59.7
1974	9639	125.2			60.5
1975	9974	128.6			61.1
1976	10206	130.9	22,992,604	6.6	61.1
1977	10498	133.7			61.5
1978	10882	137.3			62.6

Source: Statistics Canada, Catalogue 71-291; *Canada Year Book*, 1978-79.

it had been in 1966. The decline in Quebec's share was more or less offset by the increase in Ontario's share so that the labour force of the two central provinces together remained approximately two-thirds of the national total. The labour force of the Atlantic provinces grew at just about the average rate and remained approximately 8 per cent of the national total.

The unemployment rate in the Atlantic provinces continued to be far above the national average, as Table 2 indicates. All other things being equal, a persistently high unemployment rate in any region would cause an exodus of workers and a decline in that region's proportion of the national labour force. Such a decline has not occurred in the Atlantic provinces, however, presumably because transfer payments—unemployment insurance, old age pensions, family allowances—have enabled people to continue living here despite the fact that they were unemployed and earning no income.

The three prairie provinces consistently experienced the lowest unemployment rates in the country. In the case of Alberta, a low rate of unemployment was accompanied by a faster than average growth of the labour force; evidently the labour force grew at about the same rate as job opportunity. In the case of the other two provinces, low unemployment rates were accompanied by slower than average growth of the labour force; presumably here, too, the labour force grew at the same rate as job opportunity, a rate significantly slower than Alberta's, and slightly below the national average.

Table 2 1966-1979 Labour Force by Province (1000's), Share of Total Labour Force, Unemployment Rates 1975-1979

Year	Nfld. Total	%	P.E.I. Total	%	N.S. Total	%	N.B. Total	%	Quebec Total	%	Ontario Total	%	Manitoba Total	%	Sask. Total	%	Alberta Total	%	B.C. Total	%
1966	131	1.7	37	.4	251	3.3	196	2.6	2113	28.1	2787	37.1	361	4.8	332	4.4	569	7.5	716	9.5
1971	147	1.7	40	.4	276	3.1	210	2.4	2347	27.1	3290	38.0	402	4.6	346	4.0	682	7.8	899	10.4
1975	176	1.7	46	.4	317	3.1	248	2.4	2647	26.5	3818	38.2	437	4.3	376	3.7	822	8.2	1087	10.8
1979	207	1.8	53	.4	352	3.1	280	2.5	2878	25.6	4289	38.3	478	4.3	433	3.9	1015	9.1	1223	10.9
Total Unemployment Rates Both Sexes																				
1975	14.0		8.0		7.7		9.8		8.1		6.3		4.5		2.9		4.1		8.5	
1976	13.4		9.6		9.5		11.0		8.7		6.2		4.7		3.9		4.0		8.6	
1977	15.6		9.9		10.6		13.2		10.6		7.0		5.9		4.5		4.5		8.5	
1978	16.4		9.9		10.6		12.6		10.9		7.2		6.5		4.9		4.7		8.3	
1979	15.4		11.3		10.2		11.1		9.6		6.5		5.4		4.2		3.9		7.7	

Source: Statistics Canada, catalogue 71-201 and 71-529.

British Columbia was, like Alberta, an area of above-average labour force growth in the years 1976 to 1978. Here, however, the unemployment rate equalled or exceeded the national average; evidently, the rapid growth of the labour force was not in response to a corresponding expansion of job opportunity.

Sex Distribution

One of the outstanding features of the Canadian labour force since the war has been the rapid growth of the female component. That growth has been very much in evidence during the years 1966 to 1978. In the former year, women comprised 31 per cent of the national labour force; that proportion rose each year afterward; from Table 3, it can be calculated that women comprised 36.8 per cent of the labour force in 1975, 37.6 per cent in 1976, 38.0 per cent in 1977, 38.9 per cent in 1978. Much of the increase in the total Canadian labour force in recent years is therefore attributable to the entry of growing numbers of adult women.

Age Distribution

Law and customary practice strongly influence the age pattern of the Canadian labour force. Compulsory education to the mid-teens assures that it will contain few juveniles; the determination of very large numbers of young persons to acquire post-secondary education assures that a substantial proportion of the persons in the 18-to-23 age category will not be in the labour force; the widespread designation of 65 as age of retirement means that the labour force will contain relatively few persons beyond this age. Approximately 44 per cent of the Canadian labour force is between the ages of 24 and 44; persons aged 45 to 64 constitute 27 per cent; persons under 24 also constitute 27 per cent; persons over 65 comprise 2 per cent of the labour force.

The unemployment rate among younger persons, under 24 years of age, has been consistently higher than among older persons. The very highest unemployment rates have been experienced by persons in the 15 to 19 age bracket; persons aged 20 to 24 experienced significantly lower unemployment rates, though still well above those affecting persons over 24. Presumably the lower unemployment rates of persons once they reach the middle twenties reflect their greater maturity, acquisition of experience and skill, and placement in satisfactory employments that provide some degree of job security.

Labour Force by Industry and Occupation

Labour force data reveal much about the structure of the Canadian econ-

Table 3 Estimates of Labour Force by Age Group and Sex, Canada (1000's)

	1975			1979		
	Total	Empl't	Unempl't	Total	Empl't	Unempl't
Both Sexes						
Total	9,974	9,284	690	11,207	10,369	838
15-19 years	1,153	981	172	1,259	1,056	203
20-24 years	1,548	1,395	153	1,766	1,576	190
25 years and over	7,273	6,908	364	8,182	7,737	445
25-44 years	4,396	4,159	237	5,130	4,822	308
45-64 years	2,678	2,560	117	2,865	2,731	134
65 years and over	199	189	10	187	183	—
Men						
Total	6,294	5,903	391	6,799	6,347	452
15-19 years	625	529	96	678	567	111
20-24 years	860	770	90	968	861	107
25 years and over	4,809	4,605	205	5,153	4,919	234
25-44 years	2,843	2,717	126	3,150	2,997	153
45-64 years	1,817	1,746	71	1,865	1,787	78
65 years and over	149	141	8	138	136	—
Women						
Total	3,680	3,381	299	4,408	4,022	386
15-19 years	528	452	76	581	489	92
20-24 years	689	626	63	798	715	83
25 years and over	2,463	2,304	160	3,029	2,818	211
25-44 years	1,553	1,442	111	1,987	1,826	155
45-64 years	861	814	47	1,000	945	56
65 years and over	50	48	—	49	48	—

Source: Statistics Canada, catalogue 71-529.

omy and its corresponding social fabric. Typical of wealthy and highly developed economies, the pattern of Canadian economic development has been characterized by a primary sector that became an ever smaller proportion of the whole, a secondary sector that grew both absolutely and relatively, and a tertiary sector that eventually became larger than the other two combined.

Between 1961 and 1971, the labour force in the primary or extractive sector decreased by 174,335, or 20 per cent. The number of persons in the labour force in primary industries declined during this period in all provinces, with one exception: in British Columbia the number of persons in this sector rose by 24 per cent, a consequence of the very great importance of forestry and mining to the province's economy and the expansion which it enjoyed. In sharp contrast to the overall decline in the number of persons in the primary sector, the service sector rose by 1,398,091 persons, or 39 per cent for the decade, with every province sharing in the increase. The secondary sector, which includes manufacturing and construction, increased by 22 per cent over the same period.

Unemployment Insurance

Most industrialized economies have developed devices to protect workers against the hardships of involuntary unemployment, and Canada is no exception in this regard. Loss of employment is just one among a number of contingencies—such as sickness, old age, invalidity, etc.—that can induce loss of income. A few countries (e.g., United Kingdom, Norway) furnish social security through a single comprehensive scheme, but it is more usual for countries to deal with specific problems by means of separate insurance programs. Canada's case is an interesting instance of evolution from the specific to the more comprehensive approach.

Unemployment insurance began in Canada in 1940 with the passage of the Canadian Unemployment Insurance Act, when the federal government also established a National Employment Service to operate in conjunction with the Act. Indeed, this original legislation grew more directly out of the nation's need for a countrywide employment agency during wartime than from concern for the well-being of the unemployed. However, in the postwar years, the latter function grew in importance, necessitating amendments to the 1940 law and its replacement by a new Unemployment Insurance Act in 1955. A decade later, in 1965, the National Employment Service was transferred to the Department of Labour, and subsequently to the Canada Manpower Division of the Department of Manpower and Immigration. Thus, the government program which was designed to reduce the imperfections of a given labour market is no longer directed only to that portion of the labour force that is unemployed, and the formal marriage between the insurance scheme and the employment agency has been dissolved, although the interrelation necessarily continues.

The basic concept of our unemployment insurance plan involves the pooling of risks, through amassing a fund from contributions by employees, employers, and the government, out of which benefits will be paid to those who lose their jobs or are laid off. In 1971, a new Unemployment Insurance Act was passed which retained the principle of pooling but substantially broadened the scope and coverage of the system.

The new act covers three types of contingencies, all of which are related to interruption of earnings, but are now more broadly inclusive of human disabilities as well as exogenous economic factors. First, entitlement to benefits arises from those by-now traditional circumstances following dismissal, layoff, or voluntary termination with just cause. Second, payments are made in response to temporary incapacity to work because of illness, injury, quarantine, or pregnancy. Third, the program provides for benefits due to separation from employment at retirement.

Minimum Wages

Power to enact legislation in relation to labour relations became largely the prerogative of provincial authorities through a series of interpretations of the BNA Act; legal precedence was necessary in this matter because the Act makes no mention of labour relations. Thus, the provinces are the lawmakers affecting working hours, physical conditions of the workplace, apprenticeship and training, wage payment and wage collection, labour-management relations, worker compensation, and minimum wages. The latter is therefore only one aspect of a much broader spectrum of protective and control measures as it relates to the labour force.

Every province in Canada has enacted minimum wage legislation, by which all employees—with stipulated exceptions which vary somewhat from province to province—must receive compensation for work that is deemed necessary to maintain the lowest acceptable living standard for workers. These rates are not identical through the country; for example, as of January 1, 1981, the minimum hourly rates for experienced adult workers were: Saskatchewan $3.85, Quebec and British Columbia $3.65, Alberta and the North West Territories $3.50, Manitoba and Newfoundland $3.15, New Brunswick $3.05 and Prince Edward Island, Nova Scotia and Ontario $3.00. When employees are paid on a basis other than time, or on the basis of a combination of time and some other criterion, they must still receive the equivalent of the minimum wage.

The proponents of minimum wage requirements argue that they attempt to equalize the power of employer and employee in making a wage bargain, and do so in advance of conciliation and arbitration (either voluntary or compulsory). Whereas the latter come into play only after a demand has been made and refused, minimum wage laws seek to regulate the wage before any dispute has arisen. Moreover, while arbitration and conciliation are applicable only to unionized workers, minimum wages set the floor below which all workers' money wages cannot fall—a matter of considerable importance in this country, where two-thirds of the workers are unorganized. Proponents in effect urge that the initiative of the state is required to confer bargaining power on those who have not gained it through union organization.

Unionization

Workers who emigrated to Canada in the nineteenth century, following the practice of workers in their respective mother countries, sought to protect their interests through the formation of labour unions. Fledgling craft unions were founded in Canada in the 1820s and 1830s, even before the advent of industrialization and urbanization. The early establishment of unions in this country was the result of the migration here of craftsmen, the majority from the United Kingdom, who were familiar with the goals and organizational techniques of trade unionism. The union with the longest continuous history in Canada (perhaps in all of North America) was founded by printers in 1832 in the town of York, and still represents compositors today under the banner of the Toronto Typographical Union, Local 91 of the International Typographical Union. Printers were one of a number of skilled craftsmen—including masons, carpenters, coopers, shoemakers and others—who, when they discovered a pressing need to defend themselves against capital's dominance in the workplace, availed themselves of the added market power that their skills conferred on them and organized themselves into locals of unions. Their purpose was to assert control over the trade's labour supply and by their combined forces confront their employers to affect the terms and conditions under which they laboured.

It was this same desire for protection and self-assertion that induced individual unions to affiliate with other labour organizations. In the 1860s, some local Canadian unions formally associated with their counterparts who had established craft federations in the United States. This was the beginning of what was to become an extremely important feature of the labour movement in Canada, that is, the role of American unions in the formation and conduct of Canadian labour organizations. With Canadian affiliation, United States' national unions revised their names, adopting the title ''International;'' this relationship with American parent organizations is being alluded to whenever the issue of ''internationalism'' is raised in the context of the Canadian labour movement.

Initially, the inducement for Canadian locals to federate with American national organizations derived largely from the nature of the labour market for skilled craftsmen. In the case of workers with sophisticated skills and high mobility, the market for labour was broadly regional in scope—in some cases, continent-wide—and political borders were no barrier in the nineteenth century. Hence, local unions were faced with the necessity of binding themselves together with other labour bodies so that they could jointly control the supply of workmen in their trade. Although this was the original incentive, over time these connections with parent organizations became firmly institutionalized; relationships became entrenched through multiple regulations and dependence on international union welfare programs.

The first Canadian federation to include a number of craft unions was formed in 1871, with the founding of a central organization called the Toronto Trades Assembly. This Assembly in effect initiated the development of a structured labour movement in Canada. It was through the efforts of members of the Toronto Trades Assembly that the Canadian Labour Union was established in 1873, and this body, which had the short life of only five years, was the forerunner of the first successful ongoing trade union federation in this country, the Trades and Labour Congress of Canada (TLC), founded in 1886.

In that same year a formidable organization—although it hardly seemed so at the time—was set up across the border in the form of the American Federation of Labor (AFL), a loose association of national and international unions. Its influence was felt almost immediately in Canada as a consequence of the connections of local unions with their respective parent organizations. Thus, even though the TLC had no formal affiliation with the AFL, and was ostensibly a completely autonomous body, its policies were, from its earliest years, circumscribed by the philosophy and objectives of the American federation.

Disaffected union leaders who resented the dominance of the AFL formed a purely national federation which was named the Canadian Federation of Labour; they were joined in 1910 by a Nova Scotian group of dissidents who had established a body called the Provincial Workman's Association. In Western Canada, too, opposition to the craft-minded TLC and its American counterpart began to mount in the first decade of the new century. However, the significant gains in unionization in this period were made along craft organizational lines, under the banner of the TLC. Opposition continued, in both Canada and the U.S., to the reigning doctrine that only skilled craftsmen could be organized into unions. The new twentieth century industries that were mass producing goods by assembly line processes employed large numbers of unskilled and semi-skilled workers; here was a new and major component of the national labour force that was ineligible for recruitment in traditional craft unions. It was inevitable that their claims would become more pressing and more vocal.

In the U.S. in the 1930s, rebel members of the AFL formed the Congress of Industrial Organizations (CIO), which was comprised of unions that enrolled all of the members of a particular industry, regardless of whether they were skilled or unskilled. Bitter conflict ensued as the new industrial unions sought to enrol skilled workers who were already members of craft unions. The CIO unions proved to be extremely effective competitors against the rigid, unbending AFL unions with their conservative adherence to the principle of craft unionism; their federation soon attained a size comparable to that of the AFL.

In Canada there was considerable opposition to the TLC on the dual grounds that its member unions were exclusively of the craft type and that they were American-dominated. In 1927 a number of discontented groups came together to form the All Canadian Congress of Labour (ACCL), but the depression of the 1930s struck hard at the young and vulnerable association. The ACCL's career was plagued with difficulty and disaffection, and its existence was precarious. However, a nucleus survived around the one large and important union in its fold, the Canadian Brotherhood of Railway Employees, and this remnant became part of a new industrial union federation in Canada. The ACCL was joined in 1940 by the Canadian branches of eleven CIO international unions which had been expelled, in conformity to AFL dictates, from the TLC in 1939. The two elements fused to form the Canadian Congress of Labour (CCL). The CCL thus became the Canadian counterpart of the U.S. labour federation that adhered to the philosophy and applied the practices of industrial unionism.

In 1955, after years of bitter rivalry, the two great American federations, the AFL and CIO, merged into a single federation. Just a few months later, in April 1956, the TLC and CCL carried out a corresponding merger, the new organization being given the name Canadian Labour Congress (CLC).

In addition to the CLC, there are three other Canadian union federations operating in this country, all independent of American associations. The most prominent of the three is the Confederation of National Trade Unions (CNTU), a Quebec-based organization that grew out of a uniquely Québécois and originally purely Catholic form of unionization. In 1972, a second distinctly Quebec confederation was formed, called the Centrale des Syndicats Démocratiques (CSD), comprised of unionists who seceded from the CNTU because of its political militancy. Finally, at the national level, a small group of unions, opposed to domination by American internationals, founded the Confederation of Canadian Unions (CCU) in 1968.

Union Membership

Despite the long history of labour organization in Canada, which spanned a period longer than the lifetime of the nation itself, the extent of union membership remained relatively static until the Second World War. From 1921 to 1940, total union membership was always less than 10 per cent of the total civilian labour force, and hovered at about 15 per cent of the non-agricultural paid labour force. Favourable economic conditions and strongly supportive legislation during and after the Second World War enabled trade unions to enrol a great many new members. New legislation assured workers of the right to join unions of their own choosing and forbade employers to interfere as they had in the past. Unions as a con-

Table 4 Total Union Membership and Percentage of Labour Force

Year	Union Membership (1000's)	Union Membership as % of Civilian Labour Force	Union Membership as % of non-agricultural paid workers
1951	1,029	19.7	28.4
1952	1,146	21.4	30.2
1953	1,220	23.4	33.0
1954	1,268	24.2	33.8
1955	1,268	23.6	33.7
1956	1,352	24.5	33.3
1957	1,386	24.3	32.4
1958	1,454	24.7	34.2
1959	1,459	24.0	33.3
1960	1,459	23.5	32.3
1961	1,447	22.6	31.6
1962	1,423	22.2	30.2
1963	1,449	22.3	29.8
1964	1,493	22.3	29.4
1965	1,589	23.2	29.7
1966	1,736	24.5	30.7
1967	1,921	26.1	32.3
1968	2,010	26.6	33.1
1969	2,075	26.3	32.5
1970	2,173	27.2	33.6
1971	2,231	26.8	33.6
1972	2,388	27.6	34.6
1973	2,591	29.2	36.1
1974	2,732	29.4	35.8
1975	2,884	29.8	36.9
1976	3,042	30.6	37.3
1977	3,149	31.0	38.2
1978	3,278	31.3	39.0

Source: *Labour Relations in Canada.*

sequence were able to recruit close to 30 per cent of the country's non-agricultural workers and the growth trend continued into the 1950s (see Table 4).

Table 4 reflects some interesting developments. While the 1940s and early 1950s were a period of growth, the second half of the fifties and the first half of the sixties were a period when union membership stagnated and union density—that is, the proportion of the labour force unionized—actually declined. The subsequent resumption of union expansion is attributable largely to the enormous increase in unionization of workers employed by governments. The speed with which public servants became unionized was primarily attributable to the fact that they were already organized into government employee associations; it was only necessary to transform these associations into collective bargaining units.

These newly established public service unions are purely Canadian, with no international linkages. Their sudden emergence, and on a large scale, has dramatically altered the ratio between unionized Canadian workers associated with the U.S. labour federation and unionized Canadian workers who have no such association. As Table 5 indicates, in 1973, Canadians who were enrolled in international unions substantially outnumbered those enrolled in national unions. In 1978, following the establishment of the new public service unions, the total membership of national unions exceeded that of international unions. Furthermore, as Table 6 indicates, Canadian unions affiliated only with a Canadian federation, or not affiliated with any federation, included 56.4 per cent of the total membership of trade unions in Canada in 1978; in the past, they had been very much a minority. This new, more nationalistic hue of the Canadian labour movement is obviously of very great significance; however, it should not be overlooked that if 56.4 per cent of unionized workers have no international association, 43.6 per cent—still a very substantial proportion—do have such an association.

Political Role of Unions

The powerful influence of the international unions on Canadian locals and federations has left its imprint in many forms. One facet of that influence has been evident in the manner in which Canadian subsidiaries dealt with the issue of labour's role in the political sphere. The American labour movement—in particular, the AFL—has been characterized as "business unionism;" that is to say, its primary objective has been to win greater benefits for workers through the exercise of their united strength. It very definitely has not sought to devise programs or policies aimed at revising or essentially restructuring the social system. Hence socialism was anathema to the AFL; it strongly and consistently opposed the idea of participation in the formation or endorsement of a labour party. This did not,

Table 5 International and National Union Membership, 1973, 1978

	International Unions		National Unions		Total	
	No. of Unions	Membership	No. of Unions	Membership	No. of Unions	Membership
1973	96	1,443,246	87*	1,074,232	183	2,517,478
1978	88	1,553,477	121	1,637,628	209	3,191,103

*Total does not include six unions affiliated with CSD.
Source: *Labour Relations in Canada.*

however, mean that the labour movement should deny itself any political expression; it meant instead that political activity should take the form of lobbying the nation's two centralist parties. As it has turned out, organized labour in the U.S., especially since the days of Franklin D. Roosevelt, has developed political relationships almost exclusively with the Democratic party, the Republican being the party favoured by, and favouring, business interests.

Canada's counterpart to the AFL was somewhat ambivalent on the issue of direct political action. On the one hand, the TLC was certainly influenced by American labour's ideology, and demonstrated over much of its history a willingness to accommodate itself to a "business unionism" approach. On the other hand, the federation was not devoutly opposed to socialism; in the very early years of the TLC, socialistically inclined leaders were responsible for setting up one federal and several provincial labour parties that received union sponsorship. Moreover, Canada has among its three national political parties one that is founded on socialistic principles—in sharp contrast to the United States, where strict adherence to the two-party system has, to all intents and purposes, ruled out the pos-

Table 6 Union Membership by Congress Affiliation, 1978

Congress Affiliation	Membership Number	Per Cent
CLC	2,203,812	67.2
AFL-CIO/CLC	1,281,495	39.1
CLC only	922,317	28.1
CNTU	177,755	5.4
CCU	26,007	0.8
AFL-CIO only	10,573	0.3
Unaffiliated International Unions	96,278	3.0
Unaffiliated National Unions	665,088	20.3
Independent Local Organizations	60,372	1.8

Source: *Labour Relations in Canada.*

sibility of a socialist party. Even within the most conservative wing of the Canadian labour movement, the TLC, there was always some degree of receptivity to the idea of formal association with a political party.

When the Co-operative Commonwealth Federation (CCF) was established in 1932, it was a party representing farmers, Western labour and socialists. It was not endorsed formally by the TLC; on the contrary, since the CCF appeared to take a stand in opposition to international craft unionism, it lost the support of even the socialists in the TLC. With the formation of the CCL, however, opposition to international craft unionism became a positive attraction to the new and more radical wing of the Canadian labour movement, and a firm link began to emerge between organized labour and the CCF. This took the form at first of inter-relationship between the leadership personnel of the two organizations: CCF people were active in CCL unions and CCL leaders were candidates for office or held prominent positions in the party. The rapid growth of union membership in the CCL was accompanied by increasing popular support for the CCF.

This connection between one major strand of the Canadian labour movement and the CCF eventually embraced the whole labour movement, following the merger of the TLC and CCL in 1956. In agreeing to the merger, TLC leaders accepted as well the principle of political activism. At the merger convention, the idea was broached of initiating a new party —either an entirely different one or a reformed CCF—and the concept was then accepted that labour should have direct affiliation with that political party rather than continue the more passive procedure of lobbying or endorsing other parties and their candidates. Out of this initiation, and only after a great many obstacles were overcome, the CCF was transformed into the New Democratic Party (NDP) in 1961.

Perhaps the most significant new element in the NDP, as distinct from the CCF, was the commitment that it received from organized labour to be a principal source of both political and financial support. However, once the CLC helped recreate the old party to become the new one, it had to retreat from the role of leading activist. In part, this was due to the fact that it included civil servants' unions that would be jeopardized if the Congress to which they belonged had direct affiliation with a single Canadian political party. In part, this retreat was also due to the fact that some international unions that were AFL affiliates were prohibited by their constitutions from contributing money or political support to a specific political party. Even when some of these constitutions were amended to permit such support, American labour leaders, opposed to political involvement, continued to exercise strong, contrary pressure. Individual unions, however, have been free to make their own decisions with respect to formal political affiliation; since the establishment of the NDP, this has proven to be an increasingly attractive option for many. Labour unions in Canada have therefore developed a direct outlet for political expression through the support that they bring to and the influence that they exert on the New Democratic Party.

Problems

Canadian workers have had one overriding concern in the past few years: how to maintain their living standards in the face of an unabating upward trend in prices. The consumer price index, the indicator of this upward movement, rose 10.8 per cent in 1975, 7.5 per cent in 1976, 8.0 per cent in 1977 and 9.0 per cent in 1978. Food prices, in particular, inflated rapidly in 1978, when the price of the model basket of food increased by 15.5 per cent. However, according to the statistics on weekly earnings, the average working person managed until 1977 to keep abreast of, or even slightly ahead of, the rate of inflation. The struggle to do so involved a number of bitter and prolonged strikes. In 1978, average weekly earnings fell by 1.5 per cent in real terms. According to records of almost all collective agreements negotiated in 1977 and 1978, the average increase was less than the inflation rate. Both unionized and non-unionized workers have therefore felt much uncertainty and anxiety about rising living costs. Many workers are finding themselves on a treadmill: they run hard, full out and full time, in order to remain on the same spot.

There are, in addition, ominous portents for the union movement. The statistics of recent union growth are in some ways deceptive. If almost 40 per cent of the Canadian labour force is unionized, it is also the case that over 60 per cent is not. The aggregate level of union density in Canada, while higher than that in the United States, is still considerably lower than that in the United Kingdom, Australia and many European countries. What is more, examination of the situation in several specific areas reveals some serious problems. Firstly, the density of unionization in some of the most highly unionized sectors of the economy is declining. Secondly, there are industries in the economy—for example, finance, insurance, real estate—where the level of unionization has been and remains low; since these fields constitute major elements of the growing tertiary sector, it is here that the potential for union growth is greatest. There is, however, little indication that this potential will be realized soon.

Thirdly, the dramatic growth of the female component of the labour force means that here also is a major target for union organizers. In the past, for many reasons, relatively few women workers have been unionized. In large measure, this was due to the fact that women were employed chiefly in low wage, unskilled jobs where turnover and the cost of organizing was high and where employers could resist unionization by tapping an abundant and readily available labour supply. The relatively small proportion of women in unions could also be attributed to their vulnerability; earning very low incomes, they depended absolutely on regular earnings. Employer opposition to unions meant that they faced the possibility of dismissal if they participated in union organization activities. There is also reliable evidence, revealed in the records of some unions, that male leadership either discriminated quite openly against women or showed disinterest in their plight. Unhappily, factors such as these are not mere relics of the past. Although there has been some diminution of these painful impediments to the organization of women into trade unions, they still exist today. Hence, the female labour force is still a sector with low union density and progress in union organization here continues to be difficult.

Employment in the poorly organized sectors of the economy is expanding more rapidly than in the well-organized sectors. If union density in Canada is to increase, the labour movement must make great advances in the most resistant areas. An economic climate favourable to unionization must exist: low unemployment levels offer the most helpful environment for union advancement. High rates of unemployment, in contrast, reduce the relative bargaining power of trade unions, making them seem less attractive to non-union workers; as well, they generally inhibit people from venturing into new undertakings. When governments adopt fiscal-monetary policies designed to restrain inflation, as they have in the recent period of rising prices, they do so with a calculated acceptance of higher unemployment rates. The current rapid inflation, therefore, combined with the government measures designed to counteract it, have a negative effect on employment and hence on potentials for unionization. This challenge to the labour movement is not unknown or ignored by its leaders. They recognize that to make the case for unionization they must show that enrolment in unions is a rational and desirable solution to workers' problems under trying conditions.

The task of union organizers will not be an easy one. It is made more difficult by yet another structural feature of the contemporary unionized labour force. We noted the expansion of unions into the public sector; welcome as this has been to organized labour, the new element has been responsible for a hardening of public attitudes toward trade unionism. As CUPE affiliates and other government employee unions endeavoured to improve their members' working conditions—this was their *raison d'être* —they inevitably encountered management resistance, with strikes often being the result. Such an outcome is, of course, not confined to the public sector. However, a strike of government employees is likely to provoke a sharper reaction from the general public. When government employees withdraw their services, the public experiences deprivation directly and in some cases quite universally; when a private firm is struck, most people are either unaffected or unaware that they are being affected because the impact is indirect. Hostility engendered by widespread public discomfort, whether justified or not, has been directed at unions in general. Recruitment into unions of workers in highly resistant areas has not been made any easier.

There is, however, a strongly positive side to the picture of organized labour's future prospects; they are by no means all bleak. Some social scientists have noted that Western societies are becoming increasingly "organization societies" in which an individual can represent his/her interests only through some form of group representation. An individual alone cannot fight urban rezoning battles, advocate consumer protection, impress governments to legislate pollution controls. Similarly, a lone individual at the workplace is excluded from participation in decisions of vital concern to his/her well-being. Union organization is indispensable if the individual worker is to have any power in this arena; it is likely to be increasingly accepted as people become more familiar with the advantages and techniques of organization.

Chapter 7

The Regional Economies

Carl J. Wenaas,
economic consultant

A mare usque ad mare—from sea to sea—this message on Canada's coat of arms gives a unique official recognition of the regional character of Canada's economy. But not only does Canada stretch more than 5,000 kilometres from the Atlantic to the Pacific, its population is almost entirely confined to a narrow band 300 kilometres in width. This is in spite of the fact that in places Canada stretches almost as far from south to north as it does from east to west.

With such a vast territory and with such an attenuated population, it is not surprising that Canada is divided into distinct economic regions marked by several differing geographic and economic characteristics. In this chapter, we will describe the major regions into which the Canadian economy may be divided and identify the factors which distinguish them one from another. This chapter will proceed to an examination of the varied resource bases of the regions and their significance for the overall regional economies. The distribution of the various types of manufacturing activity carried on within Canada will be described. The relationship of manufacturing to the resource base on the one hand and to the market on the other hand will be explored. The chapter will then turn to a description of the nature of the services produced in the various regions.

Regional differences in productivity and incomes will be discussed, as will the factors accounting for these differences. It will be shown that the shifts in population and other economic factors within Canada have responded in part to these regional differences. But these regional shifts in economic activity have also been due to technological changes and new resource discoveries. Another shift in population within regions, namely urbanization, will be identified.

Canadian Regions Defined

There are several ways in which a region may be defined. In Canada, geographic features (mountains, rocks, water) break up the thin band of population into four main regions. These barriers are the Rocky Mountains, the Canadian Shield, the Appalachian Mountains and the Gulf of St. Lawrence; they divide Canada from west to east into the Pacific, prairie, central and Atlantic regions, in each of which population is reasonably continuous. The area north of this band of population, which is the Canadian Shield itself, makes up a fifth region. Because of its sparse population, this Northern region is generally given only limited attention in regional analysis.

These regions also roughly correspond to a number of major river drainage systems of which the principal rivers are either major transportation routes or are associated with breaks in land formations through which road and rail transport is possible. Thus, most of the population of the Pacific region lives at the lower end of the Fraser River basin. The prairie region consists almost entirely of the alluvial basins of the Saskatchewan and Red Rivers. The central region largely consists of the Great Lakes - St. Lawrence river system which provided early entry into the heart of the continent; the Atlantic region consists largely of islands and peninsulas bordering the Gulf of St. Lawrence. The North comprises many drainage systems entering into the Arctic and the North Atlantic, a feature once important to the fur trade and the early explorers, although the southern part of the Canadian Shield also drains into the St. Lawrence.

These regions also have other distinctive geography-related features such as topography and soil. The Pacific region is largely mountainous with a distinctive western mountain soil which, because of heavy rainfall, supports an abundant forest growth. The prairie region ranges from flat to slightly rolling, from grassland to lightly wooded and has the largest area of fertile agricultural land in Canada. The central region outside of the Canadian Shield possesses grey-brown fertile soils that were once completely forested but are now largely cleared and under cultivation. The Atlantic region (with the exception of Prince Edward Island) is largely forested with scattered pockets of fertile land suitable for agriculture. Prince Edward Island is different, being covered with soil that is nearly all suitable for agriculture. Newfoundland is really part of the Canadian Shield and in a geological sense is in the northern region. The northern region consists of two main zones: the rock, peat and podzolic soils of the Canadian Shield that support a forest growth which becomes progressively thinner in its northern reaches and the tundra soils of the high Arctic, with which the first zone merges.

These geographic features, together with climatic differences such as the low temperatures of the North which inhibit forest growth, have had profound effects on Canadian development.

Regions may also be defined on the basis of political boundaries, most particularly those of the provinces. In fact, most of our regional analysis is done for these regions because economic data are most readily available for them. On a west-to-east basis, some of the provincial boundaries do roughly match the geologic features which divide Canada into four main geographic regions. Thus British Columbia may be equated with the Pacific region; Alberta, Saskatchewan and Manitoba form the prairie region; Ontario and Quebec form the central region and New Brunswick, Nova Scotia, Prince Edward Island and Newfoundland make up the Atlantic region.

But each of these major political aggregations includes large portions of the Northern region as defined by geography. This means that each could be subdivided into at least two geographic regions, an exercise in analytical rigour which is not attempted here.

The individual provinces themselves are often treated as separate regions. This is becoming increasingly appropriate as diverging resource developments take place, particularly in the prairie and Atlantic regions. The prairie region once shared a common agricultural base but now oil and natural gas discoveries radically transform the Alberta economy, potash, oil and uranium developments proceed in Saskatchewan, and metal mining and hydro power are expanded in Manitoba. Ontario and Quebec have similar geographic characteristics but their ethnic and sociological differences justify a separate treatment. The Atlantic provinces have always been separated one from another by oceans (the isthmus joining Nova Scotia to New Brunswick is very narrow), conferring on each a certain geographic insularity. And some of the economic similarities among the Atlantic provinces are disappearing. Thus, agriculture was once a major industry in all of the Maritime provinces (Nova Scotia, New Brunswick and Prince Edward Island); it remains so only in Prince Edward Island. Hydro development in Labrador and major offshore oil discoveries may significantly change the Newfoundland economy from a reliance on fishing, an industry it shares with the Maritime provinces.

Regions also may be defined in terms of the relationships of hinterlands to a major urban centre or centres. Here, also, we find increased justification for considering each province as a region since more and more of the population of a province is being concentrated in one or two urban centres which provide services for the whole province. The massive growth in the service industries also means that a larger proportion of total final demand for the product of the market economy is being met within each province because services must generally be provided on the spot. This factor has been reinforced most forcefully by the expansion of provincial government services. As well, each provincial government has maintained uniform policies and programs throughout its territory, with considerable effect on provincial economic development.

The Resource Base

Many Canadians have been taught to be embarassed at the important role of natural resources in Canada's economy. This has been particularly true of residents and governments in regions and provinces which are strongly resource-oriented. Some have seen it as the highest goal of economic policy to shift out of resource-related activities as quickly as possible. They feel cheated that there are not more secondary manufacturing industries, preferably highly technical ones like the electronics industry, in which Japan with its limited resource base has been forced to specialize. Few seem to remember that, were it not for its natural resources, there would be scarcely any reason for anyone other than masochists to live in Canada.

Canada's natural resources have been, and remain, the base for much other economic activity. The resource base varies significantly from region to region and from province to province.

Farming, fishing and forestry (the three F's) were the predominant resource industries in Canada at the time of Confederation and had been for many generations. The fur trade, despite its romantic allure, has never been more than a comma on the page of Canada's history.

Agriculture

A century ago, agriculture was by far Canada's predominant industry, directly employing half the country's labour force. It remains very important today although *directly* employing less than five per cent of Canada's work force.

Despite its significance to the economy, less than 8 per cent of the vast area of Canada is occupied farmland and only a little over 4 per cent is improved farmland under cultivation or in cultivated pasture. About 82 per cent of Canada's improved farmland is in one region, that being the prairie region. Nearly all of the remainder (15 per cent) is to be found in the central region. The rest is divided about equally between British Columbia and the Atlantic region, with only a little over 1 per cent in each.

The distribution of improved farmland throughout the country does not precisely reflect the relative importance of agriculture in the different regions. Agricultural land is used less intensively in the prairie region than elsewhere so that in 1978 only about 55 per cent of the net value of agricultural production came from the prairie region. The central region produced about 37 per cent of Canada's total farm output, while the Pacific and Atlantic regions contributed about 5 per cent and 3 per cent of the total respectively (see Table 1).

While the prairie region and the central region thus produce roughly

Table 1 Agriculture production, value added, by region, 1978

	Millions of Dollars	Per Cent Distribution
Atlantic	$ 216	3.2 %
Central	2,480	36.8
Prairie	3,740	55.5
Pacific	303	4.5
North	n.a.	
Canada	$6,739	100.0 %

Source: Statistics Canada, *Survey of Production, 1978.*

equal values of farm produce, the nature of agriculture in the two regions differs substantially. Grain production is concentrated in the prairie region, with about 95 per cent of Canada's wheat and barley, about 80 per cent of its oats and nearly all the rapeseed being produced there. In addition, about 58 per cent of farm sales of Canadian beef comes from there. On the other hand, 75 per cent of Canada's milk, 55 per cent of its eggs, 66 per cent of the farm sales of its pork and 66 per cent of the farm sales of its poultry is produced in the central region.

Forestry

The area of Canada covered with productive forests is more than four times that in occupied farmland and amounts to about 35 per cent of the country's total land area. However, while this forest area extends all the way from Newfoundland to British Columbia, only a small part is actively harvested.

The industry is most important in the Pacific region (at 51 per cent of value added in 1978) with the central region coming in a strong second at 35 per cent; the Atlantic region contributes about 10 per cent, with the remaining 4 per cent coming from the prairie region (see Table 2).

Table 2 Forestry production, value added, by region, 1978

	Millions of Dollars	Per Cent Distribution
Atlantic	$ 152	9.2 %
Central	578	35.1
Prairie	69	4.2
Pacific	849	51.5
North	n.a.	n.a.
Canada	$1,647	100.0 %

Source: Statistics Canada, *Survey of Production, 1978.*

The data in Table 2 understate the importance of forestry to the Canadian economy since they include only the value added by the primary forestry industry. The value added by processing beyond the raw material stage is several times that of the primary industry, amounting to $6.9 billion in 1974[1] and even more in 1978.

There are distinct differences between the forest and wood-processing industries in the Pacific region and those in central Canada. About 70 per cent of Canada's lumber production comes from the Pacific region, while production of paper and paperboard is concentrated in the central region to about the same extent (70 per cent); something over 50 per cent of pulp production occurs in the central region.

Mining

As is the case with forestry, exploitable mineral resources are found in all regions of Canada. Mineral products are much more diversified than those of the forest industry, however, and an individual mineral resource is likely to be highly concentrated in a single region.

In 1978, over two-thirds of the value added by the mining industry came from the prairie region and only 16 per cent from central Canada. The Pacific region produced about 8 per cent of the total, with the Atlantic region producing 4 per cent (see Table 3). These figures reflect the concentration of mineral fuel production in the prairie region and the recent sharp increases in fuel prices. The central region is dominant in metallic minerals production with about 55 per cent of the total; 16 per cent occurs in the Atlantic region, 12 per cent in the Pacific region and 10 per cent in the prairie region (nearly all in Manitoba). Over 90 per cent of mineral fuel production now comes from the prairie region.

Water Power

Another major natural resource shared by all Canadian regions is in the

Table 3 Mining, value added, by region, 1978

	Millions of Dollars	Per Cent Distribution
Atlantic	$ 581	3.9%
Central	2,351	15.8
Prairie	10,549	70.7
Pacific	1,189	8.0
North	242	1.6
Canada	$14,912	100.0%

Source: Statistics Canada, *Survey of Production, 1978.*

form of waterfalls which can be harnessed for the generation of electricity. Installed hydroelectric generating capacity in Canada was slightly under 42,000 megawatts in 1978; possible undeveloped resources were estimated to be in excess of 60,000 megawatts. Over half of this developed capacity is in the central region (about 52 per cent), about one-fifth (18 per cent) in the Atlantic region (nearly all in Newfoundland), 19 per cent in the Pacific region, and 11 per cent in the prairie region.

Fishing

The fishing industry is much smaller than the others in terms of value added, the figure being only $703 million in 1978. Activity, naturally, is concentrated in the coastal regions, with 51 per cent coming from the Atlantic region and 36 per cent from the Pacific.

Furs

Even smaller is the primary wild fur industry with a value added in 1978 of only $61 million. This was about equally divided between the prairie and central regions, which contributed 41 per cent and 39 per cent respectively. Only 8 per cent of the Canadian total came from the North.

Total Primary Resource Production

Clearly, one of the important factors in determining the location of economic activity in Canada and the nature of the regional economies is the regional resource base. Let us then, by way of summary, examine the distribution of the national total of primary resource production.

The 1978 figures are startling. Fully 52 per cent of the value added of primary resources was produced in the prairie region, with 30 per cent in the central region, 11 per cent in the Pacific region and about 6 per cent in the Atlantic region (see Table 4).

Table 4 Primary resource production, value added, by region, 1978

	Millions of Dollars	Per Cent Distribution
Atlantic	$ 1,828	6.2%
Central	8,838	30.1
Prairie	15,236	52.0
Pacific	3,163	10.8
North	277	.9
Canada	$29,342	100.0%

Source: Statistics Canada, *Survey of Production, 1978.*

This quite extraordinary situation is of recent origin, reflecting primarily the sharp increases in prices of oil and natural gas. In 1972, before the spectacular increases in the price of energy, the share of the prairie region in total primary resource production was 40 per cent, compared to 39 per cent for the central region.

The regional distribution of employment in the primary resource industries is equally important, if not more important, in determining the location of economic activity in Canada. In 1978, primary resource employment was actually somewhat higher in the central region than in the prairie region, even though the value of its output was lower (see Table 5).

Table 5 Primary resource employment, by region, 1978

	Agriculture (thousands)	Non-Agriculture (thousands)	Total (thousands)	Per Cent of Total
Atlantic	18	43	61	7.8%
Central	215	121	336	42.8
Prairie	232	71	302	38.5
Pacific	27	51	78	9.9
Total	494	291	785	100.0%

Source: Statistics Canada, *Labour Force* (Cat. 71-529).

The figures are largely accounted for by the fact that much of the value added in petroleum and natural gas production does not go to employees as wages and salaries nor to companies as profits but instead to provincial governments as royalties.

The Location of Manufacturing in Canada

The net value added by manufacturing in Canada approached $47 billion in 1977 and was nearly twice the net value added of all the primary resource industries put together. Manufacturing is therefore likely to have a significantly greater effect on the location of economic activity than do the primary resource industries.

In 1977, fully 78 per cent of the value added of manufacturing was produced in the central region, compared to only 8 per cent in the leading resource region, the prairies. Even the Pacific region, with 10 per cent of the total, surpassed the prairies (see Table 6). The Atlantic region produced 4 per cent of manufacturing output, a smaller figure than its 6.5 per cent share of primary resource production.

This difference between the regional distribution of manufacturing activity and that of resource production underlies some of the sense of

Table 6 Manufacturing production, value added, by region, 1978

	Value added (millions of dollars)	Per Cent Distribution (%)
Atlantic	$ 2,203	4.0%
Central	42,420	77.6
Prairie	4,451	8.1
Pacific	5,553	10.2
Total	$54,635[1]	100.0%

[1]Includes $8,000,000 for Yukon and Northwest Territories.
Source   Statistics Canada, *Survey of Production, 1978.*

grievance of the resource-oriented regions. It is taken as partial evidence that the economic benefits of Confederation have been largely garnered by the central region.

A major question in the analysis of Canadian regions is why this concentration of manufacturing in the central region has occurred. Let us first examine the nature of the concentration, noting the industries in which the concentration is greatest. Ranked in terms of importance, the share of the central region in value added by industry group in 1978 was: food and beverage industries (68 per cent), transportation equipment (91 per cent), primary metals (85 per cent), metal fabricating (81 per cent), chemical and chemical products (85 per cent), electrical products (94 per cent), paper and allied industries (63 per cent) and machinery industries (82 per cent) (see Table 7). In addition, the central region produces around 90 per cent of the national output of a number of smaller industrial groups such as tobacco products, rubber and plastic products, leather, textiles, knitting mills and clothing. Indeed, the only manufacturing sector in which the central region produces less than half of national output is that of wood industries; here its output is 33 per cent of the national total. For all other manufacturing sectors (with the exception of petroleum and coal products), the central region share is at or above the 64 per cent share that it has of Canada's population and total employment.

The location of manufacturing activity is determined by many factors of which the location of the component resource materials is only one. In a market economy, firms will tend to locate where the most favourable relationship between revenues and costs prevails. The location of the market for the manufactured product will thus also be a major factor.

Dealing first with the resource factor, when the manufacturing process significantly reduces the volume and weight of the resource material, there will be a tendency to locate the manufacturing plant close to the site of the resource in order to reduce transportation costs. By and large, the primary resources produced in the prairie region are of the types whose

Table 7 Manufacturing, value added, central region as per cent of total, 1978

	Canada	Central Region	Central Region as Per Cent of Canada
	(millions of dollars)		(%)
Food and beverage	$ 7,463	$ 5,079	68.1
Tobacco products	441	441	100.0
Rubber and plastic products	1,541	1,346	87.3
Leather	423	401	94.8
Textile	1,498	1,410	94.1
Knitting	334	308	92.2
Clothing	1,606	1,411	87.9
Wood	3,550	1,172	33.0
Furniture and fixture	900	769	85.4
Paper and allied	4,565	2,890	63.3
Printing, publishing & allied	2,635	2,077	78.8
Primary metal	4,348	3,689	84.8
Metal fabricating	4,382	3,562	81.3
Machinery	2,720	2,240	82.4
Transportation equipment	6,469	5,887	91.0
Electrical products	3,178	2,974	93.6
Non-metallic mineral products	1,978	1,346	68.0
Petroleum & coal products	1,251	768	61.4
Chemical & chemical products	3,777	3,207	84.9
Miscellaneous	1,575	1,441	91.5
Total	$54,635	$42,420	77.6

Source: Statistics Canada, *Manufacturing industries of Canada: national and provincial areas, 1978.*

volume is not significantly reduced in processing. Crude petroleum and grain, major resource products of the region, are most effectively transported to distant markets in crude rather than in processed form. Therefore, neither the oil nor the grain industry has become the base for extensive processing activities in the prairie region. On the other hand, the crude product of forests and metal mines, resources which are important in the central region, are processed extensively before shipment. The value added by the processing of resource materials in the prairie region is therefore only a *fraction* of the value of those resources in the primary stage; the value added by the processing of resources in the central region is a *multiple* of the value of those resources at the primary stage. This is one reason for the substantially greater development of manufacturing in the central region than in the prairie region.

On the other hand, the location of the market will be the determining factor for two main groups of manufacturing industries. First, there are the ones in which the manufacturing process adds substantial volume to the most critical raw materials or where the product is perishable. Some examples are cement manufacturers, bakeries, soft-drink bottlers and breweries. Manufacturing establishments in these industries are widely dispersed across Canada to bring them close to their markets. Indeed, the food and beverage manufacturing industries as a whole are distributed among the various regions of Canada approximately in proportion to the population in each region.

The second group of industries is comprised of those which must operate on a very large scale if they are to be efficient. The scale may be so large that only a few establishments can be supported by the Canadian market. At the same time, transportation costs may be significant. Such industries will tend to concentrate in that region which, for historical reasons, already provides the largest share of the market—or which is contiguous to a large market in the United States. Three of the major new industries of the twentieth century—motor vehicles, electrical products, chemicals and chemical products—are in this category, and all are heavily concentrated in the central region. This is another major reason for the overall development of manufacturing in the central region.

There are, of course, additional factors which affect the location of industry, such as differentials in wage costs, differentials in energy costs, the availability of a wide range of technical services, access to a large pool of labour resources with many skills and aptitudes, etc.

The Location of Service Production

Approximately two-thirds of Canada's labour force is now employed in the service industries. As noted earlier, a strong case can be made that, *in general*, it is the location of the goods-producing industries in Canada that determines the location of the service industries. As the relative importance of the service industries grows, this observation becomes less valid but is still sufficiently true to be a good working hypothesis. It is true because the goods-producing industries of a region produce its major exports, and may therefore be regarded as its *basic* industries. The products of the service industries in a region are largely consumed within the region and may be described as *residentiary* or non-basic industries. This is particularly true of such service industries as retail and wholesale trade, education and health services, public administration at the provincial and municipal levels, and personal service industries such as barbers and municipal transit. All of these are highly oriented towards final demand in the consumer sector in each of the regions and indeed in the subregions.

Some service industries are export-oriented and thus may also be described as basic industries of the region. The output of business service industries, for instance, may be incorporated into exported goods, or the services may be directly exported, as is the case in sectors of the communications industry such as radio and television broadcasting and film production. Air and rail transport services may be performed on behalf of persons living outside the region, or may be incorporated in exported goods.

But, in general, the distribution of the service industries among regions closely matches the distribution of the goods-producing sector as a whole.

Productivity and Incomes

There are other distinctive characteristics of Canadian regions. One of the most significant for economic policy purposes is the chronic disparity in average incomes between the Atlantic provinces and the rest of Canada. There have been other long-standing regional differences in average incomes. Over the past 50 years, British Columbia and Ontario have consistently been above the Canadian average while the prairie provinces have generally occupied a middle position. During much of the period, Quebec had a lower per capita income than the prairie provinces (except during the Great Depression), but this margin has been much reduced in recent years. The income disparity between the Atlantic provinces and the rest of the country has also been reduced over the past several decades, although incomes there are still between 20 and 34 per cent below the national average (see Table 8).

The data in Table 8 include government transfer payments to persons (such as unemployment insurance, family allowance and old age pensions) as well as earned income. These transfer payments are a significantly higher percentage of personal income in the Atlantic region than in Canada as a whole, ranging in 1978 from 29 per cent in Newfoundland to 18 per cent in Nova Scotia, compared to 11 per cent in Ontario and 13 per cent for Canada as a whole. In the absence of these transfer payments, the income disparities between the Atlantic and the rest of Canada would have been substantially larger.

A recent study[2] by Dr. Auer of the Economic Council of Canada examines this question of economic disparities in income and productivity in some depth. It establishes that, when earned income only was considered, the gap between per capita income in the Atlantic provinces and the Canadian average ranged between 46 per cent in Newfoundland to 25 per cent in Nova Scotia in 1970-73 (see Table 9). When earned income *per worker* was considered, however, the gap was reduced to 22 per cent in Newfoundland and 13 per cent in Nova Scotia. The differences between

Table 8 Personal income per person, by province, 1978
(Index: Canada = 100)

Newfoundland	66
Prince Edward Island	68
Nova Scotia	80
New Brunswick	73
Quebec	94
Ontario	108
Manitoba	92
Saskatchewan	94
Alberta	109
British Columbia	110
Canada	100

Source: Statistics Canada, *National income and expenditure accounts, 1964-1978.*

the per capita figures and the per worker figures reflect three factors: (1) the higher proportion of young people in the Atlantic region than in Canada as a whole, (2) the lower labour force participation rates and (3) the higher rates of unemployment.

Table 9 Income and productivity levels, Canada and provinces, 1970-73
(Based on Current Dollars)

	Income[1]		Labour Productivity[2]	
	Per Capita	Per Worker	Total Economy	Goods-Producing Industries
Newfoundland	54%	78%	91%	81%
Prince Edward Island	60	n.a.	60	46
Nova Scotia	75	87	77	70
New Brunswick	68	82	82	73
Quebec	88	92	93	86
Ontario	119	110	104	107
Manitoba	94	92	89	82
Saskatchewan	80	83	99	91
Alberta	99	95	114	130
British Columbia	110	108	110	115
Canada	100	100	100	100

[1]Excludes government transfers to persons, e.g., unemployment insurance and old-age pensions.
[2]Calculated by dividing employment into value added.

Dr. Auer establishes that these income disparities reflect differences in labour productivity which are particularly marked in the goods-producing sector (see Table 9) but which are also found, to a lesser extent, in the service industries. In most cases, there is a close parallel between the index of earned income per worker and the index of labour productivity in the total economy.

What factors account for provincial differences in labour productivity? Do they reflect differences in industrial structure? Does the Atlantic region, for instance, have a larger share of low-productivity industries than other regions? Are there great differences in capital per worker?

The Economic Council study establishes that, with the exception of Prince Edward Island and Saskatchewan, industrial structure is not a dominant factor in accounting for provincial differences in labour productivity. Labour quality, especially higher educational attainment, accounts for some of the differences in output per worker. Levels of educational attainment were lower in the low-productivity provinces and higher in the high-productivity provinces. As far as capital stock is concerned, the study concludes: "In general, the variations in capital stock per worker were not nearly as closely related to provincial variations in labour productivity as were variations in labour quality." [3] The factor of capital stock does appear to be a significant one in accounting for the lower productivity in Quebec and the higher productivity levels of the three most western provinces but seems to be less important in the Atlantic region.

Obviously, other factors must account for the differences. Dr. Auer suggests that the fact that new technology was generally adopted later in the Atlantic provinces than elsewhere may be important. Scale of production was higher in a high-productivity province like Ontario. Capacity was probably more fully utilized. Differences in managerial quality may also have been important. In total, Dr. Auer suggests that factors other than industrial structure, education and capital accounted for about 30 per cent of the provincial disparities in labour productivity.

The quality of the natural resources in each province is likely to have considerable bearing on productivity. Soil surveys have shown, for instance, that the average quality of agricultural land in use in Quebec is considerable lower than that in Ontario. At an earlier stage of our economic history, when agriculture was a major industry even in the Atlantic region, the even lower average quality of soils in the Atlantic region was a major factor in income disparities and may have induced a poverty syndrome which has not yet been overcome. Density of forest growth and richness of mineral deposits are also likely to be significant factors.

Urbanization

The phenomenon of urbanization has occurred in all countries which have undergone industrialization. In Canada, urban[4] population has grown from 37 per cent of the national total in 1901 to 76 per cent in 1976: it rose from 1,990,000 in 1901 to 17,367,000 in 1976; during the same period the rural population increased only from 3,380,000 in 1901 to 5,626,000 in 1976. Moreover, the population in metropolitan areas of 100,000 persons or more grew even more, from roughly 500,000 in 1901 to 12,660,000 in 1976. In addition, even rural population is no longer largely agricultural, as it was at the turn of the century; in 1976, only 18 per cent of the rural population was in agriculture.

The present degree of urbanization varies from province to province although it is approximately the same in the four most populous provinces of Ontario, Quebec, British Columbia and Alberta, ranging between 81 and 75 per cent. The Manitoba figure of 70 per cent is somewhat lower; in Newfoundland, Nova Scotia, Saskatchewan and New Brunswick the degree of urbanization ranges between 59 per cent and 52 per cent; Prince Edward Island is in a class by itself with a figure of 37 per cent (see Table 10).

Initially, the increase in urbanization reflected a shift in commodity production from agriculture to other primary production and particularly to manufacturing. Even primary resource production such as forestry or mining typically has involved the establishment of an urban centre or centres at the site of operations. Latterly, the huge growth of the service industries has also been a major factor in the urbanization of the Canadian economy. Departments of modern government, hospitals, universities, schools, retail stores and the like have all become of such size that a single one of them can support an urban centre (i.e., a population of a thousand persons).

Each province is dominated by either one or two urban centres which contain a major part of the urban population. Ontario, Quebec, British

Table 10 Percentage Urban Population by Province, 1976

Newfoundland	58.9
Prince Edward Island	37.1
Nova Scotia	55.8
New Brunswick	52.3
Quebec	79.1
Ontario	81.2
Manitoba	69.9
Saskatchewan	55.5
Alberta	75.0
British Columbia	76.9
Canada	75.5

Source: *Canada Year Book, 1978-79.*

Columbia, Manitoba, Nova Scotia and Newfoundland each have an urban centre which is several times as large as the next largest. In Alberta, Saskatchewan and New Brunswick the pattern is distinctly different; each contains two major urban centres of approximately equal size.

Each of the metropolitan areas is at the apex of a hierarchy of urban centres in each region or province, and each size of centre performs a different range of economic activities. For the immediately surrounding area, the smallest typically perform service functions such as retail trade, primary and secondary education, some local government services such as road construction and repair, and possibly some health services. The next order of urban centres also performs these services and, in addition, may have a hospital, a small manufacturing establishment such as a creamery or bakery, lawyers and insurance agents, perhaps a provincial government office, or an agency for the electrical power utility. At a higher level in the hierarchy of urban centres there will be wholesale trade services, manufacturing functions, more provincial government services, federal government services, larger and more specialized hospitals, universities and major transportation facilities. Not all urban centres conform to this pattern, however. Oshawa in Ontario and Thompson in Manitoba have economies based on the performance of a single specialized function: automobile manufacturing in the former case and mining in the latter.

Indeed, within each region there are two systems of urban centres. One is closely linked to the regional resource endowment, with each higher order centre providing more specialized services that depend on a larger market; the other consists of urban centres that primarily serve external markets and depend very little on other centres in the regional hierarchy. The leading metropolitan centres, Toronto and Montreal, are much more than the apex of an urban hierarchy within their respective regions; they are the apexes of a national urban hierarchy.

Shifts of Economic Activity

Shifts of economic activity and therefore of population in Canada have largely reflected shifts in the nature and volume of goods production. The original distribution of a largely rural population at the time of Confederation paralleled the distribution of agricultural, forestry and fisheries resources in the new nation. The movement of population into the prairie region in the first thirty years of this century followed the opening up to cultivation of vast new areas of agricultural land. The subsequent net out-migration of population from the prairie region was due to two factors: attainment of the limits of good agricultural land, and change in the nature of agricultural production. Mechanization sharply reduced agricultural manpower requirements. The large net migration into Alberta in the last thirty years has been due almost entirely to the discovery and development of oil and natural gas. The rapid and continuing growth of British Columbia's population has reflected the steady expansion particularly of a rich forest resource but also of mining and hydroelectric power projects. Major resource developments in northern Ontario and northern Quebec have brought population to these sub-regions.

Superimposed on this pattern have been developments in manufacturing. This industry was concentrated in Ontario and Quebec at the time of Confederation and has continued to be so. While many resource-processing industries have been established near the regions of resource production and have tended to shift westward, secondary industries such as the manufacture of automobiles, aircraft, household equipment and appliances have located in the central region, thereby compensating for the relative decline in resource production and processing in these regions.

A third factor is becoming of great potential importance as the proportion of the labour force engaged in service industries increases and the proportion in goods production declines. Expansion of such service industries as television communication and air transportation has stimulated further growth in the central region; firms providing financial services have similarly become concentrated in the central region.

Overall, then, in the last fifty years, people have tended to move out of the Atlantic and prairie regions and into British Columbia and the central region (most notably Ontario). This pattern has been modified recently by the large net migration into a part of the prairie regions: Alberta.

As is to be expected, average incomes have been highest in the growing regions. Although all regions have had remarkable increases in income, Ontario and British Columbia have consistently had the highest per capita personal incomes of any region in Canada, while the Atlantic provinces have had considerably lower incomes. The shift of population can in part at least be explained as an expression of the classical economic principle that transfer of human resources must occur from lower to higher income activities. The shift has not eliminated regional income disparities, although it has reduced them. The shift of population may therefore not have been rapid enough to accord fully with economic principle; on the other hand, the continuation of regional disparities may reflect the importance of non-economic factors as well as random developments.

Within each region, there have been even greater movements of population than those that have occurred between regions. Two phenomena are involved: first, the shift from rural to urban communities as a result of the decline in farm manpower requirements; second, the concentration of urban population into the larger centres, reflecting the expansion of service industries, notably education, health, government and financial services. Within each region, the largest urban centres have had the highest rates of population growth.

These changes in the nature and location of economic activity in Canada naturally have profound implications for economic policy. They underlie the current heightening of the concerns about constitutional question, the distribution of powers between the central and provincial governments. They explain in part the rise of particularist sentiment both in Quebec, which fears its relative decline in the total population in Canada, and in the Western provinces which, benefitting from resource developments within Canada, have acquired a new self-confidence and an increased impatience with the present economic order.

---

[1] Source: *Canada Year Book 1976-77*, p. 451.

[2] L. Auer, *Regional Disparities of Productivity and Growth in Canada*, Economic Council of Canada, 1979.

[3] Ibid., p. 84.

[4] The urban population was defined in the 1976 Census as all persons living in incorporated cities, towns, and villages with a population of 1,000 and areas having a population density of at least 386/km². Also considered as urban were the built-up fringes of these cities, towns and villages if they met the same criteria of population density. The 1901 data have been estimated in part.

Chapter 8

International Economic Relations

W.H. Pope,
Department of Economics, Ryerson Polytechnical Institute

The headline described Canada's 1979 trade: "Merchandise trade surplus is a record $4.1 billion."[1] That's as far as the good news went: better a merchandise trade surplus than a deficit. But practically everything else about our international economic relations, *including* trade, is an ongoing, growing disaster.

Merchandise Trade

Table 1 summarizes Canada's 1979 exports and imports in the three broad categories of raw materials, intermediate products and manufactured goods (end products). Note the deficit in manufactured goods: just under $17 billion. Of course, the deficit here is more than made up for by the surpluses in intermediate products and raw materials; if this were not so there would be no merchandise trade surplus. The trouble is that the job content of manufactured goods is very much higher—up to ten times as high on average—than the job content of raw material production. Increasing natural gas exports in December 1979 by almost 30 per cent over the previous month's figure, as Canada did, creates few, if any, additional jobs in the natural gas and petroleum industry. How many extra people are needed to turn on the taps more? The same $88 million increase in exports of, say, cars would have increased jobs by the thousands. With over three-quarters of a million unemployed—over seven per cent of the labour force—it would seem sensible to concentrate on the export of manufactured goods, or—and this would be just as useful—on replacing our imports of these goods by Canadian production for the domestic market—in short, by increasing Canadian *net exports* (= exports less imports) of manufactured goods.

This would seem especially to be the case if the net export of raw materials were to have a depressing effect on the net export of manufactured goods, as of course it does through the operations of the foreign exchange market. If the foreign demand for Canadian raw materials should in-

Table 1 Principal merchandise exports and imports of Canada 1979
(in millions of dollars)

Exports	Amount	Per cent of Total	Imports	Amount	Per cent of Total	Surplus + or Deficit −
Live animals	$ 245	0.4	Live animals	$ 75	0.1	$ +170
Cereals (wheat, barley & others)	3,057	4.8	Fruit and vegetables	1,456	2.3	+1,601
Other agricultural produce	2,694	4.2	Other agricultural produce	2,935	4.7	−241
Raw hides and fur skins, undressed	295	0.5	Fur skins, undressed	175	0.3	+120
Fish	1,287	2.0	Fish	310	0.5	+977
Metal ores, concentrates, scrap	3,890	6.1	Metal ores, concentrates, scrap	1,075	1.7	+2,815
Coal and other bitumin	835	1.3	Coal and other bitumin	866	1.4	−31
Crude petroleum	2,402	3.7	Crude petroleum	4,430	7.1	−2,028
Natural gas	2,889	4.5	Natural gas	0	—	+2,889
Other crude materials, inedible	1,227	1.9	Other crude materials, inedible	734	1.2	+493
Total crude materials and food	18,821	29.4	Total crude materials and food	12,056	19.3	+6,765
(Raw materials)						
Wood and paper	11,623	18.2	Wood and paper	972	1.6	+10,651
Textiles	178	0.3	Textiles	1,384	2.2	−1,206
Chemicals	3,315	5.2	Chemicals	3,213	5.1	+102
Petroleum and coal products	1,882	2.9	Petroleum and coal products	446	0.7	+1,436
Iron and steel	1,599	2.5	Iron and steel	1,659	2.7	−60
Non-ferrous metals	3,649	5.7	Non-ferrous metals	1,962	3.1	+1,687

Exports	Amount	Per cent of Total	Imports	Amount	Per cent of Total	Surplus + or Deficit −
Electricity	$ 729	1.1	Electricity	—*	—	$ +729
Other fabricated materials, inedible	1,390	2.2	Other fabricated materials, inedible	$ 2,426	3.9	−1,036
Total fabricated materials, inedible	24,365	38.1	Total fabricated materials, inedible	12,062	19.3	+12,303
(Intermediate products)						
Industrial machinery	1,955	3.1	Industrial machinery	5,675	9.1	−3,720
Agricultural machinery and tractors	848	1.3	Agricultural machinery and tractors	2,109	3.4	−1,261
Transportation equipment	13,605	21.3	Transportation equipment	17,161	27.5	−3,556
Other end products, inedible	4,250	6.6	Other end products, inedible	12,699	20.3	−8,449
Total end products	20,658	32.3	Total end products	37,644	60.3	−16,986
(Manufactured goods)						
Special transactions, trade	166	0.2	Special transactions, trade	691	1.1	−525
Total domestic exports	$64,010	100.0	Total imports	$62,453	100.0	+1,557
Re-exports	1,317	2.1				+1,317
Merchandise trade balance						$ +2,874

Note: *less than $1 million.
Source: Statistics Canada, *Summary of External Trade, Dec. 1979.*

crease, so, too, would the foreign demand for Canadian dollars, since Canadian exporters would wish to receive payment in Canadian dollars, either directly or by exchanging into Canadian dollars the U.S. dollars that they would have received for their exports. (Canadian exporters would need to get Canadian dollars because they would have to make payments in Canada to Canadian factors of production). This increased demand for the Canadian dollar would raise its price in U.S. funds to, say, U.S. $0.90. At this higher external price—U.S. $0.90 instead of U.S. $0.85 —foreigners would be less willing to buy other Canadian goods, especially manufactures, *and* Canadians would be *more* willing to buy foreign-made goods, especially manufactures, for their relative prices would have dropped from Cdn $1.17 2/3 $(= \frac{\text{Cdn } \$1.00}{0.85})$ to Cdn $1.11 $(= \frac{\text{Cdn } \$1.00}{0.90})$. This change in quantity demanded as a result of a change of price is especially true for manufactured goods because of the tendency of people to be more highly responsive to the price changes of manufactures than of other commodities.[2]

Thus, it is quite conceivable that the increased net exports of raw materials may, in the long run,[3] cause a *more* than proportionate decrease in net exports of manufactured goods and thus lead to increased unemployment in Canada.

Why, then, did the Government in early 1980 authorize the export of several extra billions of dollars worth of natural gas? Partly, of course, because this is what the petroleum and natural gas industry and Alberta wished: increased profits and increased provincial royalties are involved, as well as the technical fact that, once tapped, the longer the gas is held in the ground, the less there is that may eventually be recovered. But also and more importantly, and ridiculous as it may seem to say so, the Government authorized the export partly because it does not understand enough of the *total* effect, just described, of increased exports of Canadian raw materials, and partly because of its not unnatural desire to see a stronger Canadian dollar. *Viewed in isolation,* with the employment effect *not* considered, the higher the external value of the Canadian dollar, the better, for at least two reasons. First, the higher the Canadian dollar's external value, the cheaper the imports will be to Canadians and thus the less inflation Canada will import; at the same time, the more expensive the Canadian exports are to foreigners, the less they will demand and the more that will then be available to satisfy Canadian domestic demand. Thus, *if* Canadian demand for goods is already very strong, a higher priced Canadian dollar reduces the danger of demand-pull inflation. Secondly, for a country, as for a shopkeeper, it makes sense to sell as dearly and to buy as cheaply as possible. One does not profit-maximize by having a sale when one can move the goods just as quickly at a higher price.

Table 2 Canada's balance of international payments, 1979
(in billions of dollars)

	Receipts (Exports)+	Payments (Imports)−	Balance
1. Current Account			
Merchandise (goods)	$65.2	$61.2	$+4.0
Services — travel (tourism)	2.9	4.0	−1.1
— interest and dividends	1.1	6.4	−5.3
— freight and shipping	3.4	3.1	+0.3
— other services	4.0	6.9	−2.9
— withholding tax	—	0.8	−0.8
Total services	$11.4	$21.2	$−9.8
Total goods and services (= balance of trade)	$76.6	$82.4	$−5.8
Transfers — inheritances & immigrants' funds	0.8	0.3	+0.5
— personal & institutional remittances	0.4	0.4	0
— withholding tax	0.8	—	+0.8
— official contributions (foreign aid)	—	0.6	−0.6
Total transfers	$ 2.0	$ 1.3	$+0.7
Total current account (= current account balance)	$78.6	$83.7	$−5.1
2. Capital Account			
Direct investment *(excluding undistributed profit)* — in Canada			$+0.7
— abroad			−1.9
Portfolio investment, long-term			+4.1
Portfolio investment, short-term			+7.8
Total net capital account balance			$+10.7
Net errors and omissions			$−3.9
3. Net official monetary movements			$+1.7

Source: Statistics Canada, *Quarterly Estimates of the Canadian Balance of International Payments, Second Quarter, 1980* (Ottawa, October 1980).

The Balance of Payments

Ignoring the long-run effects of a stronger Canadian dollar on net exports of manufactures, both the Government and the Bank of Canada stress the immediate favourable balance of payments effects, just described, of an increase in natural gas and other raw materials exports. So it is to Canada's balance of (international) payments that we now turn. Table 2 summarizes the balance for 1979.

The first thing to note about the balance of payments is that it is divided into three parts: 1. *current account,* 2. *capital account,* and 3. *net official monetary movements.* In the current and capital accounts, plus (+) signs indicate transactions which create increased foreign demand for the Canadian dollar and, therefore, upward pressure on its external value. Negative (—) signs in these two accounts have the opposite effect: downward pressure.

The Current Account

The current account records Canada's current international trade in goods and services as well as in international transfers. The latter are international payments and receipts of money for which no service is currently rendered; mostly they are gifts, pensions, foreign aid, inheritances, and the funds that people take with them when migrating. The withholding tax is discussed below.

The largest part of the current account is merchandise trade; that is, trade in goods. As we have already noted, Canada had a merchandise trade surplus in 1979. However, this surplus was overwhelmed by the services, or "invisibles",[4] deficit: Canadians travelled abroad more than foreign tourists came to Canada; the over-$5 billion deficit on interest and dividends is a measure of Canada's ever-growing net international indebtedness; and so is the deficit on "other services," which include all of the costs that multinational corporations decide to impose on their foreign subsidiaries, namely royalties, managerial fees, contributions to the cost of research and development done abroad (see Chapter 14).

The withholding tax of $0.8 billion, shown as a service payment, is the amount of interest and dividends payable to non-residents which is withheld at the source by the Federal government. It is shown in the payments to non-residents, or imports, column since, as far as the companies are concerned, it is paid out: it is part of their costs of doing business. But since this $0.8 billion in fact is not paid to non-residents, being withheld by the government, the services payments to non-residents entry is reversed under transfers, where the $0.8 billion of withholding tax is shown as a receipt by Canada. Of more interest than this technical discussion, though, is the smallness of the withholding tax itself: $0.8 billion is a mere

11.1 per cent of the total interest and dividends earned by non-residents of $7.2 billion [= $6.4 + $0.8 billion].

This low tax rate on non-resident earnings in Canada is deliberate: federal government policy—designed, with obvious success, to attract foreign investment into Canada. There is no withholding tax at all on interest paid to non-residents on bonds with a term to maturity of over five years; on shorter term bonds and on dividends paid to non-residents, the withholding tax is a mere 15 per cent. And a new tax treaty signed in 1980 with the United States reduces the tax to ten per cent on dividends paid to United States' residents. Contrast this to the taxes paid by Canadian residents: after receiving the first one thousand dollars of combined interest and dividend income free of tax, Canadian residents pay tax on interest income at their full marginal income tax rates—that is, at rates of up to 65 per cent—and on dividends, even with the dividend tax credit, at rates of up to 40 per cent.

Net of the withholding tax, international transfers are pretty well in balance: in total, Canada gives away just about as much as she receives. It is the services deficit of $9.8 billion which puts the total current account so heavily into deficit: a record minus $5.1 billion balance for 1979. And this despite the record merchandise trade surplus.

The Capital Account

How is this current account deficit financed? The answer is found in the capital account, which deals with *financial investment* in titles and deeds to property, and in stocks and bonds—in short, in financial instruments representing ownership and loans.

There are two fundamental types of foreign investment:[5] *direct investment* and *portfolio investment.* Direct investment is of three types: (1) the setting up in Canada of a new non-resident controlled firm; (2) the expansion in Canada of a non-resident controlled firm; and, (3) the taking over by non-residents of a previously Canadian-owned firm. In each case, it will be noted, there is non-resident *control* and always at least some non-resident *ownership*—sufficient ownership, at any rate, to ensure the non-resident control. It should also be noted that only the first two types of direct investment in themselves create jobs and meet the economist's definition of investment: the putting into place of new productive capacity. The third type, take-overs, are merely changes in ownership (transfers of title) and in themselves create no jobs, being similar in this respect to portfolio investment. Indeed, take-overs are only distinguishable from portfolio investment by the fact that take-overs involve non-resident control.

Portfolio investment is the buying of stocks and bonds by non-residents. In the case of bonds (loans to Canadians) neither ownership nor control is involved. In the case of stocks (shares), while part ownership of a firm is necessarily involved, the part is too small, by definition, to give non-resident control. Should a non-resident, or a group of non-residents acting together, buy so much company stock that control results, then what was originally classed as a portfolio investment will have become a direct investment.

As Table 2 reveals, in 1979, the balance on direct investment in Canada was $ + 0.7 billion. However, it is important to note that this does *not* mean direct investment in Canada by non-residents only increased by $700 million in 1979. By far the major part of new direct investment in Canada is carried out by reinvestment of undistributed profits made in Canada which, not having flowed across the border, are not shown in the balance of payments. Canada's direct investment international indebtedness increased by a multiple of $700 million nonetheless.

While non-residents were, on balance, increasing their new direct investments in Canada by $0.7 billion, Canadians were carrying out new direct investments abroad, on balance, to a total of $1.9 billion. Thus, the total effect of direct investments on the balance of payments in 1979 was an outflow of $1.2 billion. But this does *not* mean that Canada lost 1.2 billion of Canadian dollars. Foreigners wish payment in U.S. dollars. Canadians either acquire these before completing an international transaction or the foreigners will quickly convert the Canadian dollars that they receive into U.S. dollars. In other words, the $1.2 billion negative balance on direct investment in 1979 meant that the equivalent in U.S. dollars flowed out of Canada.

The next item in the capital account shows where these U.S. dollars came from: the balance on portfolio investment in 1979 came to $ + 11.9 billion. Mostly, this was a result of the Bank of Canada's high interest rate policy designed to encourage foreign lenders to buy higher-return Canadian bonds or—and this is simply another way of expressing it—encouraging Canadians to borrow abroad. The result was a net capital account surplus of $10.7 billion [= ($11.9—$1.2)billion].

Since the effect of so large a U.S. dollar inflow would have been to put more upward pressure on the Canadian dollar than even the Bank of Canada desired (at least in the short run), the Bank bought up Cdn $1.7 billion worth of these U.S. dollars to use either to repay past borrowings or to increase Canada's foreign exchange reserves (= official monetary assets) in the Exchange Fund Account that it manages on behalf of the Government. Note that here the convention followed in the current and the capital accounts is reversed: the plus (+) sign in the "Net official monetary movements" line indicates *down*ward pressure on the Canadian dollar: the Bank of Canada increased the supply of Canadian dollars in the foreign exchange market by $1.7 billion to buy up the "surplus" U.S. dollars. The reason for the reversal of convention is that Statistics Canada judges that it would not be logical to use a negative sign in the "Net official monetary movements" line when Canada's foreign exchange reserves have *increased*. However, the fact remains that when the Bank of Canada buys U.S. dollars in the foreign exchange market, it is putting upward pressure on the U.S. dollar in terms of the Canadian dollar, that is, it is putting *down*ward (or negative) pressure on the Canadian dollar in terms of the U.S. dollar (and other foreign currencies).

Note the remaining item not yet discussed in Table 2, "Net errors and omissions." Statistics Canada makes the best estimates that it can of the current and net capital account balances, and compares the sum of these two accounts to the precise figure for the change in foreign exchange reserves announced by the Bank of Canada. Should the sum of the two accounts not be equal to the change in foreign exchange reserves, the discrepancy is the "net errors and omissions" with sign reversed: the balance of payments must balance! For 1979, what we had then was:

	Billions
Current account balance:	$—5.1
Capital account net balance:	+ 10.7
Current and capital accounts balance:	+ 5.6
Net official monetary movements:	$+ 1.7

Therefore, net errors and omissions equal $—3.9 billion[6], the amount that must be subtracted from $5.6 billion to attain the known amount of the $1.7 billion increase in foreign exchange reserves (or decrease in official international liabilities).

There is no doubt that the capital account surplus finances the current account deficit. Even if all of the 21 million ounces of gold held in the Exchange Fund Account were sold, Canada's foreign exchange reserves could finance current account deficits of the order of $5 billion annually for barely three or four years before total reliance would have to be placed on capital account surpluses. Current account deficits mean that Canada is buying more goods and services internationally than she is selling; that is, Canada is going into debt internationally. And that is precisely what a capital account surplus is: increasing net international indebtedness.

But to say that *if* a country has current account deficits, it must have capital account surpluses to finance them, is not at all the same thing as saying current account deficits *cause* capital account surpluses. On the contrary, *Canada's current account deficits are caused by the capital account surpluses.* Whether the inflow of foreign funds is for direct investment in new productive capacity or for portfolio investment in Canadian bonds and shares, the effect is always to push up the value of the Canadian dollar to the extent necessary to bring about a precisely equal drop in net exports of Canadian goods and services.[7] Consider David E. Bond and Ronald A. Shearer:

> With a flexible exchange rate, then, the current account balance is a residual, determined by the capital account balance. The current account balance function is the mirror image of the net capital flow function. The sole determinant of the aggregate current account balance will be the level of Canadian interest rates relative to world interest rates.[8]

Or consider Lipsey, Sparks and Steiner:

> No one decides to borrow in the United States to pay for an excess of current account payments over receipts. If Canada is to have capital imports there must be a deficit on current account and the exchange rate will rise until the necessary deficit occurs. The causal sequence runs, therefore, from the capital imports to the current account deficit. If, for example, there had been less foreign borrowing during the period, then the Canadian dollar would have depreciated, with the result that the foreign exchange required to finance Canadian travel abroad and payment of interest and dividends to foreign investors would have been acquired in some other ways. There would have been higher exports or lower imports or less travel abroad or more foreigners visiting Canada, or some combination of these and other changes in individual balance of payments items.[9]

It is true that some other economics texts may contain statements such as: "We can cover a current account deficit only by borrowing on capital account and/or by drawing on our reserves." The point is that this statement does not contradict either Bond and Shearer or Lipsey, Sparks, and Steiner, for if the Bank of Canada does not run down Canada's foreign exchange reserves and if Canadians do not borrow abroad because it is cheaper to borrow at home, then there can be no current account deficit.

Foreign Investment in Canada

It is wrong, then, to view foreign investment—a net inflow of foreign currency on capital account—as always resulting in increased employment in Canada. Certainly a new foreign direct investment, such as the building or expansion of a foreign-owned plant, will, in itself, create jobs in Canada, but to the extent that the direct investment is financed by an inflow of foreign currency, the resulting increased demand for the Canadian dollar will push up its external value and bring about a precisely equal drop in net exports. It is entirely possible that the net employment effect will be *nega-*

tive; for example, a new billion dollar foreign direct investment in the capital-intensive petroleum and natural gas industry that causes a billion dollar drop in Canadian net exports of relatively labour-intensive manufactured goods will cost Canada jobs.[10] Canada's increased exports of natural gas will accomplish the same end. Moreover, portfolio investment (foreigners buying Canadian bonds and shares) will always create unemployment in Canada, for the sales of bonds and shares in themselves create no jobs while the increased demand for the Canadian dollar will increase its external value and destroy jobs in Canada as net exports fall.

If the Bank of Canada is neither buying nor selling foreign exchange, if Canada stops borrowing net abroad, and if the Government stops encouraging direct investment so that Canada has a zero balance on its capital account, then from that moment on, Canada *cannot* have a current account deficit: a country *cannot* import more goods and services than it exports, and thus go into debt, if it refuses to go into debt!

Canadian Investment Abroad

In the past five years (1976-1980), Canada's high interest rates in particular and overall unfavourable economic climate in general have reversed the century-old trend of investment so that there has been more new Canadian direct investment abroad than new foreign direct investment flowing across the border into Canada. Indeed, in one of these years, 1976, new direct investment in Canada was negative in the sense that non-residents withdrew more funds from Canada than they brought in for new direct investment.

Though the reasons for this reversal of trend are an indictment of government policy—or the lack of it—there is nothing upsetting in the trend itself. Indeed, if Canada is ever to become a net international creditor—as the wealth of her human and natural resources should require her to become—then it is a natural part of this evolution that the annual increments of Canadian direct investment abroad should be greater than the continuing annual increments of foreign direct investment in Canada, including the re-investment of undistributed profit.

The recent outflow of Canadian dollars for direct investment abroad causes concern because the investment of these funds in Canada would create jobs here rather than abroad. But, though this view is correct as far as it goes, it cannot be stressed too strongly that the view is both short-term and partial.

It is short-term because, though the direct investment *does* create jobs at once in the host country, the longer-term results tend to be favourable to the investor's country: the flow of profits home, the import-proneness of the foreign-owned subsidiary, and so on. For instance, Canadian-owned Northern Telecom's $300 million of investment in the United

States in 1978 created a permanent market that would not otherwise exist for the output of Northern Telecom's Canadian plants.

But it is of even more fundamental importance to understand why it is a partial view to be upset over the immediate loss of jobs caused by Canadian direct investment abroad. The outflow of Canadian funds abroad to buy foreign goods and services, or, in this instance, to buy title to foreign factories and to increase their productive capacity, puts downward pressure on the external value of the Canadian dollar. Alternatively expressed, the increased supply of Canadian dollars bidding for foreign currency puts upward pressure on the value of the foreign currency in terms of the Canadian dollar: Americans can buy Canadian dollars more cheaply, and Canadians have to pay more for U.S. dollars.

Thus it is that, other things equal, an outflow of Canadian dollars for direct investment abroad will bring about an exactly equal offsetting increase in Canada's net exports of goods and services. The drop in the external value of the Canadian dollar caused by the capital account deficit—the outflow of funds for investment abroad—will lead to an increase in Canadian exports and a decrease in Canadian imports until a current account surplus exactly equal to the capital account deficit has come about. There is no magic in this: the so-called "outflow of Canadian dollars" for direct investment abroad is in fact in the form of foreign currency, usually U.S. dollars, bought by the Canadian investors: Canadians can invest in a foreign country only by using that country's currency or U.S. dollars. And these U.S. dollars can only be earned by Canada running a current account surplus exactly equal to the amount of direct investment abroad that Canadians wish to carry out. And it is the carrying out of the direct investment abroad that *creates* the current account surplus!

Thus, though Canadian direct investment abroad, viewed in isolation, probably does cause an immediate loss of jobs in Canada, this loss is balanced by the jobs created by an increase in net exports exactly equal to the direct investment. Whether more jobs are created or lost in the short term will depend entirely on the labour content of the new investment compared to that of the increase in net exports. But in the longer term, it is most probable that the Canadian direct investment abroad, to the extent that it is successful, will be beneficial to Canada, in respects that include job-creation, especially if the investment is of the Northern Telecom type where investments in the United States create markets for Northern Telecom's Canadian plants.

But note that this description of the benefits that Canada can derive from direct investment abroad is correct only if viewed in isolation; that is, "other things equal." But other things decidedly have not been equal.

The small, beneficial capital account deficits caused by Canadians recently carrying out new direct investments abroad while foreigners were at the same time withdrawing direct investment capital from Canada have been massively outweighed by the inflow of loan capital induced both by the Bank of Canada's high interest rate policy and by the Government of Canada's direct borrowings abroad. The $4 to $8 billion annual capital account surpluses[11] thus created have, as intended, kept up the external value of the Canadian dollar and thus, through making imports cheaper than they would have been otherwise, helped to lessen the inflation rate by a percentage point or so.

If it were government policy to achieve a zero capital account balance, the Canadian dollar would probably sink to about U.S. $0.80. It probably would not go below U.S. $0.75 for any length of time. But even this low level would add but two percentage points to the inflation rate, for merchandise imports make up only a fifth of total expenditures in Canada. Moreover, as the cost of imports increased, less would be bought as Canadians would buy now relatively cheaper Canadian products.

Thus, for the slight advantage of a present inflation rate one or two percentage points lower than would otherwise be the case, and for the purely illusionary prestige of an 85-cent dollar instead of, temporarily, a 75- or 80-cent one, the government has forced on Canada a current account deficit averaging almost $5 billion annually for the past six years (1975-1980).

The Cost of the Current Account Deficit

The cost of the 1979 $5 billion current account deficit, for instance, was severe. It meant, first, that Canada was not producing $5 billion worth of goods and services that Canadians would otherwise have been exporting or producing for themselves in lieu of imports. Secondly, since the multiplier is about 1.2, it meant that Canada was forgoing about another $1 billion worth of production that would have been called into being by the increased employment and incomes, generated through the multiplier effect, by the $5 billion increase in net exports. Thus, the policy of high interest rates and overvalued Canadian dollar cost Canada about $6 billion worth of production in 1979—about 2 1/2 per cent of gross national production.

This lost production is a major cause of Canada's continuing heavy unemployment. Regardless of where the full employment-unemployment rate is set[12], it is clear that an increase in production of 2 1/2 per cent— with the higher level once attained being maintained—would considerably reduce the unemployment rate. In other words, so simple a policy as letting the Canadian dollar truly float by bringing interest rates down to the level necessary to ensure a zero net capital account balance would bring Canada back to something close to full employment in two or three years.

However, this "simple policy" is far removed indeed from the policies even considered by the two major parties that have alternated in office in the past couple of years. Jean Chrétien, then Minister of Finance, wrote on February 16, 1979, that "international capital [in]flows with corresponding deficits on current account should not be viewed with alarm."[13] And in the Budget he brought down on December 11, 1979, John C. Crosbie said:

> Most projections suggest that the current account deficit will continue to widen, mainly because of the growing burden of interest payments, although it does not increase as a percentage of GNP. To do better than this we must import less and export more. We need more investment and we need more skills in order to increase our share in both foreign and domestic markets.[14]

Where these "policies" lead Canada was revealed by the Economic Council of Canada in October, 1979: in none of the five policy packages that it puts forward does it foresee for 1985 a current account deficit less as a percentage of GNP than the one "achieved" in 1979.[15]

If the capital account surplus—Canada's massive borrowings abroad— were being used entirely to finance imports of machinery that made possible increases in Canada's export and import-competing capacity that were more than large enough to repay the loans with interest, then, and only then, would the Government and Bank of Canada's encouragement of these foreign borrowings make any sort of sense.[16]

But they make no sense at all when the same government which does the borrowing also criticizes Canadians for holidaying abroad. Canadians seek the southern sun in winter at least in part because their government's massive borrowings abroad allow them to buy U.S. dollars for Cdn. $1.19 (when the Canadian dollar is worth U.S. $0.84) instead of for Cdn. $1.25 or Cdn. $1.33 1/3, which would be the cost if the Canadian dollar was at U.S. $0.80 or U.S. $0.75. By enabling Canadian tourists to buy a U.S. dollar for $1.19 instead of $1.25 or $1.33 1/3, the government is encouraging them to take their holidays outside of Canada, thereby creating jobs abroad and unemployment at home.

Moreover, is it truly conceivable that Canada's net international indebtedness should increase literally forever? To borrow abroad to increase productive capacity is one thing; to borrow in order to fund government deficits, in order to pay interest on past borrowings, in order to travel abroad, is entirely different—and irresponsible. Canadians are mortgaging their children's future, for Canada's net international indebtedness can only be paid off by future net export surpluses in goods and services. Who can say that a generation from now Canada's northern need for imported energy may not be so great that Canadians would have very great difficulty in achieving such surpluses? How could this be otherwise when Canada's international indebtedness already results in a *net* outflow of well over $5 billion annually for interest and dividend payments alone? It is true that the ratio of Canada's net indebtedness to GNP has been greater in the past but this "would be relevant only if all this GNP were readily exportable".[17] Moreover, it should be noted that between 1974 and 1979 Canada's *net* payments of interest and dividends went from 1.05 per cent of GNP to 2.04 per cent of GNP—an increase of 94.3 per cent in a scant five years.

The High Interest Rate Policy of the Bank of Canada

It is undoubtedly true that the substantial decline in the external value of the Canadian dollar that has already occurred is "working to reduce Canada's large deficit in international trade in goods and services," as the Governor of the Bank of Canada said on January 3, 1979. It is also true, as the Governor added, that the "rechannelling of trade flows will take time."

However, it is precisely the actions of the Bank of Canada that are slowing this rechannelling of trade flows. If the Bank had not persisted in its high interest rate policy which started in 1974, Canada would not have had deficits in trade in goods and services of close to $5 billion annually starting in 1975. In the words of Arthur Donner and Douglas Peters: "The massive international borrowings in 1976, directly attributable to policy objectives and actions, had forced the current account into deficit, and the interest payments on that debt compounded the difficulties in bringing the current account back into balance".[18]

The longer the Bank persists in its fundamental error, the lower the dollar must eventually fall. Each year of $5 billion trade deficit caused by $5 billion of net borrowing abroad adds over $1/2 billion in interest payments to the trade deficit for the following year. And these increasing interest payments can only be met by decreasing the travel (tourism) deficit and increasing the merchandise trade surplus, both of which will require further decreases in the international value of the Canadian dollar.[19]

The Bank of Canada should never force up interest rates; increases, when they occur, should be the *result* of increasing inflation or a slowing rate of increase of the money supply in relation to real GNP. The fifteen increases in the Bank Rate that ended with the historic high of 16.2 per cent attained on April 2, 1980 were major errors of policy. The necessary reduction in the excessive rate of increase of the money supply (a consequence of earlier Bank errors) could have been achieved without a doubling of the Bank Rate. High interest rates depress real investment, creating pressure on capacity utilization. The fact that this pressure existed was acknowledged by the Governor of the Bank of Canada, Mr. Gerald Bouey, in his statement before the House of Commons Finance Committee on October 25, 1979:

. . . an important factor in our economic situation is the fact that many of our industries are operating uncomfortably close to capacity. In present circumstances we are much closer than is generally recognized to a situation in which most firms and industries, because they can readily sell just about all they can produce on a profitable basis, see little risk in incurring large cost increases or in posting large price increases.[20]

Mr. Bouey's "solution" had been announced the previous day: a further one percentage point increase in the Bank Rate! To the extent that investment was still carried out, it was now done with still more expensive money, at higher cost. Thus high interest rates add to cost-push inflation at once and continuously, and eventually, as Mr. Bouey himself showed, to demand-pull inflation because of slowed investment. At a given exchange rate, and assuming a constant rate of inflation in Canada's main trading partners, surely the result will be, again, to price Canadian goods out of world markets! And will this not lead to renewed downward pressure on the Canadian dollar, a still higher Bank Rate, still less real investment, and still higher capacity utilization? And yet the Bank maintains its high interest rate policy is helping to reduce inflation through inducing a net inflow of capital that keeps up the value of the Canadian dollar and thus cheapens imports. Certainly, this latter effect exists, but the past few years would seem to suggest it is outweighed by the two inflation-creating effects of high interest rates just cited. Moreover, the longer Canada continues to borrow, the greater becomes the net outflow of interest payments, the greater the current account deficit, the greater the downward pressure on the Canadian dollar, and the higher the Bank will feel constrained to raise interest rates to induce even greater net inflows of capital. But the result will also be an even greater shortfall of real investment in Canada, even more resulting inflation and, given the exchange rate, increasing inability to reduce the current account deficit— thus "justifying" the Bank in its foreign capital-attracting high interest rate policy!

Moreover, it is a commonplace that business hates uncertainty. Though the Bank of Canada insists that its foreign exchange dealings through the Exchange Fund Account are designed to smooth out sharp changes in the exchange rate and thus reduce business risk and uncertainty, the fact is that the Bank's actions increase uncertainty. It is commonly believed the Bank is not happy with the Canadian dollar at U.S. $0.85 and would prefer to see it at least close to U.S. $0.90, else why would the Bank have used U.S. $711 million of Canada's foreign exchange reserves in August, 1978, to keep the dollar from dropping more than from U.S. 88.11 cents to U.S. 86.97 cents?

Thus Canadian producers who compete in foreign markets and those who compete in our own market against imports cannot count on the 85 cent dollar. If the Bank is "successful," the dollar could rise 5 percentage points to 90 cents, reducing the competitive advantage of Canadian producers at home and abroad by a like percentage. And who can be sure that the Bank would be satisfied with a 90-cent dollar, should its high interest rates bring in enough foreign loans to force the dollar to this level? After all, in June, 1977, the Bank of Canada used $134 million of Canada's foreign exchange reserves to keep the dollar from dropping more than from U.S. 95.09 cents to U.S. 94.39 cents.

However, with the Exchange Fund Account dormant (or at least neutral, so that its purchases and sales of foreign exchange are equal in any three- or six-month period) and with rates of interest at the level necessary to ensure a zero net balance in the capital account, the Canadian dollar will be truly floating at last, and will *necessarily* be at whatever level is required to keep the current account's balance also at zero. Then the Canadian dollar would only rise in value as Canadian producers increase output by outcompeting foreigners in Canadian and foreign markets. With *this* rise in the value of the Canadian dollar Canadian producers can live, for it will have been set in the free market precisely because of their own increased productivity. A rise in the external value of the Canadian dollar in such circumstances cannot force Canada back into a deficit in trade in goods and services, for it will be the very fact that Canada is tending towards a trade surplus that will be pushing up the value of the Canadian dollar.[21]

However, the *Toronto Star* reported on November 19, 1980, that no less a person than Edward C. Lumley, Minister of State for Trade, in commenting on Canada's record merchandise trade surplus for the first nine months of 1980, added: "if I were an exporter I wouldn't rely on a continued lower dollar as part of my marketing strategy." But if it is not increases in our net exports of goods and services that cause our dollar to rise, then it *must* be greatly increased sales of our gold reserves or continuing and still more massive net inflows of foreign investment capital. One is left to wonder what *is* the economic strategy of the Government of Canada.

Reduced Government Interference

Should some Canadian industries producing for the domestic market seize the opportunity afforded by a dropping dollar and lessened foreign competition to raise their prices rather than increase their production, the government itself could—and should—seize the opportunity of ending its own interference by decreasing, or possibly removing entirely, the Canadian tariff in such markets.

The *total* effects of foreign investment must be clearly understood, and this most definitely includes the fact that because an inflow of foreign capital for investment pushes up the international value of the Canadian dollar, foreign investment in Canada must always be at the expense of Canada's net exports. Paradoxically, understanding this should lead the government to abolish another of its interferences in the market: the Foreign Investment Review Agency. FIRA may well be useful if the government remains committed to the notion that Canada must always have a capital account surplus;[22] that is, continually increase Canada's net international indebtedness by encouraging foreign investment in Canada. In such a case, FIRA can, as it does, induce the foreign investors to agree to increase the job-creating effects of the investment. But once the government is committed to a zero current account balance which, with a dormant Exchange Fund Account, necessarily means a zero net capital account balance, an inflow of foreign capital must *necessarily* always be balanced by an equal outflow of Canadian capital for investment abroad.

In these circumstances, the Canadian interest is amply safeguarded, not by FIRA, but by the expectation that Canadian investors abroad will be as successful as foreign investors in Canada.

The current account deficit will continue to worsen as long as the Government of Canada continues to believe that more foreign investment is desirable. The continuing *net* inflow of foreign capital is the problem, not the solution. These net inflows of foreign capital create mounting indebtedness, current account deficits together with unemployment for this generation, and decreased consumption, lost sovereignty, and possible bankruptcy for future generations.

Thus, regardless of by how much the Canadian dollar must drop for the current account to be balanced, and regardless of how wide the swings must be in the dollar's value on the way to this balance, the unalterable fact is that the current account deficit must be eliminated. Obviously, this will require major structural changes in the Canadian economy:[23] Canada must increase its international competitiveness, especially in manufacturing. But the very size of Canada's annual trade deficit in manufactures—$17 billion in 1979—is, in fact, a measure of Canada's opportunity to do better. Canada does not require a trade surplus in manufactures, the normal situation for most industrialized countries, nor even a zero balance. A yearly deficit in manufactures of around $5 billion would probably ensure a total current account in zero balance; this reduction of about $12 billion in the manufactures deficit would cover the services deficit and allow for some reduction in raw materials exports.

Reduction of imports would reduce our current account deficit just as much as an increase in our exports. In a depressed world economy, especially if the U.S. economy is slow-growing, Canada would have great difficulty increasing exports of manufactures; but, assuming the Canadian dollar is free to float downward as net capital inflows cease, Canadians will turn away from increasingly expensive imported manufactures and buy Canadian-made import substitutes. The Canadian dollar's external value will continue to decline until Canadians switch to home production sufficiently to bring the current account to zero balance.

The sooner Canada achieves current account surpluses, the sooner we will be paying back the $5 billion-a-year borrowing that started in 1975. Future generations should not have to bear the burden of such mindlessness.

This, then, brings us to our conclusion.

Achieving Full Employment Through Decreasing Indebtedness

The monetary and fiscal policies that would now be appropriate are:

1. Attainment of a zero net capital account balance through a sizable decrease in the Bank Rate in order to get the chartered banks' prime rate down. Should the prime rate not decline sufficiently to enable the attainment of a zero net capital account balance, or should it be possible to achieve a low enough prime rate only through increasing the rate of increase of the money supply, then we should increase the withholding tax on interest and dividends paid abroad to the level that will discourage capital inflows to the extent necessary to attain a zero net capital account balance.[24]

2. Through the above, achieve a depreciation in the external value of the Canadian dollar in order to increase net exports to the level allowed by Canada's present productive capacity.

3. Since bottlenecks will undoubtedly prevent net exports from increasing quickly to the point where the current account balance is zero and full employment has been achieved, run down Canada's foreign exchange reserves (including sale of gold at the market price) to import required machinery and equipment.

4. Should Canada's foreign exchange reserves, including gold, be insufficient to finance the import of all the real capital needed to attain full employment, then, and only then, borrow foreign exchange abroad to the extent of the deficiency.

5. As net exports increase because of the depreciated Canadian dollar and as real investment increases because of decreased interest rates and, more importantly, because the increase in net exports will require even fuller utilization of our capacity, increases in employment and income will result in higher domestic consumption, as

well. In these circumstances, demand-pull inflationary pressure becomes more severe unless government spending decreases as a proportion of GNP. Therefore, the tightening of fiscal policy must be accelerated with a view to ensuring that, at full employment, the government's budget is balanced.

The aim of the policies proposed here is to achieve full employment as rapidly as possible, without adding to inflation, and without adding to Canada's international indebtedness more than is absolutely necessary.

The longer-run aim—certainly within the term of the Parliament elected on February 18, 1980—is to decrease Canada's net international indebtedness while maintaining full employment. Indeed, it is *through* decreasing Canada's net international indebtedness—which implies continuous current account surpluses—that full employment will be maintained. It is not mere coincidence that Canada in the decade of the 1940s was a major net exporter of capital, had continuous current account surpluses, and had continuous full employment.[25]

---

[1] Toronto: *Globe and Mail,* February 2, 1980, p. B16.

[2] In more technical language, demand for manufactures tends to be more price-elastic.

[3] "In the long run" because one's responsiveness to price changes (price elasticity of demand) tends to increase with time.

[4] So-called because, unlike the flow of goods, nothing tangible crosses the border, except for such financial instruments as dividend cheques and interest payments.

[5] More properly, "non-resident investment": we are interested in the place of residence of investors, for it is this, not their nationality, which governs international flows of capital.

[6] This amount, which is twice as large as it has been in the past, probably indicates unsettled markets in the capital account: several billion U.S. dollars shown as having flowed in (the positive capital account balance) did not stay very long.

[7] From a longer run point of view, however, it *does* make a difference what the capital inflow is for. Portfolio investment in bonds can be reversed when the bonds mature with no greater cost to Canada than the interest payments; portfolio investment in shares and direct investment are altogether different, for in these cases, national assets are sold. The return to foreigners can quite literally be forever and, because of the productivity of the assets sold, may mount to many times the initial inflow of funds.

[8] David E. Bond and Ronald A. Shearer, *The Economics of the Canadian Financial System: Theory, Policy and Institutions* (Scarborough, Ont.: Prentice-Hall of Canada, Ltd., 1972), p. 511. (Italics in original.)

[9] Richard G. Lipsey, Gordon R. Sparks, Peter O. Steiner, *Economics,* 3rd ed. (New York: Harper & Row, 1979), p. 466. (Italics in original).

[10] See Bruce W. Wilkinson, "Long Term Capital Inflows and Balance of Payments Policy," in Canada Studies Foundation, *The Walter L. Gordon Lecture Series* 1978-79, Vol. 3, *An Economic Strategy for Canada,* (Toronto, 1979), pp. 36-37.

[11] The $10.7 billion capital account surplus for 1979 is discounted by the major part of net errors and omissions outflow of $3.9 billion—see footnote 6.

[12] See Chapter 9.

[13] Letter to author.

[14] House of Commons *Debates,* Dec. 11, 1979, p. 2260.

[15] Economic Council of Canada, *Two Cheers for the Eighties: Sixteenth Annual Review 1979* (Ottawa: Supply and Services Canada, Oct. 1979) p. 93.

[16] Though even in such a case, foreign borrowings imply a decision to favour our present consumption over that of our children. See Wilkinson, *op. cit.* pp. 35-36.

[17] Michael Hudson, *Canada in the New Monetary Order. Borrow? Devalue? Restructure!* (Toronto: Butterworth & Co. (Canada), 1978) p. 92.

[18] Arthur W. Donner and Douglas D. Peters, *The Monetarist Counter-Revolution: A Critique of Canadian Monetary Policy 1975-1979* (Toronto: James Lorimer & Co., 1979), p. 75. See also pp. 65-72.

[19] See Wilkinson, *op. cit.* pp. 31-32.

[20] Ottawa: *Minutes of Proceedings and Evidence of the Standing Committee on Finance, Trade and Economic Affairs,* House of Commons, Oct. 25, 1979, p. 2:12.

[21] The situation is similar to that of a firm which can increase prices, profits, and employment because *demand* for its product has increased. Its price increase is a measure of its success. This is the opposite of the firm which is forced to increase prices because of *cost* increases. This latter firm will sell less, earn less, and be forced to cut back staff.

[22] Consider this extract from a letter of February 16, 1979, by the then Minister of Finance, Jean Chrétien, to the author:

> "Nor does there seem to be any valid economic rationale for a country to establish a zero capital account balance as a goal of policy."

Or consider another former Minister of Finance, John C. Crosbie:

> "The first reason for generally higher interest rates in Canada is that this country uses more capital than the amount saved by Canadians. We have traditionally been an importer of capital. Our need to import capital has been intensified by the need to finance the large government deficit and private-sector investment in new plant, equipment and housing."

(Ottawa: *Minutes of Proceedings and Evidence of the Standing Committee on Finance, Trade and Economic Affairs,* House of Commons, Oct. 30, 1979, p. 4:7.)

[23] See Hudson, *op. cit.*

[24] Alternatively, it could be that, as in 1979 and early 1980, the considerably lower inflation rate in Canada than in the United States would make considerably lower interest rates appropriate in Canada. Were such large interest rate differentials in effect, the exchanging of Canadian dollars by Canadians to buy U.S. dollars with which to buy the higher return U.S. bonds, might put such downward pressure on the Canadian dollar that an excessively large current account *surplus* would be created. The excessive net outflow on capital account could be stemmed by the Government of Canada imposing higher taxes on interest payments received by Canadians from foreigners—an interest equalization tax in reverse.

[25] With the right spirit and sensible government policies, it is remarkable what Canada can do. This is the record for the war years:

	1939	1940	1941	1942	1943	1944	1945
Increase in *real* GNP	7.4%	14.1%	14.4%	18.6%	4.0%	4.0%	−2.2%
Increase in consumer price index*	0.6%	4.7%	6.9%	4.7%	2.8%	0.9%	1.1%
Unemployment rate	11.4%	9.2%	4.4%	3.0%	1.7%	1.4%	1.6%
Net exports of goods and services (in billions)	$+0.13	$+0.19	$+0.49	$+0.04	$+0.52	$−0.02	$+0.66

*By 1942 the consumer price index had merely returned to the 1929 level and after 1942 the wartime price increases were trivial, despite trivial unemployment.

Chapter 9

Unemployment and Inflation: The Post-War Canadian Experience

Anthony Waterman,
Department of Economics, University of Manitoba

Since the end of the Second World War, stabilization has been an explicit object of economic policy throughout most of the capitalist world.[1] As a direct result, internationally comparable measures of national income and the balance of payments have been estimated each year and, more recently, each quarter; indices of industrial production and price changes have been refined and elaborated; monthly time-series of employment and unemployment, international trade, financial data and the production of all classes of goods are compiled and published. In many cases, some attempt has been made to extend these estimates back to the inter-war period and even earlier; however, fully reliable data for most countries begin only in 1945, 1946 or 1947. Partly for that reason and partly because of official commitments to stabilization after 1945—but chiefly because the entire period 1914-1945 must be regarded as historically aberrant—it is usual to begin modern studies of the "business cycle" soon after 1945. Consistent Canadian series run from 1947, which is the starting date of this outline.

The particular fluctuations usually described as the "business cycle" are not always apparent from a casual inspection of these time series. This is because the actual course of economic activity, like the surface of an ocean, is simultaneously disturbed by "waves" of varying amplitude and period. Statistical procedures exist for analyzing the resulting complex wave into its components, but there is no denying a certain arbitrary character to all such procedures.[2] The usual thing is to assume that the movement of any series can be broken down into four multiplicative components: a trend of period longer than the time span;[3] the so-called "cyclical" component of period greater than one year and less than that of the trend; an annual "seasonal" cycle of months or quarters; and a residual "irregular" series of random disturbances averaging to zero over a few months or quarters.[4] The second of these, commonly supposed to be truly periodic and with an average length between 40 and 45 months, is the "short" business cycle.[5]

Since the pioneering studies of Wesley C. Mitchell in the 1920s and 1930s, it has been customary to identify these fluctuations by collating the dates of peaks and troughs in a large selection of economic time series. Such is still essentially the technique of the U.S. National Bureau of Economic Research (N.B.E.R.), which publishes the dates of Peaks (P) and Troughs (T) of a "reference cycle" purporting to represent some kind of aggregate, or average, of ("cyclical") fluctuations in the general level of activity.

It is a serious objection to this method, however, that the existence of a strong upward tend in a time series may obscure or obliterate Peaks and Troughs even when a clearly marked cyclical component is in operation. This is illustrated in Figure 1, where an imaginary "trend-cycle" of a time series (the "seasonal" and "irregular" components having been eliminated) is shown in logarithmic form. The trend-cycle stands farthest above and below trend at points a and d, which therefore represent "true" cyclical peaks and troughs, dated in the diagram as B (for "boom") and S (for "slump"). Points b and c represent the absolute maximum (peak) and minimum (trough) of TC in this cycle, and are therefore dated P and T. It is easy to see that whereas the period between B and S is independent of the trend, this is not the case for P and T. The steeper the trend, the closer together P and T. Above a certain rate of growth (represented as the angle g), P and T will disappear altogether.[6] During the period from February 1961 (T) to December 1969 (P), for example, the N.B.E.R. recognizes no cyclical turning points, treating the nine years as a single, unprecedentedly long upswing. During this decade, there was much talk of the "obsolescence" of the business cycle. Yet an inspection of trend-free data reveals signs of a weak oscillation with a peak in mid-1962 and a trough in early 1963, and a later, very clear episode with a peak in mid-1966 and a trough in late 1967.

Now if the labour force and the productive capacity of the economy are growing relatively steadily at the trend rate of growth, the trend-free peaks and troughs, B and S, will mark peaks and troughs in employment and the degree of utilization of the capital stock. Any other economic functions which vary with the overall "tightness" or "slackness" of the economy, such as interest rates, inflation and the balance of trade, will also tend to fluctuate according to the B-S cycle. Studies by the Economic Council of Canada on the relation between actual and "potential" output in the Canadian economy suggest that this is in fact the case.[7]

For reasons of this kind, the present author has devised a method for modifying the Mitchell-N.B.E.R. technique to take account of the very marked growth-trends which have characterized the post-war economy.[8] In addition to the traditional P and T points, B and S points are also identified, and it is the latter which are treated as the principal indications of the business cycle.

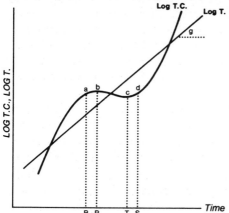

Figure 1
Cyclical Turning Points in a Growing Time-Series

Broad Outline of the Canadian Business Cycle, 1947-1978

Table 1 reveals a very marked coincidence between the U.S. reference cycle Peaks and Troughs and those estimated for Canada, especially in the first half of the period. Although the first episode (1948-49) is only weakly marked in Canada, and the very evident second episode (1950-52) not noted for the U.S.A., the third, fourth and fifth episodes (1952-61) are very similar. As mentioned above, the Canadian economy displays one (and possibly two) weak and one strong episode between 1961 and 1969, whereas the N.B.E.R. treats these nine years as a single, sustained upswing. Peaks and Troughs for both economies appear again in 1969-70, and an informal inspection of the Canadian data since 1970 suggests that in Canada, as in the U.S.A., there seems to have been a reversal in 1977 of the upturn in 1976 and hence an eleventh (post-war) episode may have begun. On average since January 1947 therefore, the "cyclical" component of Canadian economic activity has exhibited a period of about three years.

This view is somewhat modified, and the resemblance between the Canadian and U.S. business cycles made more apparent, by an inspection of Figure 2, which plots the "cyclical component"[9] of (annual) real G.N.P. for the two economies. S_1, B_3 and S_3, B_4, S_5, B_8 and S_8, B_9 and S_9, B_{10} and S_{10} are clearly visible in the annual data. The period as a whole is dominated by the long decline in activity from a high in mid-1956 to a low, four-and-a-half years later in early 1961; and a long recovery of nearly nine years to 1969, interrupted in both economies by a distinct sag in 1967. Before 1956, the 1953-54 boom and slump is very clearly marked, and so

Table 1 Turning Points of the Canadian and U.S. Business Cycle, 1947 to 1978

Turning Point	U.S.A.	Canada	
B_1			(Sept 48)
P_1	Nov 48	(Sept 48)	
T_1	Oct 49	(May 49)	
S_1			(Oct 49)
B_2			Jan 51
P_2	-	Apr 51	
T_2	-	(Dec 51)	
S_2			Oct 51
B_3			Feb 52
P_3	Jul 53	Jul 53	
T_3	May 54	Sept 54	
S_3			Aug 54
B_4			Sept 56
P_4	Aug 57	Dec 56	
T_4	Apr 58	May 58	
S_4			Jun 58
B_5			Jun 59
P_5	Apr 60	Sept 59	
T_5	Feb 61	Oct 60	
S_5			Jan 61
B_6			(Mar 62)
P_6	-	(June 62)	
T_6	-	(June 63)	
S_6			Jan 63
B_7			(Jul 64)
P_7	-	(Jul 64)	
T_7	-	(Mar 65)	
S_7			(Apr 65)
B_8			May 66
P_8	-	(Nov 66)	
T_8	-	(Nov 67)	
S_8			Oct 67
B_9			(Jan 69)
P_9	Dec 69	(Jan 69)	
T_9	Nov 70	[Sept 70]	
S_9			[Oct 70]
B_{10}			[Sept 73]
P_{10}	Nov 73		
T_{10}	Mar 75		
S_{10}			[June 75]

Source: N.B.E.R. and Waterman (1973). Parentheses enclose those dates for which the evidence is relatively unreliable; brackets, those dates estimated informally.

is the trough of the first post-war recession in 1949. After 1969, the recession of 1970 is followed by a strong recovery to 1973 in both economies, followed by a very sharp drop to 1975. For the last two years, the experience of the Canadian economy seems to have differed from that of the U.S.A.

The same broad outline is apparent in the graph of average annual unemployment rates (inverted) plotted in Figure 3. The unemployment data are more sensitive than GNP, however, in revealing the minor episode (5) which interrupted the long decline between 1956 and 1961; and less sensitive in showing the minor episode (8) which interrupted the long recovery from 1961 to 1969. The inflation series in Figure 4 show S_1, B_2, S_3, B_4, S_5, B_9, S_9, B_{10} and S_{10} fairly clearly, but the cyclical fluctuations in the middle of the period (from 1956 to 1969) are less well-marked than in the earlier or later episodes.

It is evident from Table 1 and from Figures 2, 3 and 4 both that the Canadian business cycle very closely resembles that of the U.S.A. and also that it is not identical to it. Before 1952, the Canadian average unemployment rate, though fluctuating in the same way as that of the U.S., was between one and two percentage points lower. From 1968 to 1973, however, unemployment in Canada was consistently higher than in the U.S.A.; since 1975, Canadian unemployment has increased every year whereas American unemployment has lessened. Before 1952, when Canadian unemployment was relatively low, the Canadian inflation rate was significantly higher than the American. From 1968 to 1971, when Canadian unemployment was relatively high, Canadian inflation was lower. From 1972, the Canadian inflation, whilst fluctuating in the same manner as the U.S., has been consistently higher.

Figure 2
Cyclical Component of Real G.N.P., Canada
and U.S., 1947-1978

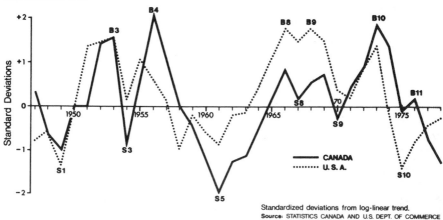

Standardized deviations from log-linear trend.
Source: STATISTICS CANADA AND U.S. DEPT. OF COMMERCE

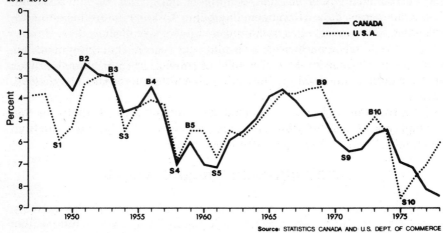

Source: STATISTICS CANADA AND U.S. DEPT. OF COMMERCE

Comparison of the trend-free GNP data in Figure 2 confirms the evidence of divergent behaviour since 1975 or 1976; it suggests that the timing of B_4, B_9 and S_9 may be appreciably different in the two economies, and shows very clearly both that the long decline from 1956 (B_4) to 1961 (S_5) was more serious for Canada and also that the long recovery to 1969 (B_9) was less complete. The two series are 59% correlated with each other, compared with a correlation coefficient of only 11% between the Canadian and comparable data for O.E.C.D.-Europe.[10] The two unemployment series are correlated with a coefficient of 78% and the two inflation rates with a coefficient of 87%.

This evidence, taken together with that of the graphs and the dates of cyclical turning points, admits of the following provisional conclusions about the post-war, Canadian business cycle.

(1) Economic fluctuations in Canada have been strongly influenced by those in the U.S.A., much less so by those of Western Europe.

(2) The broad outline of the North American business cycle may be summarized as:

-a marked check to post-war growth in 1949 soon followed by a strong recovery to a peak in 1952-53;

-a sudden and drastic decline in 1954, quickly reversed, with a new peak in 1955 or 1956;

-a long decline, somewhat interrupted in 1959, to a deep trough in 1961;

-a sustained growth of nearly nine years, interrupted in 1967, to a peak in 1969;

-a recession in 1970-71, followed by a recovery to the latest clearly recognizable peak in 1973;

-decline from 1974, reversed in 1976, but with a stronger recovery in the U.S. than in Canada.

(3) The Canadian *cycle* has followed that of the U.S.A. very closely, but Canadian *trends* have often been divergent. Although in both economies the unemployment rate has exhibited an upward trend since 1947, for example, the tendency towards a secular increase in unemployment has been greater in Canada. And although the trend of price inflation has been rising in both countries since 1961, Canadian inflation seems to have risen faster.

(4) Appreciable differences in such key indicators of activity as the unemployment and inflation rates can therefore persist between the two economies for periods as long as five or six years.

Fluctuations in Unemployment

It has already been remarked that a principal reason for the concern which cyclical fluctuations cause is the high unemployment rate which occurs during recessions. The first object of government policy in the early post-war years was the maintenance of "full employment," and for more than twenty years after 1945 the general public, haunted by memories of the Great Depression, regularly reported to the Gallup Poll that "unemployment" was among the most serious problems facing Canada.[11] It seems appropriate, therefore, to consider in more detail the cyclical fluctuations in Canadian unemployment since 1947.

Figure 3 shows that the average unemployment rate in Canada was between 2% and 3% from 1947 to 1953, never below 3% thereafter, and never below 5% since 1969. "Unemployment" as measured by Statistics Canada seems to display a secular tendency to increase. It is important to know whether this has been caused by a gradual abandonment by the government of the good intentions proclaimed in the White Paper of 1945, or whether the measure of unemployment itself conceals certain long-term structural changes in the Canadian labour market.

Measured "Unemployment" is the difference between the "Labour Force" and "Employment," both estimated by Statistics Canada each month by means of sample surveys for different age groups and regions. At infrequent intervals, the basic assumptions of the survey are revised in the light of the most recent census data. The latest revision of the Labour Force Survey was in 1976, extending the series of revised data back to 1966. Although the revised estimates are not strictly comparable with those for before 1966, the differences in the measured (national) unemployment rate for the overlapping years is never more than half a percentage point, though larger differences appear in some of the regional figures.

According to these various estimates, the average national unemployment rate during the first, major post-war boom in 1953 (B_3) was 3.0%. During the most recent comparable boom, that of 1973 (B_{10}), it was 5.6%. Table 2 analyzes this difference into its demographic components.

It is evident from this Table, first, that adult female participation[12] in the labour force has greatly increased since the early post-war years, and, secondly, that the incidence of unemployment—even at the height of a boom—has increased for all groups but relatively much more for females than for males. It is also clear that the highest unemployment rates were —and remain—among persons below the age of 25, and that these groups together formed a larger component of the labour force in 1973 than in 1953, despite the fact that participation rates for younger males actually fell and those for younger females rose less than in the older age-groups. It is also evident that the unemployment rate for young adult males has risen much more sharply than for males in other age cohorts.

These data suggest that one of the reasons for the upward trend in measured unemployment may be cultural and another may be demographic.

A much greater willingness of Canadian females to enter—and remain in—the labour market has been accompanied by a drastic increase in the incidence of female unemployment. Whereas in the early post-war years a female who was unemployed for several weeks or months would simply have given up and quit the labour force, her daughters in the 1970s seem much less ready to do so. Hence some of the increase in "unemployment" may be merely statistical: a cyclical downturn which caused a decline in the female *participation* rate in the 1950s produced a rise in the female *unemployment* rate in the 1970s.[13]

Table 2 Participation, Component and Unemployment Rates
by Age and Sex: Canada, 1953 and 1973 Compared
(Percentages)

| | Age-group | | | | | | | | | |
| | 14-19 | | 20-24 | | 25-44 | | 45 + | | Total | |
	M	F	M	F	M	F	M	F	M	F
1953										
Participation rate	52	34	93	47	98	23	75	13	83	24
Percentage of										
Labour Force	6	4	9	5	37	9	26	4	78	22
Unemployment Rate	7.2	2.9	5.1	1.8	2.9	1.2	2.8	1.0	3.5	1.6
1973										
Participation rate	44	35	86	63	97	45	69	27	77	39
Percentage of										
Labour Force	6	5	9	7	29	14	21	9	66	34
Unemployment Rate	12.9	10.8	10.0	6.5	4.2	3.9	4.1	2.8	5.8	5.1

Source: Statistics Canada

Although participation rates for under-25 males have fallen significantly, and those for younger females have risen less than for older women, this age-group as a whole comprised 27% of the total Canadian labour force in 1973 as against 24% in 1953. This change resulted from the arrival at employable age of the "post-war babies"; the entry into the labour market of this very large group was more than sufficient to offset the decline in their participation rate, resulting from extension of the period of full-time education and training. Rising technological unemployment, following the application of more capital-intensive techniques in the Canadian economy, would naturally impinge most severely upon this untrained, or semi-untrained, age-group.

The very substantial increase in the (boom) unemployment rate of males aged 20 to 24 may in part reflect a different set of causes, however. Some part of the increase may properly be described as "induced," and so, in all probability, may some portion of the increase in unemployment among the over-19 age-groups of both sexes. It has been argued by M. Feldstein, H.G. Grubel and others[14] that unemployment insurance and welfare payments, by encouraging participation in the labour force, lengthening the time that workers are willing to spend searching for preferred jobs, and also by raising the frequency of strikes and lay-offs, contribute noticeably to measured unemployment rates. It has also been argued that minimum wage legislation, by creating excess supply in the labour market, and by encouraging expectations of employment at the minimum wage among those who might otherwise work for less in the "uncovered" sector, contributes further to employment. Inasmuch as unemployment insurance and welfare payments have become more generous, and minimum wages higher and more widespread since the early 1950s, we should expect that, during similar phases of the business cycle, unemployment rates will now be higher than before.

A recent attempt by H.G. Grubel and D.R. Maki to estimate the quantitative effect of these factors in Canada concludes that their increased operation over the post-war period had the effect of raising the average unemployment rate in 1972-75 by about two-and-a-half percentage points over the average in 1952-55.[15] Assuming therefore (as Grubel and Maki do) that a measured unemployment rate of 3% represented "full employment" in the early 1950s (because of seasonal and "frictional" influences the rate could not be zero), we discover that the "full employment" rate in the early 1970s would have been 5.5%. It was noted above that average unemployment in 1953 (B_3) was 3.0%, and in 1973, (B_{10}) was 5.6%. It would then appear that both B_3 and B_{10} mark occasions of "full employment," meaning by that phrase a state of affairs in the labour market in which all non-seasonal, non-frictional unemployment is voluntary.

If this reasoning be correct then most, if not all, the seeming long-term tendency of Canadian unemployment to rise since 1947 can be attributed to a greater inclination of Canadians to declare their participation in the labour force without actually working. In terms of Figure 3, we might draw a straight line between the peaks at B_3 and B_{10}, and then measure the "cyclical" component of unemployment vertically from that line.

Three observations suggest that we regard this procedure with some caution, however. In the first place, to do so would imply that the boom of 1966 (B_8 in Fig. 3)—when the unemployment rate was just over 3% —was a time of "over-full" employment, or excess demand for labour, and hence was of greater relative amplitude than any other post-war boom, with the possible exception of B_2 (1951). Such a view is supported neither by the cyclical behaviour of real GNP (Figure 2) nor by inflation (Figure 4), nor indeed by any other aggregative indicator of the Canadian economy.[16] In the second place, it would seem from Figure 3 that the Canadian unemployment rate exhibits more of a rising trend than the American. For most of the first ten years of the period, unemployment in Canada was well below that in the U.S.A.; for nine out of the last twelve years it has been well above it. This must imply that the development of unemployment insurance, welfare and minimum wages has been significantly more rapid in Canada and/or that there are substantial behavioural differences between Canadian and American workers. In the third place, large and persistent differences in regional unemployment rates, far exceeding the change in trend for national unemployment since 1947, suggest that seasonal and "frictional" factors may be a considerable part of the explanation of unemployment rates in some parts of Canada.

Figure 5 plots annual average unemployment rates by region from 1954

Figure 4
Annual Rates of Price Inflation, Canada and
U.S.A., 1948/47-1978/77

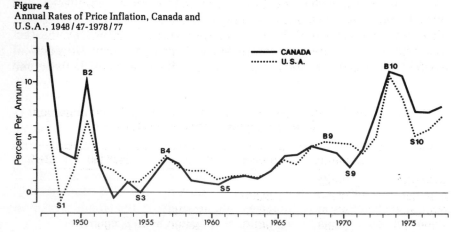

Percentage year-over-year change in implicit G.N.E. deflator
(Consumer Goods Expenditure)

Source: STATISTICS CANADA AND U.S. DEPT. OF COMMERCE

168   PART A: THE ECONOMY

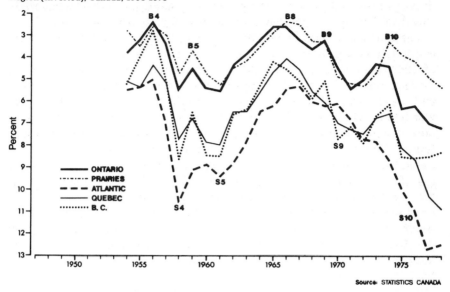

Figure 5
Annual Average Unemployment Rates by
Region (Inverted), Canada, 1954-1978

Source: STATISTICS CANADA

(when consistent data became available) to 1978; and Table 3 lists the coefficients of correlation between each of the series plotted.

It would seem from these, first, that the cyclical movement of regional
unemployment is very similar for all parts of Canada; secondly, that unemployment in the Atlantic Provinces, Quebec and British Columbia has
been consistently higher than in Ontario and the Prairie Provinces; and
thirdly, that as average rates of unemployment have risen, more regional
divergence has appeared. The last impression is confirmed by the fact
that the simple regression coefficients of unemployment in each of
Quebec, B.C. and the Atlantic provinces on that in each of Ontario and

Table 3 Coefficients of Correlation between Annual Unemployment
Rates by Region, Canada, 1954 to 1978

	Atlantic	Quebec	Ontario	Prairies	B.C.
Atlantic	1.0000				
Quebec	.9780	1.0000			
Ontario	.9706	.9878	1.0000		
Prairies	.9163	.9613	.9406	1.0000	
B.C.	.9509	.9702	.9741	.9623	1.0000

(Note: all correlations significant at 1% level)

the Prairie provinces are all significantly greater than unity. The equation relating percentage unemployment in the Atlantic provinces and the Prairies, for example, is: Unemployment rate (Atlantic) = 0.33 + 1.88 x Unemployment Rate (Prairies) which implies that for every change of a percentage point of unemployment in the Prairies, unemployment in the Maritimes has changed by nearly two percentage points. Insofar as variations in unemployment are caused by cyclical variations in aggregate demand, therefore, the effect upon unemployment of any given change in demand has been greater in the high unemployment regions of Canada than in Ontario and the Prairies.

Of the reasons which lie behind both the persistent differences in unemployment and the differential sensitivity to cyclical changes, it is only possible in this chapter to conjecture. The former may reflect both decline of regional staples (such as coal and fisheries) and a higher incidence of seasonality (as in logging). The latter may be connected with the fact that a large pool of permanently underemployed, unskilled or semi-skilled workers is only likely to be drawn into employment at times of high demand for labour in such industries as construction and mining. A thorough-going explanation lies outside the scope of this outline.

Fluctuations in Inflation

Although the inflation rate reached high levels on several occasions in the early post-war period (1946-1953), it was not very seriously regarded at the time. Unemployment rates were low, the supply of goods and services was growing more than twice as fast as population, and explanations for the abnormal character of such inflation were ready to hand.[17] Bankers and business spokesmen voiced concern about "creeping inflation" throughout the 1950s and early 1960s but the general public paid little attention. Suddenly, in June 1966, there occurred a remarkable revolution in public opinion. "Unemployment," which had headed the list of "most serious problems" for the past seven years, fell to a mere 7% of the Gallup Poll's sample. "Inflation," which had never been mentioned by more than a handful of respondents, shot into first place with 29% of the population listing it first. In October of that year, housewives staged an unprecedented demonstration in Ottawa against rising prices. Ever since 1966, the percentage of the public regarding "Inflation" as the "most serious problem" has remained high, though in recent years, "Unemployment" has again been listed by a sizable portion of the sample.

It is not easy to account for this drastic switch in public opinion in a mere six months, during which time consumer prices rose at what now seems to be the very modest annual rate of 3-1/2%. It may have had something to do with a sharp rise in interest rates caused by the desire of the United States to fight a major war on credit, and also with the acceleration in inflation (from 2% in 1964) arising from the same cause. The most probable explanation, however, is the atmosphere of alarm and despondency deliberately created by the United States government as part of a program to contain inflation by "jawboning." Most Canadians get most of their news and opinions from American radio and television. In 1966, they were deceived by American government propaganda into supposing that a severe inflationary crisis had suddenly hit the economy.

Whatever the causes, and whatever the reality of an inflationary crisis, the Canadian public has demanded since 1966 that its government should be seen to be doing something about inflation. Since the first Trudeau administration in 1968, the Canadian government has been willing to use monetary and fiscal policy to combat inflation even if this necessitated the abandonment of full employment.[18] It is appropriate, therefore, to consider in some detail the behaviour of inflation during the Canadian business cycle since 1947.

Although Figure 4 shows most of the major peaks and troughs—with the exception of B_8 (1966)—quite clearly, it is evident that more than simply cyclical forces have been at work. From 1946 to 1952, the Canadian rate of price-change (as measured by the Consumption Goods component of the Implicit GNE Deflator) fluctuated violently around an annual average of nearly 7%, quite high by the standards of the next twenty years. From 1953 to 1972, the rate of price-change fluctuated slightly about a slowly rising trend, with an average for the two decades of just over 2% per annum. For the last six years, from 1973 to 1978, the rate has fluctuated strongly again, about an average of 8-1/2% per annum.

In view of the widespread tendency, accepted by the Economic Council of Canada since 1964, to regard "creeping inflation" at 2% per annum or less as virtual "price stability," we can divide the post-war period as a whole into three clearly distinct sub-periods. From the early 1950s to the early 1970s there was, roughly speaking, "price stability." During the seven years before and the seven years following these twenty years, there was appreciable, but fluctuating, "inflation." In a still larger perspective, it is instructive to note that Canadian prices have risen in every year since 1933 save 1939 and 1953; and that the average rate of inflation (as measured by the Consumer Price Index) over the last forty-six years has been 3.8%.

Inflation is variously supposed to be caused by monetary expansion in excess of real growth, excess demand in product markets whether arising from this or from other causes,[19] excess demand in the labour market leading to "cost-push," or some combination of these. Some attention must be paid to each of these in light of the post-war Canadian experience.

On average from 1947 to 1978, GNP in real terms has grown at 4.8% per annum and the general level of prices has risen at an annual rate of 4.1%. A merely "passive" or "accommodating" monetary policy would thus have determined an annual rate of monetary expansion of about 9% over the whole period. But the actual average annual rate of monetary expansion[20] has only been 6-1/2%, sufficient to finance inflation at only 1.8% per annum and therefore distinctly anti-inflationary. It is true that peaks in the rate of monetary expansion have coincided with peaks in the rate of inflation. But as Table 4 shows, excepting for the case of B_{10} (1973)— where monetary expansion also tended to precede the general cyclical peak—the monetary increase has been insufficient to finance the growth in nominal income associated with each of the major post-war booms.

It would seem therefore, that excepting for the early 1970s, monetary policy in Canada has been relatively contractionary for the whole of the past thirty-one years. Money supply as a proportion of national income has fallen continually, and the general level of interest rates has risen steadily. Although other factors, including rising expectations of price inflation, have some part to play, it is consistent with the generally unpermissive aspect of Canadian monetary policy that the Three-Month Treasury Bill rate should have risen from an average of less than 1/2% in 1947 to 1950, to an average of more than 8% in 1975 to 1978. It would appear from these considerations that, with the possible exception of B_{10} (1973), Canadian monetary expansion has played no very obvious role in the cyclical behaviour of Canadian inflation.

If general excess demand in the Canadian economy were the initiating

Table 4 Annual Percentage Growth in Real GNP, Price Level,
Nominal GNP and the Money Supply During Booms:
Canada, 1947 to 1978

	Real GNP	Price Level	Nominal GNP	Money Supply
B_3: 1952	8.9	2.3	11.2	5.8
1953	5.1	—0.2	4.9	— 2.8
B_4: 1955	9.4	0.0	9.4	7.5
1956	8.4	1.6	10.0	— 0.2
B_8: 1965	6.7	1.9	8.6	6.5
1966	6.9	3.3	10.2	6.5
B_9: 1968	5.8	4.2	10.0	4.3
1969	5.3	3.9	9.2	7.2
B_{10}: 1972	6.1	4.0	10.1	14.3
1973	7.5	7.3	14.8	14.5

Source: Statistics Canada

cause of inflation, we should expect that the time-series in Figure 4 would show clear peaks at B_3 (1953) and B_8 (1966) in addition to those at B_2, B_4, B_9 and B_{10}. But at B_3 the Canadian inflation rate was actually negative despite the fact that this seems to have been the second strongest boom since the Second World War.[21] At B_8 inflation was less than 4% measured either by the implicit deflator or the CPI, and a slight peak actually appears in 1967, mid-way between B_8 and B_9. Moreover, the sudden spurts of inflation in 1951 and 1973 are far out of proportion to the amplitudes of the cyclical peaks in these years. Although inflation is undoubtedly somewhat cyclical therefore, this view of the matter leaves too much to be explained to be wholly satisfactory.

In recent years, various versions of the ''cost-push'' theory of inflation have become popular both among economists and in official circles. According to this view, it is some autonomous change in money earnings, whether in response to excess demand for labour or simply as a result of aggressive wage claims by powerful unions,[22] that initiates the process of inflation. Figure 6 plots the annual rates of change of average employment earning, prices, and real (or deflated) employment earnings from 1954 to 1978. The curve of real earnings shows some correspondence with the business cycle at B_4, S_4, S_5 and B_8, showing that employees were able to increase both their real and nominal earnings relatively faster in times of generally high demand. For the period 1954 to 1978 as a whole, moreover, real earnings rose at an average annual rate of 3.2%, compared with an an-

Figure 6
Annual Percentage Changes in Average
Employment Earnings, Prices and
Deflated Average Earnings, Canada, 1955/54,
1978/77

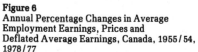
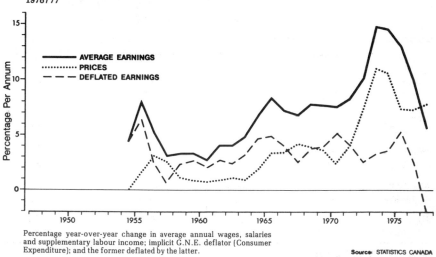

Percentage year-over-year change in average annual wages, salaries
and supplementary labour income; implicit G.N.E. deflator (Consumer
Expenditure); and the former deflated by the latter.   Source: STATISTICS CANADA

nual increase in the average productivity of labour of only 2.2%. As a result, the share of wages and salaries in national income has risen from 50.2% in 1947-1949 to 57.5% in 1976-1978, whereas the share of corporation profits has fallen between the two periods from 13.0% to 10.8%. These data are consistent with the popular view of wage costs rising faster than productivity, and of employers therefore being forced to raise prices where they can and take a profit cut where they cannot. In the latest episode, however, it is not so clear that this explanation can be applied.

Table 5 shows the inflation in the Industrial Composite Index of Average Weekly Wages and Salaries compared with that in the Consumer Price Index for 1970 to 1975, together with the resulting effect upon "real" (or deflated) wages and salaries, and the relative shares of employees and corporations S in national income. During the three-year recovery from S_9 in 1970, the increase in wages and salaries was just sufficient to keep the share of labour in national income about constant, the share of profits tending to increase. During the great inflationary surge in 1973 and 1974, the rise in wages and salaries barely kept up with the increase in consumer prices and the share of labour fell, whereas the share of profits rose to 13.5% of GNP, its highest point since 1947. Only in 1975 did real wages again begin to rise by enough to increase employees' share of national income at the expense of profits. Since that time, as Figure 6 illustrates with slightly different data, the rate of increase in real wages

Table 5 Wage and Price Inflation, and Relative Factor Shares: Canada, 1970 to 1975

	Percentage Annual Change In:			Percentage Share in GNP of:	
	Av. Weekly Wages & Sal.	CPI (All Groups)	Deflated AWWS	Wages & Salaries	Corporation Profits
1970				55.6%	9.0%
	8.5%	2.9%	5.6%		
1971				55.5	9.2
	8.4	4.8	3.6		
1972				55.6	10.3
	7.5	7.5	0.0		
1973				54.9	12.5
	11.0	10.9	0.1		
1974				55.2	13.5
	12.9	10.8	2.1		
1975				57.4	12.2

Source: Statistics Canada

has again declined, becoming negative in 1978, the first year since the Second World War in which Canadians have suffered an absolute decline in the real value of their earnings. It would be very difficult to argue in the face of this evidence that autonomous wage increases have played an initiating role in the Canadian inflation of the past nine or ten years.

It would seem from the foregoing review that none of the three common explanations of inflation is altogether satisfactory in the Canadian case. The reason for this, of course, is that they are formulated with a closed economy in mind. In an open economy—with a fixed exchange rate—a domestic monetary expansion is normally reversed by the resulting deficit in the balance of payments, excess demand in the product markets is largely dissipated in rising import surpluses, and any tendency for domestic wage-costs to increase faster than those in the rest of the world is eventually defeated by rising unemployment associated with the price-induced deterioration in the balance of trade. It is well known that Canada is a highly "open" economy which, despite the pretence of a "floating exchange rate" between 1951 and 1962 and again since 1970, has actually maintained its currency unit within 2 or 3 cents of some declared or implicit U.S. price in 28 out of the past 34 years.

It is therefore to be expected that all measures of inflation in Canada should be highly correlated with the corresponding measure for the U.S.A. For example, the Implicit Deflators (Consumption Goods) plotted in Figure 4 are 87% correlated, and the Consumer Price Index (All Groups), 91%. It may be recalled that these high correlation coefficients for inflation compare with values of only 78% for the unemployment rates and 59% for GNP residuals. Over a forty-year period from 1931 to 1971, the average annual increase in the CPI for Canada was 2.8% as against 3.2% for the U.S.A. The difference between the two averages is exactly accounted for by the average annual appreciation in the Canadian dollar in those years. These results are consistent with the fact that annual average short-term interest rates in the two countries are 92% correlated, whereas annual monetary expansion is only 45% correlated. When allowance is made for actual and expected exchange rate changes, prices and interest rates in the two countries tend to a common level, regardless of Canadian monetary policy, according to the law of one price.

It is interesting to note that Canadian inflation rates are highly correlated not only with those in the U.S.A., but also with those in the rest of the capitalist world. For example, the Canadian Implicit Deflator is correlated with that for O.E.C.D.-Europe with a coefficient of 85%, whereas GNP residuals are correlated at only 11%. Though there are considerable differences between the European and the North American business cycles, inflation since the early 1950s has tended to become a single, (capitalist) world-wide phenomenon.

[1] The Canadian government in 1945 issued a White Paper entitled *Employment and Income with Special Reference to the Initial Period of Reconstruction*, Ottawa: King's Printer, April 1945.

[2] Even spectral analysis is limited in its power to detect component oscillations by the time-span of the data.

[3] Except where the time-span is so long that "long-swings" may be identified.

[4] Then any time-series Y = T.C.S.I., where T is the trend, C the "cyclical" component to be isolated and studied, S the annual seasonal cycle, and I the series of random disturbances. Note that this postulate implies the assumption that the four components are causally independent of each other: each is a function of *time*, but of none of the other components. It is plausible enough to assume that S and I are causally independent of each other and of T and C. But to assume the causal independence of T and C implies a particular class of business cycle theory associated in particular with J.R. Hicks, (*A Contribution to the Theory of the Trade Cycle*, Oxford, 1950) according to which the forces which produce cyclical fluctuations operate independently of those which produce the growth-trend of the economy. The Hicksian theory has received some econometric confirmation and is assumed in this outline. But the reader should be aware that such distinguished investigators as Schumpeter, Harrod and Goodwin (not to mention Marx!) believed that the process of fluctuation is inextricably bound up with the process of economic growth.

[5] A recent example of the conventional wisdom is found in a pamphlet issued by Mr. Walter Gordon's Canadian Institute for Economic Policy: "The short business cycle is a well known phenomenon with an average duration of 40 to 45 months and accompanied by recessions, which seldom last for more than 12 months." *Out of Joint with the Times* (Ottawa, June 1979), p. 21.

[6] Figure 1 and the text assume that T is log-linear, implying a constant percentage rate of "trend" growth, g. But this need not be the case and T could be drawn as a curve with increasing or decreasing slope. In previous studies, the author has fitted log-quadratic trends to post-war Australian and Canadian data (see note 8).

[7] Economic Council of Canada, *First Annual Review* (1964), and subsequent *Annual Reviews* compare the performance of the economy with "potential output."

[8] For details, see Waterman, A.M.C., "The Timing of Economic Fluctuations in Australia: January 1948 to December 1964," *Australian Economic Papers*, 1967; and *The Measurement of Economic Fluctuations in Canada, January 1947 to December 1969*, Prices and Incomes Commission Staff Study, Ottawa, 1973.

[9] Deviations of logarithmic data from the least-squares log-linear trend, expressed in standard deviation units to make the two directly comparable. The log-linear trend was used rather than the log-quadratic as the latter was not significantly different from a straight line, implying that there has been no tendency for the average growth-rate of either economy to accelerate or decelerate between 1947 and 1978.

[10] Aggregate, constant price GNP data for 18 European countries: Austria, Belgium, Luxembourg, Denmark, France, Germany, Greece, Iceland, Ireland, Italy, Netherlands, Norway, Portugal, Spain, Sweden, Switzerland, Turkey and the U.K.

[11] Between 1959 and 1966, "unemployment" remained consistently in the first place among the public's perceptions of "the most serious problem." Since 1966, it has been replaced by "inflation" as the most cited problem, but still is cited by between 5% and 20% of the population.

[12] The labour force "participation rate" is that percentage of the age-group either actually employed or actively seeking—and expecting—employment. What has here been labelled the "component rate" is the percentage of the entire labour force contributed by a particular demographic cohort. For example, in 1973, 45% of females aged 25 to 44 "participated" in the labour force; that "component" comprised 14% of the total Canadian labour force.

[13] This explanation—based on an assumed change in female decision-making—is merely conjectural and, to the best of the author's knowledge, has not yet been tested rigorously.

[14] Feldstein, M., "The Economics of the New Unemployment," *Public Interest*, 1973; Grubel, H.G., and Maki, D., "The Effects of Unemployment Benefits on U.S. Unemployment Rates," *Weltwirtschaftliches Archiv*, 1976.

[15] Grubel, H.G., and Maki, D., "What is Full Employment?" Discussion Paper 79-1-1, Simon Fraser University (mimeographed), 1979.

[16] See Waterman, op. cit. (1973), Table XXXVI, for an estimate of the relative amplitude of Canadian fluctuations. According to these estimates the relative amplitude of B_8 (1.49 standard deviations) ranked fourth after B_4 (2.15 s.d.), B_3 (1.63 s.d.), and B_2 (1.53 s.d.).

[17] Spending on consumer durables of war-time savings; relaxation and eventual abandonment of war-time price controls; and the surge in world prices caused by U.S. stock-piling at the outbreak of the Korean War.

[18] "The Federal Government accepts the responsibility for high unemployment. I regret high unemployment, but inflation with high employment is not an acceptable alternative to no inflation with high unemployment." The Rt. Hon. P.E. Trudeau, Prime Minister, in a radio interview in May 1971.

[19] In which latter case rising prices would have to be "accommodated" by increasing velocity of circulation.

[20] That is, of M1: the total of currency and demand deposits in the hands of the general public.

[21] Waterman, op. cit. (1973), Table XXXVI.

[22] These could only be sustained for long in an environment of excess demand for labour, hence the latter subsumes both versions of the "cost-push" theory.

PART B

THE ROLE OF GOVERNMENT

Chapter 10

Education

Phil Husby,
Faculty of Education, University of Manitoba

Education in Canada is a complex enterprise operating within both the private and public sectors of the economy and involving all levels of government. Most educational activities are undertaken through the public sector, but private enterprise is active in many facets of education. Kindergarten and other pre-school programs are operated as private ventures in many provinces; private schools cater to some 3.5 per cent of the nation's elementary and secondary school populations; a variety of private business colleges, religious academies and other institutions operate at the post-secondary level; and fees and private donations remain an important source of revenue for the publicly operated post-secondary institutions.

As a public sector activity, education involves the three levels of government. Constitutionally, responsibility for education is vested in the provincial legislatures[1], and provincial governments play a critical role in all levels of education both in terms of operation and financial support. At the local government level, school boards are delegated responsibility for operating elementary and secondary schools by provincial statute, and, in some provinces, certain programs at the college level. The financing of programs operated by school boards is usually shared between local[2] and provincial[3] revenue sources.

The federal government in Canada is active in education in two principal ways. The first is through the direct operation of education programs that are ancillary to such federal responsibilities as Indian affairs, the penitentiary service and national defence. The second is through financial support of provincially operated programs which have been considered from time to time important to the "national interest." Federal financial support of such programs as manpower training, vocational and technical training, all forms of higher education, and second language instruction are examples that have involved national interest considerations.[4]

Because of the constitutional allocation of primary responsibility for education to the provinces, educational developments in Canada have occurred on a regional rather than a national basis. Thus there is no Canadian education system *per se.* Instead, in each province, institutions and practices have developed in response to provincial needs and circumstances, resulting in ten education systems, each with its unique characteristics.

Education in the Yukon and the Northwest Territories, while nominally under the authority of the federal government, has largely been turned over to the territorial councils for operational and administrative purposes. The elementary and secondary education systems in these territories therefore effectively constitute two more in the list of independent school jurisdictions in Canada. A thirteenth may be considered as incorporating the schools that come under the authority of departments of the federal government.

The lack of uniformity in educational practices in Canada that is a consequence of the regional nature of educational developments across the country makes for serious difficulties when comparisons of provincial education data are made. One example of this difficulty is in the area of secondary education. Each province has its definition of the secondary grades, which may begin anywhere from Grade 8 to Grade 10 and may end at Grade 11, 12 or 13, depending upon the province. With such differences, attempts to derive meaningful comparisons of such statistics as enrolments and unit costs of secondary school programs encounter serious problems of definition.

In the following sections, recent developments in education in Canada are discussed. The focus is on the post-World War II period, with special emphasis given to developments in the 1960s and 1970s. Trends relating to elementary and secondary education are first presented, followed by an examination of the post-secondary sector. Some economic implications of these post-war educational developments are noted in the final section.

Elementary and Secondary Education

Prior to World War II, elementary and secondary education was the responsibility of the school boards, whose geographic boundaries in many cases had been laid out in the nineteenth century. The school districts of the day were often relatively small, with schools staffed by few teachers, and with most classrooms servicing several grades. The typical elementary teacher's professional training consisted of one year's attendance at normal school or teachers' college after junior matriculation. School districts in the rural areas of the country had been viable when families were large, children were needed to help with the family enterprise, and seven or eight years of schooling was considered adequate for most children. In urban Canada at that time, secondary education was almost exclusively academically oriented, with programs generally designed to prepare graduates for university entrance. After the war, changes in the social fabric of the nation began to force school systems to alter their structures and procedures in a variety of ways. The societal changes that most directly affected the schools included changes in the economic activities of the country, changes in family patterns and parental expectations for their children, and changes in national attitudes towards education and schooling.

The economic life of Canada changed radically during the post-war years. As farming and fishing and other resource-based industries became more mechanized and more capital-intensive, operating units became larger and less labour-intensive, with the result that the percentage of the population engaged in agriculture and other primary industries decreased considerably. The population movements from rural Canada associated with these trends, together with the concentration of the industrial and service sectors into urban areas, have been responsible for the rapid urbanization of Canada that occurred after 1945. The percentage of rural population in Canada decreased from 43.5 in 1941 to 38.4 in 1951 and to 24.5 in 1976.

The family in Canada has undergone many changes in the decades since World War II, paralleling the changes in the country's economic structure. A recent study by Statistics Canada noted that ". . . these changes in Canadian families since 1945 can be seen in both the composition and size of the family and the roles of its members."[5] The report noted the increased life expectancy beyond age 65, the emergence of the small nuclear family as the basic family unit, the increasing tendency of women to share in the responsibility for providing for the family's economic needs, increases in family breakdown, and the increasing tendency to transfer to governmental agencies some of the responsibilities for such family tasks as child care and the satisfaction of social needs. Another major change noted was the increasing length of time that children were dependent on the family, " . . . because of the increased level of education required to meet the greater demands and complexity of modern society."[6]

After 1945, birthrates in the country were exceptionally high, resulting in the "baby boom" that extended into the 1960s. During that decade, birthrates tumbled dramatically across the nation, and family size began to show a marked decrease. Table 1 indicates the changes in birthrates in the Canadian provinces since 1945. It will be noted from the table that the declines in birthrates occurred in all provinces by 1966, with perhaps the most dramatic reductions reported from the province of Quebec.

Changing attitudes about the role of education in the lives of individuals and in the economic development and progress of the country have had considerable effects on educational developments since 1945. The concept of equality of educational opportunity became accepted as an objec-

Table 1 Rates of birth* by province — selected years, 1946-1976

	1946	1951	1956	1961	1966	1971	1976
Nfld.	36.5	32.5	35.0	34.1	28.5	24.5	18.7
P.E.I.	29.7	27.1	26.8	27.1	20.3	18.8	16.4
N.S.	29.5	26.6	27.5	26.3	20.1	18.1	15.5
N.B.	34.0	31.2	29.9	27.7	20.6	19.2	17.4
P.Q.	30.7	29.8	29.4	26.1	19.0	14.8	15.5
Ont.	23.8	25.0	26.6	25.3	19.0	16.9	14.8
Man.	25.9	25.7	25.8	25.3	18.7	18.2	16.4
Sask.	25.7	26.1	27.3	25.9	19.9	17.3	17.3
Alta.	27.6	28.8	31.1	29.2	20.9	18.8	18.0
B.C.	22.5	24.1	25.9	23.7	17.3	16.0	14.5
CANADA	27.2	27.2	28.0	26.1	19.4	16.8	15.7

*Live births per 1000 of population.
Sources: Statistics Canada, *Vital Statistics 1974*, Cat. 84.201. and *Principal Vital Statistics by Local Area, 1976*, Cat. 84.207.

tive which should be worked towards in a variety of contexts by governments, educators and the general public. This concept has been applied to such conditions as differences in the accessibility to quality education programs between urban and rural areas, large and small school jurisdictions, and rich and poor communities.[7] In addition to their acceptance of the equality of educational opportunity doctrine, governments after 1945 became interested in the notion that education can be an important factor in a nation's economic development. Studies by such researchers as Vaisey[8] in Britain, Schultz[9] in the United States and Bertram[10] in Canada suggested that a population's educational level was an important determinant of economic progress.

The *Second Annual Report* of the Economic Council of Canada illustrates very well the importance that officialdom ascribed to education as a factor in the country's economic development.[11] The document reported the Council's opinion that, "education is a critically important factor contributing to economic growth and to raising living standards."[12] Governments of Canada during the 1950s and 1960s seemed willing to pour vast sums of money into education at every level because of such convictions.

All of these various factors contributed towards remarkable changes in elementary and secondary education in Canada after World War II. Under the influence of the baby boom, immigration and increased participation rates[13] at the secondary level, enrolments grew dramatically in all the provinces from 1945 to near the end of the 1960s, as noted in Table 2. These increases in enrolments were accompanied by major changes in school organization and administration as provinces found alternatives to the small school districts for the provision of elementary and secondary schooling. Two notable organizational changes took place during this period, the first relating to school system *consolidation*, and the second to school *centralization*. The consolidation movement involved the amalgamation of small school districts into larger administrative units. In New Brunswick, for example, a 1962 Royal Commission report recommended a reduction in the province's school districts from 422 to 33, a proposal which was implemented on January 1, 1967.[14] Similar consolidation programs have been implemented in all the provinces. School centralization consisted of the closing of small schools and the incorporation of their pupils into larger and more complex school structures. Centralization led to such practices as single-grade classrooms in most elementary schools, increased specialization of the teaching force, and the development of comprehensive programs to cater to the broad range of interests and abilities present in the burgeoning populations of the secondary schools.

The increasing size and complexity of school systems resulted in major changes in the work force associated with the schools. The number of teachers employed by school boards in Canada increased from 90,000 to 262,500 between 1950 and 1970. This increase in the teaching force was proportionately greater than enrolment increases during the period as a result of two factors. The first reflected changes in the student-teacher ratio as class size gradually declined, as teachers' demands for preparation time were met in collective agreements, and as more teachers became employed in such roles as school librarians, resource teachers and counsellors where the traditional student-teacher relationships no longer applied. A second factor affecting teacher force numbers was the increasing employment of people with teacher qualifications into such

Table 2 Enrolments in public elementary and secondary schools by province, 1946-1976 (000's)

	1946	1951	1956	1961	1966	1971	1976
Nfld.	70.5	79.3	102.6	128.9	146.5	154.8	151.6
P.E.I.	18.1	18.9	21.5	24.5	27.9	30.6	28.2
N.S.	120.7	134.5	156.8	179.4	199.9	214.9	202.6
N.B.	95.2	105.7	127.1	152.3	165.2	175.9	165.0
P.Q.	625.1	696.5	959.4	1,189.3	1,360.6	1,534.5	1,328.1
Ont.	666.5	768.2	1,037.3	1,389.2	1,738.8	1,945.2	1,906.6
Man.	121.3	128.9	160.2	189.6	222.2	239.1	219.6
Sask.	173.6	167.5	181.2	208.7	238.3	245.5	214.4
Alta.	155.5	174.0	223.9	294.4	362.2	423.9	430.4
B.C.	130.6	173.4	241.5	321.3	420.8	507.9	524.1
CANADA	2,106.4	2,446.7	3,211.5	4,077.6	4,900.6	5,486.5	5,187.9

Source: Statistics Canada, *Elementary-Secondary Education - Financial Statistics*, Cat. 81.250.

positions as superintendent, director, curriculum consultant, full-time principals, etc. whose administrative and supervisory duties kept them at arm's length from direct teaching contact with students. These changes in teacher roles were directly associated with the increased size and complexity of schools and school systems.

The large school systems also became employers of large numbers of non-teaching personnel. With school board budgets often amounting to several millions of dollars, accountants, bookkeepers, and clerical help became employed in increasing numbers. The list of non-teaching employees of large school systems came to include bus drivers, maintenance personnel, secretaries, custodians, cafeteria assistants, school business managers and security officers. With the increasing tendency of such public employees to organize, school boards became involved in the collective bargaining process with several different unions in addition to their collective negotiations with teacher employees.

The growth in enrolments, programs and ancillary operations, together with general inflationary trends in Canada, caused school system budgets to escalate in dramatic fashion in the post-war years. Total expenditures of school boards rose from $178.4 million in 1946, to $648.9 million in 1956, to $2.3 billion in 1966 and $8.3 billion in 1976. Table 3 shows the growth in such expenditures by province for this period.

Funds for the support of elementary and secondary education continued to be derived principally from local property tax revenues and from provincial grants to school boards. Property tax revenues failed to increase at the rates needed by the schools, so during the years a marked

Table 3 Operating expenditures of school boards by province, selected years, 1946-1976 ($'000,000)

	1946	1951	1956	1961	1966	1971	1976
Nfld.	—	5.5	9.8	18.1	29.6	74.2	186.5
P.E.I.	.6	1.3	1.9	3.9	7.8	17.5	34.1
N.S.	6.8	12.8	21.3	38.9	61.1	124.2	263.1
N.B.	4.8	13.9	18.7	30.2	46.2	83.7	177.3
P.Q.	41.9	69.0	146.7	307.6	643.5	1,209.0	2,292.9
Ont.	67.7	136.4	250.6	478.8	876.6	1,800.2	3,147.6
Man.	12.7	18.9	30.5	60.4	91.9	180.3	337.9
Sask.	16.1	25.3	42.8	75.8	109.8	164.6	305.9
Alta.	15.2	31.5	57.8	122.9	190.8	369.2	683.7
B.C.	13.3	45.2	68.8	126.7	213.8	400.4	859.4
CANADA	178.4	359.8	648.9	1,263.3	2,271.1	4,447.2	8,336.6

Sources: Dominion Bureau of Statistics, *Survey of Education Finance*, Cat. 81.208, and Statistics Canada, *Elementary-Secondary Education — Financial Statistics*, Cat. 81.250.

shift occurred between these two sources, with boards becoming more and more dependent upon provincial grants to finance their operations. In 1952, 64.4 per cent of school board revenues came from local tax sources. This figure fell to 52.5 per cent in 1963 and to 28.9 per cent in 1976.

This shift in responsibility for financing elementary and secondary education to the central source of funds in the provinces contributed to the equalization of education expenditures on a per-pupil basis by school boards within the individual provinces. When school districts depended for most of their revenues on local resources, differences in wealth among districts made it possible for citizens in high assessment areas to contribute substantial funds for the support of local schools with often a relatively minor tax burden. Conversely, low assessment areas, even with excessively high mill rates, often were unable to finance their schools at a reasonable level.

Several measures were devised in the various provinces to equalize per-pupil expenditures across all the school systems and at the same time equalize the financial burden to pay for public schools. These measures included (1) legislation to standardize assessment procedures on a provincial basis; (2) the implementation of "foundation programs" to provide what was considered an adequate minimum level of expenditure in all school jurisdictions; (3) the establishment of mandated mill rate levels throughout a province for the support of public schools with the remainder of foundation level expenditures supplied by the province; (4) the imposition by provincial authorities of per-pupil expenditure ceilings; and (5) the virtual elimination in some provinces of local taxation as a source of funds for the schools. Several of these provisions have tended to reduce the fiscal independence of local authorities, as school system budgets have become more and more affected by financial decisions made at the provincial level.

The movement to equalize education expenditures within the provinces during the post-war period has been parallelled by a diminution in the substantial interprovincial differences that earlier were a serious concern of Canadians. To illustrate, in 1956, the average annual expenditures per pupil ranged from a low of $89 in Prince Edward Island to a high of $285 in British Columbia.[15] In that year, for every dollar spent on a student in PEI, 3.2 dollars were expended in B.C. In 1975, the corresponding range was $944 in Newfoundland to $1360 in Quebec, a ratio of 1 to 1.4. By that time, the per-pupil expenditure differentials had been substantially reduced. No programs were specifically devised on a national basis to directly influence these differences. However, it would appear that national income redistribution schemes such as the Provincial Revenue Equalization Program had significant effects in this regard.

The provincial school systems in Canada which, for more than twenty years after the end of World War II, had become accustomed to ever-increasing enrolments, expanding programs and burgeoning budgets, suddenly towards the end of the 1960s found that a new set of circumstances had to be faced. Two major elements were present in these new circumstances. The first was the phenomenon of declining enrolments that was a direct result of decreases in birthrates across Canada during the 1960s. The second factor was a developing scepticism on the part of the public and governments to the idea that constantly increasing education expenditures were in fact "paying off" in economic and other benefits.

The facts of declining enrolments have been well documented.[16] As Table 2 indicates, enrolments dropped in all provinces with the exception of Alberta and British Columbia between 1971 and 1976. The situation in Quebec is perhaps illustrative of similar trends elsewhere. In that province, elementary and secondary enrolments peaked during the 1969-70 school year at 1,657,200. By 1975-76, the corresponaing figure was 1,467,600, representing an enrolment decline of almost 200,000 pupils in a six-year period. Projections by Statistics Canada suggest that such enrolment declines will continue for several years.[17]

The effects of such enrolment drops have been pervasive. A series of reports by an Ontario commission established to study effects of declining enrolment in that province illustrate effects that are typical across the nation. Noted are a number of interrelated consequences for the teaching force, student programs and per-pupil costs. The demand for newly trained teachers drops off, affecting enrolments in teacher-training institutions. In those areas where enrolment declines are most pronounced, staff reductions become necessary with consequent negative effects on the individual teachers declared surplus and on overall teacher morale. Since school boards generally follow the practice of "last hired, first fired" when it comes to staff reductions, an overall effect of declining enrolments is an increase in the age of the teachers remaining. As job opportunities become more scarce, teachers with jobs tend to hold on to them tenaciously. As staff is reduced, program offerings are affected, with a consequent reduction in course options available to students, especially those in higher grades. And because older, more experienced, best qualified and therefore most expensive teachers tend to be retained, unit costs of education rise proportionately more quickly as enrolment drops.[18] Experience has shown that costs of elementary and secondary education will continue to escalate despite declining enrolments in the years ahead.

The fortunes of the private elementary and secondary schools in Canada during the post-war years varied in patterns different from those experienced in the public schools. Enrolment trends in the private schools compared with those in the public schools are shown in Table 4. The table indicates that private schools did not match the growth experienced in the public school systems after 1946. Growth was modest between 1951 and 1966, but a substantial decline occurred after 1966, when educational costs were rising rapidly. During this period, the Roman Catholic private

Table 4 Enrolments in private and public elementary and secondary
schools in Canada — selected years, 1946-1976

	Private School Enrolments (a)	Public School Enrolments (b)	Per Cent (a)/(b)
		('000)	
1946	107,907	2,106.4	5.1
1951	102,676	2,446.7	4.2
1956	125,464	3,211.5	3.9
1961	148,304	4,077.6	3.6
1966	203,681	4,900.6	4.2
1971	142,601	5,486.5	2.6
1976	182,001	5,371.8	3.4

schools, which enrol a majority of Canada's private school students, experienced serious difficulties in staffing their schools with teachers from religious teaching orders. The increased costs of employing lay teachers provided insurmountable obstacles for many of these schools at this time. However, after 1972, while the public schools were coping with the declining enrolment phenomenon, the private schools began a period of modest expansion, assisted in part by newly instituted grants from provincial governments to help with their financial operations.

Post-Secondary Education

Post-secondary education in Canada is made up of two major elements, namely the universities and the college systems. At one time, the universities and colleges operated almost exclusively as privately run institutions supported by tuition fees, by contributions from alumni and benefactors, and by revenues from endowment funds. Since many of the colleges were affiliated with or operated by religious organizations, the churches often provided significant funding as well. The move towards provincially sponsored and publicly operated university and college systems is of relatively recent origin in Canada. It began in the West early in the twentieth century, but did not become common practice across Canada until well after the end of World War II.

Public involvement in higher education prior to 1939 was generally limited to such operations as provincially operated normal schools which provided basic pedagogical training for elementary school teachers, schools for nurses in public hospitals, and a relatively few technical, vocational and agricultural colleges.

During the Second World War, many universities became active in the war effort through the development of programs in engineering and other technical fields for officer candidates, and for the training of doctors, dentists and other specialists for military and civilian needs. With the enactment of the federal Veterans' Rehabilitation Act in 1944, provision was made to furnish discharged veterans of the war with rehabilitation grants to enable them to attend universities in programs of their choice. The Act also provided for federal financial assistance grants to the universities based on their enrolment of veterans, to assist the universities in coping with the resulting anticipated enrolment increases. The expansion in the country's universities after 1945 was dramatic, with enrolments more than doubling from 40,000 in 1944-45 to 83,000 in 1947-48. As the enrolment bulge created by the returning veterans gradually dissipated after this, the hectic years of growth and expansion during the 1945-48 period came to an end. By the academic year 1952-53, enrolments had fallen to 63,000 and the flow of special federal grants to the universities on behalf of the veterans ceased.

But this decline in the fortunes of the Canadian universities was of relatively short duration. The country had entered a period of buoyant economic growth, university graduates were in great demand, and the youth of the nation became convinced of the economic and social advantages that attached to increased educational attainments. Since governments also viewed the growth of the universities as necessary for the economic progress of the country, provincial authorities became directly involved in their financing, and strategies were devised to permit the acceptance of massive federal grants for the support of the universities without offending the sensibilities of those concerned with provincial rights in education. From the post-war low of 63,000 reached during the 1952-53 year, full-time enrolments rebounded in exponential fashion, reaching 141,000 in 1962-63 and 322,000 in 1972-73 in a period of unparalleled and almost continuous growth. The growth in student populations was accompanied by rapid expansion of university programs in the professional faculties, the natural and social sciences, and the humanities areas. Enrolments in graduate programs in all fields mushroomed. The number of women entering and completing undergraduate and graduate programs grew phenomenally. To accommodate the burgeoning enrolments and expanding programs, new buildings had to be erected, furnished and equipped on an almost continuous basis on the campuses across the land. The growth precipitated an unprecedented demand for professorial staff which was recruited largely from the increased number of graduates from the universities' graduate faculties. Many were also recruited from the United States and abroad.

The term "college" in Canada has a variety of connotations, being applied to institutions whose programs run a whole gamut of fields. Some colleges are largely academic in nature. Other colleges offer business, technical or vocational programs that lead directly to occupations. Some religious and fine arts and other colleges have a focus that is perhaps less career-oriented. Many larger colleges offer several different programs. None of these colleges received the same kind of support that the universities received during the 1940s and 1950s.

Two types of colleges began to receive more attention during the latter part of the 1950s. One of these was the Junior College, modelled after the two- and three-year academic colleges of the United States. Junior Colleges were established in some provinces in regional centres to provide easy access to the first two or three years of study for those who lived a distance from universities. The second was the technical college, whose graduates were in increasing demand as the industrialization of the nation progressed. Perhaps the greatest impetus to the development of technical colleges was the launching of the Russian satellite SPUTNIK on October 4, 1957. This great technological achievement induced the countries of the western world, including Canada, to expand facilities to increase the pool of highly competent technologists.

The major growth of the colleges took place in the 1960s, and each province developed its unique college system. Alberta perhaps led the way with the establishment of five public Junior Colleges and two Institutes of Technology and Art in the period from 1957 to 1968. Across Ontario, twenty Colleges of Applied Arts and Technology (the CAAT colleges) were set up to provide training in a great variety of job-related fields. Following the recommendations of the Parent Commission in Quebec, which was established to plan the reorganization of the total educational system of that province, a system of CEGEP's (collèges d'enseignement général et professionnel) was established. The CEGEP's were planned to provide graduates of the province's regional secondary schools with two-year programs leading to university studies, and with three-year technical and vocational programs leading to occupations. Other college systems were developed in the other provinces during this same period.

Financing the growth of post-secondary education following 1952-53, and particularly during the 1960s, provided a major challenge to provincial and federal authorities. For many of the less affluent provinces, the costs were far beyond provincial means, with the result that federal funding schemes became necessary. Initially, federal funds were directed to individual institutions, as they had been when the veterans were in attendance at universities after the war. Later, most funds for the support of post-secondary education were paid into the general revenues of the provinces, and were presumably directed to the universities and colleges as needed. Federal funds were provided for the support of post-secondary operating costs, capital costs, research, student loans and special projects.

The growth in expenditures for post-secondary education during the post-war period is illustrated in the figures in Table 5. Costs more than

Table 5 Total expenditures for post-secondary education in Canada
selected years, 1950-76 ($'000,000)

	University		Non-University		Total
	$	%	$	%	$
1950	55.2	82.6	11.6	17.4	66.8
1955	104.4	77.1	31.0	22.9	135.4
1961	310.6	84.2	58.4	15.8	369.1
1966	991.6	88.8	125.0	11.2	1,116.6
1971	1,864.5	77.9	530.0	22.1	2,394.5
1976	3,127.5	75.0	1,039.8	25.0	4,167.4

Source: Statistics Canada, *Historical Compendium of Education Statistics*, Cat. 81.568, and Statistics Canada, *Advance Statistics of Education*, Cat. 81.220.

doubled during each five-year period from 1950 to 1970, and university expenditures made up four-fifths of total post-secondary expenditures during most of the period. The major increases in non-university expenditures occurred after 1966, reflecting the massive expansion of the college systems, particularly those of Ontario and Quebec, after that year.

Some Economic Aspects of Education

Education is an important activity in the economy of Canada, both in terms of the extent to which it is a consumer of the nation's resources and in terms of its impact on the development of the economy. Looked at from these two perspectives, education expenditures may be viewed as consumption and as investment. In this section, some aspects of these two facets of the economics of education are discussed.

Since education in Canada is largely carried out through the public sector, expenditures for education make up a part of the resources of the nation that are extracted from individuals and firms through the tax system to be expended by public agencies. Table 6 indicates changes in the total expenditures for education in Canada compared to the gross national product and to total government expenditures. The table shows that from 1950 to 1971, education expenditures rose substantially faster than did the gross national product or total government expenditures. In 1971, they accounted for 8.8 per cent of GNP, compared to 2.4 per cent in 1950. In 1971, more than one-fifth of total government outlays in Canada went to support education, which was more than double the corresponding fraction in 1955. Since 1971, however, these have declined in relation to both GNP and to total government expenditures. This decline is accounted for by enrolment drops in the public schools, by a reduction in capital expenditures at all levels of education, and by a growing ten-

Table 6 Total education expenditures in Canada in relation to gross national product and to total government expenditures, selected years, 1950-76

	Total Expenditures On Education ($'000,000)	Gross National Product ($'000,000)	Per Cent	Total Government Expenditures ($'000,000)	Per Cent
	(a)	(b)	(a)/(b)	(c)	(a)/(c)
1950	438.8	18,006	2.4	4,567.0	9.6
1955	829.1	27,132	3.1	7,386.0	11.2
1961	1,730.7	39,646	4.4	11,760.1	14.7
1966	4,155.2	61,828	6.7	18,727.1	22.2
1971	8,349.7	94,450	8.8	36,275.5	23.0
1976	15,073.9	190,027	7.9	70,758.0	21.3

Source: Statistics Canada, *Historical Compendium of Education Statistics*, Cat. 81.568.

dency for senior governments to give only minimum reluctant concurrence to revenue increases requested by education authorities during recent years.

Table 7 indicates the relative changes in revenue sources for education in recent years on a national basis. Some major changes in the proportion of funds derived from different levels of government have occurred since 1950. Local governments contributed nearly one-half of all education funds in 1950. In 1976, less than one-fifth came from that source. A major shift in the education burden occurred during this period, with the provincial government taking over most of the responsibility. The "other"

Table 7 Sources of funds for all levels of education in Canada selected years, 1950-76

	Federal Government $'000,000	%	Provincial Governments $'000,000	%	Local Governments $'000,000	%	Other $'000,000	%	Total $'000,000
1950	20.7	4.7	172.9	39.4	199.3	45.4	45.9	10.5	438.8
1955	56.8	6.9	342.8	41.3	343.3	41.4	86.3	10.4	829.1
1961	161.0	8.3	852.5	44.2	691.3	35.8	225.9	11.7	1,930.7
1966	539.9	13.0	1,984.8	47.8	1,155.4	27.8	475.3	11.4	4,155.2
1971	924.0	11.1	4,966.7	59.5	1,713.6	20.5	745.4	8.9	8,349.7
1976	1,254.4	8.3	9,941.6	66.0	2,820.8	18.7	1,057.2	7.0	15,073.9

Source: Statistics Canada, *Historical Compendium of Education Statistics*, Cat. 81.568 and Statistics Canada, *Advance Statistics of Education*, Cat. 81.220.

category, made up principally of fees paid for post-secondary education and from gifts, endowment fund revenues and the like, declined in importance after 1966.

Another major change in education finance is in the proportion of funds allocated to different levels of education. In 1950, elementary and secondary education accounted for four-fifths of total education expenditures, with post-secondary education accounting for most of the remainder. By 1976, the elementary and secondary share had decreased to two-thirds, indicating a continuing shift in the use of education resources in favour of the post-secondary sector. If governments continue to provide a reduced proportion of their revenues to education in the future, the competition for funds among the major educational divisions is likely to become severe.

Education, like most public sector activities, is highly labour-intensive. As a consequence, most education expenditures are used to pay salaries of teachers and other employees. However, unlike many other national economic activities, education has to a great extent resisted the tendency to become concentrated in a few major centres. Schools are located throughout the provinces, and teachers' and other employees' salaries tend to be spent in the areas where they live and work. In addition, the provinces appear to favour decentralization of colleges and universities to the greatest extent possible. And since education funds are derived more and more from senior levels of government which rely on progressive income taxes for their revenues, education expenditures are likely to contribute considerably to income redistribution within the nation.

Conclusion

The view that the time, energy and funds expended by individuals for their educational advancement are likely to enhance their future economic status and life chances has been generally accepted by Canadians from all social classes for decades. Parents have viewed the educational progress of their children as being the major route towards their economic security and well-being.

Governments, particularly after World War II, also became convinced of the economic advantages to the nation that could be derived from increased investments in education. They came to share the view expressed by the Economic Council of Canada when it noted,

> . . . the vital need for creating an adequate supply of professional, technical, managerial and other highly skilled manpower as a basis for future growth of the Canadian economy. We . . . place[d] increased investment in human resources to improve knowledge and skills at the head of our list of essential ingredients for attaining the goal of faster and better sustained productivity and growth.[19]

Because of such convictions, all sectors of education developed under relatively generous governmental funding during the 1950s and 60s.

During this period, governments became involved in financing a great many other social services and economic activities that were considered to be important to the public welfare. As public funds were increasingly channelled into education as well as into such areas as health and welfare programs, public housing, improved transportation networks and energy-related activities, the total proportion of the national income expended by governments rose dramatically.

Eventually, of course, people came to question the wisdom of steadily increasing their expenditures in the public sector, and "restraint" gradually became an important word in the lexicon of governments. The competition for available resources amongst the conflicting demands on the public purse has tended to become more intense in recent years, as education, health care and all other public sector activities have sought to maintain or increase their share of a relatively static or shrinking total. As was noted previously, the proportion of GNP expended on education has tended to decrease in recent years, indicating that education has not been too successful in this competition.

The recent relative decreases in expenditures for education have resulted in an increase in the competition for funds *within* the education community as well. The colleges, the universities, the public elementary and secondary school systems have all vied to maintain an adequate financial base from a relatively static revenue source. This factor, together with the rapid increases in unit costs resulting from inflation and other previously noted causes, and with enrolment declines projected to continue, has forced Canadian educators to look into the future of the 1980s with much less optimism than was justified in previous decades.

---

[1]Section 93 of the *British North America Act* states, "In and for each Province the legislature may make laws in relation to education". The power of the provinces to legislate in educational matters is limited only in respect to certain denominational rights which had statutory authority in a province at the time it entered confederation. This limitation accounts for the continued presence of denominational school systems in Quebec and Newfoundland, and of separate school systems in Ontario, Saskatchewan and Alberta, all of which have access to public funds.

[2]School board revenues from local sources are derived almost exclusively from taxes on property. In most provinces, school board property tax revenues are not collected directly by school officials. Instead, they are requisitioned from municipal authorities.

[3]Provincial grants, the major source of school board revenues in recent years, normally derive from the general consolidated revenue sources of the province—income taxes, transfer funds from the federal government, resource based revenues, etc., rather than from a particular educational sales tax or the like.

[4]See: Ernest D. Hodgson, *Federal Intervention in Public Education.* Toronto: The Canadian Education Association, 1967, for a discussion of direct and indirect federal involvement in Canadian education in recent years.

[5]"The Changing Family", Ch. 2 in: Statistics Canada, *Perspective Canada II,* Ottawa, 1977, pp. 13-31.

[6]Ibid, p. 13.

[7]W.G. Fleming, *Educational Opportunity: The Pursuit of Equality.* Scarborough: Prentice-Hall of Canada, 1974.

[8]J. Vaisey, *The Economics of Education.* London: Faber and Faber, 1962.

[9]T.W. Schultz, *The Economic Value of Education.* New York: Columbia University Press, 1962.

[10]Gordon W. Bertram, *The Contribution of Education to Economic Growth.* Staff Study No. 12, The Economic Council of Canada, Ottawa, 1966.

[11]*Towards Sustained and Balanced Economic Growth.* Second Annual Report. The Economic Council of Canada, Ottawa, 1965.

[12]Ibid., p. 71.

[13]The term "participation rate" refers to the ratio of school enrolments of a given age group to the total population of that age group. Because of compulsory school attendance laws in all provinces, participation rates of children to age 14 or 15 have been typically high in Canada during this century. The rapid increases in secondary school enrolments in the 1950s and 1960s resulted in substantial rises in participation rates of 15 to 19 year olds during this period.

[14]See: J. Donald Wilson, Robert M. Stamp and Louis Philippe Audet, (eds.), *Canadian Education: A History,* Scarborough, Ontario: Prentice-Hall of Canada, 1970, p. 449.

[15]*Financing Education in Canada,* (Second edition). Ottawa: The Canadian Teachers' Federation, 1967, p. 88. During this period, provincial per-pupil expenditures for education correlated highly with provincial personal income figures.

[16]Statistics Canada, *Out of School, Into the Labour Force,* Ottawa: The Queen's Printer, 1978.

[17]Ibid., pp. 29 ff.

[18]A summary of the reports of the Commission on Declining Enrolments in Ontario is found in: *Implications of Declining Enrolments for the Schools of Ontario: A Statement of Effects and Solutions.* Toronto: The Ministry of Education, 1978.

[19]*Towards Sustained and Balanced Economic Growth,* op. cit., pp. 71-2.

Chapter 11

Health

John Horne,
Faculty of Medicine, University of Manitoba

Introduction

Canada's health care system may be metaphorically described as a "joint venture" among the public, private, and voluntary sectors of the economy. The term is not literally applicable because the contribution that each sector makes to the working of the system is specified less by formal contract than by informal accord. In essence, the public sector assumes major responsibility for financing the costs of health services, while the private (for-profit) and voluntary (non-profit) sectors together assume major responsibility for the production and delivery of health services. Achieved only after a long and intense national debate, this broad division of labour represents a compromise between the polar alternatives of a completely public "socialized" health system on the one hand and a completely private "free enterprise" system on the other.

To most Canadians, the sectoral roles and responsibilities are likely perceived in less abstract terms. Public sector financing commonly translates into "medicare" and an awareness that care in the nation's hospitals and doctors' offices is ordinarily available free of direct charge, the costs having been prepaid through a variety of taxes levied by the provincial and federal governments. Private sector provision commonly translates into "personal physician" or "family dentist" and an awareness that these individuals are mainly self-employed fee-for-service practitioners who, like members of other "free and self-governing" professions, have the legal right to locate and organize their clinics as they choose. Voluntary sector provision commonly translates into "community hospital" or "teaching hospital" and an awareness that these are non-profit institutions funded by government but owned and governed by independent boards of private citizens.

Common knowledge of the health care system almost certainly extends beyond these basic structural details. One has only to read the daily press and its regular reporting of yet another health care "crisis" to know that the system's past performances and future prospects are matters that the principal providers and financiers debate at great and seemingly endless length. Physicians complain that Medicare is underfunded and threaten to "opt out" of the program and "extra-bill" patients on a discretionary basis unless their collective demands for higher fees are met. Hospital boards and administrators complain that their institutions are also publicly underfunded and threaten to reduce the volume and quality of patient care unless budget pressures are eased. Federal and provincial governments share a concern and frustration with the relentless increase in health care costs and the apparent inability of the system to economize on its use of scarce resources and tax dollars, but, as co-financiers of the hospital and medical care insurance programs, more often find themselves in conflict over the specifics of cost-sharing and cost control. The impression of a system working to no one's complete satisfaction is indeed inescapable. What is escapable in the surfeit of reportage on the topic is a clear perspective on the structure and function of the system and the policy options for addressing its most serious organizational and financial problems.

In this chapter, an attempt is made to provide some of the necessary perspective. Matters of important fact relating to health care as a public sector activity are discussed in the first section. Health care expenditure trends and associated shifts in the utilization and costs of health manpower and facilities are selectively reviewed in the second section. Problems of resource management peculiar to the present system and some analytical themes are surveyed in section three, followed in a fourth and final section by an assessment of current policy initiatives and some speculation on future developments.

The Role of Government

The role of government in health care was established early in Canadian history by provisions in the British North America Act that allocated to the Federal Parliament jurisdiction over quarantine and the establishment and maintenance of marine hospitals, and to provincial legislatures jurisdiction over "the establishment, maintenance and management of hospitals, asylums, charities and eleemosynary institutions in and for the province other than marine hospitals." While the BNA Act appeared to place health care squarely within the jurisdiction of the provinces, the federal Liberal Party included a health insurance program in its election platform (though did nothing to implement it) of 1919, and in 1935 the Federal government passed the Employment and Social Insurance Act that included health benefits. Although this Act was subsequently declared *ultra vires*, the 1939-45 period saw renewed federal interest in stimulating health care insurance schemes that would benefit all Canadians. To this end, in 1948 it established the National Health Grant Program that provided for extensive hospital construction, health surveys, public health, tuberculosis control, cancer control, etc.

This program was "cost-shared" with the provinces, a mechanism that was to be used again with passage of the *Hospital Insurance and Diagnostic Services Act* in 1957, a statute that provided for federal financial contributions to hospital insurance programs sponsored by the provinces. The Act effectively established national hospital insurance, the main principles of which were universal enrolment, comprehensive benefits portable between the provinces, and public, non-profit administration. It began in 1958, with five provinces participating, and achieved national status three years later when all provinces and the Northwest and Yukon Territories had established programs qualifying for the fifty per cent federal cost share. Thus, for two decades, all Canadians have been beneficiary to "free" (publicly pre-paid) hospital care.

With a federally financed and provincially administered hospital insurance scheme firmly in place, it is not surprising that pressures began to mount to introduce medical care insurance to cover the costs of physicians' services. The policy debate over private versus public funding of such a scheme was fueled by the Province of Saskatchewan in the late 1950s with its drive towards public medical care insurance. This initiative was opposed by the country's medical profession which, seeing the spectre of "state medicine" on the horizon not just for Saskatchewan but for all of Canada, urged the government (then the Conservative administration headed by John Diefenbaker) to establish a Royal Commission to look into the matter. The government responded by appointing a Royal Commission whose mandate encompassed not only medical care, but all aspects of health and health care in Canada. Hardly had the Commission begun its work than Saskatchewan implemented, in 1962, a program that provided for universal, comprehensive coverage of physicians' services at public expense. Saskatchewan doctors responded by collectively withdrawing their services, a "strike" that lasted three weeks before being resolved with minor concessions to the profession in exchange for unopposed implementation of the principles of medicare.

The "strike" and its outcome undoubtedly did not go unobserved by the Royal Commission which, notwithstanding its original Conservative sponsorship (and indeed membership), recommended in 1964 to the Liberal government of Lester Pearson the establishment of a health services program with the following features:[1]

1) "Comprehensive" - including all health services, preventive diagnostic, curative and rehabilitative, that modern medical and other sciences can provide.

2) "Universal" - meaning that adequate health services shall be available to all Canadians wherever they reside and whatever their financial resources may be, within the limitations imposed by geographic factors.

3) "Freedom of choice" - meaning the right of the patient to select his physicians or dentists and the right of the practitioner to accept or not to accept a patient except in emergency or on humanitarian grounds.

4) "Free and self-governing professions" - meaning the right of members of health professions to practise within the law, to free choice of location and type of practice, and to professional self-government.

Clearly the Commission was not proposing a system of state medicine, "a system in which all providers of health services are functionaries under the control of the state," but rather a mixed system, privately organized and publicly financed.

That government action was necessary to ensure Canadians access to medical care on a pre-paid basis was beyond dispute. In 1961, after more than thirty years of operation, the voluntary prepayment and commercial insurance plans were providing some form of protection to only fifty-three per cent of the population; over 7.5 million Canadians (forty-one per cent of the population) were exposed to the risk of random bankruptcy by having no medical care insurance of any sort. The only issue to be resolved was the scale of government involvement.

Several considerations led the Commission to recommend full-scale government action to supplant rather than supplement the existing system of private finance. First, a majority of the commercial insurance plans sought to control "excess" utilization of services by such devices as coverage limitations, waiting periods, cancellation clauses, dollar limits on the amount of benefits, and co-insurance and deductibles. Regardless of how consistent these devices were with the commercial insurers' primary aim of providing protection against catastrophic loss, they were rejected by the Commission as inconsistent with the objective of providing comprehensive benefits, irrespective of medical experience or ability to pay.

The second consideration was the comparative cost of private insurance—the cost of collecting and administering premiums and paying claims—as between group and individual contracts. Thus in 1961, for every premium dollar paid under group contracts, fifteen cents was retained to cover non-claims (including profit) expense, while for every premium dollar paid under individual contracts, fully fifty to sixty cents was retained for this purpose. These discrepancies in costs and benefits provided the Commission with strong evidence of the economies of scale associated with group contracts, economies which it concluded could be readily exploited under a universal, public plan.

Third, the Commission was impressed by the problems that would attend a partial program of the sort which was being advocated at the time by the medical profession, the insurance companies, and the Canadian

Manufacturers' Association. In the Commission's view, their proposal that the government should only subsidize the premiums of "needy" (means-tested) individuals did not realistically assess:

1) the proportion of the population that would require such assistance:[2]

2) the magnitude of the sums required for supplemental assistance;

3) the difficulty of establishing equitable criteria for assessment of need;

4) the fluctuations in incomes (for example, among seasonal workers) and the consequent continuing need for re-testing;

5) the high acquisition and administrative costs of voluntary insurance.

Finally, the Commission regarded the 1957 *Hospital Insurance and Diagnostic Services Act* that had been implemented over the period 1958-61 "as having proved that a universal comprehensive program is feasible, practicable, economical to administer and immediately effective for a total population."

The course of action advocated by the Commission was not long in coming. Indeed, the then minority Pearson government responded with uncommon haste when, in mid-1965, scarcely a year after the Commission submitted its Report, it laid before a federal-provincial conference a proposal for a medical care insurance program which incorporated the essential features recommended by the Commission. Further consultations were held with provinces—the last formal meeting took place in early 1966—and, satisfied that it had the requisite support, the government placed its "medicare" bill before Parliament in mid-1966. Following a spirited but fundamentally ritual debate, it was passed on December 8, 1966 by a vote of 177 - 2.

Although the *Act* stopped short of creating the "comprehensive-universal Health Services Program" envisaged by the Commission, it encouraged the provision of pre-paid medical care to all Canadians by offering federal financial assistance to provinces establishing medical care insurance programs that featured universal enrolment, comprehensive benefits portable between the provinces, and public, non-profit administration. The federal government agreed to pay per insured person fifty per cent of the national per capita costs in participating provinces; the remainder was to be financed provincially. As well, the *Act* permits a province to impose on its (sick) residents utilization fees and co-insurance charges, providing such "user charges" do not preclude or impede access to medically required services.

Mainly because of federal fears about the costs of operating such programs, the *Act* did not become operative until 1968. British Columbia and Saskatchewan joined at this time, followed in 1969 by Alberta, Manitoba, Ontario, Nova Scotia, and Newfoundland, in 1970 by Quebec and Prince Edward Island, and in 1971 by New Brunswick.[3] Together, the programs now cover virtually all of the nation's 24 million residents.

As with the hospital insurance program, each province has been free to finance its share of costs by premiums, sales tax, payroll tax, other provincial revenues, or by a combination of methods. To fulfil the federal government's "universality" requirement, a province choosing to levy premiums was required to enrol ninety per cent of its insurable residents during the first two years and ninety-five per cent thereafter. British Columbia, Alberta, Ontario and the Yukon Territory currently employ a combination of premium and non-premium finance. The premiums are uniform in the sense that they are not based on the individual's age and medical experience as they would be under private insurance, but vary in amount among individuals, couples, and families; other provinces finance their programs entirely from general tax revenues. Moreover, most provinces have opted not to impose direct charges on patients; current exceptions to this rule are British Columbia, Alberta, New Brunswick and the Northwest Territories, where a variety of authorized charges apply to hospital inpatients and outpatients.

Hence, by 1971, the fundamental principles of a scheme that freed Canadians from the financial burdens of hospitalization and physicians' services had passed from the realm of political and professional ideology into legislated programs. The resolution of the "public" versus "private" debate was a uniquely Canadian compromise: public financing of voluntary hospitals and private fee-for-service physicians through provincially administered insurance programs cost-shared with the federal government.

With the major hurdles in the development of a comprehensive health care system apparently surmounted, individual provinces have proceeded to introduce a variety of supplementary programs without federal financial assistance, some featuring universal enrolment and others featuring benefits targetted on specific segments of the population. Manitoba and Saskatchewan have introduced universal prescription drug programs, while virtually all of the other provinces have acted to publicly finance prescription drugs for senior citizens. Saskatchewan, Nova Scotia, and Quebec have established province-wide dental care plans for children; Manitoba and New Brunswick have established smaller scale programs providing dental services to children in rural and underserviced areas. Manitoba has implemented programs of universal home care and nursing home care and similar programs are being actively planned in many other provinces. Expanded programs for the handicapped, for alcoholics, and for the mentally ill and the retarded have been introduced in Saskatchewan and are high priority items in the other provinces.

Notwithstanding the development of these new programs, the fundamental tensions that fueled the early debates remain: federal versus provincial jurisdiction; public versus private enterprise; and above all, the concerns emanating from the magnitude and rapid growth of health care costs.

Health Care Expenditures

In both formal and informal discussion of Medicare and related topics, questions frequently arise concerning the nation's health care bill. How large is it? What are its major components? How much of it is financed through the public sector? What trends does it evidence and what factors have most affected its rate of growth in recent decades? Is it good value for the money? To answer the first four of these questions, it is necessary to make reference to the official statistics, as will be done in this section. To answer the last, most controversial question, it is well to acquaint oneself not only with the pertinent dollar details, but also with critical interpretations of these and other data by those who have made formal study of the system. This more problem-oriented discussion will be deferred until the next section.

The nation's health care bill is an aggregation of public and private spending on a wide variety of health-related items. Included in the official Health and Welfare Canada definition of "national health expenditures" are outlays by federal, provincial and local governments, by private organizations and by consumers for health goods and services broadly classified into "institutional care" (hospitals and nursing homes), "professional services" (of physicians, dentists, chiropractors, etc.), "drugs and appliances" (eyeglasses, hearing aids, etc.), and "other," the last including expenses for the administration of public and private payment plans, public health, medical research, occupational health, and the construction of health facilities. In 1976, the most recent year for which data are available, total health spending thus defined amounted to $13.6 billion, or almost $590 per person spread over a population of 23 million.

Total and per capita expenditures for the main components of the bill are shown in Table 1. Strikingly evident here is the institutional orientation of the health care dollar. Over half (54 per cent) of all expenditures in 1976 went for services provided by hospitals and nursing homes. Most of these monies were claimed by the general and allied special (maternity, chronic, convalescent) hospitals, a group comprising 1,048 non-profit and 95 for-profit institutions with operating expenses of $5.5 billion, or fully 41 cents of the 1976 health care dollar. A minority group of psychiatric institutions, tuberculosis sanatoria, and hospitals operated by the federal government comprise the "other hospitals" and they, together with nursing homes, incurred costs of $1.7 billion and claimed 13 cents of the health care dollar. Doctors, dentists and other health professionals accounted for almost $3 billion and shared 22 cents of this dollar, while the remaining $3.3 billion or 24 cents was evenly split between "drugs and appliances" and "other expenditures." Also noteworthy is the fact that general hospitals and physicians—two groups whose services are covered

Table 1 Health Expenditures by Category, Canada, 1976

	Total ($ million)	Per Capita ($)	% of Total
Institutional Care	$ 7,263.0	$315.43	53.6%
General and allied special hospitals	5,538.2	240.53	40.9
Other Hospitals	769.1	33.40	5.7
Nursing Homes	955.7	41.51	7.0
Professional Services	2,974.0	129.16	21.9
Physicians	2,078.5	90.27	15.3
Dentists	694.6	30.17	5.1
Other Professionals	200.9	8.73	1.5
Drugs and Appliances	1,655.2	71.89	12.2
Prescribed Drugs	759.1	32.97	5.6
Non-Prescribed Drugs	702.6	30.51	5.2
Eyeglasses and Appliances	193.5	8.40	1.4
Other Health Expenditures	1,660.2	72.10	12.3
Prepayment and Administration	242.8	10.54	1.8
Medical Facility Construction	636.4	27.64	4.7
Public Health, Research, Other	781.0	33.92	5.8
TOTAL	$13,552.5	$588.59	100.0%

Source: Canada, Health and Welfare, *National Health Expenditures in Canada, 1960-75*, Ottawa, January, 1979.

under the public universal insurance programs—together accounted for $7.6 billion or 55 per cent of national health expenditures in 1976.

Explicit indication of the extent to which health services are publicly financed is provided in Table 2. Here the 1975 expenditure on each major category of service is proportioned into public and private components, with the public sector portion further divided among the three levels of government. The dominant role of the public sector and of the federal and provincial governments in particular is readily apparent. Seventy-five cents of every dollar spent was publicly financed, with all but a fraction of this coming from federal and provincial budgets. Federal-provincial cost-sharing of the hospital and medical care insurance programs is conspicuously present in the figures for general hospitals and physicians' services, as is their almost complete domination of these two categories. Provincial governments account for nearly all public sector "prepayment and administration" due largely to their direct management responsibilities in respect of these two programs. Public financing of "other hospitals'' coincides with direct provision of care by the federal and provincial governments to the mentally ill and retarded, native peoples, war veterans, and the military. Public health, medical research, and medical facility construction are other categories where public financing is also synonymous with direct public sector provision. Finally, and notwithstanding the advent of the provincially funded programs of dental care for children, prescription drugs, and personal care facilities for the elderly, private sector financing heavily dominates dental care (90 per cent) and drugs and applicances (88 per cent), and accounts for a significant share (40 per cent) of nursing home care.

This present mix of public and private financing of health expenditures contrasts sharply with earlier years when the system was in a much more transitional state. Thus in 1960 when the national hospital insurance program was fully operative in nine of the ten provinces, the public sector accounted for only 43 per cent of total health spending. In 1965, when

Table 2 Health Expenditures by Category and Sector, Percentage Distribution, Canada, 1975

Category	Federal Gov't.	Prov Gov't.	Local Gov't.	Total Gov't.	Private Sector	Total
Institutional Care	40%	49%	1%	90%	10%	100%
General and allied special hospitals	46	48	0	94	6	100
Other Hospitals	23	74	0	97	3	100
Nursing Homes	24	33	3	60	40	100
Professional Services	36	39	0	73	27	100
Physicians	47	48	0	95	5	100
Dentists	2	8	0	10	90	100
Other Professionals	1	41	2	44	56	100
Drugs and Appliances	3	9	0	12	88	100
Prescribed drugs	6	19	0	25	75	100
Non-prescribed drugs	0	0	0	0	100	100
Eyeglasses and appliances	2	1	0	3	97	100
Other Expenditures	16	48	7	72	28	100
Prepayment and administration	3	66	0	69	31	100
Medical facility construction	6	46	7	59	41	100
Public Health, research, other	30	45	9	84	16	100
TOTAL	32%	42%	1%	75%	25%	100%

Source: Canada, Health and Welfare, *National Health Expenditures in Canada, 1960-75*, Ottawa, January, 1979.

"free" hospital care was a reality for everyone but when only Saskatchewanians had access to "free" medical care, the figure had increased to 51 per cent. Five years later, when all provinces except Quebec, Prince Edward Island and New Brunswick had implemented medical care insurance programs qualifying for the federal grants-in-aid, it had reached 70 per cent. Once Medicare became a national fact in 1971 the figure edged up a little higher (to 72 per cent), but it took until 1975 to reach the 75 per cent mark and the overall "three parts public, one part private" system of payment detailed in Table 2. As a consequence of these shifts, health has become a much more significant item in public budgets, increasing its share of total expenditure by all governments from 7.8 per cent in 1960-61 to 12.5 per cent in 1975-76.

The contrasts with earlier years are no less striking in respect to the $13.6 billion national health care bill for 1976. It dwarfs the $2.2 billion spent in 1960, exceeds by a factor of four the $3.4 billion spent in 1965, and more than doubles the $6.1 billion spent in 1970. Between 1960 and 1976, expenditures increased a whopping $11.4 billion on the strength of year-to-year increases averaging 12.2 per cent. Since neither the population nor the economy as a whole grew at the same rate, per capita health expenditures increased from $120.34 to $588.59, while the health share of the gross national product (GNP) jumped from 5.6 to 7.1 per cent. Though this latter fact is sometimes cited as evidence of "excessive" growth in health spending, it is notable that the share of national resources devoted to health in 1976 was slightly less than it was in 1971 when the share peaked at 7.4 per cent, and was substantially less than the corresponding U.S. figure of 8.6 per cent. In large measure, this reflects deliberate efforts by the federal and provincial governments to restrain health spending during the seventies, and thereby avoid what the Economic Council of Canada termed the "unsustainable" increases witnessed during the late sixties.[4] Thus qualified, the sixteen-year record is no less impressive; in its total, its amount per capita, and as a percentage of GNP, health spending has evidenced remarkable growth.

Each major category of health expenditure contributed to the overall growth of $11.4 billion, as shown in Table 3. The institutional care sector added a phenomenal $6.3 billion to its 1960 base of $946 million and accounted for over half of all new spending. Services of health professionals jumped almost $2.5 billion from a 1960 base of $513 million, while dollar gains of $1.3 billion were registered in both the drugs and appliances category (1960 = $310 million) and the miscellaneous group (1960 = $385 million). In each category, the tempo of spending surpassed population growth by a wide margin and in two cases, institutional care and professional services, the pace well exceeded GNP growth.

Confronted by this information and the clear indication that Canadians are spending unprecedented sums on all forms of health care, it is natural

Table 3 Expenditure Growth by Major Health Category, 1960-76
and Percentage Contribution to Total Increase

	Increase ($ million)	% of Total Increase
Institutional Care	$ 6,316.7	55.4%
Professional Services	2,461.0	21.6
Drugs and Appliances	1,344.8	11.8
Administration, Research, Construction, etc.	1,275.0	11.2
TOTAL	$11,397.5	100.0%

Source: Canada, Health and Welfare, *National Health Expenditures in Canada, 1960-75,* Ottawa, January, 1979.

to ask how much of the expenditure growth represents increased per capita consumption of services on the one hand and higher prices of health goods and services on the other. By one rather crude reckoning, using the all-items Consumer Price Index (CPI) as a deflator of per capita health expenditure, approximately sixty per cent of the increase may be ascribed to higher per capita consumption and forty per cent to higher prices.[5] While both factors evidently played major roles in fueling expenditure growth, more accurate answers to the question may be obtained by examining trend data for selected items of expenditure.

Attention focusses naturally on the two items which figure so prominently in public budgets and public debate, namely, hospital care and physicians' services. Their expenditure records, inclusive of information on prices and quantities, will be briefly reviewed in turn.

As noted earlier, the dominant providers of services covered under the federal-provincial hospital insurance program are the public (non-profit) general and allied special hospitals. Over the period 1960-75, the operating expenses of these institutions surged from $622.4 million to $4.72 billion, an astonishing increase of 658 per cent. At 14.5 per cent, their average annual growth rate was nine times that of the population (1.6 per cent), nearly one and one-half times that of the GNP (10.2 per cent), and over one and one-third times that of all other health spending (10.7 per cent). Interestingly, the lion's share of the overall dollar increase is ascribable to higher costs, not higher quantities of care. Reckoned on the conventional per patient-day basis, unit costs rocketed 417 per cent from $21.32 to $100.30;[6] concurrently, the volume of care rose by a comparatively modest 45 per cent from 29.4 to 42.8 million patient-days on the strength of both population growth and higher per capita hospitalization. By implication, only one-fifth of the expenditure growth is due to the fact that Canadians are spending more time in hospital. Small wonder, then, that most observers cite soaring daily costs as the hospital sector's number one problem.

Striking growth has also occurred in expenditure on physicians' services. Between 1960 and 1975, total spending mushroomed from $355 million to $1.9 billion, while per capita expenditures jumped from $19.82 to $83.62. Adjusting these latter figures for an estimated 64 per cent increase in physicians' fees implies that per capita use of physicians' services increased by a very sizable 158 per cent. Evidently, fee inflation contributed much less to the growth of medical costs than did utilization increases. This pattern contrasts sharply with that of the hospital sector, and, equally revealing, is almost the exact reverse of that for dental services. Per capita spending on dental services grew at the same rate as medical spending, but was driven by an unparallelled 147 per cent increase in dental fees and a relatively small 73 per cent increase in per capita utilization. Lest there be any doubt that consumers of dental services have faced extraordinary fee increases, consider that the economy as a whole experienced inflation of only 86 per cent over the same fifteen-year period! For their part, physicians may fairly claim that their fees have lagged behind the general trend, especially in the post-Medicare years when fee increases have been deliberately restrained by cost-conscious provincial governments.

Problems and Analytical Themes

The obvious question begged in the preceding review of health expenditures is, "Are they good value for the money?" Were one to demand the shortest possible and least controversial answer, it would have to be, "Yes, but." Any subsequent demand for defence of both the affirmation and the qualification would almost certainly produce a wide range of responses, many of which would doubtless reflect opposing views about the appropriate role and function of governments in the health area. Some would argue that the state has intervened to an excessive degree and because of this, the costs yield benefits lower than would be obtained under a more "laissez-faire" arrangement featuring much heavier reliance on the private sector. Others would dispute this position, and assert that the overall benefit-cost ratio is lower than it might be were governments to intervene even more than they do now. On this largely ideological plane there will always be room for vigorous debate, though the risk is real that it will generate more heat than light.

Among those who have made formal study of the system, the request for a more expansive response to the question would elicit a virtual consensus that opportunities exist for securing "more bang for the buck," an uncommon degree of like-mindedness on the major problems which beset the present system, and, as well, some considerable measure of agreement on the most viable options for addressing these problems and thereby improving the system's overall performance. To these dominant analytical themes the discussion now turns.

The most fundamental theme is that we have entered an era where the treatment-oriented health care system is limited in its ability to reduce death, disease, and disability. These so-called "limits to medicine" are not uniquely Canadian, nor are they related in any obvious way to alternative methods of organizing and financing health care associated with different divisions of health labour between the public and private sectors. Rather, they exist in all affluent post-industrial societies where the major life-prolonging and life-enhancing advances in medical knowledge have been largely exploited, and where further improvements in population health status depend much more on reducing the risks to mind and body emanating from the physical and social environment and from contemporary lifestyles. Air and water pollution, crowded and otherwise inadequate living conditions, monotonous and otherwise stressful working conditions and poverty are representative environmental factors hazardous to health, as are lifestyles involving abuse of alcohol, tobacco and other drugs, over-eating, lack of exercise, careless driving and failure to wear seatbelts. Modern medicine can and does attempt to treat the wide variety of resultant illnesses and conditions but, in the absence of a frontal attack on their root causes, is effectively reduced to fighting a flurry of rear-guard actions, many of which are widely believed to generate more costs than benefits. To illustrate, costly chemotherapy, radiotherapy and surgical interventions for lung cancer yield little demonstrable extension of life or relief of symptoms.

This theme—a variant of what the economist terms "the law of diminishing marginal returns—has been emphasized in numerous international studies of health care, but has found its clearest Canadian expression in a highly readable document entitled "A New Perspective on the Health of Canadians" tabled in the House of Commons in 1974 by the then Minister of National Health and Welfare, the Honourable Marc Lalonde. Based on an analysis of mortality and hospital morbidity, it was shown that the principal causes and underlying factors of health and sickness are environmental and lifestyle hazards of the sort just described. Specifically, the mortality data revealed that for Canadians aged 5 to 35 in 1971, the main cause of death was motor vehicle accidents, followed in second and third positions by all other types of accidents and suicide, respectively. Attributable mainly to human, environmental and social factors beyond the direct control of the health care system, these three causes together accounted for fully 6,200 of the 9,700 deaths specific to this age group. For the age group 35 to 70, diseases of the cardiovascular (heart, vein and artery) system, attributable in large part to obesity, smoking, stress, lack of exercise, high-fat diets, or combinations thereof, accounted for 25,700 of 58,000 deaths. These too represent deaths which the traditional treatment-oriented health care system can do little or nothing to prevent. Measured in terms of the potential years of life lost (PYLL), the costs to society from these and other "early" deaths (i.e., those occurring before age 70) are enormous, the total for motor vehicle accidents alone being 213,000 PYLL in 1971.

Costs of a more direct nature are incurred through hospitalization for many of these same preventable illnesses. Hospital statistics for 1975 reveal that diseases of the cardiovascular system were by a wide margin the major cause of hospitalization, consuming nearly one-fifth of the total 41.4 million patients-days in acute care general hospitals. Fractures, head injuries, burns and all other causes due to accidents and violence were second on the list and accounted for eight per cent of the total. Mental illness, some of which is ascribable to preventable social stresses, was another major cause, accounting for 2.7 million patient-days in the acute-care general hospitals and another 15.1 million patient-days in psychiatric institutions. While the dollar cost of the "avoidable" hospitalization was not calculated, there can be no doubt that it would be impressive. For the general hospitals alone, a crude estimation may be based on their 1975 average per patient day cost of $110.30 and the conservative assumption that only one-third of all hospitalization for cardiovascular diseases, accidents and violence, and mental illness is ultimately preventable; this yields the tidy sum of $382 million, equivalent to eight per cent of the total operating costs for these institutions that year. To paint a more complete picture of potential savings, one would have to include an additional sum representative of the "avoidable" costs incurred for related physicians' services, notably expenditures on the appropriate fraction of total office, home and hospital visits, consultations, psychotherapy, out-of-hospital lab tests and radiological exams, surgery, anaesthesia, etc.

In making the case for reducing our reliance on costly hospital and medical care and for redirecting our national energies from treatment of illness to prevention of illness, the Lalonde Report indeed marshalled an impressive array of facts and figures. Perhaps the most revealing single statistic was the one showing that ninety-five per cent of the total $2.5 billion expended for all health-related activities by the federal government in the fiscal year 1973-74 was directed at the hospital and medical care sectors where the overriding preoccupation has been and continues to be with the treatment of existing illness. This, and the tiny share (5 per cent) allocated to programs and activities with a focus on prevention, underscored the prevailing imbalance between treatment and prevention, and left no doubt that even a modest redistribution of funding would pay substantial dividends, if not immediately, then certainly in the long run.

The problem with prevention, of course, is that the long run may well prove to be intolerably long, especially to the federal and provincial governments whose fiscal horizons tend to be relatively short, and whose budgets are already creaking under the pressures exerted by the mounting costs of health care and all other public goods and services. Having anted-up annual dollar increments in excess of twelve per cent for hospital and medical care throughout most of their accumulated terms as the principal co-financiers, their more immediate and pressing concern is to control the growth of health spending without at the same time impairing the quality of care to which Canadians have become accustomed.

Reinforcing this concern is the analytical theme that ample room exists for obtaining more value for the money by improving the internal efficiency of the health care system itself, quite apart from whatever efforts are made to promote savings through prevention. Touched on only briefly in the Lalonde Report, but conspicuously present in numerous other official and unofficial studies, this theme entails a rich array of argument and evidence, only key portions of which will be reviewed here.

One of the most compelling arguments holds that health care costs could be reduced without consequence to care quality by placing greater reliance on low-cost alternatives to traditional diagnostic and treatment technologies. To those who make this argument, the burden of proof rests not on theoretical grounds, since the logic of such substitutions is self-evident. Rather, the obligation is to demonstrate by practical example that the substitution strategy is technically feasible and consistent with prevailing standards of quality care. The task is not difficult.

With respect to health care personnel, the two best examples are the substitution of nurse practitioners for physicians in the provision of primary medical care and the substitution of dental nurses for dentists in the provision of dental services to children. The clinical competence of nurse practitioners in diagnosing and treating a wide variety of medical problems has been evaluated in over forty studies, twenty-one of which featured direct comparisons with care given by physicians. In a recent review of this literature, Dr. Harold Sox of the Stanford University School of Medicine concluded that the accumulated evidence shows that nurse practitioners working under the general supervision of physicians "provide office-based care that is indistinguishable from physician care."[7] Moreover, in nearly all studies, patients expressed at least as much satisfaction with the care given by the nurse practitioners as they did with the care given by physicians. These findings, coupled with the fact that nurse practitioners command incomes substantially lower than those of physicians (due to lesser investment in education and other factors), clearly indicate that the costs of primary medical care could be reduced without adverse quality effects by expanding the employment of nurse practitioners in practice settings where the dollar savings accrue not to the private physician, but to society as a whole.

The competence of dental nurses in providing educational, preventive and treatment services to children under the school-based Saskatchewan Dental Plan was rigorously evaluated in 1976 by three dentists from outside the province.[8] Specialists in the fields of children's dentistry and restorative dentistry surveyed 410 children from kindergarten to grade two in whom a total of 2,107 amalgam restorations (fillings) and 97 stainless steel crowns had been placed by either a dentist or a dental nurse. Unaware of who had performed the work, they rated the restorations as follows:

	Dentist	Dental Nurse
Unacceptable	21.1%	3.7%
Adequate	62.4%	48.6%
Superior	16.5%	47.7%

These results, plus similarly conducted assessments of the stainless steel crowns, which showed the nurses performed to the same standard as dentists, leave no doubt that dental nurses (trained in only two years) offer a viable, high-quality, low-cost alternative to traditional fee-for-service dentistry for children. An added benefit of Saskatchewan's school-based program is that it reaches a much higher proportion of the target pediatric group than does, for example, the Quebec program based on private practices.

The case for much greater reliance on low-cost alternatives to traditional technologies is no less compelling with respect to health facilities. Two good examples are the substitution of surgical day care for inpatient care and the substitution of home care for institutional care. The performance of certain surgical procedures on a day care, "not for admission" basis has been shown to be a safe, cost-effective alternative to traditional inpatient care. Studies conducted at the Children's Hospital in Vancouver reveal that day surgery costs 70 per cent less than inpatient surgery and, as well, significantly reduces the risk to the patient of both psychological stress and hospital-acquired infection.[9] Equally impressive results have been demonstrated in a recent evaluation of Manitoba's universal, comprehensive home care program.[10] Of 1,167 persons admitted or re-admitted to the program in the months of February and March 1978, 822 would have been placed in a nursing home or hospital had the program not been available. For this group, cost comparisons of the home care actually received with the designated institutional alternatives indicated that the program produced total *monthly* savings of $1.23 million to the government and taxpayers of the province.

Another line of argument directly related to the general "inefficiency" theme rests on the patently logical proposition that costs could be reduced without attendant cuts in the quality of care by reducing the volume of "unnecessary" services. More contentious than the substitution argument, it obliges one to define the term and, having done so, to provide illustrative examples. On a strictly medico-technological level, an "unnecessary" service may be defined as one yielding very little or no detectable improvement in the health of the patient. Its purpose may be either diagnostic or therapeutic, but in neither case would it fundamentally alter the course of illness or provide any notable symptomatic relief. Any test or procedure of this sort would be an obvious waste of resources, of value to neither patient nor physician. In the absence of other case-management options, the implied alternative is to do nothing.

Doing nothing or even less of something is of course contra-indicated by two elemental truths of modern medicine. One is that patients expect their physicians to do something on their behalf and, at the very least, to provide reassurance that all is not as bad as it might seem. Another is that practitioners are required to make decisions amid considerable uncertainty concerning the likely risks and benefits to the patient of any particular investigation or treatment. Their failure to be fully informed is by no means deliberate. Rather, it reflects the fact that very few devices, drugs, tests and procedures have been rigorously evaluated.[11] Many others have been only partially evaluated with ambiguous results. Hence, it is commonplace to order a test or perform a procedure if the chances are it will do no harm.

Notwithstanding the dearth of definitive studies, examples may be given of services whose recorded volumes have been judged "excessive" in the light of the available evidence on their costs, risks and benefits. Thus, in a recent and widely quoted report released by the U.S. Congress, it was estimated that there were 2 million unnecessary surgical operations in 1978 at a cost of $4 billion and more than 10,000 lives.[12] Closer to home, a study conducted by a Committee of the Saskatchewan College of Physicians and Surgeons determined that 31.6 per cent of the hysterectomies performed in five large hospitals in 1970 did not conform to good gynecologic practice and hence were "unjustified."[13] In Manitoba, studies have revealed that only 23 per cent of tonsillectomy and adenoidectomy operations performed on children in 1973 complied with authoritative indications for the procedure.[14]

The volume of diagnostic radiology examinations and tests has also been seriously questioned. In an address to the Canadian Association of Radiologists in 1973, Dr. John Campbell observed that "the overutilization of radiologic examinations is a real enigma to the delivery of meaningful radiologic exposure . . . one picture may be worth a thousand words but we have reached the point where we take a thousand pictures to get one worthwhile word of diagnosis."[15] This view is reinforced by research into methods of radiological cost restraint in a teaching hospital conducted by Dr. Donald MacEwan, chief radiologist at Winnipeg's Health Sciences Centre. He concluded:

"Utilization is approximately 30% greater than necessary. Up to 10% are duplicate of ill-directed examinations. Another 10% would not be necessary if the full value of previous medical information and laboratory tests were promptly available. Another 10% would not be justified if the patient and physician were motivated to withhold services of low yield, to await a more optimum time, to eliminate so-called medico-legal protection or to recognize, on harsh analysis, that the performance of the exam will be of little benefit to the patient or society."[16]

While these findings may not be generalizable, it is interesting to contemplate the potential savings which would accrue were the volume of diagnostic radiology in all Canadian hospitals to be reduced by as little as ten per cent. Based on official hospital statistics for 1973 showing a national volume of 13.7 million tests and examinations[17] and the conservative assumption that unit costs average $10, the resultant figure is a cool $13.7 million—enough to finance annually any number of high-priority items elsewhere in the health care system, including, for example, 84,000 months of comprehensive home care at current (Manitoba) prices.

These examples should suffice to illustrate that opportunities do indeed exist for enhancing the value of the health care dollar by improving the efficiency of the delivery system. Selective substitutions of low-cost for high-cost personnel and facilities, together with selective reductions in service volumes, offer the prospect of substantial savings without at the same time threatening the quality of care. Such savings, it must be emphasized, would accrue over and above those resulting from successful efforts to promote better health through reduction of environmental hazards and the adoption of less risky lifestyles. The scope for unambiguous improvement in the overall benefit-cost ratio is, to put it mildly, considerable.

Current Policy Initiatives, Prospects, and Options

At this juncture, the obvious questions arise: what is being done to exploit these opportunities? Is it enough? What are the policy options? Taking each in turn, it is clear that the federal and provincial governments have implemented various policies and programs which should in due course have some beneficial effect upon health costs. Consistent with the Lalonde Report's emphasis on prevention, they have launched information campaigns designed to make Canadians more aware of the dangers of smoking, drinking, over-eating and lack of exercise. Speed limits have been reduced on many major highways, and, in most provinces, the wearing of automobile seatbelts and motorcycle helmets has been made compulsory. Regulatory action has also been taken in several provinces to decrease the high number of alcohol-related traffic fatalities and injuries among teenagers by raising the legal drinking age above eighteen. Comprehensive occupational health and safety legislation has been enacted in at least three provinces (Ontario, Manitoba and Saskatchewan) which provides for, among other things, new and stiffer penalties on employers who fail to comply with regulations designed to reduce the number of accidents and illnesses attributable to working conditions over which employees have no control. Other examples could doubtless be given.

Initiatives have also been taken to contain health care expenditure growth and improve the efficiency of the delivery system. One of the more promising developments is rooted in the *Federal-Provincial Fiscal Arrangements and Established Programs Financing Act, 1977.* This act provides for a more flexible approach to federal cost-sharing of provincially administered health programs and, as well, for a much less open-ended arrangement than the original 50/50 cost-sharing formula. It enhances flexibility in provincial spending priorities by eliminating the requirement that federal funds be spent only on acute care hospitals and physicians' services. Provinces may use the federal contributions to assist in the funding of, for example, nursing home care, home care and community mental health services. In effect, the provinces are now better positioned to promote cost-effective alternatives to traditional modes of delivery. For its part, the federal government has "capped" its financial commitments to the provinces by reducing its direct cash contributions from 50 per cent to 25 per cent and by indexing future increases in these contributions to GNP growth. At the same time, it has reduced federal income taxes to create room for the provinces to increase their tax rates and thereby compensate for the reduction in the federal cash contributions. Under these arrangements, the federal contributions are no longer tied to the level and rate of growth of provincial health care costs, and the provinces no longer have the incentive to spend a dollar knowing that they will automatically receive 50¢ in return from the federal government. In consequence, the provinces have a much greater stake in and responsibility for controlling health care costs.

More direct action has also been taken to restrict spending on hospital and medical care consistent with the widely accepted view that overall resources in these two areas are adequate to meet existing and immediately foreseeable needs. In 1970, the federal government terminated a twenty-two-year-old program to assist financially the provinces in the construction of active treatment hospital facilities. Under the impetus of this program, the hospital bed-population ratio rose steadily throughout the fifties and sixties and by 1970 had reached approximately 5.5 beds per thousand population, a figure consistent with then prevailing assessments of need, and substantially in excess of the 4.0 beds per thousand population ratio that has subsequently become the target figure in many provinces. Provincial moratoria on the construction of acute care hospital facilities are now commonplace and are, in most instances, an integral part of a general strategy to match resources more appropriately with needs by shifting certain elderly and chronically ill patients into less intensive and less costly institutions. Concurrent attempts are being made to contain hospital costs through prospective budgeting procedures featuring strict limits on allowable increases for new and existing services. Efforts to restrict spending on physicians' services have found expression in a tough-minded approach on the part of provincial governments to the bargaining of medical fees, and, at the federal level, in measures to restrict the immigration of physicians. Introduced in the mid-seventies, this latter policy reflected an official consensus that the overall supply of physicians was adequate and that a "surplus" was imminent. Evidence that the national population-physician ratio had improved dramatically from 740:1 (persons per physician) in 1968 to 585:1 in 1975[18] figured prominently in the achievement of this consensus, as did the World Health Organization's widely quoted "ideal" ratio of 650:1.

While it is reasonable to expect some pay-off from all of these initiatives, some cautionary notes must be registered. First, the prospects for prevention and attendant long-run savings through modification of individuals' lifestyles are highly problematic. Downtrends in per capita cigarette consumption are encouraging, but uptrends in per capita alcohol consumption are not;[19] nor are the studies showing that programs of physical fitness tend to attract those who are already fit and who presumably need them the least.[20]

Second, the prospects for implementation of innovative new modes of health care delivery on a scale justified by the evidence on their cost-effectiveness are not as bright as might be believed. The medical and dental professions have a powerful vested interest in the status quo of private fee-for-service practice, and have successfully resisted attempts to expand employment opportunities for nurse practitioners and dental nurses in settings such as community health centres where the skills of these new professionals are best exploited. Their continuing opposition to even modest public experiments in cost-effective task delegation, while consistent with their economic self-interest, remains a formidable barrier to meaningful activation of the substitution principle.

Third, the prospects for appropriately selective reductions in service volumes are dimmed at least somewhat by the likely persistence of fee-for-service as the dominant mode of physician and dentist remuneration. In a fee-for-service environment, volume reductions imply (other things remaining the same) lower professional incomes and this, needless to say, holds little appeal for the individual practitioner.

Finally, and notwithstanding the immigration restrictions, the prospects are for substantial upward pressure on medical costs due to further increases in the number of practising physicians. Projections based on the current annual flow of new graduates from the nation's sixteen medical schools, and allowance for attrition due to death, retirements, and out-migration, suggest that the population: physician ratio will by 1987 decline from its 1975 level of 585:1 to somewhere in the 540:1—460:1 range. Should this occur, and the odds are that it will in the absence of a new health manpower policy, current perceptions of a "doctor surplus" may well give way to claims of a "doctor glut." In any event, the consequent pressures to increase both hospital and medical care expenditures will be very real indeed. Thus, to the second question raised earlier, "Is it enough?", the optimist would reply, "Perhaps," while the pessimist would reply, "Probably not."

What are the options? While it might be intellectually stimulating to contemplate the polar alternatives of complete "socialization" and complete "privatization" of health care, in reality neither represents a viable political option to the present mix of public and private sector involvement in the health care system. It is, however, instructive to consider several other options, the effects of which would be to tilt the scales in either one of these two directions.

Among the options that would impart a more private character to the system, the one most frequently discussed in recent years is to "make the user pay." Less colloquially, and more precisely, the suggestion is made that users of publicly insured hospital and medical care should be required to pay some portion of the costs of the services that they receive. The argument, briefly stated, is that health costs are excessive because patients make irresponsible and unnecessary use of "free" services; to eliminate or at least reduce abuse of the system, it is necessary to introduce a system of direct charges at the point-of-service. To assess the argument, it is well to consider the relevant evidence.

In one study, an attempt was made to identify patient abuse in the utilization of medical services insured under the Ontario Health Insurance Plan (OHIP). Statistical analysis of the OHIP claims data produced two major conclusions, one, "that the major determinant of utilization of medical services is ill-health", the other, "that there is no evidence of any significant patient abuse."[21]

An opportunity to explore the nature and magnitude of deterrent effects consequent upon the introduction of user charges was afforded when, in response to escalating health costs in the late 1960s, the Saskatchewan Government implemented a policy of direct charges on patients using selected services insured under the province's universal hospital and medical insurance programs. Effective April 15, 1968, the Saskatchewan Medical Care Insurance Commission (MCIC) authorized physicians in the province to charge their patients $1.50 for each office visit and $2.00 for each home, emergency and hospital outpatient visit. Concurrently, the Saskatchewan Hospital Services Plan (SHSP) authorized hospitals to charge adult and child inpatients a utilization fee of $2.50 per day for the first thirty days and $1.50 per day thereafter, to a maximum of ninety consecutive days. These charges remained in effect until August, 1971.

The effects of these utilization fees have been the subject of extensive analysis.[22] No evidence could be found that the $2.50 a day charge on inpatients reduced either the volume of admissions or the lengths of hospital stay. Rather the charges amounted to an "illness tax," the fairness of which was seriously questioned due to its having impacted most heavily on low income families who did not qualify for social assistance and who, on this account, were required to pay the fees. Analysis of the medical care data revealed that the visit fees did have a deterrent effect. Office visits decreased by an average of 5.4 per cent, but among the elderly and the poor, service use declined by as much as 18 per cent. Again there was compelling evidence that the fees impacted more on those least able to pay. These perverse but not altogether surprising effects have served to temper enthusiasm for user charges among politicians, policy-makers, and some segments of the medical profession.

For its part, the Canadian Medical Association has recently expressed the view that point-of-service charges levied on a discretionary basis by physicians "have many desirable social features."[23] Mindful of the Saskatchewan experience with the (regressive) uniform charge on all patients, the CMA advocates "extra-billing" only of those patients who, in the judgement of the physician, have the ability to pay. The object would not be to deter use of physicians' services, but rather to "enhance accessibility" and "safeguard against (public) underfunding." Discretionary direct charges would allegedly enhance accessibility by serving as a substitute for a disruption or withdrawal of services by physicians in the event of unresolvable differences with provincial governments over appropriate compensation for provision of publicly insured medical services. As the CMA put it, "We must have recourse to influence the people with whom we are negotiating short of taking strike action." Direct charges would safeguard against underfunding from the public purse by providing supplements from the purses of selected patients.

The extra billing option does, however, have some undesirable professional and political connotations that were glossed over or ignored in the CMA's statement. First, it requires the individual physician to maintain more costly and more detailed accounting records than are associated with the alternative of accepting payments from the public programs as payment in full for services rendered; the costs, including inconvenience, of maintaining a separate set of "accounts receivable" may or may not justify the additional revenue resulting from the direct charges. Second, it places the physician in the awkward and potentially embarrassing position of "tax-man," having to determine who among his patients is taxable and, having done this, to determine the appropriate levy. He may learn to execute this task with some skill, particularly if his patients agree to providing all the pertinent data on their economic status, but on the other hand, he may not. In any event, the charges will inevitably appear arbitrary and capricious to patients. Their confidence in his clinical assessments of their ability to benefit will in most cases far exceed their confidence in his taxation assessments of their ability to pay. And, of course, there is a distinct possibility that poorer clients will simply choose to go elsewhere for their care, or worse, remain at home with their problems unattended.

From a wider political perspective, there can be little doubt that extra-billing threatens the spirit of Medicare. It is at variance with the program's basic principle that access to medical care should be available on equal financial terms and conditions. That Canadians remain committed to this principle is obvious from numerous opinion polls consistently showing Medicare to be the most popular of all public sector programs. At the same time, and throughout most of its ten-year history as a national operation, it has functioned to provide incomes satisfactory to the vast majority of physicians. In most provinces, ninety per cent (or more) of physicians have chosen over the years to participate fully in the program and have resisted periodic advice given by their respective medical associations to "opt out" and engage in extra-billing. Their revealed preference for fee bargaining with governments rather than patients is a matter of fact in post-Medicare Canada. And, it may be safely asserted, it is a preference that most politicians, physicians and patients would judge to be worth preserving.

---

[1] Canada, *Report of the Royal Commission on Health Services,* Volume 1, (Ottawa, Queen's Printer, 1964), p. 11.

[2] The Commission estimated that, depending upon the definition of inability to pay, a program of selective assistance would have entailed means-testing somewhere between 5.5 million and 9.6 million persons in 1961, and between 8.9 million and 14.9 million in 1971. *Ibid.*, p. 738.

[3] It should be noted, however, that several provinces had their own medical care insurance programs prior to joining the federal medicare scheme. Saskatchewan's, introduced in 1962, was the first in North America to provide comprehensive coverage to an entire population; as such, it required no fundamental modification to qualify for the grants-in-aid. In contrast, the plans introduced in Alberta, British Columbia, and Ontario in 1963, 1965, and 1966 respectively all featured non-universal enrolment and were intended only to supplement rather than supplant the private insurance and prepayment plans; for this and other reasons, they failed to meet the criteria for federal cost-sharing and were subsequently replaced by new programs. For further details of the historical record see Shillington, C.H., *The Road to Medicare in Canada* (Toronto: Del Graphics Publishing Department, 1972).

[4] Economic Council of Canada, *Sixth Annual Review* (Ottawa: Queen's Printer, 1969), Table 3-2, p. 29. To underscore its concern with the growth in public ex-

penditures on health and higher education, the Council predicted that "if the rate of increase of the past five years (1965-69) were to continue unabated, these two areas of activity would alone absorb the entire potential national product before the year 2000." Properly stupefied by this extrapolation, one journalist could wryly foresee "that in the end only the members of the Economic Council survived because they alone understood economics and could thrive on a simple diet of statistics." Bruce Hutchison, "Healthy, but dead," *The Globe and Mail*, (Toronto: November 19, 1970).

[5] Between 1960 and 1976 per capita health expenditures grew 10.4 per cent annually, the CPI rose 4.4 per cent annually, and per capita consumption of health care inferentially at 5.7 per cent annually. Canada, Health and Welfare, *National Health Expenditures in Canada 1960-75* (Ottawa, January 1979), p. 3.

[6] Much of this inflationary pressure emanates from the wages and salaries of hospital employees. Their share of total hospital budgets increased significantly over the period, and by 1975 represented fully 70 per cent of the average daily cost. Higher staffing levels, more skilled personnel, and collectively bargained wage gains have each had an impact on the process, and together explain why labour costs have escalated so rapidly.

[7] Harold C. Sox, "Quality of Patient Care by Nurse Practitioners and Physicians' Assistants: A Ten-Year Perspective," *Annals of Internal Medicine*, Vol. 91, September 1979, pp. 459-468.

[8] Saskatchewan Dental Health Plan, *Annual Report 1977-78* (Regina: Department of Health, 1978).

[9] Robert G. Evans and Geoffrey C. Robinson, "Day Care Surgery: Measurements of the Economic Payoff," paper presented at the Annual Meeting of the Canadian Paediatric Society, Edmonton, June 23-27, 1979.

[10] E. Thompson and C. Motuz, "The Manitoba/Canada Home Care Study: Some Preliminary Findings," paper presented at the Eighth Scientific and Educational Meeting of the Canadian Association on Gerontology, Halifax, Nova Scotia, November 1-4, 1979.

[11] Harvey V. Fineberg and Howard H. Hiatt, "Evaluation of Medical Practices: The Case for Technology Assessment," *New England Journal of Medicine*, Vol. 301, No. 20, November 15, 1979, pp. 1086-1091.

[12] J.E. Brody, "House Panel Calls for More U.S. Control of Surgery," *New York Times*, December 27, 1978, p. A1.

[13] Frank Dyck, *et al.*, "Surveillance of Hysterectomy in Saskatchewan," *Canadian Medical Association Journal*, Vol. 117, December 17, 1977.

[14] Noralou Roos, *et al.*, "A New Audit Procedure Applied to an Old Question: Is the Frequency of T & A Justified?," *Medical Care*, Vol. 15, No. 1., January, 1977.

[15] John Campbell, "Radiologic Delivery Systems and Health Care," *Journal of the Canadian Association of Radiologists*, Vol. 24, 1978, pp. 201-208.

[16] D.W. MacEwan and M.K. Kiernan, "Methods of Radiology Costs Restraint in a Teaching Hospital," *Journal of the Canadian Association of Radiologists*, Vol 24, June 1973.

[17] Canada, *Supplementary Statistical Compendium of the Hospital Insurance and Diagnostic Services Program*, (Ottawa: Health and Welfare Canada, June, 1977).

[18] Canada, *Health Manpower Inventory 1978*, (Ottawa: Health and Welfare Canada, June, 1979).

[19] Canada, Health and Welfare, *Health Field Indicators* (Ottawa, September 1979).

[20] Robert W. Morgan, *Prospects for Preventive Medicine* (Toronto: Ontario Economic Council, 1977).

[21] Alan D. Wolfson and A. Solari, "A Patient Utilization Study," (Toronto: Department of Health Administration, University of Toronto, 1976).

[22] Glen Beck and John Horne, "Utilization of Publicly Insured Health Services in Saskatchewan Before, During and After Copayment," *Medical Care*, Vol. 18, August 1980, pp. 1-21.

[23] Canadian Medical Association, "Submission to the Honourable Mr. Justice Emmett M. Hall, Chairman, Health Services Review 1979," (presented in Saskatoon, February 27, 1980).

Chapter 12

Welfare

Geoff Norquay,
Director of Programs, Canadian Council on Social
Development

Most people think of social welfare in the narrowest sense, in terms of cash payments to individuals and families who cannot meet their basic needs through their own efforts. In reality, welfare programs have a much wider focus, including financial support for the poor, but extending far beyond to include broadly based social insurance programs and universal demogrants, social services that meet a variety of personal and family needs, and programs to encourage and support local social planning and citizen participation.

Origins of Social Welfare in Canada

The principal origins in Canada's modern social welfare system can be traced to the period between the first and second world wars, when two significant income security programs were initiated at the national level. The Old Age Pensions Act of 1927 marked the first major intervention of the federal government in the field of income security. This legislation provided for federal cost-sharing of provincial pensions to persons 70 years of age and over, and was expanded to include pensions to blind persons in 1937. Also during the inter-war period, the first step towards establishing a national unemployment insurance program was made through the passage of the Employment and Social Insurance Act in 1935. Unfortunately, the Supreme Court ruled in 1937 that unemployment insurance was a provincial matter and that the Act was outside federal jurisdiction. The federal government consequently asked the provinces to waive their rights in this area. By June of 1940, all had done so and the British North America Act was amended to confirm the transfer of jurisdiction. In August of that year, the Unemployment Insurance Act became law.

A series of major national reports[1] in the early 1940s foreshadowed the development of social programs over the next twenty-five years. The Royal Commission on Dominion-Provincial Relationships, the Committee on Health Insurance, and the Marsh report to the Commons Special Committee on Social Security addressed federal-provincial roles in such areas as unemployment assistance, equalization, health care and income support programs. All urged a more activist federal role in reducing regional and income disparities and in the creation of major national social welfare programs.

The impact of these reports was both immediate and far-reaching. The National Employment Service, later the Department of Manpower and currently the Canadian Employment and Immigration Commission, had already been created in 1941. Family Allowances followed in 1945 and the Central Mortgage and Housing Corporation began operations in 1946. Finally, although comprehensive national health legislation would have to wait until the next decade, Saskatchewan and British Columbia made the first steps towards this objective by creating provincial hospital insurance programs in 1946 and 1948, respectively.

The principal developments of the 1950s centred on the creation of the Old Age Security program and the further development of public assistance programs. The Old Age Security Act of 1951 replaced the Old Age Pension Program that had been established in 1927 and administered by the provinces. The means test requirement was dropped and the new program provided flat-rate payments to all who met basic age and residency requirements. At the same time, the Old Age Assistance Act was passed, establishing a shared-cost, means-tested measure for persons between the ages of 65 and 79, and a similar program was established for the blind under the Blind Persons Act. In 1952, a program of vocational rehabilitation of disabled persons began under the authority of an Order-in-Council, and allowances for the disabled began in 1955. Another important development in this period was the creation in 1956 of the unemployment assistance program through which the federal government shared half the cost of provincial assistance to certain unemployed people.

During the 1960s, the final key elements of today's social welfare system were put into place. The Canada and Quebec Pension Plans, designed to create a comprehensive earnings-related pension floor for all Canadians, were enacted in 1966. In the same year, the Guaranteed Income Supplement was established to ensure that elderly Canadians with no income other than Old Age Security would have a more reasonable standard of living. Finally, the Canada Assistance Plan of 1966 consolidated and extended federal cost-sharing for provincial social assistance and social service programs. CAP brought together federal support for such provincial programs as mothers' allowance, unemployment and old age assistance and blind and disabled persons assistance, and thereby encouraged provinces to move toward more comprehensive social assistance programs. It also defined as eligible for cost-sharing a broad range of social services such as child welfare, counselling, services for the elderly and day care.

The Institutional Framework of Social Welfare

This historical overview is essential, not only to identify the origins of the key programs that make up the Canadian social welfare system, but also to indicate the intricate federal-provincial relationships on which the system is based.

Not surprisingly, the Fathers of Confederation did not envisage the development of the modern welfare state. Although the federal level has always had authority over such specific groups as Indians, veterans and immigrants, most of the social welfare functions that have come to be recognized as necessary in the twentieth century fall within the responsibility of the provinces.

Because the provinces have authority to levy only direct taxes, they have traditionally lacked the tax base necessary to meet these growing social welfare needs. Consequently, the provinces have generally (but not always) welcomed federal initiatives to assume shared or direct responsibility for the financing of social services. One early example of this was the 1935 attempt by the federal government to assume responsibility for unemployment insurance, but as noted earlier, this subsequently required a constitutional amendment to transfer jurisdiction from the provincial to the federal level. During the 1950s and 1960s, cost-shared programs became a frequently used response to accommodate what might be termed ''de facto'' joint responsibility in areas where provinces did not have adequate financial resources and the federal government had an interest in ensuring national program standards. The Canada/Quebec Pension Plans, the Canada Assistance Plan, medicare and hospitalization are all examples of federal-provincial cost-sharing arrangements that were developed between 1950 and 1970.

During the 1970s, the trend had begun to move away from cost-sharing and towards the ''deconditionalizing'' of federal-provincial financial arrangements. At the same time, the federal government has on occasion agreed to adjust federal programs to fit better with provincial priorities and wishes. For example, when family allowances were increased substantially in 1973, both Quebec and Alberta asked that the funds be targetted differently within their provinces and this request was agreed to by the federal government. Finally, as the 1980s begin, there is increasing pressure from provinces to obtain more authority over programs and spending priorities in social programs. This trend is likely to be reflected in extended use of tax transfer or block-funding mechanisms for social welfare programs that are currently cost-shared.

These constitutional and financial considerations have played an important role in the development of the institutional framework for addressing social welfare issues in Canada. Describing this framework concisely is no mean task, because it involves federal, provincial and municipal governments, as well as a substantial voluntary or non-governmental sector that is deeply involved in the design and delivery of social service programs. With respect to funding, there are programs that are exclusively federal, exclusively provincial, jointly funded by the federal, provincial and municipal levels, exclusively funded by the voluntary sector, and jointly funded by public and voluntary sectors. To complicate matters further, programs throughout the social welfare system are based on a variety of principles, including universal payment, insurance, and pre-defined standards of need.

Federal Programs

Federal social welfare programs are well known to all Canadians and need not be discussed in detail for the purposes of this chapter. In brief summary, the major programs are:

Family Allowances:

Provides a monthly payment to the parents or guardians of all children under 18;

Child Tax Credit:

Provides a tax credit to low-income families, with reducing benefits above approximately $18,000 yearly family income;

Old Age Security:

Provides an indexed pension to all Canadians over 65 who meet basic residency qualifications;

Guaranteed Income Supplement:

Provides a supplementary pension to the elderly who have no means of support other than old age security;

Spouse's Allowance:

Provides a pension to the spouses of old age security recipients provided that the spouse is between 60 and 64;

Canada/Quebec Pension Plans:

Provide retirement, survivors' and disability benefits to almost the entire labour force on a compulsory basis.

Unemployment Insurance:

Provides insurance against interruption of income due to unemployment, illness or pregnancy.

Provincial Programs

Social Assistance:

Through the Canada Assistance Plan, the federal government shares 50 per cent of the costs of provincial and municipal social assistance or welfare programs for people in need. Under CAP, each province has established its own program and administrative structure. Within the general guidelines set by the federal legislation, provinces provide a basic allowance that varies with family size and, in some cases, with employability of the recipient. The basic allowance covers such necessities as shelter, food, clothing, personal and household supplies. Each province has also recognized a lengthy list of special needs such as property repairs, extra shelter and fuel costs, drug, dental and optical costs, special diets, burial expenses and the like.

Social Services:

The Canada Assistance Plan permits cost-sharing for provincial, municipal and voluntary social services, including child welfare, day care, assessment and counselling, rehabilitation, homemakers services and institutions for children, the elderly, and mentally and physically handicapped. A key feature of CAP is its emphasis on preventing social problems through the timely intervention of social services.

Municipal Programs

The role of municipalities in designing and delivering social welfare programs varies from province to province. In some provinces, such as Ontario, the municipal level is deeply involved in the implementation of both social assistance (welfare payments) and social service programs. Other provinces, such as Alberta, have chosen to centralize social assistance at the provincial level while expanding the role of municipalities in delivering social services at the local level. In all provinces, where municipalities are involved in social welfare programs, they receive the benefits of federal and provincial cost-sharing for a part of their costs. In such cases, the most common cost-sharing ratio is 50 per cent federal, 30 per cent provincial and 20 per cent municipal.

Voluntary Sector Programs

The voluntary sector comprises those non-profit agencies that have an administrative structure independent of government, are accountable to an independent board of private citizens, and receive at least part of their funding from non-governmental sources. The voluntary sector in Canada involves several thousand agencies that play a critical role in the delivery of social services. Many voluntary agencies provide services to clients of all income groups while others direct their efforts towards more discrete populations defined on the basis of income, age, type of need, religion, or ethnic group.

To a certain degree, all voluntary agencies receive at least part of their funding from non-governmental sources, through such avenues as the United Ways or by separate community fund-raising efforts. Voluntary agencies also receive funding from governments through purchase of service arrangements, and through annual grants or deficit-financing arrangements.

Social Welfare Expenditures

It is not easy to arrive at a firm dollar value for social welfare expenditures in Canada. Depending on the programs included in the calculation, most estimates place social welfare spending at between $17 and $18 billion in 1979. The pattern of public expenditures for the major programs described above is presented in Table 1. The substantial growth of social welfare spending over the past decade is readily apparent, although interpretation of this trend must be tempered by recognition of the impact of inflation on the incomes of recipients and the value of government transfer payments. In addition to inflation, several major changes in program structures and benefits are evident in the expenditures presented in Table 1:

1. The upward adjustment of family allowance rates in 1974, combined with their indexation in subsequent years (except 1976), resulted in a significant increase in expenditures.

2. The more than threefold increase in Old Age Security, Guaranteed Income Supplement and Spouses Allowance reflects the effects of indexation to the cost of living, the growing population of elderly, and heavy demand on the GIS program, which is paid to needy pensioners.

3. The 1972 amendments to Unemployment Insurance more than doubled program costs in that year. Expenditures rose 85.4 per cent between 1974 and 1977 as a result of heavy demand due to high rates of unemployment in this period.

4. A similar though less spectacular trend can be observed in the growth of provincial and municipal social assistance expenditures between 1974 and 1977, reflecting the effect of inflation and the close relationship between economic conditions and the need for assisting low income earners and individuals lacking Unemployment Insurance entitlements.

Table 1 Total Expenditures for Major Social Welfare Programs 1967-1978

	1967	1969	1971	1972	1973	1974	1976	1978	% Increase 1967-78
					(in millions of $)				
Family Allowances	611	618	619	611	711	1769	1942	2224	363%
Old Age Security/ Guaranteed Income Supplement/ Spouses' Allowance	1318	1659	2114	2430	2824	3303	4305	5244	397%
Canada/Quebec Pension Plans	—	51	172	248	366	495	1036	1701	N/A
Unemployment Insurance	353	499	891	1869	2008	2121	3332	4536	1,284%
Social Assistance	515	674	1037	1059	1191	1433	2114	2456	476%
Social Services	349	456	727	769	825	1056	1602	1684	482%
TOTAL:	3146	3957	5560	6986	7925	10177	14331	17845	567%

Source: *National Income and Expenditure Accounts, 1964-1978*, Catalogue 13-201, Statistics Canada 1979, Table 50, pp. 68-69. Social Services expenditures calculated by Canada Assistance Plan Directorate, National Health and Welfare.

5. The significant and steady growth of expenditures on social services throughout the period indicates increased emphasis on programs designed to prevent and alleviate social problems.

Table 2 places the growth of social welfare spending in perspective with increases in government expenditure generally and growth in the Gross National Product between 1967 and 1978. It is apparent that social welfare expenditures increased considerably during the period, experiencing a sixfold increase, while government expenditures and GNP respectively rose by a factor of just less than four. Social welfare spending rose from 14.2 per cent of government expenditures in 1967 to 21.1 per cent in 1978, and moved from 4.7 per cent of GNP in 1967 to 7.7 per cent in 1978.

Defining and Measuring Poverty

Despite the substantial programs and expenditures just described, poverty remains a reality for several million Canadians. The definition and measurement of poverty is the subject of a lively and extensive body of literature within the social welfare field. Some definitions approach poverty from broad socio-cultural or ideological premises, but these are extremely limited in offering measurable standards. While economic definitions have their own limitations, they now form the basis for most empirical research on poverty.

Using the economic approach, poverty can be defined as inadequate command over resources relative to needs. There are two general methods used by economists to define and measure poverty: the creation of poverty lines that define a minimum amount of income necessary for basic needs, and the distribution of income throughout society.

Poverty Lines

There are two basic approaches to the creation of poverty lines: the absolute and the relative. The absolute approach creates a poverty line that identifies the resource necessary to provide the basic necessities of food, clothing and shelter. By contrast, the relative approach measures poverty in terms of income inequality by establishing necessary income standards in relation to the overall distribution of income throughout society.[2]

There are several poverty lines in use in Canada. For the purposes of simplicity, two of the five lines will be explored here: the revised Statistics Canada poverty line and the poverty line produced by the Canadian Council on Social Development. The revised Statistics Canada line is based on the assumption that any individual or family that must spend more than 62 per cent of its income on basic necessities should be considered as poor. In contrast, the Canadian Council on Social Development line is constructed by assuming that the average Canadian family income

Table 2 Expenditures for Social Welfare Programs, Government Expenditures and Gross National Product, 1967-1978

(in billions of current $)

Year	Expenditures for social welfare programs	Government Expenditures	GNP	Social Welfare as a per cent of government expenditures	Social Welfare as a per cent of GNP	Government Expenditures as a per cent of GNP
1967	3.1	21.8	66.4	14.2	4.7	32.8
1969	3.9	27.2	79.8	13.9	4.9	37.1
1971	5.6	35.2	94.5	15.9	5.9	37.2
1972	6.9	39.7	105.2	17.4	6.5	37.7
1973	7.9	45.0	123.6	17.5	6.4	36.4
1974	10.2	56.0	147.5	18.2	6.9	38.0
1976	14.3	77.1	191.1	18.5	7.5	40.3
1978	17.8	96.7	230.4	18.4	7.9	41.9

Source: *National Income and Expenditures Accounts, 1964-1978*, Catalogue 13-201, 1979, Statistics Canada, Tables 1, 17 and 50.

Government Expenditures taken from Richard M. Bird, *Financing Canadian Government: A Quantitative Overview*, Canadian Tax Foundation, Toronto, 1979, Table A7.

is representative of a family of four, which is the average size of Canadian families. The poverty line for a family of four is calculated as 50 per cent of the average income figure and adjustments are then made for other family sizes.

Incidence and Distribution of Poverty

The composition and characteristics of the poor can be presented according to several dimensions. At the national level, the numbers of people living in poverty vary according to the particular poverty line used, but they are considerable by any measure. In 1976, the most recent year for which detailed data are available, there were 2,831,000 people living in poverty according to the revised Statistics Canada line. The Canadian Council on Social Development line yields a total poverty population of 4,423,000.

It should be noted that the general incidence of poverty throughout Canada has been dropping according to the Statistics Canada line. In 1969, 20.6 per cent of Canadians had low incomes as defined by Statistics Canada. By 1977, the incidence of low incomes had dropped to 13.9 per cent.

Regional Variations

Table 3 presents the incidence of low incomes by region for 1967, 1973 and 1978 for both families and unattached individuals.

The most obvious relationship apparent in Table 3 is the continuing higher incidence of poverty among unattached individuals than families. This reflects two large groups who traditionally experience low incomes: the young, who have not yet formed family units and are not yet permanently attached to the labour force, and the single elderly, most of whom are women.

The low income statistics for 1978 indicate reasonable homogeneity

Table 3[3] Proportion of Families and Unattached Individuals in Each Region Who Have a Low Income

Region	1967		1973		1978	
	Families	U.I.	Families	U.I.	Families	U.I.
Atlantic	33.8	50.0	19.0	44.9	15.7	42.9
Quebec	19.9	41.8	15.4	40.8	13.3	39.4
Ontario	12.2	33.0	10.7	37.7	9.6	35.8
Prairie	23.0	39.1	16.5	45.5	11.5	34.5
British Columbia	15.9	30.7	8.9	37.1	7.5	34.2
Canada	18.4	38.9	13.4	40.2	11.2	36.7

across the five regions, with families in the Atlantic region experiencing a higher incidence of poverty than the national average, while Ontario families have a slightly lower incidence. It is interesting to note the steady decline in the incidence of poverty between 1967 and 1978 for families in the Atlantic and Prairie regions. In the case of the Atlantic provinces, this decline in the incidence of low incomes may well reflect the positive effects of federal regional economic expansion initiatives and equalization payments. In the case of the Prairies, this trend can probably be attributed to improving employment opportunities and the rapidly expanding economy of the region.

Age and Sex

Table 4 presents a composite picture for three key factors: income, age of family head and sex.

On the basis of this Table, a number of generalizations about the distribution of income and poverty in Canada can be made. The average income of families headed by males was $20,370 in 1978, more than twice that of families headed by women, which averaged $8,771. While 25.3 per cent of families headed by men had incomes under $11,000, no less than 71.4 per cent of families headed by women had incomes at that level.

Table 4 indicates that the incomes of those under 25 and over 65 averaged just more than half of the incomes of all age groups combined. While many of those under 25 can be assumed to be just starting their working life, the high proportion of those with incomes under $5,000—almost one-third—can also be taken as an indication of the unemployment problems being faced by many young people in Canada in recent years.

As far as the elderly are concerned, the continuing over-representation of this group among the poor is confirmed by Table 4. In 1978, the average income for all families and individuals over 65 was $9,412, in comparison to average family income of $17,710. Most striking is the fact that in 1978, 58.1 per cent of elderly women had incomes of less than $5,000. The average income of all families headed by women over 65 was only $6,819.

Social Services

Social workers and social policy analysts view the relationship between income and social problems from a variety of ideological and professional perspectives. Those who start from a more radical standpoint suggest that the inequitable distribution of society's resources is the root cause of most social problems, and there is considerable evidence to support this view. A variety of data exist that link low income status with the incidence of such social problems as marital breakdown, child abuse, mental illness, juvenile delinquency, alcoholism, poor nutrition and various

Table 4 Percentage Distribution of Families and Unattached Individuals by Income Groups, Age and Sex of Head, 1978

		Age of Head	
Income Group	All Age Groups	Under 25	65 and over
All Families and Unattached Individuals			
Under $5,000	15.7%	30.8%	36.4%
$ 5,000 - $10,999	20.2	30.9	37.5
$11,000 - $14,999	12.1	14.9	10.8
$15,000 - $19,999	15.1	12.8	6.4
$20,000 - $24,999	13.2	6.9	3.9
$25,000 and Over	23.7	3.5	5.1
Average Income	$17,710	$ 9,887	$ 9,412
Male Head			
Under $5,000	8.4%	19.6%	21.2%
$ 5,000 - $10,999	16.9	26.6	45.0
$11,000 - $14,999	12.1	18.6	13.5
$15,000 - $19,999	17.1	20.0	7.5
$20,000 - $24,999	16.2	10.8	5.9
$25,000 and Over	29.5	5.4	6.8
Average Income	$20,370	$12,297	$11,225
Female Head			
Under $5,000	40.1%	51.1%	58.1%
$ 5,000 - $10,999	31.3	38.7	26.9
$11,000 - $14,999	12.7	7.5	6.8
$15,000 - $19,999	8.6	1.8	4.8
$20,000 - $24,999	3.2	0.0	0.9
$25,000 and Over	3.9	0.0	2.5
Average Income	$ 8,771	$ 5,528	$ 6,819

Source: *Income Distributions by Size in Canada*, (preliminary estimates, 1978), Catalogue 13-206, Statistics Canada, Table 4.

forms of institutionalization. On the other hand, it is also evident that, other than poverty itself, no social problem is limited to those with low incomes. Therefore, regardless of their cause, social problems exist and they must be met by the social welfare system.

Social services are that part of the social welfare system whose function it is to deal with non-financial social problems. In the broadest sense, social services can be categorized according to four general objectives: prevention, rehabilitation, protection and development. Within these broad objectives, a range of more specific functions and types of services can be identified. A comprehensive definition of social services was included in Bill C-55, the Social Services Financing Act, which was introduced in Parliament in 1978:

> . . . "social services" means services having as their object enabling persons to lead useful, satisfying and independent lives, preventing personal and social conditions that cause disadvantage or disability, raising individuals, families and groups to a higher level of participation in social and economic life, protecting those whose personal or social well-being is at risk, or developing individual, group and community capacity for growth, enrichment and social participation, and, without limiting the generality of the foregoing, includes services that
>
> (a) facilitate access to the necessities of life,
> (b) assist disabled or disadvantaged persons to live as normally and independently as possible or support them in doing so,
> (c) prevent the need for institutional care or provide alternatives to it,
> (d) support or assist the aged, children or families,
> (e) facilitate or support the involvement and participation of people in their communities and in society,
> (f) enhance or maintain employability, or
> (g) provide information and refer people to available services
> . . . [4]

The services represented by this classification are numbered in the thousands and range from large multi-faceted agencies with hundreds of staff to small organizations staffed by unpaid volunteers. To the extent that individual social problems can be forecast, and once identified, treated and ameliorated, social services represent society's principal effort to anticipate, prevent and lessen the effects of these problems. Unfortunately, the importance of this function has not been matched by a corresponding commitment of public funds in Canada. While social service expenditures have risen from $349 million in 1967 to $1.7 billion in 1978, they still represent only 9.0 per cent of the social welfare expenditures detailed earlier in this chapter.

Several reasons for this relative lack of emphasis can be identified. First, the functions of social services are not as clearly understood by the public as are the functions of the health and education systems, and consequently, broad support for their expansion does not exist. Second, increased expenditures for social services, particularly those with preventive functions, are difficult to justify in traditional cost-benefit terms. Third, the federal-provincial cost-sharing mechanism for social services, the Canada Assistance Plan, limits cost-sharing to persons "in need" or "likely to become in need." While this mechanism has done much to encourage the development of social services since 1966, it has also tended to limit this development to services for the poor, while recognition has been growing that individual social problems are by no means limited to low-income Canadians.

Future Prospects for the Canadian Social Welfare System

In the past twenty years, Canada's social welfare system has undergone considerable improvement and consolidation. The rationalization of provincial welfare programs through the Canada Assistance Plan, the creation of a national public pension system, and the extension of unemployment insurance to cover most of the working population have together improved the security of income of practically all Canadians. While the evidence presented earlier suggests that the basic distribution of income has changed little in the past twenty years, it must also be acknowledged that the incidence of poverty would be much greater without these improvements.

This growth in social welfare expenditures has been so rapid and so considerable that it will likely prompt a fundamental change in the way that Canadians view social policy in the next decade. In the past, social policy has generally been viewed as secondary to economic policy. Social welfare expenditures were seen as a small but necessary correction to compensate for the failures of the free enterprise economy. The magnitude of social welfare expenditures now requires that greater consideration be given to the relationship between social and economic policy. Therefore, the next decade will likely witness increased pressures on governments to regard social policy objectives on a par with the objectives of economic policy, along with the traditional argument that social expenditures should be limited as part of the battle against inflation.

As the 1980s begin, the general social and economic outlook for Canada is most uncertain. Inflation is expected to remain at a generally high level, with growth of the economy expected to be modest. This suggests continuing high levels of unemployment, with the world energy situation raising the possibility of even more significant economic dislocation. While these trends will impact generally on all parts of the country, their effects will be somewhat cushioned in those provinces rich in natural resources, but regional disparities will likely heighten until potential eastern offshore energy resources are proven and begin production.

With this expected economic uncertainty, it can be expected that such issues as employment, income and the standard of living will be central in shaping the major social patterns of the decade. In areas experiencing rapid economic growth, the potential for increased social problems is great, while those areas of the country without a strong economic base will continue to suffer from chronic unemployment and prolonged individual and family dependency. Both situations—the boom economy and the stagnant economy—can be expected to create considerable variations in lifestyles and greater demand for social services to deal with family breakdown and related problems. It can also be expected that an increasing number of Canadians will be leaving or reducing their involvement in the formal economy.

The role of government is likely to be a significant issue throughout most of the 1980s. As the decade begins, there appears to be a national consensus that governments have grown too large, costly and interventionist and this view could well collide with the social and economic problems that the decade will produce. The national impetus towards less government does not augur well for efforts to deal with poverty and inequitable income distribution in the new decade, although restraint may have the benefit of initiating more comprehensive efforts to address these issues more directly and effectively.

The 1980s will see the beginnings of even more significant demographic changes forecast for the end of the century. In this decade, those children born early in the post-war baby boom will reach middle age. By the year 2001, the number of Canadians over 65 will have risen from 2.1 million in 1978 to 3.4 million at the turn of the century.[5] As Canada's population bulge reaches middle age and looks towards retirement, social programs for the elderly will clearly be under increasing pressure. Major decisions must be faced in the 1980s with respect to pension and income programs for the elderly.[6] In particular, the relationship between public and private pension programs will require resolution and it is likely that major reforms in the private pension system will be forced by an electorate that is increasingly concerned about its future. The aging of Canada's population will also create major challenges to Canada's health care system. Foremost among these will be the need to develop community-based alternatives to both hospitalization and other inappropriate institutional forms of care.

Against this general background, several major issues are likely to confront Canada's social welfare system in the 1980s.

Public Commitments to Social Welfare

Like all other public sector activities, social welfare programs must continually compete with other groups of activities for the public dollar. Historically, social welfare expenditures have tended to grow during times of general economic prosperity and growth, and decline, or at least grow more slowly, during periods of slow growth or stagnation. This relationship between public commitments to social welfare and the economy is understandable, but in the case of this particular sector, paradoxical, since the number of people requiring the assistance provided by social welfare programs increases when the economy is stagnant.

The general climate of restraint that began in the late seventies presents two broad challenges to the social welfare sector. The first and more general issue is whether the Canadian public will continue to support the levels of social welfare spending achieved in the more buoyant growth period of the late 1960s and early 1970s. The second issue is closely related to the first, and centres on the degree to which existing social welfare expenditures, particularly those aimed at reducing or eliminating poverty, can be reorganized and restructured to do their job more effectively and efficiently.

The relationship between these two issues is complex. At least part of the public ambivalence towards social welfare spending can be attributed to the fact that past expenditures have done little to reduce income disparities. Unfortunately, barring major new public commitments to income redistribution programs, obtaining financial leeway to make these programs more effective requires that current benefits available to all Canadians become less universal. Since many social welfare programs benefit all income groups, the question for the future will be whether middle- and upper-income Canadians will be prepared to give up benefits that they objectively do not need, in order that poorer people be able to receive more help.

The general social, economic and political environment does not augur well for substantial reform of social welfare programs. Continuing inflation, rising energy costs and exorbitant mortgage rates have combined to threaten the economic stability of many middle-income Canadian families. It is not likely that governments will find much public support for substantial reform of social welfare programs, particularly if that reform involves either increased public expenditures or reduced benefits for the embattled middle-income group.

Finally, any attempt to change social welfare programs in the next decade can only be achieved through an increasingly complex and political set of federal-provincial relationships. Many of Canada's social welfare programs came about in the post-war period because successive federal governments saw the need for national programs that would meet basic needs regardless of the resources or political orientations of individual provincial governments. Buoyed by increasing natural resource revenues in the late 1970s, provinces are of an increasingly independent frame of mind and their desires for more autonomy are now being felt in the social policy field. Thus in the 1980s, social policy issues will likely be characterized by arguments in favour of continued national programs and standards versus demands for increased provincial authority over the setting of social priorities. In other words, whatever degree of commitment Canadians may have towards creating a more equitable society, any consensus requires negotiation through a complicated intergovernmental relationship.

Reorganization of Income Security Programs

The character of any country's income redistribution efforts is influenced by two key variables: the nature of the taxation system and the impact of income support programs. Canada has a reasonably progressive taxation system but recently, serious questions have been raised about the equity of many tax write-offs and deductions.[7] This recognition has grown in tandem with the realization that some existing transfer payment programs could be delivered through the tax system.

Canada's many and varied income security programs represent a very rough income floor providing benefits below, at, or slightly above the poverty line. The problem is that these programs are based on a variety of principles (insurance, universality, selectivity, etc.) and have developed almost independently of each other. Consequently, their overall impact is variable, and they are increasingly criticized for being ineffective in fighting poverty.

Ten years ago, at the beginning of the last decade, most discussions of the future assumed that some form of guaranteed annual income would be created to replace all or most existing income support programs. While no such plan emerged during the 1970s, it is useful to recall the debate of a decade ago because it provides some important keys to income security options for the 1980s. There were essentially three reasons that the guaranteed annual income was proposed: to achieve administrative simplicity, to ensure equity and to fight poverty. It was argued that if all existing welfare programs could be combined into one program, the result would be a comprehensive assault on poverty that would save money and also remove the stigma often felt by recipients of provincial and municipal welfare programs.

Ten years later, Canada's income security programs are just as complicated, sometimes inequitable and much more expensive. Therefore, the major challenge facing the federal and provincial governments in the next decade is to streamline these programs into one comprehensive program that provides adequate support with administrative simplicity. Underlying the organizational options behind this challenge is a growing imperative: the need to aim income security expenditures more precisely towards those who need help most. Less than half of transfer payments in Canada go to people below the poverty line. While family allowances, old age security and unemployment insurance are all taxable, their universal nature means that millions of dollars stay with individuals and families who are far from poor:

> . . . a large proportion of social security spending, particularly through federal government programs, is not exclusively to the advantage of the poor but is also to the advantage of middle and upper income groups. This should solve at least

part of the mystery surrounding the seeming inability of society to defeat poverty, despite its "great efforts"; other factors may also be at work, but the fact that a large portion of social security spending is clearly not intended for the poor accounts for a major portion of program "ineffectiveness."[8]

Since it is unlikely that the transfer payment pie is going to get any bigger, then it clearly must be sliced differently. There are essentially two options for the future. The bolder course would be to replace the majority of our existing income support programs with one comprehensive program, preferably delivered through a negative income tax. The more modest but just as challenging approach would be to settle for incremental change to create closer and smoother relationships among income transfer programs and between these programs and the tax system.

The bold approach—creating one program to replace most existing programs—is appealing because of its simplicity. In that respect, this approach is basically the guaranteed annual income 10 years later, but we now know a lot more about how difficult it would be to create. Canada has just begun to experiment with delivering social benefits through the tax system. It is also clear that no matter how much integration of existing programs takes place, one comprehensive program cannot replace *all* existing programs. Even if all or most existing programs were combined into one, it would still be necessary for some provincial or local programs to meet emergency and short-term needs. It is also likely that special provisions for special groups would be reintroduced. Finally, the overall effect of guaranteeing incomes on the work incentive is far from clear, and consequently this aspect of the plan would be scrutinized very closely by the general public.

If the incremental approach to reforming income support programs is pursued, several interesting possibilities exist. The federal government could aim income security payments much more precisely at the poor by creating a richer child tax credit. This could be financed without additional expenditures by eliminating the current regressive children's deduction from the income tax system, or by recovering family allowances from families with above average incomes. Due to the continuing prevalence of poverty among elderly Canadians, it does not appear that appreciable savings can be gained by altering the universal nature of old age security. Another major issue to be addressed is the relationship of unemployment insurance to other income support programs. While the program was quite strictly based on insurance principles until the early 1970s, the changes implemented in 1971-72 broadened the mandate of unemployment insurance to serve other objectives and gave it a greater role in income transfers. Despite the fact that employer/employee contributions were supplemented in 1979-80 by $1.7 billion from general revenues, less than 10 per cent of unemployment insurance benefits go to the poorest 20 per cent of Canadians. Unemployment insurance could be made much more effective in combatting poverty if the program returned to a concept of self-financing, with the savings used to supplement low-income Canadians on an income-tested basis.

Special Population Groups

In the new decade, the Canadian social welfare system will face several other challenges presented by the needs of particular population groups.

The Elderly

During the 1980s, the first children born in the post-war baby boom will begin to reach middle age. As noted earlier, the Special Senate Committee on Retirement Age Policies forecasts that the number of Canadians over 65 will rise from 2.1 million in 1978 to approximately 3.4 million in 2001. This demographic shift will put considerable stress on the social welfare system unless certain reforms are made within the next few years.

If there is one myth in Canadian social policy that should be put to rest, it is that people retire in their early- to mid-sixties and live happily ever after, supported by payments from the pension plans that they have faithfully supported for many years. This is simply not the case, and one of the major reasons that poverty remains so persistent a problem among elderly Canadians is the failure of the private pension system to provide adequate coverage and benefits.

In 1976, only 41 per cent of the employed labour force was covered by a job-related pension plan. Vesting (the point at which employees earn the right to at least a partial pension and employers match employee contributions) and portability provisions of private pension plans are antiquated for a work force as mobile as Canada's; the Canadian Labour Congress has estimated that only 10 per cent of the workers enrolled in private plans actually end up receiving full pensions.

The statistics on survivors' provisions are even more discouraging. Excluding public sector employees, if death occurred before retirement, private pension plans provided a surviving spouse's pension for only 23.5 per cent of members covered by plans in 1974. If death occurs after retirement, 21 per cent of survivors are ineligible for any benefit, 32 per cent receive benefits for up to five years, and 12 per cent receive only their spouses' contribution. The impact of these failings in the private pension system are illustrated by the fact that in 1976 "of all income flowing to those aged 65 and over, only 13 per cent flows from pension income, 50 per cent from government sources, and the rest from private savings and investments."[9]

Clearly, the pressure on public income transfer programs is likely to continue unless the pension system is reformed. Some of the more progressive leaders within industry have begun to acknowledge publicly that changes must be made, but government intervention may be necessary.

It will not initially be easy to obtain widespread public support for pension reform, particularly if improvements are seen as costly to either pension plan members or taxpayers. Most Canadians think that their pension plans provide much better coverage than they actually do. On the other hand, several recent reports have documented the failure of the private pension system to provide adequate incomes for elderly Canadians.[10] It is not likely that the growing number of elderly Canadians will allow the federal government to escape this issue. Between now and the end of the century, either the private pension system will be reformed or public pension and income support programs will be forced to provide adequate incomes for Canada's elderly.

The rising proportion of elderly present another significant challenge that must be addressed jointly by the health and social welfare systems on an urgent basis. In a recent report,[11] Statistics Canada forecasts that if current hospital capacity and utilization rates remain unchanged, Canadians over 65 will require 71 per cent of all hospital beds by the turn of the century and every hospital bed in the country by the year 2021. It is not difficult to assess the social and economic implications of this forecast. While it is likely that the elderly as a group will always require a higher proportion of hospital care than other age groups, alternatives to hospitalization *must* be developed to prevent inappropriate and unnecessarily expensive institutional care of the elderly. Because many of the residential care facilities and community-based services required to prevent unnecessary hospitalization are funded by the social welfare sector, planning to meet these needs must be a joint effort between the health and social welfare systems. The natural tendency of the bureaucracies of these systems to plan within their own narrow jurisdictions could be a major deterrent to solving these issues.

Women

The participation rate of women in the Canadian economy has grown dramatically in the past twenty years, increasing by 19[12] per cent since 1960. In January, 1979, the labour force participation rate for women reached 48.8 per cent, a rate that the federal Department of Finance had previously forecast would not be reached until 1986. Further, women make up 71 per cent of the part-time work force. The data presented earlier in this chapter indicate the degree to which the incomes of women are significantly less than men. This is largely due to the segregation of women in so-called job ghettos, i.e., the clerical, service and nursing fields.

In the next ten years, the Canadian economy will likely be forced to deal with several implications of this influx of women into the work force. There will be increased pressure to enact and implement equal pay for equal work provisions in labour codes and human rights legislation. Since the majority of women joining the work force in the past ten years have done so out of economic necessity, the calls of traditional economists for women to return to home and hearth will be largely ignored. It could also be argued that society will increasingly be pushed to provide collectively for many of the community and volunteer services formerly provided by women not employed outside the home.

More firmly within the realm of social welfare policy and programs, the pressure for greater public investments in day-care facilities will definitely continue unabated as more women seek work outside the home. Another area of social policy that will demand increasing attention is the need for public expenditures for assistance to women who have been subject to assault or battering. The National Advisory Council on the Status of Women[13] recently estimated that one in ten Canadian women in a marital or common-law relationship suffers assault each year. The need for such services is likely to grow continually in the next decade as more women reject the laws and attitudes that support the traditional view of the family based on women's unquestioned inequality and which directly or indirectly condone wife battering.

Native Canadians

The Canadian social welfare system does not begin to meet the needs of Canada's Indians and Metis. Responsibility for social welfare programs for these groups is split between the federal and provincial governments and is further complicated by the variable legal status of individuals and families. The combination of poor economic circumstances on reserves and rapid urbanization has created major social problems among Indians and Metis during the past twenty years. For example, native children represent about half of the children in the care of child welfare authorities in the western provinces and about 20 per cent of all children in care in Canada.[14]

The social and economic circumstances of natives present a major and likely costly challenge to Canada in the next decade. Unfortunately, these issues are not likely to be comprehensively addressed until the question of long-standing land claims has been settled between native groups and the federal government. In the meantime, the lost economic potential of native Canadians will likely compound existing social problems, resulting in significant long-term social welfare costs.

---

[1] For a detailed review of key events in the development of social welfare institutions in Canada, see Andrew Armitage, *Social Welfare in Canada*, (Toronto: McClelland and Stewart, Ltd., 1975), pp. 213-219.
[2] For a detailed discussion of the construction of Canadian poverty lines, see

Donald M. Caskie, *Canadian Fact Book on Poverty, 1979*, Canadian Council on Social Development, Ottawa, 1979, p. 2.

[3] *Ibid.*, p. 29, updated to 1978 by the author.

[4] Bill C-55, *The Social Services Financing Act*, Section 2, p. 2.

[5] Canada, *Retirement Without Tears*, Report of the Special Senate Committee on Retirement Age Policies, Ottawa, 1979, pp. 42-43.

[6] See Canada, *One in Three: Pensions for Canadians to 2030*, Economic Council of Canada, Ottawa, 1979.

[7] See National Council of Welfare, *The Hidden Welfare System*, 1976, and *The Hidden Welfare System Revisited*, 1980.

[8] Ontario Economic Council, *Issues and Alternatives, 1976: Social Security*, Toronto, 1976, p. 11.

[9] Dr. David Ross, *Submission to the Special Senate Committee on Retirement Age Policies*, Canadian Council on Social Development, Ottawa, 1979, p. 16.

[10] See, for example, *Retirement Without Tears*, op. cit., and Canada, *The Retirement Income System in Canada: Problems and Alternative Policies for Reform*, Report of the Task Force on Retirement Income Policy, Ottawa, 1980.

[11] L.A. Lefebvre, Z. Zeigmond and M.S. Devereaux, *A Prognosis for Hospitals*, Statistics Canada, Ottawa, 1979.

[12] Judy Wasylycia-Leis, "Equality in the Eighties: Integrating Economic and Social Policies," New Democratic Party of Canada, Ottawa, 1979, p. 3.

[13] Linda MacLeod, *Wife Battering in Canada: The Vicious Circle*, Canadian Advisory Council on the Status of Women, Ottawa, 1980.

[14] See H. Philip Hepworth, *Foster Care and Adoption in Canada*, Canadian Council on Social Development, Ottawa, 1980, pp. 111-121.

Chapter 13.

Housing

Greg Mason,
Department of Economics, University of Manitoba

In most Western economies, housing policy has emerged in the postwar period as a major policy and budgetary commitment. In Europe, public intervention was inevitable, since many areas required extensive rebuilding; the scale of reconstruction made government assistance indispensable. In North America, especially Canada, postwar housing policy has evolved in response to political pressure from the middle-class whose aspirations to homeownership were too slowly being fulfilled, from low-income households who had difficulty in achieving even minimal housing, and occasionally from entrepreneurs who had to contend with cyclical market conditions.

The first part of this paper surveys postwar developments in Canadian housing policy and examines housing in the context of the economic environment. The second traces housing policy in Canada at three levels: federal, provincial, municipal. The third section suggests the likely future course of housing policy.

Housing and the Canadian Economy

Fixed-capital formation (investment) has always been one of the most volatile components of national income. Housing investment (both single family and apartment) usually forms about 20 per cent of total private and public sector investment in any given year, although with considerable year-to-year variation. Economists have been very interested in the housing sector, especially housing starts, since the construction industry tends to be labour-intensive and, from time to time, appears also to be countercyclical. That is, during business downturns housing starts have tended to increase, while economic expansion has been accompanied by a slump in house construction.

In addition to the role that housing plays in the macro economy, social planners have recently focused on housing, not as a countercyclical economic tool, but rather as a fundamental right to be enjoyed by all Canadians. The substantial price inflation in housing which occurred in the seventies caused concern about affordability and focused attention on the microeconomic issue of price formation, on concentration in the housing industry, and on the need for price (rent) controls.

Proper appreciation of the major issues involved in government housing policy requires that the role of housing in the macro economy be outlined. The long-run determinants of housing demand and supply are reviewed here, with special emphasis on demographic change, the creation of effective demand, and the role of the monetary environment in influencing the supply of new housing.

Housing in the Macro Economy

The post-war record of non-farm housing starts in Canada shows both a marked year-to-year variation in number and a pronounced change in composition. The periods 1958-63, 1965-67, 1969-70, and 1972-75 all showed significant declines in starts, reflected in the series for both single and multiple family starts. The record for row and duplex housing is much steadier and generally upward; most recently, growth in this type of housing has been associated with the expansion of condominium forms of housing.[1] These general relationships are shown in Figure 1.

Figure 1
Housing Starts in Canada

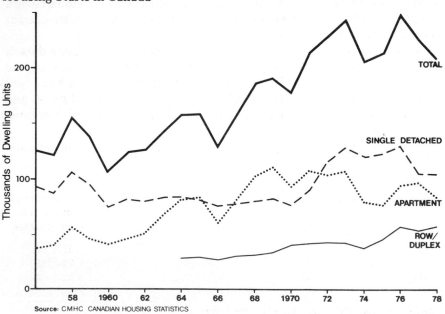

Source: CMHC CANADIAN HOUSING STATISTICS

With respect to the changing composition of housing starts, the following may be said. Until 1964, single-family unit starts outpaced those of multiple family units, but during the period 1965-70, this relationship was reversed quite sharply; after 1971, single family units were once again in the lead. The decline which occurred in apartment construction after 1971 was closely related to changes in the Income Tax Act, a matter which will be discussed below.

Housing Demand and Supply: The Long Run

Most analysts agree that the demand for housing is primarily determined, in the long run, by demographic change and growth of real income. Changes in relative prices (of housing relative to other major durables), the monetary environment, and some features of fiscal policy can also mediate the demand for housing, but these tend to be secondary.

Table 1 shows the measured rates of household formation over the period 1951-76 compared with the housing stock.

Care must be exercised in analyzing demographic data such as household formation. In most cases, the figures are crude estimates, based upon some official indicators of family formation such as registered marriages and divorces. Needless to say, these can diverge considerably from the actual rate of household formation. For example, a marriage will likely create a demand for an additional dwelling unit (if both partners lived with their parents prior to the marriage). Initially this might be an apartment, but after children are born, the demand is likely to become for a single-family home. In the event of divorce, demand may materialize for an additional apartment unit.

Another source of difficulty in the use of household formation data is that the ability to form a separate household depends critically on the supply of housing units. The ability of young people to leave home and live in their own apartments depends upon their income opportunities and the supply price of such units; the supply of housing may well determine the number of households.

One major demographic phenomenon is widely recognized, namely the

Table 1

| | Number of Households | | Housing Stock |
	Family	Non-Family	Number of Units
1951	3,024,285	384,010	3,522,162
1961	3,948,935	605,801	4,744,715
1971	4,933,450	1,107,855	6,324,690
1976	5,633,940	1,532,150	7,550,900

Source: *Census of Canada*, 1951, 1961, 1971, 1976.

so-called "baby-boom." The leading edge of this cohort was born in 1946-1950, while the last of the children who can be regarded as part of this demographic shift are now nearing their twenties. This bulge in the age structure of the population first impacted on the Canadian housing market in the mid-sixties, when increases in the demand for student housing, for small bachelor and one-bedroom apartments, reflected the large numbers of young people leaving home and entering the labour force or going to college. After a rather brief period of time, this group obtained more secure employment, formed families and redirected their demand toward single family units; they became a major factor in the housing price inflation of the 1970s.

Housing and the Business Cycle

Needless to say, general economic conditions will strongly affect the housing construction industry; the demand and supply of dwelling units will in turn have an effect on general economic conditions. The state of money markets is of critical importance: it determines the terms upon which builders obtain the large block mortgages that they need to construct apartments or row housing, and influences the demand for houses by prospective buyers. Students of housing economics have carefully studied the relationship between changes in the capital market and fluctuations in housing construction with a view to identifying precisely sensitive controls on the housing industry. They hoped to be able to "fine-tune" the housing cycle and thereby make it a superior fiscal policy tool.

Figure 2 shows the relationship between capital formation in the business sectors (plant construction, equipment purchases, and raw material purchases) and residential construction. There clearly appears to be a tendency for these two investment sectors to be opposed in phase. Other indicators of economic activity, however, show a less consistent relationship between housing and the business cycle. Figure 3 shows housing investment and the unemployment rate and year-to-year percentage change in real gross national product.

The Micro Foundations of Housing

Prior to 1970, the supposed relationship between housing and the business cycle was of far greater interest than the microeconomic problems of housing. The price inflation of the early seventies highlighted the problems of the rapidly expanding middle class in attaining their housing expectations. Questions arose of affordability, of price formation in specific housing markets, and of industrial concentration in the house-building industry, and these quickly became the focus of discussion. There was a general repudiation of the view that housing should be employed only as a countercyclical instrument; government, it was urged, had a responsi-

Figure 2
Per Cent Change in Residential and
Non-Construction Capital Formation

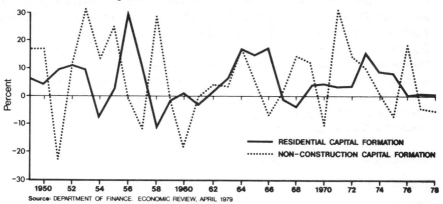

Source: DEPARTMENT OF FINANCE. ECONOMIC REVIEW, APRIL 1979

bility to provide adequate housing for every Canadian.

The so-called components of housing prices accelerated sharply from 1968 to 1978. Table 2 shows the main components of the shelter index prepared by Statistics Canada; interest rates are identified here as the major cost component faced by home buyers. In the early seventies, housing consumers were confronted by accelerating housing prices, with soaring land costs appearing to be the prime cause; at the same time, increasing interest rates placed ever heavier financial burdens on mortgage borrowers. These developments induced a series of policy measures by both the federal and provincial governments which were intended to alleviate house-buyers' burdens.

Land Costs and Housing Prices

One of the most controversial housing issues has been the relationship between housing prices and land costs. There appeared to be very strong evidence that soaring land costs were primarily responsible for the rapid appreciation of house prices. Once this connection was made, it was but a short step to a host of policies designed to moderate land prices in the hope that housing prices would thereupon decline or at least stabilize.

Actually, the relationship between land costs and housing prices is quite complex. If percentage change in land prices is plotted against percentage change in housing prices, an interesting relationship becomes apparent: housing prices appear to have increased before land prices. The data, based upon NHA information, are gross. Nevertheless, they do show what is logically the correct sequence of events. The only reason that a speculator or developer holds land is in the expectation that it will eventually (sooner rather than later) be used for housing or for some in-

Figure 3
Per Cent Change in Housing Starts and (a) Unemployment (b) Real GNP

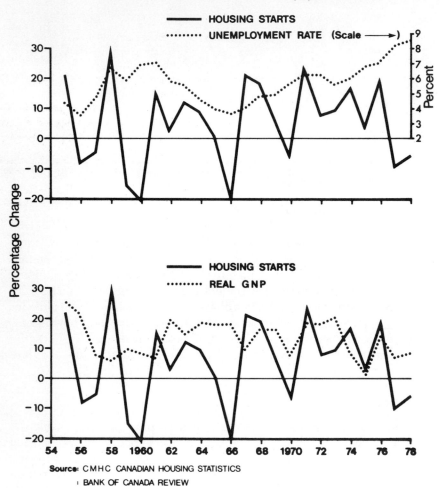

Source: CMHC CANADIAN HOUSING STATISTICS
: BANK OF CANADA REVIEW

dustrial or commercial activity. This expectation is fostered by the perception that the return on these land-using activities is increasing and that the demand for land will therefore increase in the near future. Hence, before the demand for land can increase, the demand for land-using activities must increase. Accordingly, the price of housing will rise first, in response to an increased demand for housing which presses against a supply which tends to be inelastic in the short run (say about a year). Increase in the price of land follows. Today's housing prices determine the

Table 2 Shelter Component of the Consumer Price Index   (1971 = 100)

	Rental Housing Rents[1]	Owned Housing				Housing Total
		Taxes	Interest	Repairs	Insurance[2]	
1971	100.0	100.0	100.0	100.0	100.0	100.0
1972	101.2	101.6	108.7	107.6	124.3	104.7
1973	102.6	103.5	121.0	118.6	154.7	111.4
1974	105.5	104.0	136.7	136.6	175.8	121.2
1975	111.1	111.2	156.8	146.6	212.5	133.2
1976	118.9	125.7	179.1	163.6	266.1	148.0
1977	126.3	141.1	198.8	178.8	305.6	161.9
1978	132.9	153.9	215.0	193.2	329.1	174.1

[1] It is widely conceded that the Statistics Canada rent survey contains serious downward biases due to sampling errors.
[2] Although home insurance increased more than mortgage costs, it generally forms a very small percentage of annual homeownership costs.
Source: Statistics Canada: *Consumer Prices and Price Indexes* (62-010)

demand for land, and therefore determine the price that people are willing to bid for it. Today's land prices in effect are determined by what people expect housing prices will be in the near future—the housing that will be built upon today's empty land.

Housing Prices: Micro Demand Determinants

The role of demography in determining the demand for housing has already been noted. In particular, the rising real incomes of the late sixties and early seventies and the demographic change associated with the baby boom must be reckoned as critical factors in the inflation of housing prices.

The rise in the effective real incomes of middle class families, especially young households, was an important factor in the increase in demand for housing. Increased participation in the market by women was another factor. Several significant changes to the National Housing Act removed restrictions which discriminated against women in the securing of mortgage funds. As well, households were entering the housing market earlier (partly in response to government incentives), as reflected in the declining average age of mortgage borrowers under the NHA. In 1960, the average borrower had been 35 years old; in 1978, the average borrower was 30. These figures are a significant indication of the housing improvement that Canadians were able to achieve. (The caveat should be registered that the figures apply only to NHA mortgages; data on conventional mortgage borrowers are not available).

In addition to the demand for housing as a consumption good (shelter and a personal environment), there was demand, stimulated by inflation, for housing as an investment good. Housing is always regarded as a good hedge against inflation; the spurt in inflation which accompanied the world-wide food shortages of 1972 and the energy embargo of 1973 induced many people to enter the housing market. Some were going to enter the market in any case; they simply did so earlier than they might otherwise have done. This increased demand served to confirm the expectation that housing appreciates faster than the consumer price index and is therefore a good inflationary hedge. Actually, over the entire postwar period, the price of housing increased at an average annual rate close to the banks' prime lending rate.

The demand determinants cited above are all in some sense "natural." Many analysts believe that government policies designed to assist the middle class with their affordability problems in the housing market further stimulated housing prices. More of this shortly.

Housing Price Determinants: Supply Side

Some of the more sophisticated reasoning to explain the rapid rise of housing prices in the seventies acknowledged the role of demand side factors, but stressed that the housing industry was a highly concentrated one and failed to respond competitively to market forces. It was alleged that concentration in the housing construction industry permitted a handful of firms to collude, either withholding units from the market or keeping land and building supplies from smaller competitors and thereby enhancing their own market power.

Evidence of industrial concentration is always difficult to evaluate. When the housing industry is examined at the national level, no conventional measure of concentration indicates critical levels of concentration. But housing, especially in Canada, is not a national industry; we must examine regional markets in and around large urban centres for relevant evidence of concentration. Studies of concentration in the real estate industry revealed that in some Canadian cities, three or four firms owned most of the land on which the city's growth would occur. Calgary, Edmonton and Winnipeg especially were characterized by a high degree of concentration in land holdings during the mid-seventies.

The leap from data indicating high concentration to evidence that substantial market power existed and was exploited is a rather long one. During the period 1972-77, the years when price pressures were most intense, the housing industries in Canadian cities responded in different ways (Table 3). In Calgary, Edmonton and Winnipeg, the rate of construction appeared to stall in the mid-seventies only to pick up dramatically toward 1978. In Montreal and some other cities, the rates of construction remained quite steady throughout the decade, with a slight downward trend reflecting a slowing of general economic growth. The fact that several regional, separate markets all experienced a slowdown in construction during 1974 could possibly indicate collusive behaviour. Alternatively, a pervasive change in the national economic environment could be the more appropriate explanation.[2]

Some observers claim that Montreal is an example of a competitive market while Calgary and Edmonton are examples of markets characterized by oligopolistic collusion. However, the decline in residential construction in the latter two cities in 1974-76 could also be explained by restrictive servicing and zoning practices on the part of municipal governments. Given the available evidence, neither hypothesis can be rejected; the issue needs further investigation.

The charge that vertical integration in the housing industry was responsible for rapidly rising prices is based on the fact that a number of large firms are both housebuilders and land developers. Genstar, a Belgian subsidiary, for example, assembles land, constructs houses, provides materials to builders, and markets housing. The relationship between vertical integration and market power is, however, a matter of controversy. All firms are to some degree vertically integrated. The general consensus in

Table 3 Dwelling Starts by Urban Area (Dwelling Units)

	1969	1970	1971	1972	1973	1974	1975	1976	1977	1978
Calgary	7,775	9,001	7,738	7,710	7,733	7,085	5,650	6,817	11,480	13,708
Edmonton	8,601	7,129	8,252	9,932	9,803	7,668	4,570	8,495	12,853	15,567
Halifax	1,999	2,520	1,951	220	2,760	3,255	2,679	3,662	3,678	2,705
Montreal	26,947	17,693	20,405	25,219	27,832	27,726	25,377	26,932	31,901	26,034
Quebec	5,006	5,825	8,776	7,756	5,653	4,422	3,988	4,976	7,001	8,284
Ottawa	5,140	6,917	10,396	11,469	12,541	15,036	11,313	6,556	6,730	8,492
Regina	1,657	891	955	1,010	1,731	1,372	2,397	2,665	3,372	3,129
Saskatoon	2,152	1,117	487	707	1,006	1,274	1,316	2,575	2,372	4,046
Toronto	36,289	28,276	27,423	41,156	34,701	39,448	26,055	29,251	26,691	25,866
Vancouver	14,247	13,488	14,984	14,044	15,580	15,814	15,750	13,662	15,753	14,895
Winnipeg	5,635	6,897	7,461	7,187	7,821	8,680	5,062	6,340	6,282	7,542

Source: *Canadian Housing Statistics, 1978.*

economics is that to exert monopoly power over the price of housing depends upon the degree of concentration in the final stage of production, i.e., in the retailing of housing.

The experience of some Canadian cities reveals how short-lived the market power of real estate developers can be. In Winnipeg, economic stagnation has produced a substantial outmigration together with decline in the growth rates of real income and employment, with the inevitable result that housing prices have also declined. Many builders in 1977 had an excessive inventory of completed houses which they had to carry through the winter. Several bankruptcies ensued and mergers are proceeding at all levels (land development, housing construction, and sales). For a time in the seventies, Winnipeg was considered to have one of the most highly concentrated and collusive house-building industries in Canada; currently, however, ''cut-throat'' competition appears to be the order of the day.

Housing economists have characterized the house construction industry as one with comparatively low barriers to entry. During periods of expansion, many small new firms emerge. However, economies of scale inherent in the construction of tract housing or apartment blocks favour large firms and may bring the demise of competition in the industry. Some analysts argue that the land-servicing policies of municipal authorities have also harmed small builders. It seems inevitable that concentration will increase in the housing construction industry in the next decade, and that exploitation of market power could become a problem, particularly in some regional markets.

Housing Policy in Canada

Analysis of government involvement in Canadian housing markets is complicated by the federal system and its evolution. All levels of government—federal, provincial and municipal—have had some housing responsibility since the end of the First World War, though until 1970 the activities of provincial and municipal governments were largely tertiary.

Housing policy in Canada can be roughly divided into three periods. The first commenced in 1935 with the passing of the National Housing Act (NHA) and continued, with changes in degree rather than kind, until the late sixties. During this period, the federal government had the prime responsibility for the provision of adequate housing, although only recently has that responsibility been clearly enunciated.

The second era commenced in the late sixties, and was characterized by expansion of the federal role together with the emergence of major provincial programs.

Finally, a third era, still inchoate, now appears to be emerging: an era of contraction of federal activities and modification of provincial programs, with greater emphasis on direct income redistribution and shelter allowances.

Federal Policies

Pre-1970 Federal Housing Policies

The first era in Canadian housing policy was characterized by federal support of credit accessibility for house buyers. The National Housing Act introduced a joint loan program with conventional lenders, which provided for subsidization of mortgage interest rates. The government in addition controlled loan-to-value ratios, amortization periods and other terms of these mortgages, and therefore had the capability of further stimulating the demand for houses. Variation of the terms of mortgages (the minimum downpayment, the qualifying income, the amortization period), could substantially alter the monthly cost to buyers and greatly alter as well the number of eligible borrowers. The effect on housing demand could be of major proportions.

Surprisingly, only the insurance companies found these NHA mortgages attractive in the first few decades of their availability. The absence of a viable secondary mortgage market, i.e., a market where those who had given out a mortgage could sell this asset before the amortization period expired, limited the participation of chartered banks and trust companies.

In an attempt to stimulate the secondary mortgage market, the federal government renewed supply side efforts in housing by initiating several new programs in the mid-fifties designed to stimulate the mobilization of capital for residential construction. In 1954, the Federal Loan Insurance Program replaced the joint loan arrangement introduced in the original National Housing Act. The government in essence safeguarded approved lenders against loss in the event of default and maintained the right to determine the terms upon which mortgages could be given. Certain market imperfections were also removed, such as the stipulation of a maximum interest rate on mortgages eligible for the insurance program; the interest rate limit was tied directly to the Bank Rate in 1966. In 1969, variable interest rate mortgages were accepted for insurance under the NHA.

These policies were designed to make mortgages easy to resell and therefore more liquid. Those institutions that had the capability and the willingness to initiate mortgages could now sell the assets to secondary financial agencies. They could then use the proceeds to initiate more mortgages, i.e., primary lenders would not have their portfolios saturated with illiquid assets and therefore be unable to undertake additional mortgage loans.

In 1957, the federal housing agency, Canada Mortgage and Housing

Corporation, entered the mortgage market directly and initiated direct lending programs. These reached a peak in 1970, when almost 20 per cent of all housing starts in Canada were financed directly by CMHC. The rationalization was that a good many qualified would-be house buyers were unable to obtain financing through NHA and conventional mortgages. In theory, CMHC direct lending was to be residual, drawn upon only to make up the shortfalls of other lending agencies. In fact, CMHC direct lending very quickly became a major factor and probably displaced some private lending. Nevertheless, it probably did augment the overall supply of mortgage credit, and to a considerable degree.

Post 1970 Housing Policy

While at the start of 1970, Canadians were probably the best housed people in the world, the rapid acceleration of housing prices created difficult problems for low income households. Federal housing policy did not address the basic concern of affordability felt by low income households who were anxious to achieve home ownership; nor did it deal with the housing concerns of other specific consumer groups.

In addition, economists began to assert the proposition that housing conferred substantial externalities, especially upon the generation which had least control over the housing environment: the young. Housing was no longer regarded as a privilege to be enjoyed after a mandatory period of rental accommodation, but rather a fundamental right to be enjoyed by all Canadians. Moreover, citizens in general benefited by having their fellows properly housed. The right to decent housing, it was widely held, should be acknowledged in social policy. Many studies sought to establish that inflation had effectively robbed a significant proportion of the population of this right. Federal policy was now modified and directed toward the promotion of home ownership, encouraging non-profit housing, revising the Income Tax Act to remove the tax concessions hitherto provided to the owners of apartment buildings, and assisting in the construction of "rent geared to income" apartments.

Government often influences the housing market by policy moves in areas which appear quite remote from housing. By altering credit conditions, monetary policy will have considerable impact upon the demand and supply of housing. As indicated below, municipal governments, through their control over land-use, can affect the construction of housing. Perhaps one of the most powerful instruments possessed by the federal government for affecting the housing market is the power to tax incomes and capital gains. This policy potential was highlighted in the early part of the decade.

Housing and the Income Tax Act

In 1972, significant changes were made in the Income Tax Act which removed substantial advantages hitherto enjoyed by professionals and apartment builders. The revisions to the Act removed the provision which had permitted losses incurred through the use of capital cost allowances (C.C.A.) on real estate to be deducted from non-rental income. The following example illustrates the effect of this revision. An investor who owns a concrete apartment block with an undepreciated capital cost of $200,000, annual gross income of $50,000 and expenses of $45,000 would, under the revision, no longer be allowed to transfer losses incurred on the apartment block to other, non-real estate income, thereby reducing that income and the tax payable on it.

	Under the Old Act	Under the New Act
Gross Income	$50,000	$50,000
Expenses	—45,000	—45,000
CCA @5%	—10,000	—10,000
Taxable Income	$—5,000	$\emptyset$

That is to say, the new act allows the capital cost allowances to be applied only until they reduce rental income to zero.

Needless to say, removal of these provisions significantly altered the plans and activities of many real estate entrepreneurs. Examination of Figure 1 shows that construction of multiple family units declined sharply after 1971 (the revisions were widely anticipated). The continued decline in apartment starts has been further exacerbated by the declining demand for apartments (recent demand has tended to focus on row/duplex housing and single family structures); rent controls have, as well, discouraged investment in rental accommodation. An important provision of the current tax act is the exemption from taxation of capital gains on principal residences. This provision, along with the exemption from taxation of the imputed income from home ownership, is a significant incentive to home purchase.

Subsidization of Homeownership

In the early seventies, the federal government initiated a spate of programs designed to assist lower income households to achieve home ownership. In part, the designers of these programs were motivated by the belief that substantial and desirable externalities are generated by good housing. In addition, even if middle income households were the prime beneficiaries of these measures, the "filtering" process, whereby the vacated houses of these households would be "handed-down" to the poor, could be relied upon to provide better housing for the poor—or so it was alleged.

Cash Grants

The initial programs involved direct cash grants by CMHC to lower income households toward the purchase of new houses (provided that they were priced below designated maximum figures). In some provincially sponsored programs, the purchase of existing houses also qualified for this subsidy. One of the prime reasons for this program was that the housing goal set by the government in 1970 (construction of 200,000 units) was in jeopardy, and a direct injection of cash into the housing sector appeared to be the easiest way to stimulate lagging demand. Originally budgeted at $200 million, the program was targeted for households in the $4000-$6000 range but, as Dennis and Fish report, only 11 per cent of recipient households had incomes below $5000, while 48 per cent had incomes in excess of $6000.

Assisted Homeownership Program (AHOP)

Certainly one of the most ambitious programs of the seventies was a plan designed to provide certain qualifying households with high-loan-to-value, low-interest mortgages. A cash grant was also available to those households which had secured conventional financing. Periodically the assistance was increased, and in 1975 CMHC was authorized to contribute $1200 toward the repayment of the loan. In addition, AHOP was also made available through conventional lenders, and many developers built housing in conformity with the guidelines.

The plan was introduced in 1973 with a capital budget of $133 million, and reached its peak in 1975 with an appropriation of $458 million. Since then it has been slowly phased out; by 1978, few new loans were made.

As a policy measure designed to stimulate the housing market, the plan had only limited success. It did encourage some developers to provide modestly priced homes to qualified borrowers; however, it probably also increased housing prices. Inadvertently, it gave rise to a good many defaults upon the expiry of original mortgages, when increases in interest rates and reductions in subsidies greatly increased the monthly payments required of families whose incomes had risen only marginally. The problem led to a series of federal and provincial programs (known as "AHOP stacking") to extend the benefit of AHOP.

Rental Subsidies

The federal government also undertook the stimulation of rental housing construction in the seventies. In several respects, the rental subsidies were more successful than the attempts at promoting home ownership, in that these policies were aimed at both sides of the market. Some policies, however, had negative effects on housing supply. Thus, the rent controls that were applied under the wage and price control legislation discouraged construction.

Federal programs, carried out under sections 40 and 44 of the National Housing Act, also provided for joint federal-provincial housing programs (most often public housing) and for direct federal initiatives in the field of public housing. The relative importance of these programs has declined in recent years.

Assisted Rental Program (ARP)

In 1976, CMHC initiated a program to encourage the construction of multiple, low rental units with the return on investors' equity being limited to 10 per cent. ARP provided for interest forgiveness for up to 10 years on a government-provided second mortgage (the first mortgage having been obtained in the private sector), and a tax shelter provision which permitted the builder/owner to use capital cost allowances in the same way as had been permitted under the old (pre-1972) Income Tax Act.

Non-Profit Housing

Although not strictly limited to rental housing, this program was initiated to stimulate the construction of new housing and the rehabilitation of old dwellings. The essential feature was that a conventional lender provided the bulk of the low interest capital (originally CMHC provided funds at 8 per cent), with CMHC compensating the lender for the loss incurred. The advantage of this program was that government funds were spread over a longer period since the annual compensation to lenders for a lower-interest return required far less immediate outlay by the government than did the provision of relatively large second mortgages.

Provincial Policies

It is difficult to generalize about the various provincial housing initiatives. Many provincial governments were content merely to participate in federal cost-sharing schemes under the National Housing Act and did not pass independent legislation or fund specific measures. Perhaps the most widely adopted of provincial programs was that of rent control; rent controls were in effect nationwide after 1975 under the federal wage and price control legislation (British Columbia, Manitoba and Quebec had already instituted their own legislation).

Rent Controls

Typically, under a rent control program, a public agency sets maximum annual permissible increases in rents. Most often these programs gear rent increases to cost-of-living increases, with the control agencies evaluating the claims of landlords for rent increases. Generally also they deal with tenants' complaints.

Some of the provincial programs, e.g., that of Manitoba, separated the market into a controlled sector comprised of old apartments and an uncontrolled sector comprised of new apartment units, in the hope of avoiding a slowdown in construction. In addition to causing a slowdown in construction, rent controls are likely to lead to evasive behaviour by landlords; where the rent is controlled, they may effectively compensate by raising the charge for other services or by skimping on maintenance. Some rent control agencies attempted to deal with these problems by stricter supervision and enforcement, thereby raising considerably the program's costs.

The basic problem with rent controls is of course that they treat a symptom, not the root cause—which is insufficiency of low cost housing. Accordingly, without longer term policies aimed at increasing the supply of rental units, rent controls may worsen the plight of tenants. If the private sector is to be relied upon to construct low rental units, the effective rates of return to investors must be made comparable to those realized in other areas of the economy. The government must then either provide subsidies or allow tax relief measures—either of which means that taxpayers subsidize tenants.

Land Banking

Several governments, using their own funds and assisted by federal grants, attempted to moderate the price of building lots, and therefore housing prices, by assembling tracts of urban land. These "land banks" were designed to be a competitive threat to private speculators in land who were allegedly withholding their stocks in order to inflate the price. Some advocates of land banks saw here a possibility of providing land at below-market prices to provincial housing programs. Still others saw land banks as a means whereby society could capture for itself the gain in land value that resulted from its investment in facilities that raised the value of local land. In general these aims were, however, mutually inconsistent.[3]

For the most part, land banks are being discontinued. Their substantial capital cost threatened other government programs, and, as became clear to planners, land prices were an effect and not a cause of high housing prices. Many observers have contended in fact that the massive intervention by public agencies in the accumulation of land banks served to inflate land prices even further in the short run. The public sector was often unable to be covert in its acquisitions and consequently these land banks were often assembled at above-market prices. In purely financial terms, the land banking program was perhaps the most wasteful of government initiatives in the housing market during the seventies, and provided few benefits to prospective home buyers; it did, however, enhance the gains of those people who already owned land.

Public Housing

In order to manage effectively joint federal-provincial housing programs, many provinces created provincial housing agencies which were designed primarily to accumulate the provincial land banks and to construct public housing. Public housing is usually championed on the grounds that delivery of the actual housing service ensures that economically weak groups do in fact receive the service and benefits of a decent home environment. Economists generally favour redistribution of income, which preserves consumer sovereignty, rather than donations in kind. However, housing may be a special case. It may be in the self-interest of the taxpayer to deliver housing, rather than give money, if it assists in the elimination of social problems such as juvenile crime. More cynical analysts suggest that public housing acts as a facade behind which social problems can be concealed.

Shelter Allowances

Public housing often involves high operating costs. Furthermore, critics argue, the per-unit construction costs can be prohibitive, and such units may be politically and socially disruptive to neighbourhoods, who fear that the problems associated with poverty are contagious. Several provinces have now begun to provide shelter allowances, consisting of regular cash subsidies that are geared to income, to assist specific groups. Two programs currently in existence are the Rental Assistance to The Elderly (RATE) in New Brunswick and the Shelter Allowance for Elderly Renters (SAFER) in British Columbia and Manitoba. Proponents of these programs argue that they permit a precise targeting of funds to deserving people, do not interfere with the market process, subsidize people rather than property, and allow poor people to integrate into existing neighbourhoods.

Just as federal housing initiatives have been reduced by increasingly nervous politicians, so provincial housing programs have also been cut back. Shelter allowances are basically seen as a device for replacing the increasingly expensive direct provision of public housing with programs which also appear to satisfy basic social requisites. It is still difficult to evaluate these programs since they are very new. They do, however, appear to reflect the emerging nature of government housing policies.

Municipal Influence on Housing

Few local governments maintain significant programs which are designed to provide housing directly; however, each municipality, through the zoning process, does have significant authority over the supply of residential land. In addition, most municipalities have strict building and neighbourhood regulations which require developers and builders to conform to designated standards and provide specific development services.

Many developers have identified municipalities as prime culprits in the housing price escalation of the seventies. In particular, they have cited restrictive zoning which limited the supply of residential land and complex regulatory processes which delayed the approval of subdivision plans. They contend that difficulties in the land use regulatory process were responsible for delays in bringing housing onto the market, especially during the crucial period of 1974-1977 when effective demand so rapidly expanded. Municipal officials counter by arguing that despite the increase in time required for approval, developers in many cities were in possession of more than adequate amounts of serviced land to permit accelerated construction; they allege that developers were more interested in maintaining their stocks of land than in meeting the expanded demand for housing.

Housing Policy in the 1980s

It appears clear that Canada Mortgage and Housing Corporation is in a transitional stage. Its role as redistributor of income through the provision of housing assistance will probably be cut back increasingly. Its prime function of administering NHA mortgage provisions will undoubtedly remain; however, more flamboyant housing programs such as AHOP and ARP have already been liquidated. In all likelihood, CMHC will remain a source of funds for sewage treatment, for some federal-provincial public housing programs, and the like. As provinces increasingly use shelter allowances as a substitute for the direct provision of housing, the federal government will likely be asked to share some of the cost.

The third period of housing policy will probably reflect government's growing faith in the market. "Privatization," or the removal of government interference and initiative, is becoming a dominant theme which reflects public (middle-class) pressure on government to trim budgets and alleviate tax burdens—and a declining demand for housing assistance by this group. Before a complete withdrawal of housing initiatives by the government is mandated, however, several fundamental issues need to be considered.

First, advocates of income redistribution regard shelter allowances, as opposed to direct public housing, as almost a miracle cure that is free of drawbacks of public housing programs; experience with social policy intervention during the past fifty years indicates, however, that mere income transfers are unlikely to erase the needs of the very poor. Although only the most naïve would suggest that public housing alone can eliminate the emotional and physical scars of poverty, it will probably remain a significant means of income redistribution, especially to dependent generations.

Second, now that the baby boom has subsided, many would be tempted to believe that the affordability problem has also subsided. This assumption ignores an emerging problem faced by a growing number of aged people in Canada. The present solution of institutionalizing them is unlikely to remain either financially or socially acceptable. By the same token, old people who own their homes either face increasing financial hardship as their fixed incomes are eroded by escalating costs of home maintenance or utilize housing stock inefficiently. Governments will probably be called upon to participate in such arrangements as reverse annuity mortgages, whereby the owner sells the house back to the state, acts as a mortgagor and uses the monthly payments to maintain income. Work should begin now to gauge the costs of such programs, since widespread predictions of impending pension fund inadequacies urge that the problem is a pressing one.

Finally, the inevitable future increases in energy costs are likely to induce housing consumers to direct their interest to more centrally located areas. In the same way that governments heavily subsidized the explosion of cities into suburbs by underwriting an extensive street program, the next decades may see governments assisting the cities to "implode." The Neighbourhood Improvement Programs may well have to expand rather than contract. In addition, a major social problem could arise if, because inner areas become much more attractive, the market value of houses on the periphery substantially declined, so that their owners suffered heavy losses.

---

[1] The term condominium has come to mean a townhouse, rowhouse, or in some cases an apartment with extra amenities. In fact, the term "condominium" is a legal concept describing and delimiting property rights in three-dimensional space. Recently, many previously undistinguished apartments have been legislated as condominiums without any structural alterations to the building.

[2] Housing data on a Census Metropolitan Area basis are difficult to evaluate. The growth of subdivisions outside what Statistics Canada defines as a city may well be significant, yet not recorded as growth for an urban area. For this reason, interurban comparisons of housing starts must be treated with care.

[3] One cannot recapture the full gain in value by selling at below-market prices. To acquire a significant inventory of land that would constitute a genuine competitive threat usually requires that much valuable land be assembled; once the land is sold the competitive threat evaporates.

Chapter 14

Research Support

R.D. Voyer,
Executive Director of Research Administration,
Canadian Institute for Economic Policy

Canadians like to believe that they live in one of the world's most technologically advanced countries. However, consider the following:

> Gross Expenditure in Canada on Research and Development (R&D) amounts to less than 1 per cent of the Gross National Product, a much smaller percentage than in any other major industrialized country.

> Business in Canada provides about a third of R&D expenditures and performs about 40 per cent of R&D. In most industrialized countries, the business sector is the source of some 40 to 50 per cent of R&D expenditures and performs 50 to 65 per cent of all R&D.

> For every scientist and engineer in R&D in the government sector there is slightly more than one in the business sector. In the U.S.A., Japan, Germany and Sweden, there are approximately five scientists and engineers in the business sector for every one in government.

We do differ from other industrial countries. The amount spent on R&D is low and the distribution of the R&D effort shows a serious deficiency in industrial research. These indicators reflect the unique history of the development of science and technology in Canada.

Some History

Our early experience in science and technology was related principally to the support of resource development in such fields as mining, forestry, fisheries and agriculture. The federal government was the prime agent in providing R&D support through institutions such as the Geological Survey of Canada (established in 1842) and experimental farms. Government expenditures were justified as providing a public good—that is, a good which everyone wants but the private sector is unable to supply because no private person finds it profitable to do so. For example, an individual farmer cannot afford to undertake research on new varieties of crops; it can be undertaken only by the government, which would act on behalf of the entire agricultural industry. The government becomes involved in a wide variety of scientific endeavours for the same type of reason: no individual firm can afford to undertake research that would be of great value to an entire industry.

The urging by industrialists for university research aimed at improving Canada's industrial performance was instrumental in allotting responsibility to the National Research Council, established in 1917, to promote industrial research in Canada. However, the universities were reluctant to undertake industrial research, feeling that this would lead to the erosion of their more familiar role of advancing the frontiers of knowledge. The NRC then separated academic and industrial research. It instituted a program in support of university research and established its own laboratories to conduct industrial research in support of Canadian industry.

The "National Policy" which predates NRC and is based on tariffs designed to encourage the production of goods in Canada led to large inflows of direct investment in Canada. The establishment of subsidiaries to serve the Canadian market behind a tariff wall stunted the development of an indigenous technological capability; subsidiaries could depend on the R&D capability of their parents and it was unnecessary for them to set up elaborate research facilities in Canada. Canada's dependence on foreign technology and capital (particularly American technology and capital) grew to unique proportions over time. By 1970, Canada's dependence on U.S. capital was some ten times higher than in thirteen leading member countries of the OECD.[1] With such a high level of foreign ownership of Canadian industry (e.g., 60 per cent in the case of manufacturing), it should not be surprising to find a weak industrial R&D effort (Table 1), since foreign-owned firms are so highly dependent on technology developed by their parent organizations. Also, the fact that the vast majority of Canadian firms, because of their small size, do not have the capability to undertake R&D and are not attuned to the potential of R&D, exacerbates this situation.

In Canada, both the federal and provincial governments have played a key role in the development of scientific activities. Governments have not only provided public goods to support the private sector but have also become directly involved in activities where the private sector considered the risks too high (e.g., Panarctic Oils), where the private sector failed (e.g., Canadair) or where the market system was deemed not to act in the national or provincial interest (e.g., uranium mining, potash, asbestos). Both the direct and indirect role of governments in economic devel-

Table 1 Comparison of Industrial R&D Effort for
OECD countries—1974 (Expressed as % of GDP)

Country	Industrial R & D Performance	National Gross Expenditure on R & D (GERD)	Ratio Industry/GERD
U.S.A.	1.6% GDP	2.4% GDP	0.69
United Kingdom	1.3%	2.1%	0.63
W. Germany	1.3%	2.0%	0.65
Japan	1.1%	1.7%	0.66
Netherlands	1.1%	1.9%	0.58
Sweden	1.1%	1.6%	0.67
France	1.0%	1.7%	0.59
Belgium	0.78%	1.3%	0.60
Australia	0.70%	1.2%	0.41
Norway	0.55%	1.1%	0.50
Italy	0.52%	0.9%	0.58
Finland	0.48%	0.8%	0.60
Denmark	0.41%	0.9%	0.45
Canada	0.36%	1.0%	0.36
Ireland	0.24%	0.7%	0.34
New Zealand	0.17%	0.7%	0.24

Source: O.E.C.D. DSTI/SPR/76.32

opment have resulted in a large amount of R&D being sponsored by and performed within government agencies.

As a result of this process of historical development, we have become burdened with a difficult problem. Academic research was separated from industrial research early in this century; a large part of Canadian industry has come to depend on foreign technology; governments, particularly the federal government, have acquired extensive in-house R&D facilities. As a result, communications and the technology transfer process between sectors are very difficult indeed. It is no wonder that when it comes to describing the R&D system in Canada, the three sectors, government, industry and university, are known as the three "solitudes."

The Economic Context for R&D in Canada

Because of our close economic ties with the U.S.A., Canadians tend to believe that we have a similar economy. However, a careful look at the two economic structures reveals substantial differences between the two economies. If the economic structures of the U.S. and Canada were approximately the same, there would be little relative spread in the output of various industrial groups between the two countries. However, as can be appreciated from Figure 1,[2] Canada's greatest relative strength (shown

Figure 1

Canadian Industrial Structure Compared to That of U.S. (1973)

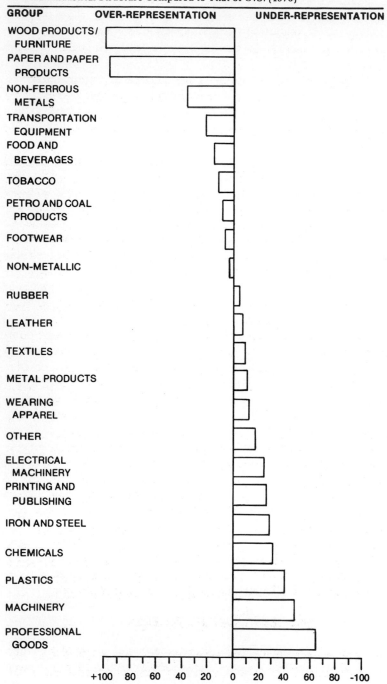

as "over-represented") is in primary manufacturing industries which are linked to resource development. In Canada, resource-based exports represent more than 60 per cent of total exports, while these exports amount to less than 40 per cent of total exports in the U.S.A. (1975). These resource-based industries are capital-intensive and consume much energy per unit of output.

The middle group of Figure 1 represents a more or less normal distribution vis-à-vis the U.S.A. This group contains industries that are labour-intensive and technologically static. Many of these industries have grown rapidly in low-wage Third World countries and are therefore subject to high risk here.

The industries at the bottom of Figure 1 are those in which Canada shows serious underdevelopment because of the large number of foreign controlled firms in these areas. In Canada, technology-intensive exports represent some 33 per cent of total exports, while in the U.S.A. these exports represent 54 per cent of total exports (1975). Those industries in which the level of foreign ownership is high in Canada are at the forefront of industrial development in the OECD countries. They employ skilled workers, involve a great deal of R&D and stimulate the creation of new industries. This phenomenon is truncated in Canada, however, because subsidiaries of foreign-controlled firms are rarely given the independence necessary to develop leading-edge technology.

The structure of the Canadian economy complements rather than competes with that of the U.S.A. This relationship is also reflected in the two countries' balance-of-payments situation. While the U.S.A. has a surplus in manufactured goods and a deficit in the rest of its merchandise trade (particularly energy), Canada has a rapidly growing deficit in manufactured goods—$17 billion in 1979—and a surplus in the other items in its merchandise trade account. In the manufactured goods or end-products category, two areas stand out in the Canadian deficit; the deficit in machinery and equipment alone approached $5 billion in 1978, while the auto-parts deficit stood at $3.6 billion. Such deficits indicate a failure to translate large domestic demand into domestic production. This failure means that we are importing much R&D embedded in imports, thus limiting the potential of Canada's scientific and technological capabilities.

The levels of expenditure on R&D, about 0.9 per cent of GNP in Canada and over 2 per cent of GNP in the U.S.A., are reflections of the different economic structures of the two countries; that is, they indicate how much R&D can be absorbed effectively in a particular industrial structure.

Recent R&D Initiatives

There has been a growing debate regarding the low level of R&D expenditures in Canada. This debate is intensifying as science and technology come to be more fully recognized as primary determinants of economic growth and competitiveness. For example, E.F. Denison of the Brookings Institute has estimated that technology accounted for 45 per cent of U.S. economic growth between 1929 and 1969. Also, it is becoming recognized that research-intensive industries outperform other industries. The Ministry of State for Science and Technology (MOSST), in comparing highly research-intensive with low research-intensive industries, found that the former registered, over a fourteen year period, 50.3 per cent greater growth in employment, 23.5 per cent more growth in output, 29.4 per cent more growth in productivity and 55.6 per cent *smaller* price increases. The contribution of high-technology industries to economic well-being runs counter to the assertion made by some economists that the support of R&D is merely a scheme to employ scientists and professors.

The federal government has recognized the importance of science and technology to the economy (particularly that which is related to industrial development) and, on June 1, 1978, announced a target of R&D expenditure of 1.5 per cent of GNP by 1983. The Conservative government, elected in May 1979, was committed to the even higher target of 2.5 per cent of GNP. As part of this policy, the private sector has been selected as the main performer of R&D. The implications of this policy are far-reaching, considering the structure of the economy, the high levels of foreign ownership and the compartmentalization of the sectors referred to earlier.

If industrial research in 1983 is to be 50 per cent of a total R&D effort costing $1.5 billion (in 1978 dollars), then it must triple its 1978 size by that year. This will require a massive alteration in the structure of the Canadian economy, with a shift away from low-technology industries towards selected promising high-technology areas.

Industrialized countries are finding that they must specialize. Even large countries such as the U.S.A. and the U.K., which traditionally have stimulated technological development across a broad spectrum, are finding that they must be more selective in order to meet the competition of a restructured Europe, Japan and the Third World. In the U.S.A., a current review of innovation has recommended specialization in specific sectors. The U.K. has already given top priority to the development of a microprocessor technology.

In Canada, the Science Council has argued for a strategy of Technological Sovereignty; that is, support of *those* technological developments necessary to maintain and enhance the country's political sovereignty. In a country which is as vast, underpopulated and resource-endowed as Canada, communications, transportation and industrial development linked to the extraction and further processing of our resources are obvious areas where we must have indigenous technological supremacy.

In the energy sector alone, some $300 billion is expected to be invested between now and 1990 to bring on-stream new energy supplies. Complex new technologies will be needed to extract in-situ oil sands and to produce and handle coal, not to mention the opportunities in the newer areas of renewable energy, such as solar and biomass.

Canada's new 200-mile offshore limit is putting pressure on government to develop the technology needed to exploit and properly manage the ocean resources within that zone. There are immense opportunities related to the fisheries and offshore petroleum exploration.

The mining sector presents new challenges and opportunities now that the era of "easy ores" is over. New technologies will be needed to exploit mineral resources in frontier areas and at greater depths; new processing techniques will be needed as well.

In the traditional field of agriculture, there will be needs and opportunities in respect to such matters as processing, storage, nutrition, food safety, horticulture, pest control, energy use, and so on.

Since natural resources and commodities must be brought to markets, transportation has always been central to Canadian concerns. As well as the traditional east-west rail and marine links, which have brought resources to international markets ever since the days when Canada was a colony, we now require northern extensions of this transportation system to move frontier resources; modernization is needed of the southern systems (e.g., light rail comfortable LRCs). The special nature of Canada's north (cold, ice, tundra, muskeg, permafrost) presents particular challenges. Moving liquid natural gas from the Arctic islands will require special ships, northern posts and specialized equipment to deal with the constraints of that harsh environment. Northern oil and gas exploration is furthering the development of specialized vehicles (air cushion vehicles, off-road tractors) that operate on muskeg and permafrost.

The vast and sparsely populated country that is Canada needs to be tied together by an efficient communications system. The ground network is now being supplemented by satellites for communications and remote sensing. New computer technologies leading to interactive visual communications systems (Videotext), coupled with fibre-optics, are creating important new opportunities in a country that has been described as the most wired country in the world.

Achievement in these priority areas would help correct the imbalances in our industrial structure and, by doing so, would help improve our balance of international payments as well as generally stimulate the economy. By importing fewer high technology products and exporting more of them, we would create the highly skilled jobs that are the hallmark of a modern economy.

Policies and Instruments to Enhance Canada's Scientific and Technological Capability

The key policy directions and instruments needed to redress the imbalance in Canada's industrial structure and improve our scientific and technological capability are captured in the elements of a Technological Sovereignty Strategy proposed by the Science Council. These are:

1. The control and enhancement of those technologies considered vital to Canada;
2. The encouragement of Canadian ownership of technology-based firms;
3. The establishment of government policies (especially procurement policies) that support the development of selected technological capabilities;
4. The encouragement of the establishment of a small number of large firms of international stature;
5. The encouragement of the development of a range of small innovative firms;
6. The establishment of major industrial and technological programs that address national needs; and
7. The strengthening of our basic research effort to ensure scientific capability.

The realization that industrial strength creates the proper environment for successful R&D is at the heart of the Technological Sovereignty argument.

The Control and Enhancement of Technologies Vital to Canada

As a small country, Canada can generate only a very small fraction of the world's pool of scientific and technological knowledge. We must use the knowledge generated elsewhere if we are to keep abreast of advances in international science and technology. However, the conditions under which this knowledge is imported must serve Canadian interests.

In the past, Canadians have not been overly concerned with how technology was transferred to Canada. As mentioned earlier, much technology has been obtained from multinational firms. Subsidiaries purchase the knowledge embedded in a product or process and are charged service fees by their parent for the management of the technology. Such service charges have been a growing drain on our balance of international payments. One estimate places service payments from subsidiaries to foreign parent companies at $44 billion in the last 30 years.[3]

Because of the lack of autonomous decision-making capability in branch plants, Canadians do not control many of the industries essential to act on the priorities mentioned earlier (See Table 2). It is therefore imperative that, in future, Canadians control development in key areas. This means altering the manner in which Canada imports most of its technology. Specifically, more emphasis needs to be placed on licencing agreements, joint ventures and government participation; there should be less emphasis on intracorporate transfers of technology which lead to dependence on decision-making organizations outside of this country. Through a licencing arrangement, a Canadian firm can adapt and develop the technology necessary not only for the domestic market, but also for penetration of international markets. Equity participation through joint ventures will also ensure that Canadians are involved in the key decisions surrounding the development and deployment of technologies important to Canada.

The economic history of Canada is one of government involvement in

Table 2 Rank Order of Canadian Manufacturing
Industries By Degree of Foreign Ownership
(Based on Sales in 1974)

	Percentage Foreign-Owned
Tobacco Products	99.8
Petroleum and Coal Products	95.7
Rubber Products	90.6
Transport Equipment	88.9
Chemicals and Chemical Products	81.0
Machinery	69.4
Electrical Products	65.6
Textile Mills	56.1
Non-metallic Minerals	51.7
Miscellaneous Manufacturing	47.8
Paper and Allied Industries	42.9
Metal Fabrication	38.5
Primary Metals	35.8
Food	33.3
Beverages	24.9
Leather Products	22.2
Wood Industries	22.2
Knitting Mills	18.6
Furniture Industries	16.0
Clothing Industries	12.0
Printing and Publishing Industries	11.2
TOTAL	56.3

economic development, either directly or indirectly. As noted by Herschel Hardin,[4] the Canadian genius is that of public enterprise. This historical experience needs to be marshalled and applied to attain national objectives. In many ways, Canada resembles European countries more than the U.S.A. because European governments, too, are active participants in economic development. Unlike Canada, however, they use all possible public levers and instruments to their advantage. Even in the U.S.A., where free enterprise rhetoric is rampant, the Buy America Act and the new Trade Agreement Act of 1979 are used as instruments for the protection of markets that are vital for American enterprise. The label "Japan Inc." reflects the partnership between the government of that country and its industry in economic development; a host of non-tariff barriers are applied to protect domestic markets. The traditional Canadian genius for public enterprise must adapt to the world of the 1980s if we are to control and enhance the technologies that are essential to Canada's development.

The Encouragement of Canadian Ownership of Technology-Based Firms

Canada is the odd man out. Where other industrialized countries favour domestic firms over foreign firms, Canada adheres rigidly to the principle of non-intervention. But where else is non-intervention to be found? Even in the U.S.A., the new Trade Agreement Act 1979 states that fair import competition can be curbed if found politically intolerable. Industrialized countries implement nationalistic policies while Canada hesitates. The economically successful nationalistic policies of the U.S.A., Japan and European countries should guide our actions.

The encouragement of the development of indigenous industry is a cornerstone of industrial development strategy in all industrialized countries. In Canada, we need to emulate other industrialized countries, reserving strategic areas of economic development for Canadians and encouraging the establishment of Canadian core companies, consortia and joint ventures that would lead to indigenous industrial growth. Such an activity would stimulate technological development and employment, not only in key areas of national interest but in allied areas as well, through the spin-off of smaller firms. A good example of this strategy is Canada's aerospace and telecommunications industry. Large companies that have been encouraged by government have created a market for high-technology electronic and engineering components in the production of satellites, aircraft and telecommunications switching equipment. This has led to the development of a number of firms supplying the larger firms with specialized components. The economy is stimulated and employment for highly-skilled people is generated.

This Canadian experience should be sufficient to show that we can only benefit by encouraging Canadian ownership of firms operating in areas vital to Canadian development.

The Establishment of Government Policies that Support the Development of Selected Technological Capabilities

The Canadian government, like all governments, has a number of legislative tools at its disposal which can be used to direct technological development in selected areas. The Foreign Investment Review Agency can be used for this purpose, as can tariffs.

The Buy America Act and the Trade Agreement Act are used by the U.S.A. to protect essential domestic markets; Canada's legislative and fiscal tools can be employed in like manner. Governments use their purchasing power as well to favour domestic enterprises. In a recent Canadian government study of international government purchasing policy, the Comptroller-General of the U.S.A. is quoted as follows:

> The Buy America Act and other buy-national legislation have been effective in limiting foreign procurement by government agencies of the U.S.A.

> In terms of national governments exerting influence over the procurements undertaken by nationalized industries . . . discussions with procurement officials showed that the governments exert substantial influence over the purchasing policies of the nationalized industries.[5]

Canada has been slower to realize the potential of government purchasing power to stimulate industrial development in the Canadian interest. The government market is huge. The federal government purchases more than $6 billion annually of goods, services and construction projects. Seventy per cent of government procurement is concentrated in only eight sectors. In 1975 the procurements of the main government purchasing agent, the federal Department of Supply and Services represented:

30 per cent of all shipments in the area of aircraft and parts
12 per cent of all shipments in the area of shipbuilding and repairs
12 per cent of all shipments of communications equipment
12 per cent of all shipments of scientific and professional equipment
10 per cent of all shipments of office machinery and equipment

The impact of the federal government on some industrial sectors is obviously of major dimensions. But federal procurement represents only some 23 per cent of total procurement by all governments in Canada; the size of the total government market is very large indeed.

The potential exists. Governments in Canada should recognize that the purchase of goods and services is not only an end in itself but a means of stimulating national industrial development.

The Encouragement of the Establishment of a Small Number of Large Firms to International Stature

There are Canadian-owned firms that can ensure technological sovereignty (e.g., Northern Telecom, C.N., C.P., Noranda). Such firms, however, need assurance that government policies will be supportive in the long term. To help these firms reach international markets, the federal government needs to promote Canada's trade and commercial interests actively and to enter into agreements that will provide the long-term framework for the development of Canadian scientific and technological expertise.

Also, government needs to direct its instruments toward the development and support of large Canadian firms. Such a policy, which has come to be known as the policy of "maximum unfairness,"[6] is applied now in other countries.

However, since Canada is unique in the industrialized world in respect to the level of foreign ownership of its economy, special policies will have to be developed to harness the potential of multinational firms. In 1975, the Canadian government issued a set of principles or guidelines for multinational firms operating in Canada. The major thrust of these guidelines was to foster in subsidiaries independence in decision-making and in their innovative and entrepreneurial capabilities. Among the specific guidelines was the following:

> . . . foreign-controlled firms in Canada should strive for a full international mandate for innovation and market development, where it will enable the Canadian company to improve its efficiency by specialisation of productive operations.

This guideline is directed at establishing in Canada a World Product Charter for the typical foreign-controlled firm; that is, assigning to it total and world-wide responsibility for a given product line. This may run counter to the tendency of many multinational firms to rationalize their investment on a continental basis, with their Canadian operation being considered as only a minor element. However, certain firms, such as Canadian General Electric (hydro generators), Canadian Westinghouse (turbines) and Pratt-Whitney (PT-6 engine), have found the world product charter to be profitable. From a national perspective, world product mandates contribute substantially to Canadian employment and exports. The fact that design, research and development, and managerial responsibility are allotted to the Canadian subsidiary as well as responsibility for manufacture and assembly creates employment for Canadians that is more highly paid and generally more desirable, and requires workers who are more highly skilled.

The Encouragement of the Development of a Range of Small Innovative Firms

Small firms can be the source of much innovation. However, the innovator or entrepreneur needs to be assisted if he is to establish himself in a keenly competitive environment.

As in other countries, small firms in Canada tend to be technologically backward and unprogressive. They often lack the technological capability and marketing strength needed to compete effectively. They can, however, overcome the problem of small size through joint ventures; they can thereby achieve the scale economies enjoyed by larger firms. Such ventures need to be encouraged. The Japanese, for example, have recognized that smaller firms are frequently the indispensable complements of larger ones; they provide specialized goods and services that could not be provided economically by larger firms. Japanese authorities have set in place a group of policies designed to nurture small firms; arrangements have been made for business groups, for the elimination of excessive competition, for the modernization of facilities. Canadian policy-makers could benefit by reviewing the Japanese experience.

To strengthen the capacity for technology absorption within small firms, there is a need to improve the flow of technical information reaching these firms. Industrial technical centres geared to the needs of smaller firms, in particular industrial sectors, could serve as effective means for providing them with the technological and marketing skills needed to bring new product ideas to the market. Prototypes of such centres are the Sulphur Development Institute of Canada, the Canadian Welding Development Institute and the Canadian Gas Research Institute.

The emerging university-based innovation centres could also provide much needed technical and commercial assistance to smaller firms. Mechanisms to promote better university-industry co-operation and government-industry co-operation are sorely needed.

In recent years, the Canadian Federation of Independent Business and other commentators have certainly raised the level of public awareness as to the potential of smaller firms and have made valuable suggestions regarding small business policy in Canada, including the development of technological capability. Now that there is a Minister of State for Small Business and Industry, there is a focal point for government action relating to this sector.

The Establishment of Major Industrial and Technological Programs that Address National Needs

The growth and well-being of science and technology is best assured by the channelling of funds through large programs aimed at reaching specific objectives within the areas of national priority identified earlier in this paper. Examples of successful programs in which all sectors of the economy have participated are the development of the CANDU nuclear reactor and Canada's satellite program. Such programs necessitate the development of a technological capability in the private sector and scientific expertise in the universities. This activity stimulates the economy and provides employment for highly skilled Canadians in advanced technology areas.

Historically, Canada has been very innovative in putting in place the mechanisms needed to operate major programs where the initial risk is so great that government participation was indispensable. Crown corporations (e.g., Atomic Energy of Canada Limited) and public utilities have come to be regarded as successful public mechanisms in areas where government leadership is essential. A variant is the public-private consortium such as Panarctic Oil. One particularly innovative management structure is the Alberta Oil Sands Technology and Research Authority (AOSTRA) which was set up to capture, hold and manage the intellectual property surrounding in-situ oil sands research and development. By entering into joint ventures with the private sector and controlling the activity, AOSTRA becomes an important instrument for the implementation of the Alberta government's policies regarding the development of the Alberta oil sands.

The experience gained from such management innovations can be used to deal with the challenges facing us in other areas of national interest.

The Strengthening of our Basic Research Effort to Ensure Scientific Capability

While it is important to develop the technological capability needed to capture the opportunities available to us, it remains essential that Canada's fundamental research effort be nurtured since it is the fount of the new knowledge and talent needed to ensure the long-term viability of the stance of Technological Sovereignty.

The 1960s were a period of major expansion of higher education and university research. This expansion was sustained by a healthy economic environment; it was felt at the time that Canada's basic research effort was finally reaching international standards. The efforts of the provincial governments to provide for the flood of aspirants to higher education were supported by a variety of grants from the federal government for both educational purposes and for research. It was a period of extremely rapid growth. Thus, between 1960 and 1970 the number of full-time university teachers grew at the average annual rate of 14 per cent. Effective planning was most difficult when growth was occurring at such a rate.

The era of rapid growth in the field of higher education came to an abrupt end in the early 1970s. In 1970-71, total Canadian expenditures on university education were 11.6 per cent greater than in the previous year. The increase for 1971-72 was 4.1 per cent; for 1972-73, it was 0.2 per cent. Such increases did not match the inflation rate so that the 1970s began with cut-backs in real terms, jeopardizing the effort of the 1960s. New approaches are needed to ensure that the research capability now in place is not lost because of financial cut-backs and a declining clientele for higher education.

The period of restraint that the 1980s prospectively will be, will provide the opportunity of moving from a complete laissez-faire approach to basic research, to one which attempts to orient university research activity toward national and provincial objectives. The newly formed National Science and Engineering Research Council is devoting part of its budget to research aimed at specific objectives. At the provincial level, Quebec has been leading by putting in place mechanisms, as early as 1964, to orient university research in particular directions (e.g., bio-medical research, action concertée). Ontario has taken initiatives in the health field while the newly formed B.C. Science Council is intending to provide direct support to research aimed at areas considered important for the development of the province. Alberta is using its Heritage Fund to support health research.

There also are attempts to set up mechanisms to bridge the university/industry interface and thereby diversify the sources of research funding.

As the golden era of university research is succeeded by the constraints of the 1980s, we can expect more initiatives that will tie basic research more closely to national objectives.

Conclusion

Policies related to the use of science and technology in Canada cannot be separated from other policies related to the socio-economic well-being of the country. The socio-economic context in which research and development are undertaken will determine how R&D will effect change.

The socio-economic benefits of science and technology are becoming increasingly evident. Science and technology can no longer be viewed as "exogenous" variables in formulating economic policy. If we are to become competitive internationally in the difficult environment of the 1980s and advance from a semi-industrialized to a modern industrial state, then science and technology strategies will have to be integral elements of overall national socio-economic policy.

[1] *Forging the Links*, Science Council of Canada Report No. 29 (1979), p. 38.
[2] J. Britton and J. Gilmour. *The Weakest Link*. Science Council of Canada, Background Study No. 43, 1978.
[3] Hurtig, M. *Canadian Business*, July 1979, p. 36.
[4] H. Hardin. *A Nation Unaware*. Vancouver: J.J. Douglas Ltd., 1974.
[5] J.J. Shepherd. *In Search (Enquête)*. Summer, 1979.
[6] *Technology Transfer: Government Laboratories to Manufacturing Industry.* Science Council of Canada Report No. 24, 1975.

Chapter 15

Labour Legislation

John Crispo,
Faculty of Management Studies, University of Toronto

A good many aspects of employer-employee relationships are subject to government regulation in Canada. The governing legislation is mostly provincial: labour matters are deemed to affect property and civil rights and are therefore subject to provincial jurisdiction. However, the federal government has jurisdiction over a small number of industries that are interprovincial in character, such as the railways and the banks, and parliament legislates in respect to labour matters in these industries. The legislation, of all the provinces and of the federal government, is broadly similar in character. Every jurisdiction lays down standards of safety and hygiene that must be maintained at work places, sets minimum rates of pay and maximum hours of work, requires that workers be given holidays and vacations with pay.

The labour legislation which is probably the most significant is that which regulates the bargaining that takes place between employers and workers in respect to pay and terms of employment. Every jurisdiction assures the right of any group of workers to bargain collectively with its employer; the employer is forbidden by law to interfere with attempts by workers to organize themselves into a union for the purpose of collective bargaining. In each jurisdiction, a government-appointed board considers whether a union does in fact have the support of the majority of the workers in any enterprise; if it concludes that the union does have such support, it will "certify" the union as the exclusive bargaining agent of that group of workers. Once the union has been "certified," the employer must bargain "in good faith" with its representatives.

Legislation exempts trade unions from two provisions of the common law which, if applied, would critically impair their bargaining power. The common law prohibits conspiracy, defined as planning by two or more persons aimed at injuring someone else, and the law declares that when someone's actions are injurious to another person, the injured party may sue for financial compensation. If these provisions of the law were applied to trade unions then they could never legally call a strike since that would amount to a conspiracy; and if any strike harmed an employer, he would be able to launch a suit against the union for financial compensation. Obviously, it is absolutely essential that the unions be exempted from these provisions of the common law if they are to be able to resort to the strike weapon as a means of putting pressure on an employer.

Public servants, i.e., the employees of the federal, provincial and municipal governments, also have the right to bargain collectively with their respective employers, though not necessarily the right to strike. Except for some designated categories, federal employees have the right to strike if they do not opt for arbitration. Some, but not all, provincial governments have given their employees the right to strike. Municipal employees have that right, though most jurisdictions forbid strikes by policemen and firemen.

Every jurisdiction provides for government assistance when a union is negotiating a contract with an employer. The federal government, and every provincial government, have on their staffs "conciliation officers" whose services are available upon request to help the two negotiating parties reach an agreement. And if, despite the good offices of a conciliation officer, agreement cannot be reached, the government may appoint a board of conciliation to consider the issue and make recommendations, the board being composed of a representative of the workers, a representative of the employer and a neutral chairman. The recommendations made by a conciliation officer or conciliation board are not mandatory; either of the disputing parties may refuse to accept them.

The Public Interests
in Collective Bargaining

The most useful way in which to approach the role of law and public policy in industrial relations is in terms of the public interests in collective bargaining. There are essentially three such interests to be considered.

After briefly outlining the nature of the three major public interests in collective bargaining, it is the purpose of this chapter to review how our laws and public policies endeavour to cope with them. In the space available, it will obviously be impossible to do justice to these responses in any one of the designated areas, let alone three of them. Nonetheless, it should prove possible to illustrate the basic framework of legislation that we have thus far developed, and to indicate what further steps need to be taken.

The concluding section will emphasize the competing and conflicting nature of our public interests in collective bargaining.

Overview

The first public interest in collective bargaining is to preserve it as an integral part of our overall social, economic and political system. Collective bargaining represents one of the important components of the hierarchy of values and institutions that form the essence of this system.

Undoubtedly, the key component in this hierarchy consists of what we loosely describe as fundamental Western values. Traditionally, these have ranged from freedom of speech and assembly to freedom of contract and property. More recently, such values might be said to include equality of opportunity and protection from deprivation, sickness and suffering.

Two other important components of this hierarchy of values and institutions are liberal democracy and mixed free enterprise, or modified capitalism. Liberal democracy can be described as government of, by and for the people whether in a congressional or parliamentary form. Mixed free enterprise, or modified capitalism, entails an economic system in which the bulk of decisions is largely determined by the interaction of supply and demand in relatively free markets. Like liberal democracy, such an economic system can cover a fairly wide variety of possibilities.

To understand how collective bargaining fits into this hierarchy of values and institutions, one need only refer to the propensity within our economic system for business and corporate interests to charge what the traffic will bear for their goods and services. Other groups in society cannot be expected to accept such profit maximization unless they, too, are allowed to extract all that they can for their talents. Many workers have discovered that they cannot do so on their own and have therefore resorted to unions to engage in collective bargaining on their behalf.

The second public interest in collective bargaining is in the procedural results of the process. These cover the strikes, lockouts and other forms of industrial strife which occur when organized labour and management cannot resolve their differences amicably. Although such strife is inevitable under any form of free collective bargaining, the public has every right to be concerned, particularly if the strife threatens to do real harm to society.

The public also has a legitimate interest in the substantive results of collective bargaining. These results include the many terms and conditions of employment that emerge from the process, all of which entail increased labour costs. While these cost increases are seldom the prime cause of inflation, they can aggravate the task of trying to achieve price stability. For this reason alone, the public is understandably concerned about the outcome of collective bargaining.

The Public Interest
in the Preservation of Collective Bargaining

It is difficult to generalize about the role of labour relations legislation in Canada because there are so many different jurisdictions and laws. Since, by constitution, over ninety per cent of our labour relations falls under provincial jurisdiction, there are eleven different sets of laws to be considered: one federal and ten provincial. Moreover, within both jurisdictions, there is more than one applicable law. At the federal level, the Canada Labour Code governs employees of the private sector and of crown corporations, while the Public Service Staff Relations Act applies to government employees. A similar breakdown applies in all of the provinces, but it is compounded in most cases by other special laws pertaining to particular groups, such as firemen, policemen and teachers. The comments herein relate primarily to those more general laws which apply in the private and quasi-private sectors of the economy.

Most labour relations legislation in Canada at both the federal and provincial levels is designed to facilitate, if not indeed to encourage, collective bargaining among groups of workers who choose to take advantage of it. Thus, just as we have statutes promoting corporate forms of business organization, our labour relations acts enable collective forms of employee organization. To this end, the law provides for the certification of unions that can demonstrate majority support among the workers in an appropriate bargaining unit. In many cases, a secret ballot vote is taken to decide the matter. Once certified, a union is granted exclusive bargaining rights for all of the workers within its bargaining unit. In return, it has an obligation to provide fair representation. Both a certified union and the employer of the workers involved are required to negotiate with each other in good faith.

Behind each one of these general statements lies a multitude of fine and not so fine legal points. Among other matters, there is the need to decide on the appropriate bargaining unit, to determine who is eligible to join a union within that unit, and to ascertain the majority wishes of those involved. The fact that matters such as these are now the subject of so much legalistic manoeuvring is grounds enough to question the efficacy of our laws in this area. The need for appropriate legislation is indisputable but unfortunately the concomitant abundance of rules and regulations gives rise to arguments and, frequently, litigation in their interpretation. Doubtless much could be done to simplify some of the existing procedures.

Just as there is a certification procedure, so also must there be a decertification procedure. A union may lose its certification and exclusive bargaining rights if it is proven to have won them by fraud, if it abandons them by in effect "sleeping on its rights," or if a majority of the affected workers decide that they no longer want to belong to it. Here again, a great deal of unnecessary legalism has come into existence, although less so than in the area of certification.

Today, in almost all Canadian jurisdictions, a group of employers can seek to have an association accredited to represent them in negotiating with a common union or group of unions. This employer counterpart to certification on the worker's side was originally developed to help stabilize labour relations in the construction industry, which were plagued by many difficulties caused by the seemingly unmanageable divisiveness on the contractor's side. Since then, accreditation has been extended to other industries where this has proven a problem, especially in British Columbia.

Aside from providing for the formation of unions and in some cases employer associations, our labour relations acts determine the reciprocal rights and responsibilities of labour and management. Violations of these provisions of the law give rise to what are known as unfair labour practices, for which various types of penalties and remedies may be prescribed. Two major restrictions normally apply to management. In the first place, management is not allowed to discriminate against a worker for engaging in union activity unless that activity occurs during working hours on the job. If management is found to have so discriminated it can be fined, and the worker or workers involved may receive redress. In the extreme cases of firing, those affected will likely be reinstated with back pay. Even this may not prove an effective remedy, however, since anyone so reinstated may find that he or she has no real future in the enterprise.

Certain curbs are also placed on management's right to speak out during a union-organizing campaign. In essence, management is barred from saying anything that would amount to a promise to do something if the employees reject a union, or a threat to do something else if they decide on one. These strictures are based on two considerations. One is that management should only be allowed to stand on its past performance, which it is free to defend. The other is that management has a natural advantage growing out of the traditional superior-subordinate relationship between employers and employees—a relationship that it should not be allowed to exploit while a group of workers is in the process of contemplating unionization.

Where an employer exhibits a pattern of blatant anti-union behaviour, special remedies are available to compel adherence to the law. Thus, a union may be certified without demonstrating majority support by way of a secret ballot if the employer's conduct has involved so much intimidation that it is deemed impossible to determine the true wishes of the employees. Furthermore, in several jurisdictions, the law now provides for what is termed first-agreement arbitration in extreme cases. This means that an employer may be forced to accept a first-agreement imposed by a neutral or third party if its track record is such as to indicate that a union will be unable to secure a fair contract even after it is certified.

The major stricture placed upon unions is that they cannot strike legally except over an initial contract or over the renewal of an outstanding one. Even then, as we shall see in the next section, they cannot legally take strike action until they have complied with the applicable dispute settlement machinery. Thus, they cannot strike to gain recognition, to win a grievance, or to stop an employer from engaging in an unfair labour practice. In each of these cases there exists alternative machinery intended to obviate the need to resort to direct action.

Just as there is a procedure for certification, similarly the law now requires grievance and arbitration procedures to deal with contract interpretation disputes arising during the life of a collective agreement. These procedures culminate in binding third-party adjudication—again designed to ensure that workers get justice without their having to engage in a strike.

With regard to unfair labour practices, the remedy lies in an appeal to the labour relations boards, which administer our labour relations acts. As already noted, this recourse is not always satisfactory because of the numerous problems involved in the enforcement of our labour laws. In the first place, these laws are not enforced as a matter of course: no action is taken unless the aggrieved party chooses to seek redress on its own.

Monitoring of our labour laws by an independent party might seem more equitable, in which case each jurisdiction could establish an equivalent to what the Americans call their Office of General Counsel. This is an autonomous division of the National Labor Relations Board in that country, which, like a crown attorney, can pursue violations of the law whether or not the aggrieved party is in a position to do so.

Neither are some of the penalties and remedies under our labour relations acts sufficiently effective. Alluded to earlier was the fact that reinstatement and back pay do not always prove sufficient to offset improper discharges for engaging in union activity. Often our boards appear even more powerless when it comes to the termination of illegal strikes. The most successful remedy in these cases usually is a cease and desist order with the full force and effect of a court order. However, few of our boards have sufficiently extensive powers in this area.

Although some of the provisions dealt with in the latter part of this section do not lead to the facilitation or encouragement of unions, that does remain the primary purpose of our labour relations acts. That they do have other purposes is by now apparent, if only in the sense of reducing and regulating the incidence of industrial conflict. It is now time to look at that purpose in more detail.

The Public Interest in the Procedural Results of Collective Bargaining

Strikes and lockouts and other forms of industrial conflict are the catalysts that make our collective bargaining process work. Labour and management have a number of natural differences which they attempt to reconcile during the course of collective bargaining. The two most important issues that typically divide them are the employees' share of the employers' total revenue in the form of wages, salaries and fringe benefits, and the employees' legitimate concern over income and job security versus the employers' equally legitimate quest for minimization of labour costs. What ultimately leads labour and management to compromise their differences is the fear of the damage that they can inflict on each other through a test of economic strength by means of a work stoppage.

Industrial strife is thus an integral part of the collective bargaining process. The public, even when it does appreciate the importance of this inherent relationship, becomes irritated by work stoppages, especially when they occasion inconvenience, not to mention hardship. Reflecting this public concern, Canada has long practised various forms of state intervention designed to reduce the incidence of lost time due to industrial conflict. In the previous section, it was noted that we ban virtually all strikes except those associated with the actual negotiation of a collective agreement. It is now appropriate to review how the latter type of impasse is handled.

Canada's traditional approach to this kind of labour strife has been to impose upon the protagonists a compulsory form of conciliation or mediation before they are allowed to take direct action against one another. Today the standard procedure calls for a government conciliation officer to enter a dispute before the old contract expires. The conciliator's assignment is to act as an honest broker between the parties. He or she will employ any number of means in an attempt to narrow the outstanding differences, endeavouring to persuade the parties to trade off various demands and counter demands. Only after the conciliator fails to reconcile their differences are the parties free to engage in industrial conflict.

It is legal for labour to strike or management to lockout at this point. Occasionally, as in the case of the 1978-1979 INCO impasse, a very protracted strike results. Compared to most other Western industrial countries, Canada tends to have fewer but much longer strikes. This is why we consistently rank very high in the international strike league. Our record in this respect upsets a good many people, yet many of our tests of industrial strength cause very little harm to the public at large. This is because substitute goods and services are available from other suppliers, or stocks have been built up in preparation for the work stoppage. Only when a vital public service is involved is there likely to be appreciable harm or inconvenience. Even then, as recent experience proves, it is remarkable how many so-called essential services can be shut down without causing undue disruption.

As a consequence of public sensitivity over the interruption of government services, it is only recently that civil servants have been granted the right to strike in most jurisdictions in Canada. Ontario has been the major holdout in this respect. It does not allow its civil servants the right to strike; rather, it compels them to accept third party arbitration. While the Ontario Government is pleased with the results, the union that represents its employees is critical. It wants the right to strike, as do almost all public service unions in the country. The governments which have granted that right find it difficult to rescind it. Some governments, such as that of Quebec, do not want to withdraw the right, because they would rather submit to strikes by their employees than to arbitration by an outside party.

While compulsory arbitration appears to be a very attractive alternative to industrial conflict, it does present awesome problems of its own. Some are straightforward, such as the questions of who is to do the arbitrating and on what basis. But even these issues are not easily resolved. Consider the criteria that arbitrators should employ. Typically, they weigh such variables as the cost of living, productivity and external comparisons with other similar workers. But it is no easy matter to apply these criteria fairly or objectively, particularly when they are in conflict. Moreover, some relevant criteria, such as whether or not the employer is having any recruitment or retention problems with various types of labour, seldom seem to be considered.

When arbitration is the chosen route under the Public Service Staff Relations Act of Canada, one of the criteria that the arbitrator is supposed to weigh in the balance is the famous "truck drivers' clause." It bears that name because, figuratively, one could drive a truck through it, so wide open is it to interpretation. It allows, in effect, the inclusion of any other factor that the arbitrator deems germane to his ruling. This, to me, epitomizes the risks inherent in the arbitration process from the point of view of both parties. It can prove to be a very subjective and value-laden process. And what ultimately applies is the judgment of a third party who does not have to live with the results.

Two more formidable problems result from the imposition of arbitration. In the first place, it can have a serious corrosive effect on collective bargaining by inducing the parties to avoid making concessions. After all, every time they do so they have to assume that the arbitrator will move them further in his or her award. This is because arbitrators invariably opt for a compromise somewhere between the positions of the parties.

Also to be noted is the adverse effect which arbitration can have upon decision-making within a union. Often more collective bargaining takes place within a union than between union and management. This is because unions have to engage in the very unpopular process of trading off the various demands of their different membership factions. This is an unavoidable process when the only alternative is a work stoppage. But it can be avoided under arbitration by leaving it to the arbitrator. Needless to say, this is hardly conducive to responsible union decision-making.

Like the vast majority of unions and a growing number of public employers, I would not resort to compulsory arbitration except on an ad hoc basis, as a last resort, when all else fails, and the public health, safety or welfare is jeopardized. In saying this, of course, I am acknowledging that neither the right to strike nor the right to lockout can be an absolute right in our society. Obviously if either right is carried to the point of really injuring the public, it must be qualified. But the right to strike and lockout is too fundamental in a free society to be tampered with lightly.

To ensure that interference with these rights occurs as seldom as possible, and to assist governments and our legislatures in their search for alternatives, I have long advocated the establishment of a public interests disputes commission. Such a body could prove especially useful in the sector under federal jurisdiction, which has a high proportion of industries in which work stoppages can eventually do a great deal of damage. The commission would be available to advise the government on how best to cope with situations likely to cause a great deal of public anguish. If nothing else, it might delay the kind of premature intervention that is induced by political pressures, even when such intervention does more harm than good. Of course, no commission or comparable agency could detract from the fact that ultimately it is the politicians who must decide when a work stoppage is so detrimental to the body politic that some action must be taken to cope with its consequences.

Before concluding this section, it should be noted that our politicians have already done a great deal to limit the extent and scope of industrial conflict. In the previous section, it was stressed that strikes are not permitted over recognition, grievance or unfair labour-practice disputes. As well, in most jurisdictions, our laws also ban secondary disputes—that is, strikes involving enterprises other than those directly involved in original or primary disputes. In effect, all general or political strikes are also banned in Canada because of the proscription against disputes arising during the life of a collective agreement.

Without going into any detail, it should also be noted that the combined effect of our civil and criminal laws is to circumscribe precisely the why, when, where and how of picketing and other forms of industrial action. Although, as in other areas of labour law, these limits do present some enforcement problems, the net effect is to protect the public from many of the potential procedural results of collective bargaining.

Perhaps it would be best to conclude this section by pointing out that there can be worse things than strikes or lockouts or other forms of industrial conflict. Although work stoppages can prove costly to society, unreasonably high settlements designed to avert them can prove even more costly. So too can high awards by arbitrators who are interested more in making their awards acceptable than in dealing with the merits of a case.

The Public Interest in the Substantive Results of Collective Bargaining

Just as the public has little protection from extravagant fees in the professions, unnecessarily high prices set by farm marketing boards, and profiteering by individual companies and even entire industries, so also is it vulnerable to excessive wage increases. It is in this most fundamental sense that the public has a stake in the substantive results of the collective bargaining process.

As in the aforementioned areas, it has been traditionally assumed that there are enough checks and balances operating in our system to ensure that no group can gain unfair economic advantage over the rest. That is why we have striven under our labour relations laws to maintain an overall balance of power between unions and employers. In selected situations, however, there can—and does—exist a real imbalance in favour of one side or the other. For present purposes, our concern lies with those situations where the imbalance clearly favours organized labour. When such an imbalance became patently obvious in the construction industry, accreditation of contractors' associations was introduced to help correct the situation. In several jurisdictions, special measures have also been taken in construction to bring about more industry, or at least trade-wide negotiations. This has removed some of the undue fragmentation in the negotiating process, which had allowed the unions involved to extract well above-average settlements by playing off the contractors against one another.

These are examples of the kinds of actions that we should be taking to deal with any organized group in our society that is clearly out of line. Unfortunately, however, such examples are few and far between. Consequently, when the country runs into a period when several groups seem to be demanding—and winning—increases from the economy that it cannot afford, we are driven to try wage and price guidelines, or even controls. The difficulty with these desperation measures is that they deal with the symptoms of our problems rather than their underlying causes. If we do, in fact, have a problem with excessive wage or salary increases— or any other kinds of income and cost increases—the solution does not lie in rolling them back. At best, that is a temporary palliative. What we really have to tackle is the basic power structures of the groups that are able to extract such increases.

Thus it is no use relying on anti-inflation boards, which only provide band-aid relief while causing all manner of anomalies, distortions and inequities. Rather, we must work toward the establishment of some form of federal-provincial incomes and costs board that would have a mandate to zero in on power and its abuse whenever it occurs in our economy. Its task would then be to recommend what could be done to reduce the privileges and prerogatives of any of these overly powerful groups. To do its job effectively, the board would have to have the status of the auditor-general and should be representative of the various interest groups in our society.

Organized labour could probably be persuaded to work with such a board, provided that its terms of reference were such that they covered all of the other economic interest groups in our society. And, of course, to have any hope of success, any such board would have to be meticulously fair in its recommendations. Certainly organized labour would resist having its powers subject to review unless it was convinced that the powers of other groups were going to be subject to equally vigilant scrutiny.

The establishment of a board along the lines described could be preordained to failure because of the unwillingness of our politicians to follow the advice given, should it run counter to the interests of any major pressure group. There is little evidence to date of our politicians being willing to tackle abuse of power at its roots. This is because we are gradually becoming a corporate or private interest state, within which there is a tradition of trading off the various power blocs against each other, with little or no regard paid to the public interest.

Conclusion

My conclusion must focus on still another kind of trade-off. In this essay, I have discussed the three major public interests in collective bargaining. It is difficult enough to satisfy our needs in any one of these areas separately; it is much more difficult when one comes to appreciate the competing and conflicting nature of these public interests. At times, it seems almost impossible to reconcile them. In the course of trying to avoid industrial conflict, for example, government conciliators often pressure employers to concede higher wage increases than they otherwise would. Aside from raising their costs and prices, these increases can establish precedents for other unions to follow. The outcome of this escalation process can contribute to inflation, thereby exacerbating the difficulties of those in government who are concerned about the results of collective bargaining.

About all one can say about the challenge of reconciling the various public interests in collective bargaining is that one should be ever mindful of the trade-offs involved. In terms of priorities, I would place the public interest in the preservation of collective bargaining at the top of the list. I am convinced that it is too fundamental a right in a free democratic society to risk being jeopardized, but this view is hardly shared at large. The public seems far more concerned about the perceived negative consequences of our collective bargaining system, mainly strikes and inflation. Consequently, the politicians are perennially under pressure to take steps like banning strikes and imposing controls, both of which are inimical to the survival of collective bargaining. Indeed, it is remarkable that our politicians have so seldom yielded to that pressure and one can only hope that they continue to resist it in the future.

Restraint notwithstanding, there are more constructive forms of government intervention than we have witnessed in the past. We obviously require more imaginative and innovative measures to cope with work stoppages that are doing real harm and with wage and salary increases that are aggravating our inflation problem. Resorting to measures such as those discussed in this chapter would lessen the public pressure for more drastic measures and thus ensure a more viable reconciliation of the various public interests in collective bargaining.

Chapter 16

The Regulatory Role of Government

Warren Blackman,
Department of Economics, University of Calgary

Introduction

Two centuries ago, Adam Smith enunciated the principle that a government should confine itself to three responsibilities: national defence, the administration of justice, the construction and maintenance of roads. We have departed a long way from his dictum. Governments today intervene in the economy in a great many ways to achieve a great many different purposes. To protect purchasers against the possibility of excessive prices, governments maintain boards which regulate the prices charged by public utilities that are "natural" monopolies or oligopolies. To preserve the competition that safeguards purchasers in many industries, governments forbid monopoly and oligopolistic collusion. Other boards and regulations serve sellers' interests: marketing boards, tariffs and non-tariff barriers to imports, minimum wage legislation—all of these aim to arrange that sellers of goods or services receive higher prices than they otherwise would do. Finally, some governmental interventions in the economy are designed to achieve public purposes beyond the interests of buyers and sellers. In this category are anti-pollution measures, Quebec language requirements, the Foreign Investment Review Agency, regulation of oil and gas exports, regulation of the professions, transfer payments, measures of economic stabilization.

A fundamental law of the free market system is that price is the product of two independent functions: supply and demand. One might lay stress on the word "independent" because any interference with either of the functions will not yield an optimal product, i.e., a result which is appropriate to a truly *free* market. Even more important, any direct interference with the price itself, whether in the interests of the general welfare or of a particular pressure group in the economy, must have a corresponding impact upon the supply and demand functions themselves, given sufficient time for the functions to adjust to new conditions. Thus, instead of the price being the product of two independent functions, the functions adjust to the price—a kind of tail-dog relationship. The end result of such an inversion of cause and effect is demand and supply functions which are different from what they would have been had the *conditions* of supply and the *conditions* of demand been free of the arbitrary price influence. Ultimately, this can only result in economic inefficiency.

Aside from public utilities, we rarely encounter in a democratic society prices which are arbitrarily dictated by governments. What actually happens is that policies are developed with the objective of influencing prices so that they are either lower or higher than would ordinarily have obtained. In some ill-defined manner, we attempt to "improve" upon the free market system such that a desired distribution of wealth is effected via the price mechanism. Any policy which is the consequence of political pressures will likely have little or no economic rationale. For example, Canadian anti-combines legislation, if designed to promote (or, rather, "encourage") competition, would mean lower prices for the consumer than would have existed otherwise. On the other hand, legislation to permit (and encourage) marketing boards means that prices will be higher than they otherwise would have been. Perhaps the extreme is reached in the case of public utilities where strict price regulation by public authorities is the general rule; here we actually encounter a negatively sloped supply curve which encourages *increased* consumption, so that consumer prices may be lower at the same time that more is consumed.

The objective of this chapter is to explore the possibility that economic efficiency may indeed be sacrificed in the interest of some form of income distribution criteria. In particular, economic policies which directly conflict with one another cannot contribute to efficiency but must, in the end, be self-defeating. This, it would appear, is the history of Canadian government regulation and policies.

Price Regulation Through Competition

It is obvious, even at first glance, that Canada has never adopted a policy toward competition in the sense that competition has been rigorously pursued as an objective. Indeed, Professor Skeoch has argued that there has never been any genuine support for competition as a desirable economic state.[1] This is obvious not only from early debates and discussions surrounding the subject, but also from the deliberate exclusion of banks and other service-oriented industries from the legislation itself.

The principles under which competition was to be encouraged were set forth in the original legislation of 1889 and modified somewhat in the Combines Investigation Act of 1910. This Act considered only the detrimental effects of combinations as objectionable, preferring, as stated by Mackenzie King, to "control the actions of combinations" rather than their actual formation. There were, however, procedures for investigating the actions of combinations included in the Act.

The Combines Investigation Act of 1923, as amended through the years, forms the basis of the current Canadian policy toward competition and, as such, does not prohibit monopolies or mergers unless competition is completely restricted. A somewhat weakened version of similar legislation in the United States, it emphasizes the word "unduly" which appears to be the key to the entire legislation. Since the word is not defined in the Act, it is entirely the responsibility of the courts to decide as to its interpretation.

However, the most interesting aspect of the Act is not the competition that it encourages but the monopolies that it avoids forbidding. For example, the Act prohibits conspiracies in restraint of trade. Thus, "*Everyone* who unduly limits facilities for transporting, manufacturing, supplying, storing or dealing in any article . . . is guilty of an indictable offense" (Sec. 411 of the Criminal Code). As every Canadian knows, those who are certainly the most active in the restraint of trade are trade unions which use the weapon of strikes, but trade unions are specifically excluded from the Act (Secs. 409-411). Again, to take another exception, most urban dwellers must be aware, or at least suspicious of, monopoly powers enjoyed by land development companies. By restricting the supply of land from the market until prices reach a certain level, developers' profits can be increased. It would seem simple enough, therefore, for six persons (residents of Canada over the age of 21) to apply for an investigation under the Act, *except* for the fact that real estate companies are excluded from its provisions along with B.C. fisheries, professional organizations, services, trades and the like. So it is that the Act really only applies to the narrowest segment of our economy—only the manufacture, transport, and sale of commodities and not even the labour which is included in the processes of production.

Within this relatively narrow area, Canadian law seeks to encourage and enforce competition. This it does as much by exposing suspected offenders to the glare of publicity—which itself tends to act as a deterrent to anti-competitive practices—as by legal enforcement. Any complaints or objections against a company are investigated by the Combines Investigation Branch of the Department of Consumer and Corporate Affairs which, in turn, reports to the Restrictive Trades Practices Commission. The Commission then holds hearings for the purpose of making recommendations to the Minister of Consumer and Corporate Affairs who in turn decides to prosecute or not. Since the Commission's report is normally published, the offender often voluntarily complies with the recommendations. The result is that relatively few cases have ever come before the courts. It is interesting, however, that U.S. law applies to the American parents of Canadian subsidiaries so that these firms are disciplined by the more severe U.S. law—a "violation," as it were, of Canadian sovereignty, but effective nonetheless in promoting competition within a large sector of Canadian manufacturing.

An attempt in 1971 to introduce a much stiffer law—the Competition

Bill (C-256)—was unsuccessful. Based upon a report of the Economic Council for Canada, it extended and strengthened the government's powers to include very many of the "normal" business and professional practices, so much so that opposition from the business and professional community was extremely strong. The result was inevitable—the bill expired with the dissolution of Parliament before the 1972 election year. Since then, modified versions of the Competition Bill have been introduced in stages, though final passage of the complete Act has not yet been accomplished.

The fundamental difficulty underlying all anti-combines legislation lies in the fact that no juristic definition of "competition" has been satisfactorily developed. To the economist, competition is an analytical tool, no more, and is not appropriate for universal application in the practical world. This is why the attempt to define monopolies, for instance, necessarily involves concepts such as "substantial or complete control" of markets, "public detriment," etc. which are themselves vague and subject to individual rather than universal interpretation. It is, therefore, understandable that the record of the government for successful prosecution for monopolization is poor. A similar problem exists in the case of mergers. The new Competition Bill provides for mergers only when there is a " 'clear probability' that the merger has or will bring about substantial gains in efficiency . . . ." But here too the ambiguity is obvious and the task for the courts a monumental one. Professor Gideon Rosenbluth argues that since the objective of the corporate enterprise is profit maximization, a great deal of the corporation's time and energy will be devoted to the development of monopoly. We are, as it were, trying to stem a tide with inadequate legislative tools. He concludes that activities of large corporations are not effectively restricted and that such corporations are not held responsible for those activities. Indeed, the record has shown that the larger the corporation, the less effective the Combines Investigation Act is.

While the federal government attempts to guarantee a minimal domestic competition policy, the same is not true for foreign competition. Here the objective is to effectively *eliminate* competition through the imposition of customs duties which increase the price of imports by the amount of the duty. The justification for such a policy is that Canadian industry must develop and grow to provide employment. The tariff of 1879 was the practical outcome of this policy. In subsequent years, the tariffs were adjusted generally in response to pressure groups within Canada, but always the ultimate objective remained—the development and encouragement of manufacturing industry. During the Great Depression of the 1930s, a Conservative administration sharply raised tariffs in the expectation that this would increase employment at a time of severe unemployment.

The Canadian tariff is actually designed to do more than encourage domestic manufacturing; it attempts to discriminate amongst exporting countries. Thus, there is, first, the British preferential rate which is applied to Commonwealth countries; secondly, the "most favoured nation" or reciprocal rate which is applied to nations that have negotiated trade agreements with Canada; and, third, the highest or "general" rate applicable to all other imports. There is, in addition, a special rate structure applied to some imports from less developed countries. The application of these differential rates, combined with a general trend toward lower duties since the Ottawa agreements during the early 1930s, has resulted in an overall decline in average rates from a peak of 30 per cent to about 15 per cent today. This is largely the result of GATT agreements and the so-called Kennedy round of tariff reductions. Nevertheless, our tariffs are still amongst the highest in the world, ensuring that Canada is truly a protectionist country. These tariffs aid our manufacturers: they are the prime beneficiaries of the income redistribution involved.

By now there is hardly a Canadian who does not accept customs declaration forms, customs inspectors, and the inevitable duty to pay as a natural, though annoying, consequence of foreign travel or purchase of imported goods. In defence of these arrangements, manufacturers have used appealing arguments such as the following:

> The foundation of our tariff policy must always be the development and maintenance of well-balanced and diversified primary and secondary industries, capable of providing a growing population with profitable and stable employment opportunities now and in the future.
> The Canadian Manufacturers' Association has the utmost faith in the industrial potential of this nation. It is convinced that the present and future welfare and prosperity of the Canadian people are predicated on Canada's continuing to be one of the leading industrial nations of the world.[2]

In a word, the principal thrust of the pro-tariff argument still lies in the job-creating function of tariffs. We know, however, that tariffs can create additional jobs if *and only if* other countries continue to import from Canada, despite the fact that our imports from them are reduced in favour of domestic production. Thus the argument, while sounding impressive enough at first sight, is precisely one-half complete at best. The truth of the matter is that instead of increasing job opportunities for Canadians, manufacturers actually raise the prices of their products to maximize their profits at existing levels of production; they are able to charge these prices because tariffs, as well as transport costs, raise the cost of imports to the Canadian buyer.

The result of the government's "Competition Policy" is actually quite different from what was originally intended. A largely ineffective Combines Investigation Act means that manufacturers can set their own domestic prices at levels which will maximize profits; this is made possible by the complete elimination of effective foreign competition. The upper limit of their prices is determined by the cost of competing imports plus the duty. Thus, should producers lower their prices, their total revenues will fall; should they raise prices, consumers will likely switch to competing imports. It follows that manufacturers will tend to set prices just under the cost of imports plus the duty.

At the same time, it is likely that manufacturers' production costs will be high because, without export markets, economies of scale are not readily available. Further, without the pressure of competition from imports, little incentive toward efficiency will exist. Hence government policies alter the characteristics of supply and demand; the supply/demand functions will have different characteristics from those that they would have had if a free trade policy had been followed and a truly effective Combines Investigation Act existed.

Marketing of Agricultural Production

While government policy toward manufacturing is one of classic ambivalence, varying from complete protection against foreign competition to an uncertain domestic "competition policy," the same cannot be said for agricultural output. Here the objective is clear—100 per cent monopoly in the case of marketing boards which account for about one-half of all farm cash receipts. Immediately the question comes to mind, how is it possible to have 100 per cent monopoly when the Combines Investigation Act prohibits it? The answer is simple. The same clause which defines a monopoly excludes those which exercise a "right or enjoyment of any interest derived under the Patent Act or any other Act of the Parliament of Canada." Agricultural marketing boards are statutory monopolies, specifically authorized by Parliament.

In agriculture, too, one finds a substantive conflict of goals in the form of two opposing policy objectives: one, an implied cheap food goal, to be achieved by subsidized credit, agricultural research and resource development, all of which contribute to agricultural efficiency and lower costs; and, two, a small-farm-maintenance goal, which means high prices for farm products. But high prices and stable farm incomes—the farmer's dream—do not encourage the innovations or cost-cutting techniques which the Ministry of Agriculture tries to make available to farmers. The insulation from the harsher realities of the free market provided by both the marketing boards and the Wheat Board discourages the technical innovations which make possible economies of scale and lower production costs.

For the justification of what is an apparent economic anomaly, one must seek other than purely economic motives. Farmers produce under conditions of perfect competition. At the same time, they are acutely aware of the relatively small number of firms in agribusiness—i.e., the firms that supply them with machinery, materials and services—as well as the very substantial difference between the price received for food by the producer and the price paid by the ultimate consumer. During certain periods, this consciousness of "injustice" can assume the proportions of a popular rural movement. This was especially true for the farmers of western Canada, for whom the idea of producers' co-operatives during the earlier years of their formation became a virtual religion.

Co-operatives are likely to be successful enough when producers are selling in global markets for which world prices exist. They are much less likely to succeed, however, where their market is local or regional and where membership is voluntary. A single supplier who chooses not to join a co-operative can materially affect the price in a local market, making it impossible for the association to achieve its price objective.

This was the experience of the Okanagan fruit growers who had formed a co-operative in 1913. During the years following 1920, increased output and larger numbers of producers resulted in falling market prices, so that members had an incentive to withdraw from the co-operative and sell their production independently before prices fell further. The inevitable result was a collapse of market prices and, for that matter, the cooperative.

It was obvious that the voluntaristic co-operative idea could not be successful where the power to exercise compulsion over producers was absolutely indispensable. In 1927 the British Columbia legislature passed the Produce and Marketing Act which provided for the establishment of a Committee with power to regulate the marketing of fruit. A similar provision was made for the marketing of dairy products in 1929, just two years later. However, both these Acts were declared by the courts to be unconstitutional because they depended upon levies to be imposed on producers to defray the Committees' expenses. Such levies were deemed by the courts to be indirect taxes which provinces were not entitled to levy.

Economic forces often triumph in the end over legal and constitutional obstacles. The bitter experiences of the Great Depression pressed home the necessity for more stable prices and incomes for agricultural producers and, in 1934, the federal parliament enacted the Natural Products Marketing Board Act, which provided for a federal marketing board with the power of delegating authority to local boards. These local boards would be empowered to regulate the marketing of produce and to raise revenues by collecting fees from both producers and dealers.

This legislation too had to run the gamut of court action and in June 1936, after many marketing boards had begun operating, the courts declared the Act to be unconstitutional because it involved invasion by the federal government of a jurisdictional area from which it was barred by the BNA Act; the Act had allocated to the provincial governments jurisdiction over trade within their respective boundaries. It remained, therefore, for provincial governments themselves to provide their own legal foundation for the already existing marketing boards, and this they proceeded to do forthwith. Conflicts occurred from time to time between the marketing boards of different provinces as one board attempted to sell its product in another province—thereby interfering with the selling plan of the marketing board of that province. To eliminate this problem, the federal government passed the Agricultural Products Marketing Act in 1972 which now provides for federal marketing agencies that will co-ordinate the activities of provincial boards. Hence we now have two levels of government providing a statutory basis for marketing boards in Canada.

Much of our food production is now sold at prices which are not strictly competitive from the producer's point of view. Prices are either set or influenced by marketing boards with the objective of maximizing profits for producers; since marketing boards are cost-free (any administrative, storage costs, etc. are met by producers themselves), prices will be set so as to maximize the revenues of the marketing boards. A board will not lower its price in order to increase sales if, as a result, its total receipts would decline. Little incentive exists for the introduction of larger-scale, more efficient production methods because, if any additional output is to be sold, it requires a reduction in the selling price and therefore in total sales receipts. If this is to be avoided, additional output must be stored, thereby adding to the boards' expenses and requiring further levies on the producers. The supply, therefore, is likely to be relatively inelastic so that increases in demand will result more in price increases than in output increases.

Marketing boards have been only partially successful in dealing with the problems inherent in a situation where farmers operating under conditions of perfect competition buy from and sell to monopolists and oligopolists. In negotiating with food processors they have not always been able to secure prices that are satisfactory to producers. Industrial milk is an excellent example. Dairy farmers in the 1960s were bitterly discontented with the low prices they were receiving—even though these were the prices negotiated by milk marketing boards with processors. In response to that resentment, the Canadian Dairy Commission was established in 1967 primarily, it appeared, to reduce the number of small producers.

Of all the government's agriculture-related programs, the operations of the Canadian Wheat Board are probably the most successful, so far as producers are concerned. The Board's success derives from the fact that it addresses directly the problem of the market relationship between farmers and agribusiness. Unlike marketing boards, which attempt to achieve a monopoly for a specific product within a local area, the Wheat Board maintains an export monopoly of western-grown wheat, oats and barley.

Its operating principles are simple. It buys wheat from farmers, making an initial payment upon delivery and a subsequent payment when it has sold the wheat. The size of the subsequent payment is governed by the average price that the Board realized on that grade of wheat during the year. The size of the initial payment is set by Order-in-Council, having regard to farmers' costs and prospective selling prices. That initial payment is a guaranteed minimum price since, if the actual sale price to customers turns out to be lower than the initial payment made to farmers, they will not be asked to hand back any part of that money—the government will make up the shortfall.

Since 1976, the incomes of western grain farmers have been underwritten in yet another way. The Western Grain Stabilization Act, passed by Parliament in that year, provided assurance to farmers that their income in any one year would not drop below the average of the preceding five years. Farmers are required to pay premiums into a fund but if the available moneys turn out to be inadequate they will be supplemented by government contributions. Hence the possibility exists that the Canadian taxpayer may subsidize the western grain farmer.

It would be difficult to argue that Canada's farm assistance programs should be abandoned on the grounds of economic efficiency lost. Certainly there has been in the past considerable hardship in a depressed agricultural industry. However, there is little doubt that the price stabilization program of the Wheat Board was more effective and "just" in the days when supply was inelastic and prices and farm incomes were subject to very great variation. Such was the case during the 1930s when the Wheat Board was first introduced. Today, however, it appears that because of the price stabilization program, the wheat supply function has become more elastic. As a consequence, we have had big wheat surpluses during periods of low export demand. These surpluses must result in economic inefficiency since they would not exist in conditions of a free market. It is this inefficiency which constitutes the true cost of farm income stabilization.

In the case of marketing boards, the opposite is likely true. Supply is inelastic; producers are assigned quotas to ensure that they do not "overproduce." Such a quota is often included by the market itself in the selling price of a farm when ownership is transferred, thus artificially increasing the value of the land. The consequence of this is that the consumer is forced to pay a monopoly price for the product, the price which maximizes total revenue. *Then* the supply is adapted to that price, the result again being economic inefficiency. In the case of both marketing boards and the Wheat Board, therefore, substantial economic cost is involved in maintaining farm assistance programs through government intervention. The Canadian public must decide whether these programs are worth the cost involved.

Public Utility Pricing

Of all the areas of economic analysis, the regulation and pricing of public utilities is probably the most complex and, at the same time, one of the most important in terms of welfare. It is important because the services of utilities are indispensable to our economic system. Energy to run factories, transport facilities to move products and communications networks to identify markets are all basic to our industries, regardless of the specific nature of the output. A further complicating factor is that the product of the utility is used both directly as a consumer good or service and also as an input into the production process, and this necessarily involves two separate methods of pricing.

Perfect consumers' equilibrium (Pareto Optimality) is achieved when no single consumer can be made better off without reducing the welfare of someone else. This implies that the relative marginal utilities of all goods consumed exactly correspond to the ratio of their prices. In that case, when the price of every product equals its marginal cost of production, resources are allocated precisely as they should be to maximize profits. If the price of anything exceeds marginal cost, producers can increase profits by increasing output; the market price is a signal from consumers that their satisfaction will be increased if output is increased. On the other hand, if the price of anything is below marginal cost, over-production is taking place and profits can be increased by reducing output.

In a world where perfect competition prevails, marginal costs invariably are rising so that profits may be increased or decreased by altering the amount of output. Unfortunately, such a world of perfect competition does not exist. Many industries produce under conditions of increasing returns (decreasing marginal costs); it is not possible in their case for price to equal marginal cost and still equal *average total costs*.

Much of our public utility production takes place precisely under these cost conditions. Our entire public transport system, requiring fleets of buses, railroad tracks and rolling stock, as well as much of our electricity production, are specific examples. Consider for a moment civic transit systems and the dilemma in which most modern cities find themselves. Daily commuters require transport from their suburban residences to downtown core areas. Consciously or otherwise, they will seek Pareto Optimality and attempt to equate their marginal utility with price which, in turn, should equal marginal cost. In this case, the price is the marginal cost of operating their private car, their alternative to public transit. Assuming that this alternative costs anything less than a bus or rail ticket, it follows that the civic transit system is unable to meet its average total costs; indeed, there is scarcely a North American city which does not operate its transit system at a loss. Someone (the taxpayer) must provide a subsidy. If civic authorities wish to run their transit systems on a fully self-supporting basis, with users paying the full operating cost, then they should stop providing free accommodation for automobiles (road systems, parking facilities, etc.). In that case, the marginal cost of the automobile as a competing form of transport would rise to such a degree that the public would shift from private to public transit. A lower average cost of public transit systems and lower prices for consumers could result. However, at the same time that the transit system would pay its way, it would be violating the principle that an optimum result is achieved when price equals marginal cost; for this there is no practical solution.

The downward sloping supply curve is a common characteristic of public utilities in general and poses the greatest problems in price determination. The difficulty is compounded because the consumer is often not in a position to have freedom of choice as in an ordinary competitive market. Hence the price is not the reflection of competing supply-demand relationships at all; there simply are no alternatives. Pareto Optimality becomes even more remote.

The whole area of communications (telephone, telegraph, broadcasting, etc.) exhibits this problem. In some cases, e.g., the telephone system of the three prairie provinces, there is public ownership, but it does not eliminate the problem of rate setting. In other cases, e.g., broadcasting and transport, government commissions (CRTC, Canadian Transport Commission, etc.) control both prices and licences to operate. In these cases, a certain public responsibility is involved which does not lend itself to free market pricing. The "Canadian content" rule of broadcasting is an example of such a responsibility that cannot be included in the free market system for the reason that Canadian talent could not meet foreign competition in a free market situation.

A similar situation prevails in the case of airlines, railways, pipelines, etc. which are under the jurisdiction of the Canadian Transport Commission. These are "natural monopolies" in the sense that if there were more than one operating firm each would have a reduced share of the market; available economies of scale would not be captured. Licencing is therefore employed to limit entry and rate regulation in order to protect buyers against the monopolistic exploitation which is thereby made possible. The classic case of Air Canada and CP Air and the division of routes between them is an example of the problems facing not only the companies themselves but also government regulatory bodies. Competition is simply not feasible in such cases.

Probably the industry that comes closest to being a true *natural monopoly* is that of electricity supply. Every user is linked to a single supplier only, and simply cannot do without the service. All kinds of industries absolutely depend on electrical power. The cost and availability of electric power determine not only the amount of leisure time available to us (our appliances are truly domestic servants) but how we use it—watching television and the like. It is no accident, therefore, that in

Canada most electrical power generating capacity is publicly owned. The enormously successful Ontario Hydro has demonstrated both the feasibility and the desirability of public ownership. The industrial complex of southern Ontario has been made possible by the availability of cheap power, particularly hydro power. The electricity supply industry is practically the textbook case of a natural monopoly faced by highly inelastic demand.

Just as in the case of other public utilities, the capital-intensive nature of electricity generating capacity produces a downward sloping supply function. Average cost decreases as increasing amounts are consumed. Cost and demand are therefore interdependent. This interdependency is expressed in the circular logic often used by utility companies when pressed to explain high rates: "Charges are high because consumption is low." The recent energy conservation "fad" is a case in point. A utility company in California protested that unless electrical consumption increased to something like its former level, *rates* would have to be increased.

In the final analysis, the hydro electricity industry, like reserves of oil and gas, is the clearest candidate for public ownership. Since there are virtually no substitutes for such scarce resources, revenues derived from their sale are really in the nature of economic rents. The pricing of electricity, therefore, is quite arbitrary as far as economic analysis is concerned. Since no substitutes exist for energy resources, pricing on the basis of competition is not possible; hence free market pricing is impossible. This means that the "just" price or "fair" price (whatever that may mean) is the only solution. This is another way of saying that when economic analysis fails, the politicians and the courts make the decisions, based on their criteria.

The Government and Pollution Control

The principle that social product can be different from private product is by no means new. A.C. Pigou clearly enunciated it many years ago in his *Economics of Welfare* and justified the intervention of the state in cases where self-interest failed to make the "national dividend" as large as it might have been. The question of *how* to interfere efficiently and *how* the value of the social product is to be measured was not answered by Pigou, nor has it been answered by any other economist to this day.

The problem of industrial pollution abatement springs from the fact that the marketplace is not equipped to price the social satisfaction—or harm—generated by the consumption of any product. One person's satisfaction gained from the consumption of gasoline in a high-powered automobile may be measured in cents per litre, but we cannot evaluate in the market the social discomfort attributable to the inhalation of his exhaust fumes. All we know is that such externalities (the exhaust fumes in this case) do exist; they are very real, and pollution causes a decrement in the social net product.

The degree of cleanliness of our air and water should be the outcome of a conscious trade-off between production of commodities and having clean air and water. The public would have to choose among all of the "things" that it wishes to enjoy in terms of consumption and the degree of purity that it desires of air and water—it cannot have both 100 per cent purity and everything that industry is capable of producing. Since this is fundamentally a non-economic decision (it cannot be decided within the free market), the public would have to make its wishes known by way of the democratic process of voting for a particular option. Political parties at all levels of government would be required to include regulation of the quality of air and water as an issue in their party platforms. Having determined the desired level of purity, a tax would be applied to polluters, related to the amount of pollution that each caused and scheduled to deter pollution beyond the acceptable level. The free market system would include this tax as part of its cost. The hitherto "free" resources of air and water would now have a cost to users who degraded their quality.

While mineral resources are the property of the provinces, ownership of the "scarce" resources, pure air and water, could be assigned to either the federal or provincial level of government. An "economic rent" would be collected from polluting industries which in turn would recoup this cost from the public. The price level of consumer goods, therefore, would ultimately reflect the cost of the now "scarce" resources of clean air and water. Furthermore, the *relative* price structure of all consumer goods would reflect the amount of pollution which each producing industry contributed; hence the consumption pattern of the public would be altered in favour of less-polluting industries.

The proceeds of the rents collected in this way could be used, presumably along with other revenues, to defray the cost of waste disposal arrangements. The revenue so realized, however, would be part of the total public revenue out of which all public services are financed, including police and fire protection, education, etc. Since the capacity of a public authority to provide all of these services is limited by the size of its total revenue, and the other demands on its revenues compete with waste disposal and cleanliness, the public would be required to choose, on the basis of trade-offs, that portion of its financial resources which should be allocated to the achievement of cleanliness. The public preference would be revealed by the democratic process, i.e., candidates for office would be adjudged in part by the degree of cleanliness that they proposed for their constituency.

It is not proposed that *all* problems of pollution could be solved by means of the mechanism of the free market or by the expenditure of public funds directed through a voting procedure. When pollution crosses provincial or national boundaries, the problem takes on an interprovincial or international dimension. It is to be hoped that the legal and jurisdictional questions generated can be resolved by men of good will in both provinces and nations. Within a single jurisdiction, free market mechanisms may be employed. It would be a mistake to overlook their capacity to contribute to the achievement of a superior solution—if applied along with the public's revealed preferences.

---

[1] L.A. Skeoch, *Restrictive Trade Practice in Canada*. McClelland and Stewart, Toronto, 1966; reprinted in *Business and Government in Canada*, Rea and McLeod, eds. Methuen, Toronto, 1969, p. 147.
[2] "Tariff Policy for Canada," Canadian Manufacturers' Association. Submission to the Canadian Tariffs and Trade Committee, May 1964.

Chapter 17

Regional Assistance

Roy George,
Department of Economics, Dalhousie University

Just as some countries are poorer than others, so some regions are poorer than other regions of the same country. Scotland is economically worse off than south-eastern Britain; southern Italy is poor compared to northern Italy; malnutrition in northern Ghana is worse than in the south; residents of Calcutta suffer more than their compatriots in and near Bombay; New Zealand's south island is less prosperous than its north; Americans in the deep south live at economic levels below Californians; and poverty is more pronounced in Mexico's countryside than it is in its capital.

Canada exhibits the same disparities, as Table 1 shows. Ontario, British Columbia and Alberta are the "have" provinces, while the Atlantic provinces are the "have-nots," with lower personal incomes.

It is often objected that personal income per person is an imperfect measure of well-being. This is true. Official statistics have difficulty in catching all of the incomes that people receive: housewives' services are omitted, a particularly important omission in provinces where relatively few women have jobs outside the home; and the value of products grown and used by farmers and fishermen is probably understated. And the advantage of living at a slow pace in the clean air of a small Maritime town is considered by many Haligonians to be of value, a non-monetary form of income, of which Torontonians living in their polluted rat race are deprived. Official statistics do not reflect it, however.

Nevertheless, imperfect though it may be, personal income per person is as good a measure of economic well-being as we have, and the general picture it presents is realistic. Other measures confirm this; for instance, as Table 2 shows, figures of unemployment, another indicator of the state of prosperity, point in much the same direction, and figures showing the proportion of the population aged 15 to 64 in the labour force (the "participation rate"), a measure of concealed unemployment, paint a similar picture.

Economic disparities do not, of course, stop at provincial boundaries.

Table 1 Personal Income per Person, by Province, 1978

| Province | Personal Income per Person | |
	Actual	% of Canada
Newfoundland	$5,313	66%
Prince Edward Island	5,574	69
Nova Scotia	6,447	80
New Brunswick	5,984	74
Quebec	7,628	95
Ontario	8,735	109
Manitoba	7,456	93
Saskatchewan	7,432	92
Alberta	8,407	104
British Columbia	8,784	109
Canada	8,049	100

Source: Statistics Canada, *National Income and Expenditure Accounts 1964-1978* (Cat. 13-201).

Within provinces, there are areas which are much poorer than others. Newfoundlanders in the outports are still (notwithstanding the recent prosperity of the fishing industry) economically worse off than the average resident of St. John's, and people in parts of Northern Ontario live on less than does the average Torontonian. The smaller the parts into which one divides the country, the more disparities are revealed. However, for convenience, provincial boundaries have traditionally defined the boundaries for most discussions of regional disparities in Canada, and we will keep to tradition in our subsequent discussion.

In talking about income levels in Canada and the "haves" and the "have-nots," one should keep a sense of perspective. The poor in Canada

Table 2 Rates of Unemployment and Participation, by Province, 1979

| Province | Unemployment | Participation |
	(average of months)	
Newfoundland	15.4%	52.7%
Prince Edward Island	11.3	59.3
Nova Scotia	10.2	56.9
New Brunswick	11.1	55.3
Quebec	9.6	60.1
Ontario	6.5	66.6
Manitoba	5.4	63.7
Saskatchewan	4.2	62.6
Alberta	3.9	69.4
British Columbia	7.7	62.7
Canada	7.5	63.3

Source: Statistics Canada, *Historical labour force statistics—actual data, seasonal factors, and seasonally adjusted data* (Cat. 71-201).

are fabulously rich compared with the poor of countries like India; indeed, their standards of living are superior to those of the relatively rich in some countries. And the Canadian poor are rich compared with Canadians of fifty years ago who were then considered quite comfortably off. But our standards are naturally based upon contemporary conditions in our own country, and we consider ourselves poor if our living standards fall short of our contemporary compatriots.

In this chapter, we will explore the reasons for disparities among regions of Canada and discuss the attempts made by federal and provincial governments to reduce those disparities. Since there are ten provinces and two territories in Canada, with eleven governments at the federal and provincial levels, the pattern of disparities is complex, government policies designed to reduce these disparities are numerous, and the success of these policies differs greatly from one jurisdiction to another.

To describe the essential nature of the problem and the main features of remedial action, this chapter will concentrate on the case of one province, Nova Scotia, whose experience is broadly typical of Canada's "have-not" regions.

Reasons for Regional Disparities

A region becomes relatively poor if the industries upon which it has come to depend decline or grow less rapidly than industries elsewhere, if new industries do not arise to take their place, and if natural economic forces do not come into action to correct the disparities.

Decline or Slow Growth of Industries

Due mainly to economic forces, regions tend to specialize in economic activities for which they are best suited. If a region has good soil and climate, it will tend to have strong agricultural and food-processing sectors. If it is near water containing plentiful fish stocks, fishing and fish-processing will tend to be important. If it is forested with accessible trees of the right type, it will tend to do much lumbering and perhaps pulp- and paper-making. If it has easily mined minerals, mining will tend to be a prominent industry. If it has a good climate and a beautiful countryside, tourism will tend to thrive. If it has good harbours and is strategically placed, it will tend to become an important shipping and transportation centre. Finally, if it is situated near markets and materials, it will tend to develop manufacturing industries.

The word "tend" has to be used in discussions about the location of economic activity because many factors are relevant, and the existence of some conditions that are favourable for the establishment of an industry does not guarantee that it will become established. For instance, the local availability of good lumber and a sizeable local population does not ensure that a furniture-building industry will develop. The existence of an enterprising spirit, skills and energy in its population, and other factors still not well understood, together with government policies and accidental occurrences, seem to be important in deciding in which direction a region develops, if at all. Certainly, the answers to questions about regional wealth and poverty do not all lie in the nature and extent of local natural resources.

Having, over a long period, developed and based its economic existence on certain activities, a region may find that conditions change. Its industries grow less rapidly than those of other regions, and it becomes a relatively depressed region.

This is what has happened to Nova Scotia. In the early nineteenth century, it was a prosperous part of British North America and prominent in international trade. It exploited its natural resources and made effective use of its position on world trade routes; it exported fish to other parts of North America and the West Indies; it was an important world supplier of lumber and a shipbuilder of renown; it boasted one of the largest merchant fleets in the world; its agriculture was reasonably healthy; and it maintained many robust little manufacturing establishments. In the 1830s and 1840s, deterioration occurred as a result of economic and political changes. Railway building slowed and with it the demand for wooden ties, the United States raised its tariff on imported lumber, and Britain ended the prohibition of U.S. trade with the West Indies, thereby exposing Nova Scotians to powerful competition in trade with those colonies. Soon afterward, Britain destroyed Nova Scotia's protected trading position by adopting free trade in the British Empire. Then came a reprieve: mainly due to general world prosperity, the Crimean and American Civil wars, another railway building boom, and the 1854 Reciprocity Treaty in raw materials with the U.S., the years just before and after Confederation are referred to by Nova Scotians as their "Golden Years."

But the reprieve was short-lived and the tone of the next century was set in the 1870s. Economic power, and with it political power, shifted westwards. Confederation and the new tariff policies cut Nova Scotia off from its traditional markets; new transportation links with the rest of Canada brought in foodstuffs and manufactured goods rather than carrying Nova Scotia's products westwards; technological changes and overseas developments deprived it of the advantages that it had enjoyed in fishing, lumbering, shipbuilding and international trade. Times of war have been good for Nova Scotia because of its geographical position, but peace-times have seen the relegation of the province to the status of an economic backwater of Canada, relying on doles from Ontario and the West and on federal expenditure for defence. Though far from poor by world standards, and not the poorest province of Canada, it is now one of the "have-not" provinces and part of Canada's "regional problem."

Its main misfortune was that the industries upon which it relied (and, because it was small, it tended to be more specialized and more reliant upon a very few industries) have generally been the older ones which have suffered decline or relatively slow growth in the world in general; but even compared with similar industries elsewhere, its industries have languished.

Take agriculture. As societies grow richer, they tend to spend a smaller and smaller proportion of their income on food. Though the agricultural industry has its good periods along with its adverse ones, it is a relatively slow-growth industry over the long term, and retains its present size only because of massive subsidies and protection in all of the developed countries of the world. But Nova Scotia's position is particularly poor. It has no first class farmland—what good growing land it has is uneven, stony, broken up by streams and hills into small parcels unsuitable for the application of mechanized techniques; and though its climate is equable by Canadian standards east of British Columbia, its growing season is too short for some crops. While it was isolated from the rest of Canada, local agriculture could prosper on the basis of the local market; however, the building of the Transcontinental Railway and the later development of road traffic and refrigeration destroyed this monopoly and exposed it to the severe competition of products from Ontario, the West and the U.S.A. Apples, its only agricultural export of importance, lost the British market upon which it primarily depended, partly because of economic conditions in that country in the period immediately following the Second World War.

Fishing was, and is, one of Nova Scotia's principal industries. During the last twenty years, and especially during the last five years, the industry has been relatively prosperous, thanks to government financial assistance toward investment in modern boats, the proclamation of the 200-mile limit and world conditions. But this prosperity follows a long period of depression. Being a food industry, demand for its product did not keep pace with demand for other products as societies became richer, though in this respect Nova Scotia has not fared too badly, partly because lobsters, a luxury food, are an important part of its catch. But salt cod, once its most important product, is not as acceptable in Europe, North America and the West Indies as it was when the populations of those areas were poorer and refrigeration was not available. Also, trade with Europe and some of Nova Scotia's other traditional markets was interrupted by, and never recovered from, the exchange restrictions imposed in those countries. And its traditional fishing areas became badly over-fished after the Second World War by the fishing fleets of other countries, as well as Canadian fleets—a problem which is now being rectified through the imposition of a Canadian 200-mile international fishing limit.

Lumbering is another of Nova Scotia's important industries. As substitute materials have become available and the stands of easily accessible lumber have been exhausted, world demand for lumber in some of its traditional uses (shipbuilding and construction, particularly) has declined or grown relatively slowly; nevertheless, the growth of the pulp and paper industries and technological improvements in the industry (the introduction of chain saws, mechanical barkers, chippers and planers, for instance) have kept world conditions for lumbering fairly healthy. The world demand for lumber for boat building, so important to Nova Scotia, almost disappeared with the introduction of steel ships; the opening of the Panama Canal exposed the province to competition from the west coast, where the trees are bigger, faster growing, and of superior varieties. Nevertheless, there is considerable pulp and paper manufacturing in the province, and the story of the lumbering industry is much less dismal than some others.

Coal mining was one of Nova Scotia's primary industries. Up to the first world war, world demand for coal advanced at a comfortable rate as the demand for energy rose, but afterwards coal mining went into decline all over the world and became one of the world's most depressed industries. During the interwar period, this was mainly due to world depression, but in addition coal was being displaced by oil and hydroelectricity, a process which has continued up to the present. Only with the very sharp rise in world oil prices during the last six years has a somewhat brighter picture for the industry emerged. But again, coal mining in Nova Scotia has had to contend with greater difficulties than coal mining in other regions. Its seams are thin and faulted and its main field lies under the sea off Cape Breton, involving very high costs of production. American coal mining, with its lower production costs and shorter hauls, pushed Nova Scotia coal out of Ontario markets. To make matters worse, the Sydney steel mill, one of the principal customers of Nova Scotia mines, has been in decline since the First World War.

Shipping presents a similar story. In the era when British Empire ships enjoyed a privileged position in world trade, when navigation of the St. Lawrence was impeded by rapids and ice, and when international trade was expanding, Halifax was a bustling port and the Nova Scotian merchant fleet was large and important in the world context. By the twentieth century, all of these advantages disappeared. The privileged position of the British colonies was abolished in the first half of the nineteenth century; canals and locks on the St. Lawrence gave ships access to the Great Lakes for about nine months of the year; ice-breakers enabled Montreal to become a virtually year-round port; the development of U.S. ports and railways on the eastern seaboard resulted in much trade to and from central Canada that by-passed Nova Scotia. Furthermore, the shipping industry of the whole world declined with the contraction of international trade in the inter-war period. While the world's seagoing fleet recovered after the Second World War, the merchant fleet of Nova Scotia, together with that of Canada as a whole, virtually disappeared and shows little sign of being revived. (See Chapter 4, on Transportation.)

Though Nova Scotia was never a manufacturing centre of great consequence, it did once have many healthy little industries servicing local markets and the shipping trade. However, improvements in transportation between Nova Scotia and central Canada destroyed most of the local monopolies, and technological developments favouring large-scale production in central locations near major markets rendered Nova Scotian manufacturers non-competitive.

One manufacturing industry, steel-making, merits special mention because of its importance. About 1900, a steel plant was established in Cape Breton and prospered for a quarter of a century; but, like steel-making elsewhere in the world, it ran into hard times after the First World War. Its problems were aggravated by two circumstances: first, the plant's only significant final product was steel rails, which have not been in high demand since the pre-World War I era of large-scale railway construction and, second, a location remote from the main Canadian industrial centres has meant that shipments of steel were burdened with heavy transportation expenses. Its private owners ran it with no significant investment for many years until it was decrepit; in 1967, they abandoned it. It has since been run by the provincial government and its scale of operation has been gradually reduced.

The overall picture of the major industries, upon which Nova Scotia relied for its prosperity, is therefore not a bright one. With the possible exception of fishing and lumbering, all have suffered decline over the long term, partly because they were of the types which have declined in many countries, and partly because they could not hold their own against Canadian competitors in other regions of the country.

Failure of Other Industries to Fill the Gaps

There is nothing novel about the decline of an industry as a consequence of a decline in profitability caused by either a rise in costs or a dwindling of demand. If other local industries arise or expand, then the region may hold its own.

But this does not necessarily happen. While industries did indeed come into being in Nova Scotia to produce pulp and paper from the province's forests and to process the fish brought in by its fishermen, they were not enough. Inadequacy of natural resources was, to a large extent, responsible. If a large pool of oil had been found, the province might now be as rich as Alberta; if rich deposits of nickel and copper had been discovered on its territory, it might have equalled the wealth of Ontario; if it had had plentiful salmon and fast-growing forests, it might have vied with British Columbia for a position near the head of the economic table; if it had had large, fast-moving rivers, it might have thrived as the provider of electricity to the adjacent provinces and to New England; if it had had longer summers, it might have rivalled the Niagara Peninsula as a market garden and developed into a major tourist region. But it had none of these advantages.

But why did new manufacturing industries not develop to fill the void? Many industries are relatively "footloose" and are not tied to natural resources. A few did appear. Small manufacturing firms of various kinds were established in the province, and one or two larger ones, including Michelin Tire—the largest of all. But they were not of sufficient scale to compensate for the decline in the older industries; the entrepreneurs and managers who make the decisions regarding the location of manufacturing industry in Canada have considered Nova Scotia to be a high-cost location compared to locations in the corridor running from Montreal to Windsor.

It is probable that they have been right in the majority of cases, for the following reasons:

1. While wage rates in Nova Scotia have been relatively low (about 80% of those in Quebec and Ontario), low labour productivity has, to a considerable extent, counterbalanced this advantage;

2. Materials, parts and supplies have typically been more expensive because they have to be brought into the province at high freight costs. Their availability has also been an issue of considerable importance. The long haul from their point of production has meant delays between the time that materials have been ordered and the time that they have been received. To avoid being caught short, a plant in Nova Scotia either has to bear the expense of keeping unusually high inventories of materials, parts and supplies, or pay the high cost of bringing in rush orders by air or other expensive means;

3. Electricity, though not an important element in most manufacturers' costs, has been relatively expensive in Nova Scotia, partly because of the lack of sites for the generation of hydroelectricity and partly because of the fact that a population that was not concentrated in large cities could not be served by large and efficient thermal plants;

4. While fuel was until recently not a great problem, since local coal was available together with cheap imported oil, the huge increases in the cost of oil since 1973 have put Nova Scotia at a marked disadvantage;

5. The shipment of Nova Scotian finished goods to their markets has tended to be expensive. Because of the province's small population (now only slightly over 800,000), a manufacturer seeking to avail himself of economies of scale in production has had to export to markets outside the province. In doing so, he incurred heavy freight charges; and

6. Difficulties in maintaining necessary contact between producers and customers have also tended to inflate Nova Scotian manufacturers' costs. The farther a producer is from his customers, the greater the difficulty he has in ensuring that he understands their wishes and can satisfy them quickly. Ultimately, he may feel obliged to go to the considerable expense of keeping representatives and maintaining inventories in the main market areas.

All of these reasons have contributed to the belief of business decision-makers that, for most manufacturing activities, Nova Scotia is a higher-cost location than other regions of Canada, particularly the industrial areas of Ontario and Quebec. But these reasons do not entirely explain the slow growth of manufacturing in Nova Scotia. Though the manufacturing industry in general has been at a cost disadvantage compared with its counterparts in Quebec and Ontario (estimated at 3-4 per cent where there is no difference in management competence[1]), there must have been a considerable range of manufacturing industry which would have done as well or better in Nova Scotia than it would have done elsewhere in Canada. That it has not developed in Nova Scotia must be attributed to a local shortage of entrepreneurs—people who see business opportunities and put together the labour, land and capital to exploit them.

Why there should have been a shortage is a matter of conjecture. The age of the province and its insulation from disturbing influences, such as large-scale immigration, have probably resulted in the development of cozy, non-competitive attitudes in the classes from which entrepreneurs normally spring. Outside entrepreneurs have known little of the province, have preconceived ideas about it and, when making decisions about plant location, have tended to stay almost as a matter of course in the regions in which they were already established. Hence, owing to a shortage of home-grown and outside entrepreneurs, the opportunities that Nova Scotia has offered for successful manufacturing activity have not been exploited to the full and new manufacturing industries did not fill the gap left by the decline of traditional industries.

Failure of Economic Forces to Correct the Situation

Economic forces are very powerful—as governments find when they try to oppose them—and it used to be thought that the problem of depressed areas would automatically be eliminated by simply letting these forces operate without intervention or restraint. It was thought that the relative fall in incomes in depressed areas would induce people to migrate to prosperous areas where they could get better jobs. Labour would thus become more plentiful in prosperous areas and more scarce in depressed areas, each worker left behind in a depressed area would have more capital equipment at his command, and employers (the old firms plus new firms attracted by the cheaper labour) would then bid up local wage rates. Meanwhile, the abundance of labour in the prosperous areas would tend to depress wage rates. Equality, at least in the income of labour, would thereby be achieved.

This theory is not entirely unrealistic, since large-scale migrations have taken place from depressed provinces like Nova Scotia to prosperous provinces like Ontario. Unfortunately, however, migration does not necessarily restore parity, for several reasons. First, as labour moves out, the size of the local market shrinks, thereby further depressing industries producing for the local market. A cumulative process tends to set in: further migration resulting from the loss of local markets depresses local markets even more, and so on. Total depopulation could occur without equality being restored.

Second, those persons who leave the region are not a representative sample of its population. By far, the most mobile people in the community are those aged between about sixteen and twenty-five who have not already established themselves in careers or assumed family responsibilities. And it is generally the most enterprising and confident members of that age group, the ones with the most marketable skills, who migrate; the less enterprising stay behind. Older people generally find it much more difficult to move away: the cost of moving can be high and their acceptability to new employers may be limited. Since they belong to the age groups that did not migrate when younger, they are probably less enterprising or have fewer marketable skills. The out-migration consequently tends to lower the quality of the labour force, making the area even less attractive.

Finally, wages in a declining area do not respond very readily to changes in the demand for labour. Workers are very reluctant to accept wage reductions and, if unionized, are usually successful in preventing such reductions. Employers, on the other hand, are reluctant to agree to wage increases, often preferring to tolerate labour shortages. Consequently, while in the long run wage rates react to change in the labour supply situation resulting from the outflow of workers, the reaction may well be long delayed.

Hence, the economic forces which might be expected to eliminate disparities between regions are very unreliable. Even worse, they are likely to create unwelcome indirect effects within depressed regions. The general depression and out-migration are likely to diminish the tax revenues of the provincial and municipal governments of those regions, and authorities will usually respond by reducing their expenditure on the infrastructure (roads, public buildings, harbours and the like) and on public services (such as education, vocational training and health care). In the long run, therefore, the quality of labour (its skills and health) will deteriorate, tending to repel new firms. A listlessness eventually settles on the population and the downward slide continues.

During the present century, the out-migration from Nova Scotia, mainly to Ontario and the New England states, has been very considerable. Whether it has reduced or increased the degree of depression in the province is debatable. It certainly has not eliminated the disparities between Nova Scotia and the rest of Canada.

The situation described in Nova Scotia, and the reasons for it, are similar to those occurring in other "have-not" provinces where industries have been depressed for long periods and insufficient new industry has grown-up to maintain their position relative to Ontario. A realignment of the prosperity table of Ontario and the western provinces has taken place due to the very recent escalation of the world prices of oil, food and fertilizers, but the position of the "have-nots" in the east has remained substantially unchanged.

Government Policies to Reduce Regional Disparities

Governments of most developed countries, and those of many less-developed ones, have adopted policies designed to reduce the economic disparities among their regions. Canada is no exception, though systematic regional policies date back only to the 1960s.

Justification

Traditional economic thinking would deny any justification for a government interfering with the "natural" distribution of income among regions. Any attempt to change the distribution would only result in people and industry being located in the wrong places, and the income of the nation as a whole would be reduced below what it might have been. If natural forces were allowed to work freely, the ideal distribution of people and industry would result, and the national economic well-being would be maximized.

Though there cannot be many who now adhere to this doctrine in its extreme form, there is still widespread concern about government policies that encourage people to stay in areas where they cannot be fully employed, that bribe or coerce private firms to establish themselves in locations that they believe to be high-cost and that keep alive failing industries by subsidies or nationalization. In the view of many people such policies must, in the long run, result in high-cost, inefficient industry, with average living standards consequently lower than they need be.

While there is some justification for this outlook, it depends heavily on two dubious assumptions:

  1. That private firms, which make the decisions about the location of

much of the nation's industry, take into account all factors which influence the national economic wellbeing. In fact, they do not. In a good many instances, the costs and benefits to the nation of having a plant in a particular area may be quite different from the costs and benefits to the private firm which owns it. For instance, if a depressed area contains a large number of unemployed workers who are producing nothing, then that labour could be put to work in a new local factory without the country forgoing any other output (as it would if the workers were withdrawn from other productive activities). Labour employed in the new factory may therefore be costless from the national point of view. However, the private firm that owns the factory will have to pay wages to induce people to work for it, so, from its point of view, the labour is not costless. Private costs here exceed public costs. Similarly, there may be inequality between the private benefits and public benefits derived from the establishment of a new factory in a depressed area. Training given to the employees may upgrade the quality of the local labour force and may be of benefit to other regions if the new workers subsequently relocate elsewhere. For such reasons, the decisions of private firms in respect to the location of new economic activities may not optimally serve the public interest; and

2. That private decision-makers are infallible and always choose locations which are optimum from their own private viewpoints. Many decision-makers have small horizons and tend to choose locations in areas with which they are familiar, without examining possible locations in other areas. Since decision-makers in expanding firms are likely to be in the areas which are already prosperous, these areas are likely to receive a disproportionate share of new investment. Government regional policies, which induce firms to consider poorer areas and induce them to venture farther afield than they would normally be inclined to do, may prevent mistakes that would be made by private decision-makers through ignorance and excessive caution.

Virtually no one argues today for complete *laissez-faire* in industrial location on economic grounds. But, even if anyone did, he would not likely win the day since there are important non-economic considerations involved. There is general agreement that every Canadian has the right to an acceptable standard of living, wherever he or she may live, and that it is simply wrong to have wide disparity in the living standards of different regions. There is also the political view that the unity of Canada depends on each element of the nation believing that it is getting a fair deal, and such a unity is endangered if Canadians in one region of the country feel that, from an economic point of view, they are being treated as second-class citizens.

On one ground or other, therefore, diminution of regional disparities is now a generally accepted element of national policy. Few Canadians would go as far as to advocate policies which sought to eliminate all disparities, but most would agree with policies designed to reduce them.

Types of Policies

Governments nowadays play a very large role in the Canadian economy, with different impacts upon the various regions of the country. Many government policies serve to increase or decrease regional disparities, even though they were not specifically designed for these purposes. Thus the "National Policy" introduced in 1879 by the Macdonald government provided for the imposition of high tariffs on imported goods. Though this policy was intended to serve the national purpose of fostering manufacturing in the country, it benefited central Canada greatly while harming the Maritimes.

Similarly, unemployment insurance, introduced to serve a national purpose, favoured the poorer regions on account of their higher rates of unemployment; and the progressive income tax, levied for the sake of social justice, has a much heavier incidence in the richer regions than in the poor ones, thereby tending to reduce regional disparities.

While the regional impacts of these policies are no doubt substantial, they would be very difficult to trace. We shall therefore focus our attention upon those policies which have been specifically designed to reduce regional disparities.

Most of these policies have been introduced within the last two decades, during which period interest in regional disparities and the urge to reduce them have grown enormously. Five types of policy are now in effect. First, there are transfers of income from the richer areas to the poorer areas; second, subsidies are given to bolster ailing industries in poorer areas; third, inducements are offered for the establishment of new economic activities in poorer areas; fourth, assistance is provided toward the relocation of persons from poorer to richer areas; and, fifth, government offices have been moved from Ottawa to the poorer areas. Most of these policies have been introduced by the federal government, but provincial governments have also developed programs of regional assistance.

Each of the five types of policy is discussed below.

Transfers of Income

The principal measure specifically designed to redistribute income from the richer to the poorer provinces was the system of "equalization payments." Introduced in 1957, this system provides for payments from the federal government to the governments of the poorer provinces, given to enable them to provide public services of roughly the same quality as those provided in the richer provinces. The size of these payments is based upon the average tax yield per head of population in each province and the payments are designed to bring the poor provinces' yields up to the national average. Equalization payments are very important sources of revenue for governments of the poorer provinces; for instance, the equalization payments received by the government of Nova Scotia constitute one-fifth to one-quarter of its revenue.

Bolstering Ailing Industries

The nearest thing to a systematic policy under this heading has been the program established under the Agricultural and Rural Development Act (ARDA) of 1961. Though all provinces are eligible to participate in the program and all did do so in varying degrees, it was designed primarily for the benefit of small farmers scratching out a meagre existence in eastern Canada. The objective was to improve land use and to provide technical training, which would enable farmers to farm more efficiently or to take up alternative occupations. The program was operated jointly by the federal and provincial governments under a shared cost arrangement.

Though not explicitly a regional program, support of the coal mining industry was directed to just one region, indeed, to a single province: Nova Scotia. The assistance program was of long standing, having had its roots in the 1920s. The federal government then began to pay subventions toward the cost of transporting Nova Scotia coal to markets in Quebec and Ontario; otherwise, it could not have competed with the U.S. coal that was mined in nearby deposits. The supports required to keep the Nova Scotia industry alive became ever larger, however, and the financial burden ever heavier. In 1967, the decision was taken to phase the industry out of existence, and the Cape Breton Development Corporation (DEVCO) was set up to arrange a painless, if lingering, death and to fill the gap by attracting other industrial activities to Cape Breton. As a consequence of DEVCO's failure to attract new industry, political considerations and, recently, the improved prospects for coal, emphasis has shifted toward the improvement and expansion of the mines.

A number of other industries of regional importance have also been supported. The federal government has assisted the fishing industry—of major importance in the Atlantic provinces—through the maintenance and improvement of harbours and facilities (though some harbours are really too small to justify their continuance), subsidies for fishing boats and equipment, compensation for storm damage, price supports and technical and research services. It has aided the steel industry of Cape Breton, which had been simply abandoned by its private owners in 1967, and has provided subsidies and other assistance to shipbuilding in Nova Scotia and the other Atlantic provinces. Under the Maritime Freight Rates Act, Ottawa provides subsidies toward the cost of shipping goods by rail westward out of the Atlantic Region. Though not directed at any specific ailing industry the Act, passed in 1927, was intended as a general prop to producers in Nova Scotia and other Maritime provinces who sent commodities by rail to other parts of Canada. (It was subsequently extended to cover shipments from Newfoundland and shipments by truck).

The government of Nova Scotia, by a variety of means, has also attempted to bolster industries within its jurisdiction. It shared the cost of the ARDA programs within its boundaries, played a role in the affairs of DEVCO and took over the Sydney steel mill—which meant assuming responsibility for its increasingly heavy operating deficit and its capital needs. The government poured money into a number of industrial enterprises, notably the Clairtone Sound Corporation, to prevent their liquidation; and to support various industries, it provided consulting and other services.

Encouraging New Industries

The federal program of regional assistance which has attracted the most attention has been that administered by the Department of Regional Economic Expansion (DREE), formed in 1969. DREE took over the work of previously established agencies, notably the Area Development Agency (ADA), set up in 1963, and the Atlantic Development Board (ADB), formed in 1962.

The Area Development Agency had administered a tax rebate scheme designed primarily to induce manufacturing firms to establish or expand in Quebec and the Atlantic provinces, a scheme which was changed two years later to a system of grants for the same purpose. Parts of other provinces were subsequently made eligible as well.

The Atlantic Development Board was formed to finance infrastructure improvement, including the construction of roads and power plants, pollution control and improvement of civic services. The object was to make Nova Scotia and the other selected areas more attractive places in which industry might locate. The Board, as well, financed the building of industrial parks as a further means of attracting new industry.

Other devices for attracting industry to Nova Scotia and other areas have been used by the federal government. As mentioned above, one of DEVCO's roles was to attract industry to Cape Breton by offering financial inducements; Mainland Investments Ltd. (originally called Metropolitan Area Growth Investments Corporation (MAGI)), has been charged with taking an active role in promoting industry in Nova Scotia; and accelerated depreciation allowances have been granted to firms in certain development areas.

The government of Nova Scotia has also been very active in the pursuit of new manufacturing industry. Its principal instrument has been Industrial Estates Limited (IEL), which has made loans on attractive terms to new firms (as well as for expansions of existing firms); it has from time to time sought to stimulate industrial activity in other ways as well, such as by the setting up of industrial parks and the supplying of some equity capital. In one or two special instances, it has given outright grants (it gave the Michelin Tire Manufacturing Company several million dollars), and it has entered into joint projects (notably with the Deuterium Company, which built a plant to produce the heavy water required in nuclear reactors). The government of Nova Scotia has also been a party to federal programs, notably MAGI and DEVCO.

Facilitating Mobility

We discussed earlier the obstacles that people face if they wish to move from a poor area like Nova Scotia to a location elsewhere in Canada. In an attempt to remove one of those obstacles, the federal government, through the Employment and Immigration Commission (formerly the Department of Manpower and Immigration), has made grants in certain circumstances towards the cost of an unemployed person's movement from Nova Scotia or another development area to take employment elsewhere in Canada.

Relocation of Government Offices

Governments have sporadically, in special circumstances, moved some of their offices and branches in order to provide employment opportunity in lagging areas (though in some instances the action was taken in response to political pressure and to gain political advantage—as well as to bolster a weak local economy). The overall extent of such relocations has not been large, though several have been of quite significant assistance to the reception localities. Examples of this discretionary relocation of government establishments have been the construction of a military training ground at Gagetown, New Brunswick, the proposed relocation of the federal Department of Veterans' Affairs from Ottawa to Prince Edward Island, and the removal by a former Manitoba government of two provincial offices from Winnipeg, one to Beausejour and another to Portage la Prairie.

Effectiveness

Table 3 provides a comparison of income per person in the ten provinces of Canada over the period 1928 to 1978. The first half of the table indicates that the disparities between the five most easterly provinces (those provinces to which the regional programs have been primarily directed) and the rest of Canada have fallen in every case since the programs have been in force. Those who believe in regional programs might be inclined

Table 3 Personal Income per Person, including and excluding Transfer Payments, by Provinces, Percentages of Canada 1928-78 (ten-year intervals)

	Including Transfer Payments						Excluding Transfer Payments					
	1928	1938	1948	1958	1968	1978	1928	1938	1948	1958	1968	1978
Newfoundland	-	-	-	54%	61%	66%	-	-	-	48%	53%	54%
Prince Edward Island	53%	55%	54%	53	64	69	54%	55%	50%	48	58	61
Nova Scotia	69	78	72	74	77	80	69	79	69	72	73	75
New Brunswick	63	64	69	66	70	74	63	65	89	62	66	68
Quebec	86	89	85	87	89	95	87	90	85	86	88	91
Ontario	115	125	116	119	117	109	116	126	117	122	119	112
Manitoba	104	92	106	99	97	93	103	91	107	98	96	94
Saskatchewan	100	59	96	83	85	92	101	52	93	79	84	92
Alberta	107	95	109	104	100	104	107	96	110	103	101	108
British Columbia	122	130	117	116	108	109	122	131	118	113	108	110
Canada	100	100	100	100	100	100	100	100	100	100	100	100

Source: Statistics Canada, *National Income and Expenditure Accounts* (Cat. 13-531 & 13-201)

to take encouragement from these figures. However, three qualifications need to be made:

1. If one were to extract payments by governments to persons in the form of unemployment benefits, welfare payments, pensions and similar "transfer payments" (as done in the second half of Table 3), the apparent improvement is much reduced. Consequently, the reduction of disparities has been achieved mainly by the richer provinces paying doles to the poorer ones. Little in the figures would indicate that the productive capacity of the poorer provinces has been built up so that they are closing the gap by dint of their own ability to create economic wealth. Independent assessments of the programs to attract manufacturing industry to the poorer areas have generally indicated doubt about their success. One researcher[2] talked to a number of large firms which had received industrial incentive grants and gained the impression that such grants had had little effect upon those firms' decisions as to the region in which to locate new manufacturing plants. Another researcher[3] did a cost-benefit analysis of Industrial Estates Limited and concluded that, while its activities had been better than nothing, effects not markedly inferior could have been achieved by simply giving the money away to Nova Scotians. Another investigator disclosed the extent to which some provinces had been duped by unscrupulous promoters, and how their expensive attempts at industrial development had come to very little. (The plant built by the Deuterium Company was a striking example; built at the cost of some $150 million of public funds, it was a complete failure, never producing a drop of heavy water.) Similarly, few researchers have had much good to say about the results of the attempts to improve agriculture in the eastern provinces, and the propping up of ailing industries has generally become an expensive, endless and joyless process;

2. Canada's population grew by 25 per cent during the period 1963-1979, while the corresponding percentages for the five eastern provinces were: Newfoundland, 21 per cent; Prince Edward Island, 14 per cent; Nova Scotia, 13 per cent; New Brunswick, 15 per cent; Quebec, 15 per cent. These provinces were not attractive to new immigrants to the country, and they lost population as many of their young people moved to Ontario and the West. Consequently, though on average those remaining caught up a little in terms of personal income, the economic importance of each of the eastern provinces declined; and

3. Measurement of the effectiveness of any program is very difficult, since many forces unrelated to it are bound to be operating at any time. For instance, the high prices of grain and potash on world markets have raised the relative economic position of Saskatchewan,

and the world energy situation is promising to put Alberta at the top of the provincial prosperity league. Consequently, improvements in the relative position of a province that is the target of a regional program may have nothing to do with the program. Similarly, a fall in its relative position does not prove the program is ineffective; without the program, the fall might have been even greater.

One must therefore conclude from the available information that the success of regional programs has not been proven,[4] and one is prompted inevitably to ask why more obvious success has not been achieved. Part of the explanation must lie in the nature of the programs and the way in which they have been carried out. Certainly, the objectives of the programs have often been confused, and the programs themselves have floundered about because their directors were unclear or divided on precisely what they are trying to achieve. Political pressures have diverted them from their original paths (for instance, the areas eligible for industrial development grants have been extended several times so that they now include most of the populated portion of Canada), and changes of governments and responsible ministers have led to organizational changes and disruption.

But even if programs had been well-conceived and executed, they would have encountered severe resistance from economic forces. Some of the industries upon which the poor provinces rely (the textile industry of Quebec is a good example) are those which are relatively sick throughout the developed world. Propping them up by subsidies, tariffs and quotas does not overcome the pressure of economic forces, and they tend to become permanent invalids. Because of transportation and other real cost disadvantages, few new industries which might replace the declining ones are keen to enter a poor province unless they intend to confine their attention to local markets—which usually denies them economies of large-scale production.

Many researchers are now tending to the conclusion that what holds back a poor area is its lack of entrepreneurs—those persons who pursue business opportunities and create new enterprises. In any society, the proportion of entrepreneurs is tiny, most of the population being content to work for others. But, in backward areas, the proportion seems to be even tinier, opportunities are not exploited, and the areas do not develop as quickly as they might. Why this should be is a matter of conjecture. In a province like Nova Scotia, it may be due to the loss of enterprise suffered by society when it ages, loses its competitive urge through intermarriage within the business community, and lacks the stimulation brought by large immigration; and when a society becomes accustomed to being poor, apathy spreads and further quenches the spirit of enterprise. Governmental regional programs such as those offered under ARDA, DREE and IEL have sometimes indirectly sought to stimulate local enterprise and make it easier for potential entrepreneurs to enter the field. But attitudes of mind, which largely determine the proportion of entrepreneurs in any society, are slow to change, and most existing government programs affect them only indirectly, if at all. (A small program to identify and develop entrepreneurial talent has recently been introduced in Nova Scotia entrepreneurship, but it is too soon to judge its success.)

The lack of local entrepreneurial talent in poor areas would be of less importance if outsiders filled the gap. But there is evidence that the entry of new firms into poor areas is deterred by the erroneous preconceptions of decision-makers, rather than by real locational disadvantages. One study[5] of decision-makers in manufacturing showed that they were ignorant of the situation in the poor areas of Canada and very seldom took steps to dispel their ignorance; had they investigated the situation thoroughly, a significant proportion would have found that Nova Scotia, and perhaps other poor provinces, offered locations for their particular processes that were better than those in the other provinces. It may well be that the principal merit of incentives to firms to locate in certain areas is that the offer of sums of money may induce decision-makers to consider suitable locations in the poorer provinces which they should really have considered anyway.

[1] R.E. George, *A Leader and A Laggard Revisited,* mimeo, 1979.
[2] D. Springate, *Regional Incentives and Private Investment.* C.D. Howe Research Institute, 1973.
[3] R.E. George, *The Life and Times of Industrial Estates Limited.* Dalhousie University Institute of Public Affairs, 1974.
[4] P. Mathias, *Forced Growth.* James Lewis and Samuel, 1971.
[5] R.E. George, *A Leader and a Laggard.* Toronto University Press, 1970.

Chapter 18

Public Finance

Allan M. Maslove,
School of Public Administration, Carleton University

Government in the Economy

The growth of government and its increasing impact on the Canadian economy have been major topics for recurring public discussion. But, often, the terms of the debate are ill-defined. What is meant by "growing government"? What is meant by the "impact" of the public sector on the economy?

The purpose of this chapter is to explore these questions and a number of other related issues. The intention is not to provide any definitive solution to the debate over the role and impact of government; to attempt this in one short chapter (or even in several long books!) would be foolhardy. Rather, our aim is much more modest: it is to examine some of the data and explore the dimensions of some secondary, but nevertheless important, related issues. If government in general is growing, then by how much and which levels in particular? What are some of the consequences of the differential growth rates of the different levels of government, especially in the context of our federal system?

To begin, we must decide how to measure the size of government and thereby its rate of growth. The most common measure is, of course, the amount of government spending. Two measures of public expenditure will be employed later in this chapter. The first is total spending and the second is spending on goods and services.[1] A measure of total spending is meaningful if we wish to examine the proportion of the total economy that, in one way or another, flows directly through the public sector. The second indicator, expenditures on goods and services, provides a measure of the public sector as a resource user.

For some purposes it may also be sensible to measure public sector size and growth in terms of manpower. Labour as a resource or a factor of production clearly deserves to be, and is, treated in unique ways. It therefore makes sense to concern ourselves with the proportion of the labour force employed in the public and private sectors of the economy. In addition, it has been argued that a large and growing public sector (in terms of manpower) may ultimately affect the functioning of democratic governments. According to this argument, public servants (and to some extent private sector workers whose incomes are largely dependent on governments) have a vested interest in the public sector and will tend to vote in their interests. As their numbers grow, and with it their electoral power, a significant force for still larger governments develops.[2] Without passing judgment on this argument, we can see why it may be desirable to measure government size in terms of manpower.

We could devise other measures of the size of government, at least conceptually. For example, a measure of the value-added by the public sector in total GNP would be useful. However, the data for these indicators are not readily available. In this chapter, we will deal only with the spending and manpower measures of the size of government.

The second question posed at the beginning concerned the impact of government on the economy. To derive a satisfactory measure here is even more difficult than to measure the size of the public sector. One obvious possibility, and what in fact is usually done, is to (implicitly) assume a direct correlation between size and impact. That assumption is not fully justified, however. Total government spending as a proportion of GNP is simultaneously an overstatement and an understatement of the impact of government on the economy. It is an overstatement because some of the expenditures of government may be largely displacements of what would have occurred anyway. Thus, expenditure levels overstate net impacts, at least with respect to the allocation of resources. To illustrate the point, let us consider primary and secondary education. These are major expenditure items of provincial and local governments;[3] indeed, at the local level education expenditures are about equal to all other spending combined. Yet, if there was no direct public sector participation in this way, much, and perhaps most, of the country's educational activity would occur in the private sector. Certainly the government makes a difference (consider the distributional impacts, for example) but public spending on education as a measure of the net impact of government in allocating resources to this activity is an overstatement. Public spending on medical care services is another example of this kind of overstatement.

Public spending levels also understate the net impact of government. Regulatory activities are a prime example. The budget of a typical regulatory agency is a minor portion of a government's total spending,[4] yet its impacts on the private sector may be immense. Indeed, it is the very purpose of regulation to alter the behaviour of private-sector decision-makers (producers and consumers) rather than to rely on direct government actions to achieve desired objectives. The regulatory agency itself is established mainly to act as an enforcer of the regulatory statute.[5]

Government spending may also understate government impact because the government "spends" funds that are not recorded in its financial statements. It does this by using the income tax system to grant tax relief to individuals and corporations who meet certain conditions or pursue certain courses of action. These instruments are referred to as "tax expenditures" because they are expenditures in the sense of being money that the government could have collected but has chosen not to collect, by granting tax concessions to corporations and individuals who comply with its requirements. Since they do not enter into any public accounts, these concessions cause underestimation of the impact of the government on the private sector. Judging by the size of tax expenditures in Canada, their impact is potentially quite large. One recent study estimated that in 1976 personal tax expenditures were $5.5 billion and total (personal and corporate) tax expenditures exceeded $8 billion.[6] Current totals (1980) are probably well over $12 billion.

Thus, we can see that a government has a variety of tools or instruments[7] available to it in its pursuit of policy goals. A comprehensive evaluation of its impact must recognize this and attempt to include the effects of all of these instruments, difficult as this may be. We should also recognize the relationships among all these alternatives; some may reinforce others, and some may (at least partially) negate the effects of others (i.e., work at cross purposes).

Despite all these caveats, it is nonetheless a very useful exercise to examine the size and growth of government (as measured both by expenditures and by manpower levels), because the public sector is the largest spender and employer in our economy and because its activities have large and important impacts. Moreover, as we shall see in the following sections, the different levels of government have had substantially different growth rates. This fact has resulted in changes that may importantly affect the way in which our federal public sector responds to the demands of its citizens.

Public Sector Spending

Table 1 provides us with a picture of the growth of the relative size of government on a National Accounts basis.[8] That growth has been substantial indeed. From a post-war low of 22 per cent in 1950, total government spending has increased to 42 per cent of GNP in 1978. While most casual observers might attribute this increase to the federal government, the data show otherwise. The relative size of the federal government in 1978 was only slightly different from what it was in 1959. The largest change in relative size occurred in the provincial government sector. Local government also grew significantly over the period and the transfer of hospitals into the public sector has been another significant source of

Table 1 Total Government Expenditure Expressed as a Percentage of Gross National Product
For Selected Calendar Years, 1926 to 1977 Before and After Exclusion of Intergovernmental Transfers

Year[a]	Federal		Provincial		Local		Hospitals	CPP & QPP	Total, excluding transfers
	Including transfers	Excluding transfers	Including transfers	Excluding transfers	Including transfers	Excluding transfers			
1926....	6.2	5.9	3.6	3.2	6.7	6.6	—	—	15.7
1933....	10.9	9.3	8.8	8.2	10.2	9.9	—	—	27.4
1939....	8.6	7.2	8.3	7.8	6.6	6.5	—	—	21.4
1943....	39.9	38.6	3.8	3.5	3.4	3.4	—	—	45.4
1946....	24.2	22.7	5.3	4.6	7.6	4.2	—	—	31.6
1950....	12.8	11.5	6.7	5.7	4.9	4.9	—	—	22.1
1955....	16.8	15.3	6.4	5.2	5.9	5.8	—	—	26.3
1960....	17.6	15.0	9.2	7.3	7.4	7.3	—	—	29.7
1965....	15.4	12.9	11.4	6.8	8.2	8.1	2.1	—	29.9
1970....	17.8	13.8	16.5	10.2	9.5	9.4	2.8	.2	36.4
1975....	21.5	16.8	19.1	12.2	8.8	8.8	3.0	.5	41.3
1978....	21.3	16.6	19.6	12.7	8.9	8.9	3.0	.8	42.0

[a]Includes Newfoundland for 1949 and subsequent years.
Source: The Canadian Tax Foundation, *The National Finances*, 1979-80.

increase. The latter represents a case of public spending largely substituting for private spending without necessarily (at least in the short-run) changing the allocation of resources in significant fashion. If we include intergovernmental transfers as part of the expenditures of the granting government, the data reflect the growing importance of federal transfers to the provinces and the even greater relative growth in provincial transfers to local governments. What the growth pattern indicates is that the levels of government which have grown most are those which are responsible for social welfare, education and health care services, the fastest growing areas in the public sector.

The importance of governments as consumers of goods and services is illustrated in Table 2. The total public sector has grown relatively steadily since World War II and currently accounts for about one-quarter of total GNP through its expenditures on goods and services. Again, however, it is not the federal government that is the source of this growth, as so many people appear to believe; federal expenditures on goods and services receded from their wartime peaks to a relatively constant 5 to 6 per cent of GNP. The biggest source of growth has been the provincial government sector, while the government and hospital sectors have also grown in relative terms, though somewhat more slowly.

Table 2 also shows the split between current and capital expenditures on goods and services. The capital expenditures represent public sector investment in facilities and infrastructures, the benefits of which accrue in the years following the investment. Over most of the period shown in Table 2 (particularly since about 1950), we can see that capital spending as a proportion of GNP has remained at about the same level or declined slightly. As a percentage of total spending on goods and services, capital spending has remained roughly constant at the federal level (about 10 per cent) while declining at both the provincial and local levels. However, both of the latter two continue to direct a larger proportion of their spending to investment than does the federal government.

Table 3 shows the major categories of government spending. As the public sector grew, was that growth focused on particular areas? The most striking development in federal spending patterns is the relative growth of transfer payments, both to individuals and to other (mostly provincial) governments. Currently, transfers account for more than one-half of total federal spending. Federal interest payments to service the public debt have increased since 1975 but are still not out of line with the historical pattern. In the provincial sector, we note a discontinuity in 1961 when hospitals became part of the public sector and provincial transfers to hospitals began to be included as part of the transfers to other governments. Beyond that year, we see some decline in the relative share of these transfers, balanced by modest increases in the shares of provincial spending devoted to transfers to persons and debt costs. Finally, in the local sector

Table 2 Government Expenditure on Goods and Services Expressed as a Percentage of Gross National Product For Selected Calendar Years, 1926 to 1978

Year[a]	Federal Defence, Current	Federal Nondefence, Current	Federal Total Current	Federal Total Capital	Provincial Current	Provincial Capital	Local Current	Local Capital	Hospitals Current	Hospitals Capital	Combined total
1926....	.3	1.6	1.8	.6	1.3	.6	4.4	.9	—	—	9.6
1933....	.6	2.2	2.8	.7	2.3	.8	6.1	.9	—	—	13.7
1939....	1.2	2.1	3.4	.6	2.4	1.3	4.3	.7	—	—	12.7
1943....	32.3	1.0	33.2	.5	1.3	.3	2.5	.3	—	—	38.2
1946....	7.1	2.1	9.3	—.9	1.9	.8	2.8	.9	—	—	14.8
1950....	2.7	2.3	5.0	.4	2.1	1.1	3.3	1.2	—	—	13.1
1955....	6.2	2.1	8.3	.6	2.0	1.2	3.8	1.5	—	—	17.5
1960....	4.0	2.3	6.3	.6	2.6	1.6	4.9	1.7	—	—	17.7
1965....	2.8	2.3	5.1	.6	2.7	1.6	5.4	1.9	1.8	.3	19.5
1970....	2.2	3.1	5.3	.5	4.8	1.2	6.8	1.7	2.5	.3	23.1
1975....	1.7	3.4	5.0	.7	5.8	1.5	6.5	1.5	2.8	.2	24.0
1978....	1.8	3.4	5.2	.6	6.0	1.2	6.9	1.3	2.8	.2	24.1

[a]Includes Newfoundland for 1949 and subsequent years.
Source: The Canadian Tax Foundation, *The National Finances*, 1979-80.

Table 3 Government Spending by Major Categories as a Percentage of Total Spending
(National Accounts Basis)

Year[a]	Federal				Provincial				Local			
	Current Spending on Goods and Services	Transfers to Persons	Transfers to Other Governments	Interest on Public Debt	Current Spending on Goods and Services	Transfers to Persons	Transfers to Other Governments	Interest on Public Debt	Current Spending on Goods and Services	Transfers to Persons	Transfers to Other Governments	Interest on Public Debt
1926	33.0%	13.5%	5.2%	45.1%	42.4%	16.5%	14.6%	26.6%	75.5%	3.0%	2.0%	19.5%
1929	36.6	14.1	5.6	39.9	42.4	19.7	14.8	23.2	76.8	2.6	2.0	18.7
1933	27.6	13.0	15.8	39.4	29.1	38.9	7.2	24.8	65.9	8.1	3.1	22.9
1939	42.4	12.5	19.2	29.9	34.5	38.1	8.1	19.0	72.1	6.0	2.1	19.8
1943	84.4	1.6	3.4	5.7	37.7	32.1	10.3	18.5	78.8	3.8	2.0	15.4
1946	37.0	31.0	0.6	14.9	41.3	30.1	14.7	13.0	84.0	4.1	1.8	10.2
1950	40.3	26.8	11.0	18.6	37.8	37.1	16.5	7.3	88.9	3.5	1.6	6.1
1955	50.9	26.5	9.7	10.5	39.5	30.7	22.4	6.4	88.2	3.3	1.8	6.8
1961	37.5	29.1	16.4	11.4	30.6	18.4	45.2	4.7	85.4	3.4	1.5	9.7
1965	34.5	28.2	17.5	12.8	27.6	18.8	47.0	5.0	86.8	2.5	1.1	9.6
1970	30.8	27.4	23.0	12.6	31.4	20.0	41.3	5.8	86.9	3.2	1.0	8.9
1975	24.2	30.9	23.0	10.8	33.0	18.8	38.9	6.3	89.5	2.1	0.6	7.8
1978	25.0	30.7	22.9	13.5	31.6	20.8	37.7	7.5	90.9	1.6	0.4	7.2

[a] Includes Newfoundland for 1949 and for subsequent years.

we see the most stability in spending patterns, with goods and services expenditures accounting for the overwhelming proportion of the total.

Another, more detailed breakdown of federal government spending for selected years is shown in Table 4. The two most notable secular trends are the large increase in health and welfare spending (largely transfer payments) and the decline in defence spending as a proportion of total federal spending. It is also interesting to note that debt charges, while having grown in recent years along with the federal deficit, still constitute a smaller portion of total spending than over most of the period shown in the table.

We can highlight the discussion of this section in the following four summary points:

1. The public sector in Canada has indeed grown in Canada over the last 50 years, both in terms of total expenditures and expenditures on goods and services as a proportion of GNP;
2. This relative growth has not been accounted for by the federal government but by the provincial and, to a lesser extent, the local government sectors;
3. Transfer payments have been the major areas of relative growth in federal spending and transfers now account for more than one-half of the federal total; and
4. There has been a large growth in the amount of provincial transfers paid to local governments.

Later in this chapter we will turn to a discussion of the implications of these trends.

Public Sector Revenues and the Public Debt

The growth of government revenues in Canada is shown in Table 5 and the National Accounts surplus/deficit position of the public sector is shown in Table 6. Total public sector revenues as a share of GNP have more than doubled over the period, with the most rapid growth occurring in the last half of the 1960s (excluding the war period).

Federal government revenues stabilized at about 16 per cent of GNP after World War II and have increased only slightly since then. We can also note that, excluding transfers to the provinces, the federal government has generally been in a surplus position but, with these transfers included, the federal surplus is either drastically reduced or turns into an actual deficit.

Provincial government revenues (from their own sources) have increased relatively much more than have the federal government's revenues, with the 1960s being the major growth period. In addition, federal transfers to the provinces amount to about 4 to 4.5 per cent of GNP. The provinces, which receive transfer payments from the federal government

Table 4 Federal Spending on Selected Functions as a Percentage of Total Spending
Selected Years 1954-79 (Financial Management Statistics)
(%)

Year	General Government	Transportation & Communications	Health & Welfare	Education Assistance	Recreation & Culture	Defence	General Purpose Transfers to Other Governments	Debt Charges
1954	4.4	3.2	17.8	0.4	0.3	34.3	7.4	10.6
1957	6.0	4.2	18.3	0.7	0.3	32.2	7.8	10.2
1961	4.0	5.3	24.2	1.0	0.4	25.1	8.6	12.1
1965	3.3	6.5	28.4	2.6	0.6	19.1	4.8	12.8
1967	4.3	6.7	26.0	4.3	0.9	16.6	5.6	11.9
1969	5.4	4.7	28.5	4.7	0.7	14.2	7.3	11.8
1971	6.3	6.6	36.9	5.5	0.7	11.0	8.4	7.8
1973	6.0	6.6	41.4	4.0	1.0	9.1	7.8	7.2
1975	5.5	7.1	40.6	3.4	0.9	7.4	8.2	7.4
1977	5.5	6.6	41.6	3.3	0.9	7.8	8.2	8.1
1979 (est)	6.0	6.9	41.0	4.2	0.8	7.7	6.3	8.8

Source: Statistics Canada, *Federal Government Finance*.

Table 5 Total Government Revenue Expressed as a Percentage of Gross National Product
For Selected Calendar Years, 1926 to 1977 Before and After Exclusion of Intergovernmental Transfers

Year[a]	Federal	Provincial		Local		Hospitals		CPP & QPP	Total, excluding transfers
		Including transfers	Excluding transfers	Including transfers	Excluding transfers	Including transfers	Excluding transfers		
1926....	7.6	3.4	3.0	6.7	6.3	—	—	—	16.8
1929....	6.8	3.8	3.4	6.6	6.1	—	—	—	16.3
1933....	7.6	7.0	5.1	10.2	9.7	—	—	—	22.3
1939....	8.6	7.1	5.5	7.2	6.6	—	—	—	20.7
1943....	22.3	4.7	3.3	4.0	3.6	—	—	—	29.3
1946....	22.1	6.1	4.6	4.4	3.7	—	—	—	30.4
1950....	16.3	6.6	5.2	4.4	3.5	—	—	—	25.1
1955....	17.6	6.5	4.8	4.9	3.8	—	—	—	26.1
1960....	17.0	8.7	6.1	6.8	4.8	—	—	—	27.9
1965....	16.4	11.4	8.9	7.5	4.8	2.2	.1	—	30.3
1970....	18.1	16.2	12.3	8.9	5.2	2.8	.1	1.5	37.3
1975....	19.2	18.0	13.5	8.5	4.4	3.0	.1	1.7	38.9
1978....	16.3	19.9	15.3	8.7	4.5	3.0	.1	1.8	38.1

[a] Includes Newfoundland for 1949 and subsequent years.
Source: Canadian Tax Foundation, *The National Finances*, 1979-80.

Table 6 Surpluses and Deficits of All Levels of Government Excluding and Including Intergovernmental Transfers

National Accounts Basis

Selected years 1958-1978   ($ million)

		Federal	Provincial	Local	Hospitals	CPP & QPP	Total
1958	— excluding intergovernmental transfers....	−104	−162	−812	—	—	−1,078
	— including intergovernmental transfers	−767	−50	−261	—	—	−1,078
1961	— excluding intergovernmental transfers....	+718	+144	−968	−729	—	−835
	— including intergovernmental transfers	−410	−281	−128	−16	—	−835
1965	— excluding intergovernmental transfers....	+1,975	+1,181	−1,844	−1,105	—	+207
	— including intergovernmental transfers	+544	0	−367	+30	—	+207
1967	— excluding intergovernmental transfers....	+1,908	+1,261	−2,389	−1,519	+887	+148
	— including intergovernmental transfers	−84	−334	−337	+16	+887	+148
1972	— excluding intergovernmental transfers....	+3,992	+1,683	−4,171	−2,796	+1,373	+81
	— including intergovernmental transfers	−566	−691	−171	+136	+1,373	+81
1973	— excluding intergovernmental transfers....	+5,194	+2,704	−4,926	−3,189	+1,469	+1,252
	— including intergovernmental transfers	+387	−102	−485	−17	+1,469	+1,252
1974	— excluding intergovernmental transfers....	+7,274	+3,730	−6,066	−3,914	+1,771	+2,795
	— including intergovernmental transfers	+1,109	+652	−819	+82	+1,771	+2,795
1975	— excluding intergovernmental transfers....	+3,865	+2,007	−7,201	−4,723	+2,003	−4,049
	— including intergovernmental transfers	−3,805	−1,756	−568	+77	+2,003	−4,049
1976	— excluding intergovernmental transfers....	+5,166	+2,926	−8,077	−5,638	+2,183	−3,440
	— including intergovernmental transfers	−3,356	−1,501	−781	+15	+2,183	−3,440
1977	— excluding intergovernmental transfers....	+2,274	+4,706	−9,127	−6,117	+2,259	−6,005
	— including intergovernmental transfers	−7,693	−511	−227	+167	+2,259	−6,005
1978	— excluding intergovernmental transfers....	−500	+5,906	−10,062	−6,707	+2,449	−8,914
	— including intergovernmental transfers	−11,357	+565	−565	6	+2,449	−8,914

Source: Canadian Tax Foundation, *The National Finances*.

and pay transfers to their respective local governments, on balance find their net financial position in deficit or moving towards deficit. We should be aware that the overall picture of revenues and deficits of all the provinces together is considerably complicated by the very uneven distribution of natural resource revenue among them.[9] The current surplus position of the total provincial sector masks the fact of large surpluses in the western resource-producing provinces and deficits in most of the others.

Finally, the revenues actually collected by local governments, as a percentage of GNP, have decreased over the period shown. When transfers (almost entirely from the provinces) are included, however, local government revenues almost double. In large part, this secular pattern reflects the fact that the revenues actually collected by local governments are derived almost entirely from property taxes. Property tax revenues grow considerably more slowly than does GNP, partly because in established cities the new land developed each year is a small fraction of the existing total, and partly because the assessments of individual properties (the tax base) in most cities are badly out of date and bear little relationship to market values, which have increased very greatly in recent years. Accordingly, local governments are becoming more dependent on transfers from their respective provincial governments to relieve the large and growing deficits that the municipalities are experiencing because of the slow growth in the revenues they collect themselves. We can see this trend in Table 6.

Again we can sum up the major trends in point form:
1. Federal revenues as a proportion of GNP have been relatively stable in the post-war period;
2. Provincial revenues have, in relative terms, been the fastest growing; and
3. Local governments are relying more and more on transfers from their respective provincial governments to finance their activities.

Intergovernmental Transfers

Thus far we have seen that intergovernmental transfers—from the federal government to the provinces and from the provinces to local governments[10]—have grown substantially over the years. It is now time to look at these payments more directly and to note some of the potential consequences of their growing importance.

Broadly speaking, there are two varieties of intergovernmental transfers. Unconditional or general purpose grants are simply transfers of funds from one government to another; as the name implies, there are no restrictions placed on the uses which the receiving authority can make of the funds. Currently, about 40 per cent of federal transfers to the provinces fall into this category. Equalization payments made under the terms of the Fiscal Arrangements Act constitute the largest single unconditional transfer from the federal government to the provinces. Unconditional grants from the provinces to local governments are much smaller, accounting for only about 10 to 12 per cent of total transfers.

Conditional grants, by contrast, are transfers paid on the condition that the receiving government undertake certain specified activities or provide a service that meets a specified set of conditions. In other words, conditional or special purpose transfers are payments made "with strings attached." In the sphere of federal-to-provincial transfers, conditional grants have, in recent years, grown more slowly than unconditional (although they still are about 60 per cent of the total) and, in addition, the strings have been loosened. The move to Established Program Funding Grants[11] (block grants) in major areas like health and education has greatly relaxed the conditions applicable to the transfers and has provided much more discretionary room to the provinces.

In contrast, conditional grants with relatively more rigid conditions constitute the bulk (up to 90 per cent) of grants paid to local governments by the provinces. As we have already seen, over the years, local governments have been able to finance a declining proportion of their expenditures out of the revenue that they collect themselves, primarily the property tax. The provinces have acted to make up this gap, but they have placed restrictions on local government decision-making while doing so.

Why has this provincial aid been conditional rather than unconditional? The orthodox argument for conditional grants is that they are a means of securing efficient resource allocation in the public sector in the presence of inter-jurisdictional externalities or spillovers. Thus, suppose that one local government supplies a service to its citizens and that some benefits of this service also accrue to the residents of another, neighbouring jurisdiction. The decision-makers in the first jurisdiction will normally consider only those benefits that will be realized by their own citizens. They will not take into account the full benefits of the service and therefore their (formal or informal) benefit and cost calculations will lead them to undersupply the service. To attain an optimal supply, a more senior authority (the province) can intervene and, via a conditional grant, effectively "bribe" the local government to increase the service level by lowering its perceived (to the local government) cost.[12]

The counter to this orthodox argument is that a system of conditional grants distorts the spending priorities of the receiving government. In order to receive provincial aid, a local government must spend funds according to provincial direction and this may differ from what the local government would have done on its own. A first response to this argument may be, "That is precisely the point!" The grants are intended to change local priorities because they do not sufficiently take into account externalities or spillovers. But the argument deserves a more extended response.

While senior governments are presumably in a better position than local jurisdictions to recognize spillovers, it is not always clear that they are motivated to correct the perceived misallocations when they deal with the issue in specific cases. A provincial government may utilize conditional grant programs in pursuit of its own interests and the services it promotes may be ones for which interjurisdictional externalities are not particularly significant. By the same token, a government may neglect to establish a conditional grant program in a situation where the externalities are very significant.

Further, even if the initial motivation is to improve the allocation of resources, the standardized formulae under which the programs operate bring their efficacy into question. Because of political, equity and administrative considerations, a grant program typically is made available to all potential recipients on the same terms (e.g., a 50-50 cost-sharing arrangement). It is far from obvious that the reallocation of resources that this will induce will automatically make appropriate allowance for all the non-standardized externalities that will be present in different situations involving different local governments.

An extensive system of conditional transfers from provincial to local governments results in a diminution of meaningful discretionary decision-making authority at the local level. We will return to this point in the final section of this chapter.

Public Sector Employment

Earlier in this chapter, we noted the possibility of using manpower utilization as a measure of the size and growth of the public sector. In this section we briefly look at these data and the relationships that they reveal.[13] First we must define what we mean; we must indicate those individuals to be designated as public sector employees. For the purpose of the present discussion, we adopt a broad definition which includes as public employees full-time civil servants, other regular federal, provincial and municipal government employees, teachers, hospital employees and employees of government enterprises.

The composition of public sector employment, as a proportion of total employment in Canada, is shown in Table 7. We can note that there has been some growth in the relative size of public sector employment over the period shown, with slightly under one-quarter of all employees working in the public sector in 1975. In relative terms the size of the federal government sector has decreased, the provincial sector has grown substantially and the municipal sector has grown modestly. Some relative growth is also seen in the education and hospital sectors.

Since almost all public employees are in the service sector of the economy, Table 8 compares public employment to total service employment. Here we can see that the proportion has actually decreased over the

Table 7 Public Employment in Canada as a Percentage of Total Employment, 1961-75

Year	Federal Gov't.	Provincial Gov't.	Municipal Gov't.	Education	Hospitals	Enterprises	Total
1961	5.2	2.7	2.3	4.7	3.4	3.8	22.2
1965	4.6	2.8	2.3	5.1	3.9	3.5	22.2
1970	4.2	3.2	2.6	6.1	4.2	3.3	23.6
1975	4.2	4.0	2.7	5.5	3.9	3.5	23.7

Note: Rows may not add to totals because of rounding.
Source: R.M. Bird and D.K. Foot, "Bureaucratic Growth in Canada: Myths and Realities," in G.B. Doern and A.M. Maslove (eds.), *The Public Evaluation of Government Spending*, 1979. Montreal, Institute for Research on Public Policy.

period. Most of that decrease is accounted for by the decline in the proportion of persons in federal employment. The proportion of persons in municipal and education employment has remained more stable, although there was a period of significant growth and subsequent decline in the field of education.

To summarize:

1. While the public sector has grown somewhat (in terms of employment) relative to the total economy, it has declined relative to the service sector of the economy. This is because the private service sector, over the period shown, has grown very rapidly, more rapidly than have governments;

2. Corresponding to the pattern we observed in the expenditure and revenue data, the federal government has not been the source of public sector expansion. Indeed, there has been a modest decline in its relative size; and

Table 8 Public Employment as a Percentage of Service Employment, 1961-75

Year	Federal	Provincial	Municipal	Education	Hospitals	Total Non-Enterprise Civilian	Total Public Employment[a]
1961	6.1	5.1	4.3	8.9	6.4	31.0	40.4
1966	5.3	5.0	4.0	9.2	7.0	30.5	38.1
1971	5.1	5.2	4.1	9.3	6.8	30.7	37.2
1973	5.2	5.2	4.2	8.9	6.1	30.4	36.5
1975	5.2	5.2	4.2	8.7	6.1	30.4	36.6

[a] Although all the other columns in this table exclude both enterprise employment and the armed forces, the last column includes both of these elements (and correspondingly adjusts total service employment to include the armed forces also).
Source: See Table 7.

3. Again consistent with our earlier findings, the provincial governments have been the major agents of expansion in the public sector.

A Balanced Public Sector: Problems and Options

The data presented in this chapter clearly show that there have been marked differentials in the growth rates of the different levels of government in Canada. The provincial governments have grown the most rapidly relative to GNP, the local governments less so; the ratio of the federal government to GNP has remained roughly constant. We have also seen that the revenue growth of each level of government has generally not matched its expenditure growth. The most striking case is the revenue shortfall experienced by local governments. Partly as a consequence of this revenue-expenditure mismatch, we have also seen the development of an extensive system of intergovernmental transfers.

The consequences of these developments are not one-sided. From one perspective, we might view the fiscal transfers from the federal to the provincial level as evidence of the basic healthiness of our federal system: there is sufficient flexibility in the system to accommodate the expenditure responsibilities of the two levels when they grow differentially over time.[14] Moreover, in the case of federal to provincial transfers, revenue adjustments are made without any conditions attached or with very loose restrictions imposed on the recipient.

In other cases, however, fiscal transfers do not seem to be a satisfactory method of accommodating a revenue-expenditure imbalance. Conditional transfers paid to local governments by the provinces fall into this category. We have already noted the complaint that these grants constrain local government decisions, thereby lessening their responsiveness to local needs and demands and promoting provincial standardization and uniformity. There is, moreover, a considerable body of literature that argues for more diversity rather than uniformity in public services. For example, in the economics literature on this subject, variation of service levels and characteristics amongst different jurisdictions to match the heterogeneous tastes and needs of their residents are linked with the notion of economic efficiency.[15] Hence, from this perspective we might conclude that local government complaints against conditional grants are valid, at least in part, and that these grants are not a particularly attractive solution to the fiscal imbalance problem that these governments are experiencing.

What, then, are the alternatives? One possibility is to transfer the spending responsibility for particular services to the provincial or, conceivably in some instances, to the federal level. In fact, this has been done to some degree. Some provinces have largely taken over the provision of primary and secondary education. However, solutions of this sort do not resolve the diversity problem; rather, they likely result in even more standardization.

In this context, conditional grants, which shift part of the authority over spending upward to provincial governments, may be seen as a mechanism for the reallocation of jurisdiction over services within the public sector.

A more promising alternative is to make additional unconditional funds available to local governments. While there are several variations on this theme, we might include them all under the general rubric "revenue sharing." The basic idea is to tie the local government revenue structure to the federal and/or provincial income tax base.[16] A small portion of the tax levied on this base would be earmarked for local governments.[17] The effect of this form of revenue-sharing would be to make available to local governments a new source of tax revenue.

One formula for dividing this revenue among local jurisdictions could be in accordance with the residence of the taxpayer. This formula would in effect mean that local governments have a tax claim on the incomes of their residents and the federal government would act only as a collection agency as it does now for the provincial personal income tax (except in Quebec). The only difference would be that the local authorities would not have the power to individually set their tax rates. If this formula were adopted, higher income municipalities would receive more revenue than those with lower incomes. Some would argue that this is a drawback of the scheme because it is the latter municipalities which tend to need the extra revenue the most.

An alternative formula would be to distribute the money among municipalities in a manner that would effectively bring about some redistribution from higher- to lower-income jurisdictions. A straight per capita grant formula would be somewhat redistributive; more complicated schemes could take into account factors such as average incomes and the tax efforts of local governments.

Whatever the specifics of the plan, this new (to Canada) form of unconditional transfer would ease the revenue-expenditure gap that local jurisdictions are facing, without putting additional constraints on their decision-making authority.

---

[1] To put them in perspective, both measures will be expressed as a percentage of GNP, a measure of the economic activity of the economy as a whole.

[2] See, for example, Winston C. Bush and Arthur T. Denzau, "The Voting Behavior of Bureaucrats and Public Sector Growth," in Thomas E. Borcherding (ed.), *Budgets and Bureaucrats*, 1977 (Durham, North Carolina: Duke University Press).

[3] In this chapter, municipal expenditures and education expenditures are both included in the local government category.

[4] The Canadian Transport Commission's estimated budget for its regulatory work in 1979-1980 was approximately $25 million (5/100 of 1 per cent of the estimated total spending of the federal government). The Canadian Radio-television and Telecommunications Commission's estimates for 1979-1980 amounted to $16 million (3/100 of 1% of the total). A third example is the Anti-Inflation Board whose budget peaked at about $24 million.

[5] For a recent report on the impacts of regulation on the economy, see Economic Council of Canada, *Responsible Regulation*, November 1979.

[6] See Allan M. Maslove, "The Other Side of Public Spending: Tax Expenditures in Canada," in G. Bruce Doern and Allan M. Maslove (eds.), *The Public Evaluation of Government Spending, 1979* (Montreal: Institute for Research on Public Policy).

[7] Another potential instrument of public policy, although quite different than those discussed above, is exhortation. Perhaps the most current example is the appeal by governments to Canadians to conserve energy as a partial solution to our energy problems.

[8] The National Accounts basis is generally regarded by economists as the most comprehensive and reliable measure of government and its relationship to the total economy. For an explanation of the differences between the National Accounts and other accounting concepts, see the *Report of the Tri-Level Task Force on Public Finance*, Vol. 2, Appendix.

[9] For the fiscal year ending March 31, 1979 the total natural resource revenue of all provinces was $4,982 million, 10.4% of total provincial revenues. Almost all of this revenue was concentrated in the three western provinces: Alberta received 73.4% of the total (55.2% of its gross revenues), British Columbia earned 11.2% of the total (10.8% of its gross revenues) and Saskatchewan earned 9.5% of the total (23.7% of its gross revenues). See Statistics Canada, *Provincial Government Finance*, cat. no. 68-205.

[10] There are also substantial transfers from the provinces to hospitals and other, insignificant, transfers between the levels of government. These are not dealt with in this discussion.

[11] In 1977, federal conditional transfer programs to the provinces were replaced by Established Program Financing

> "to provide more flexibility in the financial assistance to the provinces in the program areas of Hospital Insurance, Medicare, Post-Secondary Education and Extended Health Care Services."

Federal contributions are determined independently of program costs in the provinces and are paid in the form of cash and tax transfers. The provinces, by the same token, are not committed to spend the funds on any of the above programs in any particular amounts. See Canada, Federal-Provincial Relations Office, *A Descriptive Inventory of Federal-Provincial Programs and Activities*, as of December 1978. Ottawa: June 1979, pp. 74-75.

[12] For example, a 50-50 cost sharing arrangement for the provision of a particular service means that for every dollar that the local authority spends, the province will also contribute one dollar. Thus, the effective cost to the local government of providing $2's worth of the service is reduced to $1.

[13] Readers interested in a more extensive discussion of this topic may wish to consult David K. Foot (ed.), *Public Employment and Compensation in Canada: Myths and Realities, 1978.* (Montreal: Institute for Research on Public Policy).

[14] The flexibility is in both directions. Because of the war, in 1939-45 there was a major shift in expenditures to the federal government and revenue agreements were reached with the provinces to finance this federal spending.

[15] This literature flows from a seminal article written in 1956. See Charles M. Tiebout, "A Pure Theory of Local Expenditures," *Journal of Political Economy*, 1956, v. 64, pp. 416-24.

[16] The revenue sharing may be defined to include either or both of the personal or corporate income tax.

[17] For example, in 1977 the personal income tax base (total taxable income) was approximately $86 billion. A tax of 1 per cent would have yielded a total of $860 million in revenue.

Chapter 19

Past Stabilization Policies

John H. Hotson,
Professor of Economics, University of Waterloo

Economic Theorists: Laid End-to-End or Side By Side, They Still Point in All Directions

The world economy is sick. It is only natural for a world with a sick economy to turn to its economists for succor and solution, much as a sick person turns to an M.D. However, one of the first things that one learns when consulting economists is that they disagree among themselves. Therefore, the advice given—the cure prescribed—depends greatly upon which economist is consulted. The urgency of the questions, coupled with frustration at the lack of agreed-upon answers, has of late led to the old saw, "If all of the economists in the world were laid end-to-end, they still wouldn't reach a conclusion," being sharpened to, "If all of the economists in the world were laid end-to-end across the Sahara Desert, that would be a damned good thing."

But instead of ordering economists end-to-end across the desert, let us sort them out by laying them side by side in a spectrum from right to left. Our organizing principle will be the degree of government regulation or control of the economic system which the economist prescribes as necessary to cure our economic ills. The governments of the world are asking the economists questions something like the following:

"What should we do to be economically healthy, wealthy and wise; instead of sick, poor and foolish? More specifically, how can we maintain full employment, stable prices, a sustainable balance of international payments and a healthy rate of growth of total output? Still more specifically, can you give us a quick, preferably painless, cure for a combination of: excessive unemployment, galloping inflation, persistent payments disequilibria and a lack of growth?"

If we array the world's economists according to their answers to these tough but vital questions in a semicircle from "ultra-right" for complete non-interventionists to "ultra-left" for advocates of complete govern-

345

ment management, we will become aware that instead of there being a uniformly dense spectrum of prone professional persons, there are distinct clusterings or "schools"; soon, we will have to decide whether to stack them vertically or horizontally. Since only the top professors in each of the larger schools would survive the former ordering, it would be only humane to place them end-to-end in vectors or rays within schools. It also would be logical to reserve spots on the innermost semicircle for the most famous economists—the brightest luminaries—placing the lesser lights in the rays behind them in ever-widening circles.

When the doctors disagree, however, how is the patient to choose? By the sheer number of adherents to the various schools? By assuming that "the truth lies somewhere in the middle"? Or by picking the doctor who tells the patient what he wants to hear, and thus be his own doctor? The last has invariably been the case. Thus, the governments of communist countries choose "leftist" doctoring based on doctrines going back to Karl Marx because that is what they want to hear, while the capitalist countries took their "rightist" medicine from Adam Smith's pharmacopeia until the ailments of the Great Depression and Adolph Hitler panicked them into shifting to John Maynard Keynes' "centrist" restoratives.

Mention of these, the three greatest names in economic theory, aids greatly in bringing order out of the seeming chaos of contending economic schools. In the innermost ring of all of the economists who ever lived we may place just these three and recognize that all schools of living economists radiate from the positions established by the "big three" long ago. Smith (1723-1790) argued for *laissez-faire* or "let well enough alone": since the economy guides itself to an optimum outcome, that government governs best which governs the economy least. Marx (1818-1883) totally rejected Smith's doctrines, maintaining that "capitalism" was doomed to destruction through recurring booms and busts and would eventually be replaced by a "socialist" economy. Keynes (1883-1946) rejected both extremes, calling for a limited amount of active doctoring to even out the business cycle, to achieve high growth rates and stable prices.

Economists of today range from somewhat to the right of Smith to somewhat to the left of Marx. However, since Marxism does not sell well in the West and extreme *laissez-faire* suits neither the instincts of most governments nor that of most economists (it being hard to make a living from patients by telling them that nothing can be done), in every sense of the word, J.M. Keynes has become the central economist. We may describe the three predominant tendencies of economists of the non-communist world as "SmithoKeynesian, Keynesian, and MarxoKeynesian."

SmithoKeynesians

SmithoKeynesians accept those aspects of Keynes' analysis which are least disturbing to their prior commitment to Smithian pre-established harmony. They seek the minimum of government intervention in the economy that is compatible with tolerable levels of unemployment and inflation. All SmithoKeynesians agree that Keynes was too radical in his rejection of *laissez-faire* and his claims that the capitalist economy has no tendency to find its "equilibrium," or resting place, in a condition of full employment and stable prices. They agree that Keynes also went too far to the left in advocating three particular programs: a near-comprehensive socialization of investment, which he considered necessary to maintain growth; a considerable levelling-down of the incomes of the very rich, which he considered necessary to maintain adequate demand in a "mixed" capitalist economy; and wage controls, which he considerd necessary to prevent inflation. SmithoKeynesianism is the predominant economic doctrine of North America and indeed of the non-communist world. Thus, in terms of our body count, most of the West's economists would be laid out in rays at varying degrees to the right of Keynes and to the left of Smith. Paul A. Samuelson, one of the world's leading SmithoKeynesians, and as such in the front rank of living economists, behind and somewhat to the right of Keynes, gives the following succinct statement of SmithoKeynesianism, or as he names his position, the "neoclassical synthesis."

> " . . . by means of appropriately reinforcing monetary and fiscal policies, our mixed enterprise system can avoid the excesses of boom and slump and can look forward to healthy progressive growth. This fundamental being understood, the paradoxes that robbed the older classical principles dealing with small-scale "micro-economics" of much of their relevance and validity will now lose their sting. In short, mastery of the modern analysis of income determination genuinely validates the basic classical pricing principles . . . ." [1]

Samuelson accepts the first two of the three government interventions that Keynes advocated (monetary, fiscal, and income policies). Samuelson's version of economics has been highly influential in western universities and western governments since shortly after World War II and we will say more about it presently. Somewhere to the right of Samuelson —and also in the same rank, since both have been awarded the Nobel Prize—we lay the recumbent form of Milton Friedman, the leading light of the "Monetarist" version of SmithoKeynesianism. As Friedman once put it, "In one sense we are all Keynesians now; in another, no one is a Keynesian any longer." [2] Friedman accepts from Keynes' analysis of the Great Depression the conclusion that *laissez-faire* must not be carried so far as to allow a financial collapse of the kind which both see as having been the trigger of the Great Depression, and, in his own writings, he accepts and extends Keynes' analysis of the demand for money. However, Friedman rejects Keynes' and Samuelson's prescription of activist use of government monetary and fiscal policies to "fine tune" the economy. Thus, Friedman maintains that all macroeconomic ills can be cured by a sound monetary policy. More on the monetarists later.

Keynesians

To the left of SmithoKeynesians and directly behind Keynes, we lay a small band of Keynesians. It is paradoxical, but true to the facts, to hold *a)* that Keynes is the central economist of the twentieth century and *b)* that he has very few followers who take his doctrines "straight."

We may distinguish Keynesians by *1)* their advocacy of some kind of permanent incomes policy intervention to reconcile full employment with stable prices *2)* their emphasis on lack of knowledge of the future, of "uncertainty," as central to the instability of a market economy *3)* their emphasis upon uncertainty as explaining the significance of money and contracts *4)* their demonstration that "fully flexible" prices, assumed by Smith and advocated by many SmithoKeynesians, are not only undesirable but impossible.

In the first rank of the Keynes school, also known as the "Post Keynesian" school, we may place John Kenneth Galbraith and Sidney Weintraub. I am a member of this school and my spot is behind Keynes' right shoulder blade, but how many rows back, I am too modest to specify.[3] Like the Monetarists, the post-Keynesian doctors are doing better business of late as the "Great Stagflation" erodes confidence in the Samuelsonian establishment. More on this below.

MarxoKeynesians

MarxoKeynesians or "left Keynesians" are more to be found in England than in North America and even there, they are rather rare. Joan Robinson[4] is in their first rank as are Piero Sraffa and Luigi L. Passinetti. MarxoKeynesians are distinguished from Keynesians by *a)* their acceptance of a planned or socialized economy as the ultimate goal (to be achieved by evolutionary rather than revolutionary means) *b)* their rejection of the marginal productivity theory of income distribution and their replacement of it by Sraffa's model *c)* their focus upon a class analysis of capitalists and workers.

MarxoKeynesians argue that although monetary, fiscal, and incomes policies can, and perhaps should, be designed to keep a mixed capitalism going a while longer, these policies cannot, even if well-designed and implemented, heal the class struggle between the rich and the poor within the advanced countries and the corresponding struggle between the rich and the poor nations. Therefore, they hold that Keynesian "uppers" to cure depression and "downers" to cure inflation do not treat the real disease. I shall say little, perhaps too little, concerning the views of the MarxoKeynesians.

Let us turn now to a closer look at past stabilization policies in Canada. Before doing so, however, we should mentally dismiss the world's economists to wander off about their business: advising governments, teaching school, and harassing their secretaries.

Past Stabilization Policies in Canada

It is reality which forces changes in economic theory and policy, not breakthroughs in theory which force changes in policy or change reality. There had been many business cycles before the Great Depression of 1929-1939 and yet the Smithian stabilization policy had survived. Smith's advice had been to maintain a fiscal policy of taxing the same amount that the government spends (a balanced budget) in every peacetime year and a monetary policy based on the "real bills doctrine" by which the money supply is limited to the amount required by the "legitimate needs of trade." Smith was mildly favourable to labour unions to offset the superior bargaining power of the "masters," and unalterably opposed to any attempts of government to regulate wages or, indeed, any price. Smith was in favour of an automatic gold standard to link national currencies to gold and thus to assure fixed exchange rates between currencies. He also favoured free trade internationally.

From Confederation to World War II, Canada was a moderately well-behaved patient of the Smithian doctors. Her worst bad health habit, as economists saw it, was her propensity to interfere with the market through high tariff walls—to keep out cheaper U.S. products—and to grandiose government aid to such enterprises as the CP and CN railroads.

Government policies based on Smithian doctoring proved woefully inadequate in the depression decade. As tax collections fell during the downswing from 1929 to 1933, tax rates were increased, particularly tariffs; government expenditures fell in 1932-33 by more than private expenditures did and government investment virtually ceased. While Canada was spared the banking collapse of the U.S., her money supply nevertheless shrank by 15 per cent from 1929 to 1933, while real output and employment fell by 30 per cent.

The chaos of the collapse forced the brighter economists to the realization that their prescriptions were at best ineffective and at worst were making the patient sicker. Among the brightest of these economists was England's J.M. Keynes, who prescribed a dose of expansionary public works: the construction of schools, roads, post offices, airports, etc., to be paid for not by taxes but by bonds sold to the banks, thereby effecting an increase in the money supply. Keynes advocated abolition of the gold standard and compared gold mining to digging holes in the ground and filling them up again. He wrote his famous, and very difficult, book, *The General Theory of Employment Interest and Money* (1936), to support his policy advice, and within a few years, many economists were converted to his views.

However, it is an ironic fact that Keynes and his medicine of peaceful public works had nothing to do with ending the Great Depression and launching the Great Boom of the next thirty-five years. One man, and one man alone, ended the Depression. His name was Adolph Hitler. First, he ended unemployment in the hardest hit country, Germany, with immense expenditures on public works and rearmament. When German expansion threatened her balance of international payments (as her imports rose and her exports remained at a low level because of the world depression), he imposed exchange controls. When full employment and diversion of increasing percentages of resources to war preparations brought inflation, Hitler imposed wage and price controls. Germany's rising military power frightened Poland, Czechoslovakia and France into defensive expenditures, ending their depression. World War II brought full employment to England and the drastic escalation of our war effort that followed the fall of France in 1940 finally ended Canada's depression. Even Hitler could not end the U.S. depression, but here he got some help from his friends. After the Japanese bombed Pearl Harbor, even those slow students, the Americans, learned the lesson that enough government borrowing and spending will end any amount of unemployment, and that wage and price controls can, if one is serious about them, allow truly full employment to co-exist with stable prices. A Canadian gone south to seek his fortune named John Kenneth Galbraith gained the job of administering U.S. wage and price controls and learned many lessons which he has since urged upon the world.

With wartime planning, therefore, there was a triumph of sorts for the "Keynesian Revolution," and a combination of Keynes' and Hitler's methods—the "welfare state" and the "warfare state"—have been used to keep the economy expanding ever since.

The maddest expedient Keynes could think of to create employment was to dig holes in the ground, bury money in them, fill the holes up with town rubbish, and then dig the money up again. Today in the U.S. and Russia, holes are dug in the ground, lined with concrete and capped with yards-thick lids. Into these holes are inserted the latest products of the missileman's science, tipped with enough megatons to destroy all life should they ever be set off, and expensive enough to account for much of the inflation of our time. Thus does "rational" economic man solve the unemployment problem.

Few SmithoKeynesian practitioners, however, have advised their governmental patients that they are subject to serious mental illness in addition to depression-inflation, or "stagflation," tendencies. Instead, SmithoKeynesians have been content to prescribe "restrictive" monetary and fiscal policies of high interest rates and tax hikes when inflation has been the more serious complaint, and to prescribe "expansionary" lowered interest rates, tax cuts and government expenditure boosts when depression tendencies were noted. Most SmithoKeynesians also maintain that incomes policies, such as wage and price controls, should be saved for dire emergencies only and that they be discontinued as soon as they start to work.

Canada holds pride of place as one of the first avowedly "Keynesian" countries in the world because her White Paper on Employment and Income of April 1945 came just after a British White Paper which promised to apply Keynes' ideas and just before the U.S. enacted a "full employment" law to this effect.

Canadian SmithoKeynesian stabilization policy has been far from an unmixed disaster. In the thirty good years from 1945 to 1974, Canada's real output nearly quadrupled, unemployment never exceeded 10 per cent, and the price level "only" tripled. Sometimes the doctors prescribed the wrong medicine—they expected a depression right after World War II and therefore dosed the economy with "easy money"—a strategy which they later came to regret. Canada, to mixed reviews, experimented with floating or "flexible" exchange rates from 1950 to 1962. Under the Governorship of James Coyne, the Bank of Canada, despite rising unemployment, determinedly applied tight money policies in the late 1950s. Eventually Coyne was pressured into resigning and the error was rectified—more than rectified, some people would maintain. The Trudeau years brought a rapid expansion of the central government's role in welfare, but not warfare, the socialization of medicine at the provincial level being especially notable. Canada went back on to a floating exchange rate in 1970 and, in 1972, with the breakdown of the Bretton Woods system of fixed exchange rates, the rest of the world followed. Economists are still arguing as to whether floating rates are as good a medicine in practice as many people held them to be in theory. (They provide countries with more freedom to use monetary and fiscal policy in order to achieve domestic stability, but increased freedom is also an increased freedom to blunder.)

Precisely when the good years of SmithoKeynesianism ended is a matter of dispute, as is the question of whom, or what, to blame. Certainly the U.S.'s long blunder in Vietnam with its never-ending balance of payments deficits played a part, a part which was aggravated as the "Eurodollar" market learned to create U.S. dollars which the U.S. had never spent! The world-wide inflationary fever of the early 1970s, in which the price of wheat, coffee, sugar, and many industrial raw materials increased sharply, turned into an inflationary recession in 1974 when O.P.E.C. quintupled the price of oil and then failed to spend promptly all of the $100 billion increase in the world's "oil bill." Canada was able to avoid the first year of the oil recession by a policy of aggressively easy money and deficit finance. However, her immunity was short-lived and her level of unemployment and rate of inflation eventually exceeded those of the U.S., in part because of political instability generated by Quebec nationalism. At this juncture, government policy shifted first left —with the Anti-Inflation Board experiment that aimed at tapering off wage and price inflation, and then right—with the decision of the Bank of Canada to taper off inflation through successively slower rates of increase in "the" money supply.

Why Has SmithoKeynesianism Failed?
—A Keynesian Critique

Three major weaknesses of SmithoKeynesian analysis account, in my opinion, for the inability of the doctors subscribing to this school to cure their patients' stagflationary—let alone mental—ills.

1) They focus solely upon manipulations of Aggregate Demand, neglecting the perverse effects of their medicines on Aggregate Supply.

2) They pay inadequate attention to the structural changes and new power relationships in the world economy which account for much, perhaps even all, of our inflation.

3) Changes in the payments system make it increasingly difficult to define, much less control, "the" money supply.

Both the Samuelson (fiscalist) and Friedman (monetarist) versions of SmithoKeynesianism seek to "fight inflation" by cutting Aggregate Demand and the level of employment. However, the tax and interest rate increases that they use reduce Aggregate Supply even as they reduce Aggregate Demand. Moreover, in the "good old days" before unemployment insurance, it was doubtless true that increased unemployment would slow the pace of wage increases, or even reverse inflation, as the unemployed competed wages down. Nowadays, it is evident that increased unemployment reduces the *supply* of goods more than it reduces *demand* because the unemployed cease producing but, thanks to unemployment compensation and welfare, are still able to demand a large fraction of their former consumption level. The result of "Smitho-Keynesian" "anti-inflationary" monetary and fiscal policy has therefore been a lower level of real output (*stag*nation) together with a higher price level for the goods which are produced and sold (in*flation*), thus *stagflation.*

Occasionally, SmithoKeynesian economists have admitted the force of these arguments in the short run but have maintained that in the long run the restrictive policies, if maintained, will slow and eventually eliminate inflation. Raising prices in order to stop prices from rising is a bit like going west in order to get to the east. Magellan demonstrated long ago that since the world is round one can, indeed, get to the "far east" by sailing west. However, recent "anti-inflation" efforts have been as inefficient as travelling from Toronto to Calgary by way of London, Paris, Berlin, Moscow, Tokyo, etc.

The structural changes and new power relationships which the Samuelsonians neglect as causes of inflation and whose existence monetarists deny include: 1) the rise of big government, taking and respending for us an enormously greater "slice" of GNP in taxes than it did in pre-World War II days, and regulating more and more aspects of production and distribution,[5] 2) an increasing degree of concentration among vertically and horizontally integrated transnational corporations with consequent increases in the monopoly power that Smith so greatly feared, 3) the granting to public service unions of the right to strike, and an increasing determination among all unionists to demonstrate that wages cannot be held down by unemployment administered at the suggestion of Smitho-Keynesian doctors, 4) O.P.E.C.'s 1973 and 1979 oil crises which demonstrate, to all but the most pure-minded monetarist, the power of a strong cartel not only to change relative prices but to set off a price, wage, money increase spiral.

In short, our price level has risen because of a growing bundle of unpriced government goods whose costs have "conflated," to use David Warsh's useful term, into the price of the goods that we buy, and because big business, big labour and now the big oil cartel are all playing more roughly than ever in a struggle over the sharing of income. In today's world, access to credit and the creation of new money are weapons in this struggle and consequences of this struggle, rather than initiating causes.

This brings us to the third weakness, one which particularly plagues the Monetarists: that it is increasingly difficult to define, much less control, the money supply.

In Friedman's "monetarist" vision of things, the economy is so close to Smith's original picture of pre-established harmony, and activist government interventions so often and so badly mess things up, that the best medicine is the following: the government's central bank must keep the money supply growing at a constant low rate. (Friedman used to advocate 5 to 6 per cent a year, or as fast as real output can grow, to keep prices stable; more recently, he has favoured 2 per cent, to induce gently falling prices.) As for fiscal policy, Friedman would have the government set its tax rates so that taxation is equal to expenditures in a "normal" year of only "natural" unemployment and accept that "temporary departures" from the natural unemployment level will mean deficits in depressed years and surpluses in years of inflationary boom. Both conditions will be short-lived, Friedman believes, if the government will continue the slow, steady growth of the money supply and avoid destabilizing the economy by discretionary tax or expenditure changes—which are usually too late and too big.

Friedman maintains that strong labour unions do not cause inflation, but rather that inflation causes strong labour unions. Friedman shares Smith's admiration for small competitive business firms, but is less concerned than Smith was about the possibility that "big business" may cause great distortions in a market economy. He believes that the power of big business, as well as of big labour, is greatly exaggerated. To Friedman, inflation is always and everywhere a monetary matter caused by excessive growth of the money supply, and to be cured, solely and surely, by ending that excessive growth. Thus, Friedman opposes activist fiscal policy (discretionary tax and expenditure changes) as being unnecessary, and condemns incomes policies, such as price and wage controls, as being worse than useless because they distort allocative efficiency.

Hence, according to Friedman, controlling the money supply will control the economy. But what is the money supply?

Unkind critics have pictured monetarists as reduced to saying, "I don't know what the money supply is, but whatever it is, it ought to grow at 5 per cent."

At one time, money and the precious metals were coextensive. Then paper currencies and bank deposits were developed and the question arose as to whether these were "money" or merely "money substitutes." After a long "recognition lag" involving considerable controversy, it became accepted that paper currency and deposits subject to cheque were indeed money, both because they were commonly used to fulfil all of the functions of money, and because it was so clear that the level of prices could not be accounted for by the volume of gold and silver alone. But what about personal savings accounts and other time deposits? Are not they also so highly liquid that transactors consider them to be part of their "cash balances" once it becomes customary to pay depositors immediately upon presentation of the savings account book? At present, the Canadian definition of money includes such time deposits while the United States definition excludes them. Friedman and other monetarists generally favour the broader definition "M2" which includes time deposits rather than the narrower, more slowly growing "M1" concept. But this is not the end of the difficulty. If time deposits are to be included within the charmed circle of "money" rather than considered as poor relation "near moneys," what about deposits in "near bank" financial intermediaries, short-term public debt issues, credit cards, Canadian Tire certificates, and so on? "Moneyness" or "liquidity" is a matter of degree rather than of kind.

As he has done with many subjects, Kenneth Boulding has summed up the basic difficulty of monetarism in doggerel verse:

> We must have a good definition of Money,
> For if we do not, then what have we got,
> But a Quantity Theory of no-one-knows what,
> And this would be almost too true to be funny,

Now, Banks secrete something, as bees secrete honey;
(It sticks to their fingers some, even when hot!)
But what things are liquid and what things are not,
Rests on whether the climate of business is sunny,
For both Stores of Value and Means of Exchange
Include among Assets no better than mine.
Still, with credit-card-clever computers, it's clear
That money as such will one day disappear;
Then, what isn't there we won't have to define.

Recently Robert Mundell has argued that the U.S. "Fed," the Federal Reserve System, has lost control of the supply of U.S. dollars, because of the existence of the "Eurodollar" and "Petrodollar" markets. European branches of U.S. banks, and European banks as well, have become accustomed to lending dollars free of the reserve requirements which limit U.S. banks in the U.S. and correspondingly limit, say, German banks when lending Deutschemarks.

The point of this discussion is that, time after time, governments have attempted to stop inflation by holding back the growth of the official money supply only to find that "near monies" or "money substitutes" took on some of the aspects of money. Thus, in Canada today, where we have "double digit" interest rates, I no longer keep any money in my chequing account. Instead, I keep all my "liquid funds" in my savings account and write cheques against my empty chequing account. The bank pays me (as of July 1980) 12 per cent interest on the daily balance in the savings account and transfers the funds, without charge to me, to my chequing account only as my cheques come in. Why are the bank and I willing to do all this shuffling of accounts? (1) Because interest rates are high, (2) Because bank reserves are low, and (3) There is an unsatisfied demand for loans even at high interest rates.[6] The eleven chartered banks of Canada are required by the Bank Act to keep a 12 per cent cash reserve against all demand deposits and only a 4 per cent cash reserve against notice, or savings, deposits.[7] Thus, if I transfer $1,000 from my chequing account to my savings account (under the lure of $10 a month in interest), this "frees" $80 of the bank's reserves to make new loans. All students of economics become familiar with the "black art" of the multiple expansion of deposits by which cash deposited with bankers multiplies into "bank money" as they make loans and buy securities. Thus, with a 12 per cent reserve requirement, $100 in cash can multiply, throughout the banking system, into $833.33, but with a 4 per cent reserve requirement, $100 can multiply into $2,500. Thus, as a tight money policy squeezes the reserves of the chartered banks, interest rates rise, inducing the banks to co-operate with customers who want to switch to time deposits—indeed, to urge them to make the switch—and the computer revolution makes it all quite easy. Milton Friedman is eloquent in showing that government regulations are frequently evaded by "the market" and that they often have results which are the opposite of what their authors had intended. Could it be that "tight money," because of its perverse interest cost effects, plus the costs of evasion entailed, plus the costs of inventing clumsy "money substitutes," may actually raise the price level? An increasing number of economists now answer "yes."

Boulding's Law and Incomes Policies

Fervent SmithoKeynesians maintain that "government incomes policies never can work, never have worked, and never will work," in clear violation of Boulding's Law. Boulding's Law, propounded by the poet Kenneth Boulding we met above, states, "Whatever is, is possible." All countries always have had, and always will have, incomes policies and they always work.

Incomes policies are the net result, whether intended or unintended, of all government policies upon the rate of growth and distribution of income. The present incomes policies of Canada include her corporation laws, which allow super concentration in manufacturing, banking, and land development; her labour relations laws, which allow even those providing life and death services, such as prison guards and operating room nurses, to go on strike if they wish to; her tariff laws, which exclude foreign goods because they would lower the price level; her agricultural marketing boards, which have converted agricultural prices from laggards to leaders in the inflationary process; minimum wage laws, and much more. Is it any wonder that, with incomes policies like these at work, we manage to have double digit inflation together with near double digit unemployment?

Monetary policy is itself a potent incomes policy. It is also a very indirect and unjust way to attempt to slow inflation. What tight money does is to decrease the income of small businessmen, particularly those in the construction industry, who are denied loans, and their employees, who are laid off, while at the same time increasing the incomes of bankers and others with money to lend. All this is done in the hope that if there is enough "slack" in the economy—sufficient unemployment and bankruptcy—the next round of wage and price increases will be smaller. Surely we can do better than that.

All sensible discussions of incomes policies must start from the recognition that we already have incomes policies which work, and work to give us stagflation. What we need to design are incomes policies which will give us the desirable outcomes—full employment with stable prices, etc.—that the "patient" desires. The description of a good incomes policy outcome is easy to specify: *A good incomes policy works to cause money incomes to grow only as rapidly as the full employment of human and nonhuman resources allows Canada to grow, and for these growing incomes to be equitably distributed.* Thus, if real output can grow only 6 per cent a year, then total money incomes should grow by 6 per cent a year, not by 15 per cent, as at present.

Some prescriptions to reach this desired goal are considered in the next chapter of this book.

---

[1] Paul A. Samuelson, *Economics: An Introductory Analysis.* 6th ed. (McGraw-Hill, New York and elsewhere, 1955). Now in its 11th U.S. edition and 5th Canadian edition. (Samuelson and Scott).

[2] Milton Friedman, *Dollars and Deficits* (Englewood Cliffs: Prentice Hall, 1968), p. 15.

[3] I am a bit to the right of Keynes because I worry about the inflationary effect of the rapid rise of the government sector in recent decades while he, apparently, did not.

[4] Lady Robinson, never one to mince words, dismisses the SmithoKeynesians as a bunch of "bastard Keynesians." Doubtless the world's "true" Marxists dismiss the MarxoKeynesians as "bastard Marxists." Thus is economic debate carried on at the highest intellectual level.

[5] Robert L. Heilbroner puts this point as follows: "When we look at the historical picture, the root cause of the inflationary phenomenon suggests itself immediately. It is a change that profoundly distinguishes modern capitalism from the capitalism of the prewar era—the presence of a government sector vastly larger and far more intimately enmeshed in the process of capitalist growth than can be discovered anywhere prior to World War II. If we wanted to stop inflation dead in its tracks, we would only have to turn off the government spigot for arms and welfare, and in all likelihood the price level would begin to fall. So would the economy as a whole, which is the reason why there is no possibility of such a massive disengagement from government." *Beyond Boom and Crash* (New York: W.W. Norton, 1978).

[6] As long as people believe that inflation will continue at, say, 10 per cent, they are not deterred by a 15 per cent rate of interest, as they expect it to be a "real" interest rate of only 5 per cent.

[7] As noted earlier, these required cash reserve ratios were revised downwards with the passage of the new Bank Act effective December 1, 1980. This does not affect the principle involved in the following discussion.

Chapter 20

Alternative Stabilization Strategies

Ruben Bellan,
Department of Economics, University of Manitoba

A growing number of economists have become persuaded that contemporary inflation is essentially a cost-push phenomenon. As they see it, the current generation of workers is better educated, more knowledgeable, and more democratic in spirit than any previous generation. These workers aspire and feel entitled to levels of pay that will enable them to achieve a middle-class lifestyle. The strong trade unions in which many are organized apply their substantial bargaining power to extract the biggest possible wage increases from employers. Episodic occurrences affect the size of the pay norms assumed and insisted on by trade union representatives in their bargaining with employers. A large gain fortuitously achieved by one group of workers becomes a goal for all. A rise in the cost of living caused by shortages or increases in the price of imports produces insistent demands for higher rates of pay to offset the increase in living costs. The higher wage rates raise production costs, requiring corresponding increases in prices which generate another round of wage increases, and so on: a one-time occurrence that raises the price level may thus generate a continuing process of inflation. Firms with market power may, for whatever reason, increase their profit margins and thereby contribute to inflationary pressure.

The anti-inflation strategy of fiscal-monetary restraint has so far been a failure, without exception. It has imposed severe unemployment and business losses—without stopping inflation. Exponents stoutly claim that restraints are bound to end inflation if applied long enough and firmly enough. Of this there is no assurance. In any case, the unemployment and business reverses imposed by a restraint program are heavy costs and may rise to frightening levels. There is in fact a strong likelihood that the claim that tough enough restraints will end inflation, will in fact, never be validated. Intense public concern over high rates of unemployment and business bankruptcy are likely to force political authorities to ease the restraints despite continuing inflationary pressure.

Sceptics of the fiscal-monetary option believe that the only sure way to prevent cost-push inflation is to prevent increases in costs. They advocate some form of "incomes policy" which will limit the increases in the rates of pay of all factors of production. They believe that an effective incomes policy would, besides ending inflation, make full employment possible. Once an apparatus were in position that prevented inflationary increase in the pay of factors of production, fiscal-monetary stimulants could be safely applied to propel the economy to the full employment level.

The restraint techniques applied in the past have been ineffective or unacceptable. Voluntary guidelines, i.e., appeals for self-imposed restraints on wage and profit increases, have generally fallen on deaf ears. "Controls" in the form of government-decreed maximum increases or increases that required the sanction of a public authority were effective in wartime but intolerable in peacetime—save on a temporary basis. They obviously violate the principle that wage rates shall be determined by collective bargaining and are therefore anathema to workers and trade union leaders; they deny businessmen the opportunity to capitalize fully on opportunities and straitjacket them with bureaucratic regulation. Controls distort the pattern of productive activity: the nation's productive capacity is directed not in response to market forces but in conformity with bureaucratic judgment. What is needed is some new strategy for restraining increases in wage and profit rates that is free of the limitations and drawbacks of the strategies attempted thus far.

Three possible "income policies," developed fairly recently with these considerations in mind, are described below.

The Tax Income Plan (TIP)

As first proposed by Professors Sidney Weintraub and Henry Wallich, this plan sought to achieve limitation of wage increases by imposing a financial penalty on all increases above an announced guideline figure. The guideline might be set at a figure which was somewhat above the rate of productivity growth and therefore would permit some degree of inflation. However, the inflation that could occur if the plan were successfully implemented would be at or below the currently experienced inflation rate so that the economy would be safeguarded against a worsening of inflation. Presumably the guideline figure could be lowered in the future so that the degree of inflation could be further reduced.

The size of the penalty imposed on any firm would vary with the degree to which a wage increase exceeded the guideline; the greater the excess, the greater would be the penalty. Each firm would be regarded as a single unit; it would be the average wage of all of its employees that would have to meet the guideline requirement. Hence the firm need not raise the pay of every employee by exactly the same percentage. It could differentiate, giving some increases in excess of the guideline; provided that it gave others a smaller increase, so that the average was within the guideline, it would not be subject to penalty.

The presumption would be that every firm, knowing that it would incur a financial penalty if it gave its employees increases in excess of the guideline, would determinedly resist demands for such increases. Hence, essentially the same result would be achieved as that obtained by a system of controls which absolutely forbade increases above a figure designated by a central body. The regulations would leave room for such increases, however; a firm willing to pay the penalty could give them. Hence, the program would accommodate those situations where there was extraordinarily powerful pressure for wage and salary increases beyond the guideline figure. In this critical respect, it would be superior to a system of rigid controls which allowed no exceptions.

The plan further presumes that the level of profits is always closely governed by the level of wages, so that effective limitation of wage increases would, indirectly, serve to limit profits as well. The absence of formal control over profits would not be a damaging deficiency.

An alternative version of this plan has been developed which in effect provides for carrots rather than sticks to induce adherence to a guideline figure for wage increases. Under this scheme, the government would offer a reduction in their personal income tax to workers who agreed to accept a wage increase that was within the guideline. The presumption is that the combination of a guideline increase in wage rates plus a tax reduction would make workers better off than they would be if they were to receive a larger wage increase but no tax reduction.

The plan could be applied on a voluntary rather than compulsory basis, with each firm constituting a unit for administrative purposes. If a majority of its employees voted in favour, a firm would be a party to the program; so long as the average of its wage increases conformed to the guideline, all employees would be eligible for the promised tax reduction. As with the penalty version, there could be variation among the increases given to individual employees; it would only have to be the average of increases given to a firm's personnel that conformed to the guideline figure.

Under this version, the owner of the firm could also qualify for a tax reduction, by keeping his markup at or below some designated figure, say the level of the previous year. Thus, this version of the plan would treat profit in substantially the same way as wages rather than rely, as in the penalty version, on market forces keeping profit increases in line with wage increases. It would, as well, be applicable to government employees, whereas the penalty version could not be applied to them in a way that fully corresponded with its private enterprise application. A financial penalty imposed on a government department which gave its personnel extra large increases in pay could not possibly have the same significance as a penalty imposed on a private firm which exceeded the guideline. The promise of a tax reduction that was conditional on acceptance of wage increases at or below a guideline figure would, however, have exactly the same significance for both public and private sector employees.

There is yet another significant advantage of the carrot approach over the stick approach. When a penalty is decreed for any designated form of behaviour, it is in fact imposed only upon those transgressors who are apprehended and against whom a case is proven. Transgressors who are never discovered escape scot-free; so do those who, by taking advantage of the inevitable loopholes, are able to avoid conviction. Where rules are complex and the data incomplete or fuzzy, the likelihood of such evasion is high. Hence, a penalty scheme would inevitably generate substantial inequities: the actual incidence of penalties would be heavily affected by happenstance and arbitrary judgments made on the basis of information that was complicated, contradictory, inadequate. What is more, in all likelihood, minor transgressions would be typically overlooked for the practical reason that the amounts involved were too trivial to bother about. Where carrots are being distributed, however, it can safely be assumed that all eligible persons will come forward to demand their rightful share. In short, while not all of the people who should get sticks will get them, all of the people who are entitled to carrots will get their carrots. A reward program will have the intended effect on all the persons at whom it is directed; a penalty program will not.

Finally, the reward approach to achieve compliance is more likely to be acceptable both to the public and politicians. Both labour and management are likely to be hostile to a program providing punishment for transgression. Politicians would probably prefer to administer an alternative program that called for them to benevolently distribute rewards for compliance rather than one in which they harshly imposed penalties for violation.

The disadvantages of even the reward type plan are severe. A very considerable administrative apparatus would be required to verify that firms had in fact given their employees wage increases which, on the average, adhered to the guideline, and that markups adhered to their guidelines. The administrative authority would have to keep continuous check on each and every firm, noting all changes in output and personnel. Due allowance would have to be made for reductions in personnel as a result of layoffs, quits, retirements; the skill and experience level of all new employees hired would have to be taken into account. As a result of such complications, the judgment as to whether and to what degree a firm was paying its employees more than before would involve a good many arbitrary assumptions. Proponents, however, claim that administration of the plan would not be terribly difficult, nor would it require many personnel.[1] They declare that a program of this type would probably be no more difficult to apply and would require no larger an administrative apparatus than a program of conventional wage and profit controls. The program would not be able to control import prices since it would have no power over the foreign wages and profits which made up those prices. A substantial degree of inflation could still occur, purely as the result of increases in the price of imports. Finally, there could be workers who were confident that their bargaining power would enable them to achieve wage increases far above the guideline figure, and would end up better off with those increases than they would with only a guideline increase plus tax reduction. If the number of such workers was large, the price level would be given an upward heave. Similarly, the owners of firms might elect to impose a bigger-than-guideline markup; the tax reduction offered would be insufficient to induce them to apply only the guideline markup. If the penalty were applied, there might be workers who successfully insisted on above-guideline wage increases, despite the penalty that their employer would suffer as a consequence. Where such increases occurred, the effect of the guideline program would actually be to exacerbate inflationary pressure: the firm would have to raise its prices not merely to cover the large wage increases that it was giving its employees, but also to recover the amount that it paid in penalty. If the number of workers and owners who violated the guideline were substantial, then the price level could be given a heavy upward push, despite the fact that the anti-inflation program was in effect.

If the reward version of TIP were employed, the cost to the government could be very large. Whether the necessary funds were raised by taxation or borrowing, they would constitute a major fraction of total government spending. The need to raise funds on this scale could require the government to alter drastically its fiscal arrangements; there might be adverse reaction to a major increase in government taxation or borrowing. What is more, if the government were to pay out large sums in rewards, it would therefore be very much involved in the issue of national income distribution. A substantial part of the income actually received by any individual might be in the form of government tax credit. To a far greater degree than now, the size of the incomes of different individuals would be determined by politically made decisions.

Across the Board Cuts on Deflation Day

Professor Hotson's ABCD Proposal

Professor John H. Hotson, Head of the Economics Department of the University of Waterloo, has advanced a bold proposal aimed at ending quickly the paradox of stagflation. His proposal is a forthright answer to those who argue for the "sound" and "conservative" policy of maintaining slack in the economy until inflationary psychology ebbs, and applying job-generating stimuli only after inflationary psychology has totally vanished. While the policies he advocates are radical, the goals he seeks are conservative: the maintenance of an essentially free enterprise economic base for a liberal democratic society.

The proposal advocated is a "short sharp shock" to end inflation by (1) equal percentage cuts to all wage and non-wage personal incomes and (2) price cuts equal, on the average, to the incomes cut plus the average annual productivity gain. Once inflation had been thus decisively checked, stimulants could be applied to generate additional jobs. Henceforth, the money supply and government spending would be allowed to grow at closely limited rates related to the growth of real GNP; some form of "incomes policy" would be maintained to assure that increases in the aggregate of money income corresponded to increases in real output.

Professor Hotson ascribes the germ of his policy proposal to H.A. Turner's summary and conclusion to the book *Do Trade Unions Cause Inflation?* written by Turner, Dudley Jackson and Frank Wilkinson. In the text, the authors had concluded that, in Britain, the neo-Keynesian tactic of raising taxes to curb inflation inevitably boomeranged: tax increases applied to eliminate excess demand triggered wage increases which pushed up the price level—and therefore proved to be inflationary. Professor Turner wrote

> . . . our study indicates (fairly decisively, one might think) that "orthodox" fiscal policy against inflation, which as it was practised in Britain in the 1960s was conceived as mopping up excess demand by increasing taxation—or, even more, by allowing direct tax receipts to rise disproportionately to income —had in fact a perverse effect. Increases in indirect taxation (of several kinds) raised prices and increased the pressure behind wage-demands: and that was particularly the impact of the increasing marginal rate of deduction, by income tax and other levies, from wage income.

Professor Turner argued that the traditional response of British trade unions to inflationary increases in the price level was in fact self-defeating. Unions as a matter of course demanded wage increases to compensate for rises in the price level. But higher wages meant higher production costs and, therefore, higher prices. Increase in money incomes failed to bring an increase in real incomes because it was accompanied by a corresponding rise in prices. A single union might increase its real income substantially by getting a big increase in rate of pay—provided that no one else got a like increase. If only one union got the increase, the price level would barely rise. But if all unions get increases of the same size (and they inevitably would insist on them), then the overall price level would rise equally with the general increase in rate of pay, with the result that no one would achieve any increase in real income. In Britain there was a strong possibility that a general increase in workers' pay might actually lead to a reduction in their real incomes. For, aggravating the effect of higher prices, would be the fact that they would now have to pay higher income taxes. The steep progressiveness of the British income tax schedule ensured that a large segment of anyone's increase in pay would be siphoned off in tax. The combination of higher prices and higher taxes could easily mean that if British workers generally got a wage increase then, with the higher prices and the higher taxes that they now had to pay, the end result would be a reduction in their real incomes.

If the government used its larger tax collection to provide services beneficial to workers, then of course this real income effect would not occur. It would merely mean that instead of having private sector goods and services which they bought, workers would have equally desirable public services and benefits financed by taxation. In fact, however, it was all too likely that the government's additional tax collections would be used not to provide additional useful services but to raise the pay of civil servants and to increase the number of its redundant personnel. An associated result would be reduction in the rate of productivity growth. Some of the additional private income taken by the government in tax would have been used to finance investment that would have contributed to national productivity gain; having had to surrender those funds to the government, the private sector would not be able to make that investment.

Professor Turner accordingly recommended that Britain's trade unions demand, all together, a reduction in their rates of pay to be accompanied by the reduction in prices that would be made possible by this general reduction in wages. With their incomes reduced they would pay less income tax; the combination of lower prices and lower taxes would more than offset the effect of the reduction in their money incomes; hence, their real incomes would rise. Since productivity gains would be occurring, the actual reduction in prices ought to exceed the reduction in wage rates by an amount corresponding to the degree of productivity gain. The real income of workers would rise, therefore, by an average figure which reflected the reduction in their taxes plus the annual rate of productivity gain.

Professor Hotson makes the same recommendation for Canada: that a reduction be applied to all wage and non-wage incomes, to be accompanied by the reduction in prices that would be made possible. Since the Canadian income tax is indexed for inflation, the effects would not exactly correspond with those that would occur in Britain: a decline in workers' incomes would be accompanied by a relatively smaller reduction in the income tax that they had to pay. Nevertheless, Professor Hotson believes that, with the accompanying reduction in prices and the slight reduction in income tax, Canadian workers would benefit from a general reduction in their rates of pay. Since the trade union movement is in fact most unlikely to demand such a reduction, it ought to be imposed by the government—for labour's own good.

In introducing the program, it would be necessary to make allowance for the fact that there is great variation among industries in the rate of productivity gain each year and that such gains, in any industry, are spread out over the whole year, rather than occurring entirely at the beginning of the year. Hence, it would be necessary to order larger price reductions in those industries which were experiencing the larger productivity gains, and to space out all required reductions over the year; i.e., an initial reduction would be required at the beginning of the year, to be followed by further reductions every three or four months.

The abrupt elimination of inflation would bring large windfall gains to bondholders. In anticipation of inflation, the bonds that bondholders had bought would have been issued at high rates of interest to ensure that, during a period of rapid inflation that eroded the real value of money, bondholders would get a decent rate of real return. Now, inflation having been eliminated, the government would lower interest rates in order to foster investment and thereby achieve increase in employment and productivity. The owners of previously issued bonds would continue to receive rates of interest well above current levels and not warranted by a high rate of current and prospective inflation. Professor Hotson believes that this would be a turnabout which was fair play. In the past, bondholders suffered windfall real losses when inflation occurred following a period of price stability: they continued to receive the low interest rates that had constituted a fair return when prices were stable but which were inadequate once rising prices eroded the real value of a fixed rate of return.

In an example designed to demonstrate how his proposal would work out in practice, Professor Hotson assumed a 10 per cent cut in all rates of pay and a 3 per cent rate of annual productivity growth. Given these figures, the required average reduction in prices would be 13 per cent. If such a reduction did occur, however, it would probably generate an even steeper reduction in real estate values, these having been bid up sharply by inflationary expectations. Individuals and firms whose assets were largely in the form of real estate would be hit very hard. For this reason, Professor Hotson suggests that it might be preferable to make only small reductions in rates of pay and prices in order not to generate the trauma of a severe reduction in real estate values.

Scale-Down of Income Increases
(The Bellan Plan)

The object of this strategy is twofold: to limit the aggregate of all income increases in the country to equality with the national increase in real output; secondly, to arrange that this permissible aggregate of income increases be distributed among individuals in accordance with free market principles. In implementing the plan, the government would first allow market forces to determine every individual's increase in money income. Then, once the total of all increases was known or could be confidently estimated, the government would uniformly scale down all increases to reduce their aggregate to a non-inflationary magnitude. Thus, if a year-to-year increase in the country's real output was 3 per cent but income increases averaged 12 per cent, the government would scale down every individual's increase to one-quarter of its original size. The person who had got a 16 per cent increase would have it reduced to 4 per cent; the person who had got an 8 per cent increase would have it reduced to 2 per cent, and so on. Through this procedure, both objectives of the strategy would be realized: the aggregate of income increases would be non-inflationary, and each individual's real income increase would be in market-determined relationship to everyone else's increase, since the uniform scaling-down of all increases would preserve exactly the original ratios that had been produced through the unhindered operation of market forces.

In real terms, the effect would be that all persons who obtained an addition to their money incomes would be certain to obtain an increase in real income, this increase being their pro rata portion of the national increment to real output. Each individual's portion would correspond to the ratio between his/her original increase in income and the national total of such increases. A person whose money income increased by $1,000 when the national total of increases was $1,000,000,000 would get 1/1,000,000 of the national increase in real buying power. Every person whose money income was unchanged would have exactly the same real income as before.

The procedure would directly come to grips with the simple reality that the total of real purchasing power in a country always corresponds to the amount of actual goods available and can never increase faster than the amount of those goods. Whenever money incomes rise faster than real output they are automatically scaled down now—by inflation. Inflation scales down the real value of each monetary unit to maintain consistency between purchasing power and real output. What is proposed here is that increase in the number of monetary units be scaled down instead, to maintain that implacably required consistency.

The scaling-down could be implemented through purely fiscal procedure. A tax could be imposed on everybody's *increase in income,* levied at a rate which would reduce the aggregate of all post-tax increases to the acceptable figure. Since the country's business firms would collectively have paid inflationary increases to the country's factors of production, it would be necessary to give them financial assistance if they were to be able to sell their output at non-inflationary prices. In order to preserve firms' normal resistance to pressure for cost increases, this assistance would have to be given on a basis quite unrelated to their individual cost experience. For example, all firms might be given a uniform grant per employee. The total of this financial contribution by government to firms would be exactly equal to the amount realized by its tax on increases in income; the stabilization program would have no net effect on the public finances. The government's grant would have to be reliably anticipated by all firms so that they took it into account in setting their prices. If that were done, then the business community as a whole would charge a stable price for the aggregate of its output. The price rises of firms that paid above-average increases to factors of production would be offset by the price reductions of firms that paid smaller than average increases to their factors, but received a grant equal to the average increase.

A good many people, union members particularly, are paid at rates that have been contracted long beforehand. This fact would enable the utilization of an alternative procedure for scaling down their incomes. Once all of their contracts had been negotiated, then, if it was evident that their aggregate would turn out to be inflationary, the government could order that all negotiated increases be appropriately scaled down before being implemented. In the case of all other persons, the scaling down would be achieved by taxation of increases in income.

While administratively less desirable, the combined use of both procedures would offer one very substantial benefit: it would likely reduce inflationary pressure to a very large extent throughout the entire economy. Thus, if the average pay increase of all unionized workers could be held to equality with national productivity growth, the incomes of all other factors of production would likely also increase at about the same rate. Non-unionized workers would get little, if any, more than unionized workers; since their customers' incomes had risen only moderately, business firms could not significantly raise their markups. Only a very small tax would have to be levied on increases in income, and a correspondingly small amount of financial assistance given to the country's business community.

A paramount criticism of the plan comes immediately to mind. Knowing that all income gains were going to be scaled down, many people would demand much larger increases to start with; inflationary pressure would be greater than ever.

This objection is unlikely to be critical. The fact that some people will anticipate the scale-down and demand big pay increases does not necessarily mean that they will get them. Employers do not blithely grant workers everything they ask for today and would oppose large pay demands even more determinedly if the price level promised to be absolutely stable. At present, their resistance to large demands is vitiated by the consideration that these increases will soon be swallowed up in the general inflation. If the price level were reliably stable, an employer who acceded to inordinate pay demands would become burdened with costs that were seriously out of line with those of competitors and the purchasing power of customers. Even when scaled down, a pay increase granted by an employer that was larger than that given by competitors could place him at a disadvantage; if the general price level were absolutely stable, even the scaled-down version of an extraordinarily large wage increase would constitute a potentially ruinous burden. The employer would have just as much reason as now to oppose demands for large wage increases and to put forth maximum effort to keep wage increases to a minimum. Furthermore, there really is no reason to suppose that workers will effectively insist on larger pay increases than they are getting now. It is a safe presumption that they are now going after the maximum attainable; to argue that they would get bigger increases if the proposed program were implemented is to make the highly questionable assumption that employees have reserves of bargaining power upon which they do not at present draw but which they would bring to bear if incomes were scaled down, not by inflation as is the case now, but in the manner proposed here.

In any case, no matter how large negotiated pay increases were, their aggregate could always be scaled down to the desired figure. An accumulation of very large individual pay increases would simply mean that the scale-down percentage would have to be larger than if smaller increases had been negotiated. Indeed, a large, uniformly applied scale-down of pay increases could serve the useful purpose of reducing the absolute magnitude of large disparities. If one union negotiated a 40 per cent increase while another won only 10 per cent, then, if both were scaled down by four-fifths, the increases would become respectively 8 per cent and 2 per cent. The difference between the two increases would now be a matter of only 6 per cent of original income, not 30 per cent.

To help make the program acceptable, the government could give categorical assurance that every individual's real income would rise by an amount that corresponded to the scaled-down size of his income increase. This it could do by undertaking to give an income tax rebate of whatever size was necessary to bring each person's take-home purchasing power to the appropriate level. Thus, say that a union had negotiated a 12 per cent pay increase which was scaled down to 3 per cent—the expected rate of national productivity growth. The government could promise that if the price level rose, despite the program, it would reduce the income tax obligation of each union member by an amount that would leave him with a net increase in purchasing power of 3 per cent. Strictly speaking, the price level simply could not rise if the program were correctly applied; the guarantee would never have to be implemented. Its existence would, however, allay the concerns of those people who felt that in accepting the program, they would be exposing themselves to the hazard of decline in real income.

In principle, the authorities could apply the program to achieve any predetermined degree of restraint. To overcome the opposition of persons who were fearful that they would somehow be harmed by it, the program could be introduced in stages. The first scaling-down of negotiated pay increases, with its associated tax on increases in other forms of income, could be relatively small, designed merely to reduce inflation rather than end it totally. Sceptics who were implacably opposed to a sharp scaling-down of increases in their incomes might be prepared to accept a modest reduction. If all went well, the experience would demonstrate that the strategy was a feasible one for reducing inflation and that it contained no grievous faults or inequities. Having established that the procedure was effective and fair, the authorities could subsequently apply it firmly enough to eliminate inflation entirely, i.e., they could eventually scale down all increases in income so as to shrink their aggregate to a size that would correspond exactly with the increase in real national output.

If everything went according to plan, the procedure outlined here would absolutely ensure price level stability;[2] since the economy would be firmly confined within a non-inflationary frame, fiscal-monetary stimulants could be safely applied to whatever degree was required to generate full employment. Conflicts about wage rates and profit margins should be less acrimonious than they are now because the stakes would be much smaller. Today, anyone whose income increase turns out to be lower than the inflation rate suffers decline in real income; negotiations about pay rates are imbued with a desperate anxiety to avoid this traumatic adversity. Adoption of the program proposed here would limit conflict to the issue of how each year's increment to national output was to be distributed. Everyone would be secured against the possibility of decline in real income (so long as their money income remained the same).

Even if successfully applied the program would not produce a panacea. It would achieve one, and only one, object. It would eliminate inflation without requiring government intervention in the marketplace by reproducing, on a reduced scale, the array of income increases achieved through the operation of market forces. The reproduction, while on a smaller scale, would be exact, and would contain all the warts of the original. The fortunate, powerful and unscrupulous would still get more than the weak, the kindly, the unlucky. Individuals who had undeservedly achieved high incomes in the past would retain them; the justifiable efforts to achieve advancement by persons whose incomes were unfairly low would be cramped. If these inequities are to be corrected, it will have to be by other means.

---

[1]At a conference held in the U.S. in 1978, two representatives of the U.S. Treasury Department expressed the view that a TIP plan was administratively feasible. It was their opinion that the penalty version of the plan would be easier to administer than the reward version and that, to be workable, the plan would have to be confined to a relatively small number of large firms; the administrative problems would likely be overwhelming if it were universally applied. They were confident that direct control over profits was unnecessary: effective limitation of wages would, through indirect effect, assure that profits did not rise unduly. Finally, they expressed the belief that the program would have to be a permanent feature of the economy, rather than merely a temporary arrangement that could be dissolved after a year or two.

[2]This would hold true provided that the available aggregate of consumer goods and services was at least as great as it had been previously. If the output of these goods and services falls as a result of, say, crop failure, labour unrest, decline in productivity, worsening of the terms of trade, or diversion of capacity to war production, a decline in national real income is unavoidable. For the country as a whole, purchasing power must decline, with the decline appearing in the guise of a rationing program which legally limits the quantities purchasable by individuals, or reduction in monetary incomes, or price inflation which exceeds the growth of monetary incomes. Given the hostility to rationing and to reduction of monetary incomes, a reduction in national purchasing power that is inexorably imposed by a reduction in the amount of goods and services available is most likely to appear in the form of price inflation. For such inflation there is no remedy; it would simply have to be endured.

Chapter 21

Summary
The editors

While the aggregate of Canada's natural resource endowment is substantial, it is far short of the promise implicit in the country's huge size. Much of Canada's land area is totally unproductive, merely useless ground that must be traversed. Of its nearly 4 million square miles, only about 260,000 square miles are arable; about one million square miles are covered by commercially exploitable forests; the rest, about two-thirds of the country, is comprised of tundra and non-productive forest in which there is only the occasional mineral deposit and the odd waterfall that can be harnessed for the generation of hydroelectricity. And many of these mineral deposits and waterfalls are in the northern reaches, far from the centres of habitation to which their product must be transported, and therefore subject to extremely heavy costs of transportation.

Our resource endowment is by now a largely known quantity. The limits of the arable land were delineated decades ago, as was the extent of commercial forest. All waterfalls have been mapped; some mineral deposits and some oil and gas pools may yet be discovered, but it is unlikely that their extent is large. If our earnings from the export of natural resources are to increase significantly in the future, it will be primarily as a result of increase in price rather than in quantity. Our output is in fact likely to decline with the exhaustion of deposits of non-renewable resources. And price may not rise substantially: other countries have resources similar to ours and compete keenly on world markets.

Our various resources have contributed unequally to the country's overall economic development. Cultivable land contributed the most: large numbers of people settled on the land, swelling the national population. To transport the land's produce to markets, major transportation systems were built, including canals, port facilities, railways and roads. These became major elements in the national infrastructure, supporting additional development in many directions. When new technology rendered a large farm labour force unnecessary, redundant agricultural population moved to towns and cities, swelling the country's urban labour force. Natural resources other than land—furs, fish, minerals, forests—

373

contributed much less to overall national development. Far fewer people were involved than in agriculture and they did not require a massive national infrastructure. In the case of fisheries, a good deal of the operation was done from foreign vessels which came and went. A good many mineral deposits generated only small enclaves of settlement and activity that had little economic contact with the rest of Canada; the companies obtained their equipment from outside the country and exported practically all of their output. The only benefits to Canada were the small royalties paid to provincial governments and the jobs provided in the construction and operation of mining plant. Most of these jobs required little skill and provided meagre wages. Nor did Canadians always get them; a good deal of the work was done by transient foreigners who came, worked and went.

We are endowed adequately, but not superabundantly, with one critical natural resource: energy potential. Within our borders are large oil and gas deposits and tar sands from which oil can be extracted; off our Arctic and Atlantic coasts, more oil and gas have been discovered. As well, we have major deposits of coal and uranium ore, and waterfalls from which hydroelectricity can be generated. Most of this we need ourselves, however. Our cold climate requires us to consume vast amounts of fuel for heating; the extreme distances that must be traversed require huge amounts of fuel for transportation; the processing of several of our major resources requires immense amounts of energy. We have indeed exported, and still export, coal, oil, gas, uranium and hydroelectricity, but will shortly end altogether the export of oil, and are likely soon to limit exports of gas and electricity.

The geographical distribution of many of our energy sources is flawed. Major waterfalls are located far from major centres of electricity consumption, requiring long and costly transmission systems. While the two central provinces, Ontario and Quebec, constitute the chief markets for oil, gas and coal, our oil and gas deposits occur chiefly in Alberta, in the high Arctic and off our Atlantic coast. Our major coal deposits lie in Alberta and British Columbia. Long and costly pipelines are needed to supply Canadian gas and oil to their major markets, and those markets have traditionally obtained the bulk of their coal requirements from more proximate U.S. sources.

The development of each energy source has been characterized by a distinct type of entrepreneurship. It was mostly Canadian and British capital and experience that built Canada's coal mines; U.S. capital and experience supported the discovery and exploitation of Canada's oil and gas resources. The Canadian government began to participate in the industry in the 1970s through the medium of two crown corporations. Private enterprise initiated the generation of hydroelectricity, but the industry became a provincial government responsibility very early in Ontario and eventually in most of the other provinces. From the very beginning, the federal government assumed responsibility for the generation of nuclear power in Canada through a crown corporation established for the purpose.

The sharp escalation of oil prices after 1973, and the consequent increases in the prices of all energy sources, generated an acutely divisive issue in Canada: the distribution of the economic rents derived from the exploitation of natural resources. The British conquest had made Canada, in 1760, a property of the British crown. The several colonial governments became legal custodians on behalf of the crown and were deemed to have the ownership of all lands within their boundaries and to be entitled therefore to all moneys paid for the purchase of such lands, all rents for their use, all royalties paid for the right of extraction from them of useful materials. The BNA Act designated provincial governments as the successor authorities to the colonial governments in this regard and they received the revenues derived from natural resources. Until 1973, such revenues were relatively small. The market value of natural materials was usually very little above the actual cost, in terms of labour, capital and materials, of extracting them; the royalty that could be claimed by the proprietary authority was correspondingly small. The wild escalation of world oil prices that occurred after 1973 drastically altered the situation, however, in respect to oil and all its close substitutes. Market value substantially exceeded production cost and, with the very large quantities being produced, the aggregate of economic rents became enormous.

The magnitude of these amounts made their distribution an issue of critical importance. As long as they were small, there had been no challenge to the constitutional right of a provincial government to be sole recipient through the royalties that it charged to the private enterprise firms that actually conducted the industry's operations. Now, however, these economic rents amounted to billions of dollars a year and there was no longer ready acceptance of the traditional rule that provincial governments should be the sole recipients. Four different claimants today demand shares in the bonanza. Provincial governments insist on their constitutional and traditional right to all financial benefits derived from natural resources of which they are legal owners. The federal government demands a substantial share, to be obtained through its power to tax the profits of the private corporations involved. The corporations demand that they be allowed to keep a large share of their profits as legitimate return and for the financing of future development activity. Canadian consumers demand that the products be sold to them at prices substantially lower than world levels so that they, too, will share in the benefit yielded by the availability of the resources within Canada. The issue is an intensely political one: it was a major factor in the defeat of the Conservative government in the federal election of February 1980 and is likely to remain highly contentious for years to come.

Canada has today a comprehensive transportation system, a major part being a natural endowment and the rest having been laboriously built at heavy cost. The St. Lawrence River-Great Lakes System is a major transport artery that reaches deep into the continental interior, making possible cheap, water-borne carriage of products over a long stretch of their journey to markets. Optimum use of this magnificent waterway required the construction of a series of costly canals around waterfalls, which have now been built. Two transcontinental railways span the country. One was constructed as an integrated unit, and the other came into being as an amalgam of previously built lines, several of which were in direct competition with one another: large sections were redundant from the moment that they were completed. Newer modes of transportation have rendered many branch railway lines unprofitable and the railways are anxious to abandon them. Since these lines still provide useful service to some communities, abandonment proposals are opposed, the opponents appealing to the government to exercise its regulatory authority in the matter and to forbid abandonment. Despite the opposition, a considerable mileage of railway line has been abandoned and more trackage is scheduled to be abandoned in the future.

Inter-city freight traffic is now carried by rail, truck and water, depending on the nature of the cargo, the region of the country and the length of the journey. Heavy, bulky products are carried by rail and water in Eastern Canada which has available to it the St. Lawrence-Great Lakes waterway sytem, and by rail only in Western Canada where no alternative water route exists. Light, valuable products are generally carried by truck, particularly if the distances involved are short. Inter-city passenger traffic is chiefly by air and private automobile, with buses and railways dividing up the small remainder. Air traffic is handled chiefly by two national airlines which operate international services and, in Canada, are supplemented by regional and local airlines that serve small and remote communities. All of the larger cities have public transit systems. In Montreal and Toronto, density of traffic has justified subway lines on several routes. In Toronto, streetcars still operate on some routes; otherwise, public transit systems are buses.

The inevitably monopolistic nature of most forms of commercial transportation has moved the government to establish regulatory authorities to protect consumers and generally safeguard the public interest. A requirement frequently imposed by regulatory authorities has been that transportation firms provide some services that are unprofitable, subsidizing them out of their profitable operations. Public boards also regulate forms of transportation where monopoly is not a problem, such as taxis and inter-city trucking. Here, the justification is the apprehended need to ensure orderly competition. Regulatory authorities fix the maximum tariffs that may be charged; the fact that fixed cost is usually a very large fraction of total cost inevitably results in a high degree of arbitrariness in rate setting. Evidence suggests that the present high structure of rates deters the fuller utilization of rail, public transit and taxis that would be economically appropriate.

There exists in Canada today a wide diversity of manufacturing firms. Food preparation for a local population is a ubiquitous activity: every city has its bakeries and dairies; every larger city has as well its breweries and meat-processing plants. The processing of natural materials is a major industrial activity, carried on typically in large plants located near the source of the raw material. Thus, we have pulp and paper plants in forested areas, smelters at the site of mineral deposits, fish canneries on the coast where the fish are caught, fruit and vegetable canneries where the products are grown, wineries near vineyards. Thanks to special freight rate arrangements, wheat is milled into flour in plants located along the route taken by wheat as it proceeds to overseas markets. Our major steel plants are in southern Ontario, located at sites to which American coal and iron ore could be conveniently delivered—and are favourably located in relation to Alberta coal and Quebec-Labrador iron ore that began to be used when new transportation possibilities made them available.

The country's manufacturing activities are concentrated in the two central provinces, much of it in their two big cities. With their large and diversified labour forces and their big local markets, Montreal and Toronto are by a wide margin the country's leading industrial centres, producing a wide array of consumer goods and industrially required products. Quebec's industrial centres include some heavy engineering firms—notably in shipbuilding and aircraft-making—and large numbers of labour-intensive clothing and furniture-making firms.

Practically every one of southern Ontario's cities and larger towns contains a few big manufacturing plants, a large proportion of them branches of U.S. firms. Location in southern Ontario provides the advantages of convenient access to the bulk of the Canadian market, availability of necessary materials and services, and proximity to the U.S. headquarters organization. Practically the whole of the Canadian automobile and automobile parts manufacturing industry is located here, along with other industries established and still controlled by U.S. interests. Since so many of the industrial firms are branch plants, they do very little research and development. The operations of many consist of the assembly of parts sent in from the U.S.; others manufacture products according to designs developed by the foreign parent. Only a few branch plants innovate products. Production is almost entirely for the Canadian market only, though a small number of firms are able to sell their products outside the country as well; thanks to the Auto Agreement of 1965, Canadian auto plants produce a few models for the entire continental market. Some manufacturing activities are carried on outside the major concentrations in central Canada: a few firms, in a variety of industries, turn out products for regional, in some cases national, and in a few cases international, markets.

Of Canada's population of 24 million, nearly half, about 11 million persons, are in the labour force. The composition of that labour force is significantly different from times past, reflecting the social attitudes and expectations of our times. Women constitute an ever-growing proportion of the national labour force, 39.3 per cent by 1979. Persons under 20 years of age constitute a relatively smaller portion of the labour force than in the past, reflecting the longer period of time spent nowadays by young persons in educational institutions before entry into the work force. Their education and training has been imperfectly synchronized with the needs of the national economy. A larger proportion has tended to qualify for white-collar, clerical and professional employment than the economy has usually required, while a smaller proportion has acquired manual skills demanded by industry. The consequence has been that substantial numbers of young Canadians have emigrated to the U.S. following graduation from their educational institutions and Canada has been forced to seek, chiefly from European countries, persons who have acquired specialized skills through apprenticeship programs.

The operational characteristics of the Canadian economy have generated a substantial corps of transient workers. Major construction projects in remote areas (of mines, hydroelectric generating plants and the like) required temporary work crews for periods of up to several years; a high rate of turnover has been commonplace among the operating staffs of plants remote from the country's settled areas.

A comprehensive financial system has evolved through which Canadians make payments to one another and through which the monetary savings of individuals and business firms are channelled to borrowers. Advancing technologies and changing market situations have generated constant alteration in the nature of the system's component organizations. New types of financial institutions keep being born, in some cases to specialize in functions hitherto performed by generalist firms; existing firms keep adding to the range of their functions.

While the great bulk of the financial operations of the country is handled by Canadian organizations, foreign firms operate here as well, either directly or through affiliates. Legislation restricts the role of foreign financial institutions, reserving the major portion of the business for Canadian firms. Major Canadian firms operate on a substantial scale outside of the country, particularly in the fields of banking and insurance. Our financial ties with the U.S. are very close: institutions that accumulate the savings of Canadians regularly invest large proportions in that country, and entrepreneurs who require risk capital in large amounts tend to obtain it from the U.S. The flow of investment funds between the two countries is large and continuous in both directions.

Through its control over interest rates and the national money supply, the Bank of Canada exercises a good deal of regulatory authority over the financial system. Its freedom of manoeuvre is restricted by the need—or what is apprehended to be the need—to keep interest rates in Canada closely aligned with those of the U.S.

Inflation, particularly in the last few years, has gravely weakened public confidence in the financial system. The constant and, at times, accelerated decline in the purchasing power of the monetary unit has impaired its serviceability as a means of payment and particularly as a store of value. A good many people have anxiously sought to protect themselves against erosion of the real value of their savings by exchanging their money for gold and silver or by investing in properties that offered the prospect of being good "hedges against inflation." One consequence of such purchases has been to increase drastically the market values of some types of property, thereby generating serious allocative distortions. Because houses were reckoned to be good "hedges against inflation," many people bought them earlier than they needed to, larger than they needed, and retained them longer than they needed to. Housing construction was excessively stimulated in some areas of the country, with the pace of construction far outdistancing the growth of demand derived from demographically based need. Meanwhile, lower-income persons, who genuinely needed housing, were unable to buy—or could buy only with great difficulty—because of the levels to which housing prices had escalated.

Several features highlight our economic relationships with the rest of the world. Roughly 70 per cent of our exports go to the U.S. and about the same proportion of our imports come from that country. Our chief exports (aside from the automobiles that we ship to the U.S. under the Auto Agreement) are processed raw materials. Our chief imports are sophisticated machinery and consumer products that we do not produce ourselves, and food products that we cannot grow for climatic reasons. We spend very large amounts on foreign services as well: Canadians travel in great numbers to other countries, particularly for winter holidays. We hire large numbers of foreign entertainers, athletes and consultants. Our numerous branch plants must make remittances to their respective head offices toward outlays by parent organizations for administration, advertising, research and development.

For years now, our net international indebtedness has obliged us to pay the rest of the world more than we have earned there, and we have had to borrow even more foreign money to make up the difference. The sum of our indebtedness to foreigners is now frighteningly large: a major part of what we have to pay foreigners each year is now the interest on all our past loans from them. Much of what we borrow each year from foreigners is used to pay interest on debt. In order that Canada obtain the foreign funds it needs to cover its annual balance of payments deficits, the Bank of Canada has kept Canadian interest rates closely linked to those of the U.S., and usually slightly above. A good many economists have become highly critical of this policy, arguing that it is because we borrow abroad that we have the current account deficit in the balance of payments. This, indeed, is the argument of Chapter 8. If we did not borrow, then, as a matter of course, we could spend in foreign countries no more than we earned from them.

The Role of Government

As in all countries nowadays, government plays a major role in the operation of the Canadian economy. As a matter of course, our public authorities assume the responsibilities for national defence, justice and police, which only governments can handle. In addition, however, they now provide a good many services which originally were provided by private enterprise, and still could feasibly be so provided. Governments have entered these fields for a variety of reasons: to ensure that a highly desirable service, such as education, is available to absolutely everyone; to ensure that a necessary service which must inevitably be produced by a monopoly organization is not exorbitantly priced; to ensure that socially desirable services are produced even though their production is not commercially feasible. And finally, governments provide aid and succor to those persons who cannot effectively fend for themselves, here taking over almost entirely the responsibilities once handled by charitable individuals and organized religious groups.

At the insistence of French Canada, the BNA Act decreed education to be a provincial responsibility. As the previous colonial administrations had done, the new provincial legislatures arranged for the establishment of public schools to be administered by local bodies that would be subject to provincial supervision and financially aided by a small provincial contribution. While initially the public schools required contributions from the parents of attending children, they were eventually made entirely free, supported totally by the provincial grant and a levy on local property. The funds available and the extent and quality of education provided varied greatly among the numerous school administrations that came into being. Wealthier provinces were able to make larger grants to local school boards. The levy on property was far more productive in some communities than in others, reflecting wide differences in both property ownership and willingness to support educational institutions. The relative sparsity of population in rural areas and the slow pace of travel in pre-automotive times inevitably required that rural schools be tiny affairs with limited curricula and facilities; each school could have as its student body only the small number of school-age children who lived within walking distance and depended for financial support on the value of the real property within that limited land area. Higher level education became generally available in due course. Religious denominations very early established colleges for the preparation of young men for their respective ministries; curricula included subjects in arts as well as divinity, and these colleges were attended as well by young persons who did not intend to enter holy orders. Eventually, every provincial government established a provincial university; several of those were in effect grafted onto institutions that had been established by religious bodies. The necessary funds came from tuition fees, private endowments and provincial grants.

Massive change occurred following the Second World War in the scale and character of Canada's educational establishment. The "baby boom" of the first post-war decade produced a greatly increased school-going population that required a corresponding development of educational facilities at every level. Much increased emphasis on the value of education as the means of qualification for highly desirable careers, together with widely demonstrated proof thereof, persuaded the typical young person to acquire far more schooling than his/her counterpart of previous generations. Educational facilities were elaborated as well as enlarged; many new features and programs were introduced. A huge increase occurred in the number of teachers and associated personnel, and the education industry became one of the country's major employers. The character of rural education underwent a drastic transformation. With the availability of automotive transportation, it became possible to "bus" students to central locations from wide surrounding areas, making feasible large schools that could offer curricula and programs comparable to those of city schools.

The national outlay on education became many times larger than in pre-war times; it became as well somewhat more evenly distributed across the country than previously. Thanks in good part to the "equalization payments" which the federal government made to poorer provinces after 1957, they were able to make larger financial contributions to their respective educational systems, reducing disparities between them and the educational systems of the "have" provinces. As well, the federal government began in 1952 to make contributions toward the financing of the country's universities, thereby both enlarging their revenue sources and making them more equal.

The end of the "baby boom" brought a consequent decline in the size of the school-going population, particularly in those regions of the country where economic growth was slow or nil and the overall population grew little or not at all. The stagnation which started in 1974 that characterized the Canadian economy significantly reduced the range and scale of opportunity for rewarding careers, provoking scepticism about the value of education, particularly at the university level. Declining enrolments caused a substantial portion of the educational establishment to become redundant, necessitating the closing down of schools and reduction in the numbers of teaching personnel.

For some years now, health care arrangements have been in effect throughout Canada under which hospital and medical services are provided without charge to the users. The necessary funds come from several sources. The federal government has been contributing roughly half of the cost, with provincial governments covering the rest, obtaining the money in some provinces entirely through taxation and in other provinces through a combination of taxation and monthly premiums charged to all residents. Individuals are free to choose their own doctors, who are paid for their services in each province by a provincial authority, at rates negotiated between the provincial government and the provincial medical association. Hospitals are administered by private, autonomous boards which obtain their funds from their respective provincial governments.

The explosive increase which has occurred in health care costs, far outstripping the rate of population growth or increase in GNP, has given rise to great concern on the part of the political authorities called on to meet those costs. Various measures have been suggested—and some applied— to prevent continued increase in health care costs at the same rapid rates. Provincial governments have allowed only relatively small increases in the fees for service that may be charged by doctors, prompting some doctors to demand the right to "extra bill," i.e., to request patients to make payments to them over and above the fee paid by the government. Consideration is being given to increased emphasis on preventive medicine, to greater use of nurses to perform medical services that do not require high levels of training, to the elimination of questionably useful tests and treatments and to small "user charges." Proposals along these lines encounter stiff resistance from entrenched interests that would be adversely affected, from persons concerned that the quality of medical care would be reduced, and from persons who fear that the present feature of universal availability would be impaired.

Until well into the twentieth century, the care of indigent persons had been a purely local responsibility to be handled by each community in its own way and out of its own resources. The widespread unemployment experienced during the Great Depression of the 1930s generated problems of indigence on a scale far beyond the capacity of local governments, particularly when that same unemployment was causing shrinkage of their revenues as property owners became unable to pay their taxes. Of necessity the federal government intervened, making large financial contributions toward welfare costs. Since then, the federal government has implemented a number of programs under which it provides financial allowances to large categories of persons, many of whom would otherwise be destitute and obliged to seek welfare assistance from their local authorities. All persons over 65 now receive pensions, families receive contributions toward the maintenance of children, and persons who are without work get unemployment insurance. By no means are all the recipients of such federal payments in financial need. The payments are made to designated categories of persons, a large proportion of whom are likely to have no real need. While it would be possible to restrict payments only to the individuals actually in need of them, that would require investigation of each person's circumstances, involving substantial administrative expense and provoking furious objections to the indignity of "means tests." As well, so long as no invidiousness attaches to payments made by government to individuals, every person who is remotely eligible insistently demands that he or she too be given them. The government does, however, manage to make larger payments to persons in need: supplementary allowances are given to persons over 65 who have no source of income other than their public pension. Recently, the government has revised its procedure for the payment of family allowances in order to channel more money to the lowest income families and less to others.

Thanks to these programs, the main burden of supporting Canadians in need is now borne by the federal government. Local governments are called on to give assistance only to persons who are not eligible for payments under one of these programs or who have special needs and problems. And the federal government pays about half of the cost of all such assistance provided by local authorities.

Particularly since the Second World War, the federal government has played a major role in the housing sector of the Canadian economy. Its object has been twofold: to arrange that all Canadians have adequate housing; and secondly, to help stabilize the national economy by maintaining a high and steady rate of house construction. Its method has been primarily to manipulate demand by liberalizing the terms of purchase whenever a boost was required, thereby enabling and encouraging a larger number of persons to buy a home. The assistance given by the government was only marginal; buyers still had to put up most of the money themselves, which meant that the government was giving its help to reasonably well-to-do people who were nearly able to make a house purchase out of their own resources. Demand was in any case very strong in the immediate post-war years, reflecting the prevailing prosperity, the high rates of marriages and births and the near universality of automobile ownership, all of which made suburban home ownership desirable and feasible. Builders responded to the demand; many anticipated it. Year after year, new housing subdivisions came into being on the periphery of the already built-up areas of Canadian cities. The level of demand was strongly affected by other considerations besides demography, prosperity and government assistance. During the early 1970s, desire to buy a house was fortified by its desirability as a hedge against inflation and also by the favoured tax treatment accorded to capital gain realized from the sale of a residence.

It was not only through its various aids to house buyers that the federal government played a role in the housing market. It provided financial assistance on favourable terms to private individuals and provincial governments, to be applied toward the construction and maintenance of low rental housing. As well, it offered financial assistance to provincial governments that acquired tracts of land that were likely to be required as building sites in the proximate future. The expectation was that a government agency would make the land available to builders at lower prices than would private land developers, thereby reducing the cost and market price of new housing.

Some provincial governments introduced programs of "shelter allowances"; i.e., they contributed to the rent paid by designated categories of persons for privately provided accommodation. A good many municipal governments also became involved in housing through the construction and operation of low rental units for lower income families. Local authorities always played a significant role. In fact, their decisions helped to determine the direction and pace of local development. Their zoning regulations specified the types of structure that could be erected on each building site. The speed at which they added to the local infrastructure markedly affected the speed with which new land could be serviced. Finally, the locations that they chose for new thoroughfares, bridges, trunk sewers and watermains determined the direction of new development.

Besides engaging itself directly in some business activities, government exercises supervision over the operation of private sector firms. It prohibits designated types of behaviour that are likely to harm the public interest, such as activities which cause environmental pollution. It prohibits firms from engaging in collusion in order to extract higher prices from their customers. It regulates the relationships of firms with one another, forbidding practices which might prove unfair or harmful. To induce particular types of production, the government offers subsidies and tax concessions. To reserve a larger share of the Canadian market for domestic firms, it imposes tariffs and other impediments to the importation of foreign goods. To support farmers, it guarantees at least minimum prices for designated agricultural products, actively encouraging the formation of marketing boards which have the power to limit output and thereby ensure higher prices than would otherwise prevail.

A crucially important area in which government exercises regulatory authority is that of employer-employee relationships. Except in the small number of industries that are subject to federal jurisdiction because of their interprovicial character, these relationships are governed by provincial legislation. With relatively minor differences between one province and another, this legislation lays down minimum rates of pay, requires designated holidays to be observed, stipulates minimum requirements of hygiene and safety. Workers are guaranteed the right to associate in unions for the purpose of collective bargaining with employers, and provision is made for the orderly resolution of disputes between employers and workers. These provisions are not always effective; strikes of long duration involving very large numbers of workers have occurred all too frequently.

Nearly half of Canada's unionized workers are members of "international" unions which have their headquarters and the bulk of their membership in the U.S. Large numbers of public servants have become organized into unions in recent years as a consequence of new legislation which authorized such organization.

Since the early 1960s, the federal government has been intervening in the economy in a wholly new way: it has carried on programs designed to assist regions of the country that were experiencing economic difficulty. The problem was particularly acute in the Maritimes and Quebec. Here, unemployment rates were well above those experienced elsewhere, incomes were lower, and growth was slower or did not occur at all. The federal government provides its aid in a variety of forms. It gives larger cash grants to "have-not" provinces. It contributes to the cost of improving the infrastructure of lagging regions. It offers financial assistance to firms that propose to build or expand plants there and thereby increase the volume of local employment opportunity. It proposes to transfer a number of government offices out of Ottawa to these regions and thereby broaden their economic base. In some localities where economic development is lagging, it has built government facilities such as a prison, a military training camp, a research establishment.

Provincial governments as well have instituted programs that aimed to accelerate their economic development and to provide assistance to regions that were experiencing special difficulty. The results of these initiatives have been mixed. While solid economic expansion has been achieved in some localities that were falling behind, there have also been spectacular failures. A number of government-aided ventures, some of them lavishly supplied with public funds, have proven to be commercial disasters. Controversy continues as to whether government should simply accept the population decline of particular localities that follows the erosion of an original economic base, or whether it ought to take vigorous action to restore that economic base by attracting new firms, thereby enabling the local population to remain at its original size and possibly even to grow.

The much larger role played by government in the national economy nowadays is reflected in financial statistics: government expenditures constitute a much larger percentage of Canada's GNP than in times past. The increase has occurred mainly at the provincial level. Local government spending is only a slightly larger percentage of the GNP than it was twenty years ago; federal spending amounts to about the same percentage of the GNP as it did twenty years ago. Inter-governmental transfers have increased substantially. The federal government currently gives large sums each year to provincial governments—currently in excess of $10 billion—some in the form of conditional grants and the rest as unconditional transfers. Provincial governments in turn hand over a roughly equal total amount to local government bodies, most of it to school boards and the rest to municipal governments as contribution to the cost of local public services. Increasingly, inter-governmental transfers are being made on an unconditional basis, to the great satisfaction of recipients who firmly believe that they know better how to spend the money than do the senior, donor governments.

Canada's cyclical experience has, for the most part, closely parallelled that of the U.S., though in recent years there has been a fairly significant degree of divergence. Until recently, anyhow, inflation and unemployment rates tended to be of the same order of magnitude in the two countries and to rise and fall at about the same time. Since 1966, however, the unemployment rate in Canada has tended to be distinctly higher. In both countries, unemployment of young persons just entering the labour market has been an especially severe problem in the last decade or so.

The conjuncture of unacceptably high inflation rates and unacceptably high unemployment rates has posed severe problems for policy makers. Subscribing to the widely held view that inflation was caused by excessive government spending and excessive increase in the money supply, federal authorities relied primarily on fiscal-monetary restraint as anti-inflation strategy. The federal government kept its spending down to the lowest levels that were politically acceptable and administratively feasible; the Bank of Canada, particularly after 1975, applied severe monetary restraints. It replicated the sharp increases in interest rates introduced in the U.S. by Federal Reserve authorities, justifying the actions by the claim that the increases were needed both to curb borrowing and to attract the foreign funds needed to cover Canada's current account deficits in the balance of payments and buoy up the value of the Canadian dollar. The Governor of the Bank repeatedly emphasized the need for preventing a decline in the foreign exchange rate of the dollar which would aggravate Canada's inflation problem by increasing the prices of all imports. The sharp escalation of inflationary pressure in 1975, highlighted by wage increases averaging over 20 per cent in the first six months of the year, prompted the federal government to introduce a program of wage and profit controls which remained in effect until 1978. Fiscal-monetary restraints continued to be exercised during the period when the controls were in effect, and were applied even more vigorously when the controls were lifted.

While attempting to curb inflation by its restraints, the federal government sought to ease the unemployment problem by programs of direct job creation aimed at categories of persons deemed to be in greatest need. Summer jobs were created for university and high school students, winter jobs were created for persons who would otherwise have been unemployed during this season, and wage subsidies were given to employers who took on additional workers.

A good many people are convinced that Canada's contemporary inflation is primarily of the cost-push variety, originating in the wage and profit increases achieved by labour organizations and business firms which vigorously exercise their market power. Against such inflation fiscal-monetary restraints are useless and harmful: they impose unemployment without stopping the inflation. There is significant possibility that they actually worsen the inflation. If this kind of inflation is to be curbed, then direct action is needed to curb the increases in pay to factors of production. Some kind of regulation is needed to ensure that the aggregate of year-to-year increases in pay throughout the country corresponds to the increase in real national output.

Three different types of program have already been applied, in other countries as well as Canada, to achieve this kind of correspondence. Appeals have been made to labour and business to show voluntary restraint in their income demands. Governments have decreed the maximum income increase that any person might be allowed to receive, the guideline figure being one that corresponded to the expected increase in the country's real productivity. Finally, governments have established control boards whose approval was required for any increase in rates of pay or profit and which allowed only such increases as they deemed to be appropriate and acceptable.

None of these anti-inflation strategies has proven to be durably successful. Appeals for voluntary restraint have generally fallen on deaf ears. Guidelines and controls have been bitterly opposed by labour leaders because they abrogate collective bargaining. They have also been strenuously opposed by business executives because they prevent corporations from realizing opportunities for legitimate profit and require them to abide by rigid, bureaucratic regulation.

What is needed to stop contemporary inflation is some arrangement that ensures that wages and profits increase no faster than productivity, but that does not violate the principle of collective bargaining and does not impose unacceptable curbs on entrepreneurial freedom. Several "income policies" have been suggested to achieve these objectives. The Tax Income Plan (TIP) devised by Professor Sidney Weintraub of the U.S. proposed in its original version that a tax penalty be imposed on all firms that gave their workers wage increases in excess of a designated guideline figure. A later version proposed a reward, in the form of income tax reduction, to workers who accepted wage increases below a guideline figure, and a corresponding tax reduction to business firms that limited their profit margins. Professor John Hotson of Waterloo University has proposed a sharp cut in prices, wages and other factor payments, to be followed by some kind of incomes policy. Professor Ruben Bellan of the University of Manitoba has proposed that all wage and profit increases be uniformly scaled down to bring their aggregate to equality with the national increase in real output. This procedure, while reducing the aggregate of pay and profit increases to non-inflationary magnitude, would preserve the ratios between individual increases that had been produced originally by the unhindered operation of market forces.

Index